China's Quest for National Identity

Written under the auspices of the
Center of International Studies,
Princeton University

A list of other Center Publications
appears at the back of the book.

CHINA'S QUEST FOR NATIONAL IDENTITY

Edited by

Lowell Dittmer

and

Samuel S. Kim

Cornell University Press

Ithaca and London

First published 1993 by Cornell University Press.

International Standard Book Number 0-8014-2785-1 (cloth)
International Standard Book Number 0-8014-8064-7 (paper)
Library of Congress Catalog Card Number 92-27284
Printed in the United States of America
*Librarians: Library of Congress cataloging information appears on the
last page of the book.*

⊗ The paper in this book meets the minimum requirements of the
American National Standard for Information Sciences—Permanence of
Paper for Printed Library Materials, ANSI Z39.48-1984.

Contents

Contributors   vii

Preface   xi

1. In Search of a Theory of National Identity   1
   Lowell Dittmer and Samuel S. Kim

2. National Identity in Premodern China:
   Formation and Role Enactment   32
   Michael Ng-Quinn

3. Chinese National Identity and the Strong State:
   The Late Qing–Republican Crisis   62
   Michael H. Hunt

4. Rites or Beliefs? The Construction of a Unified
   Culture in Late Imperial China   80
   James L. Watson

5. Change and Continuity in Chinese Cultural Identity:
   The Filial Ideal and the Transformation of an Ethic   104
   Richard W. Wilson

6. China's Intellectuals in the Deng Era: Loss of Identity
   with the State   125
   Merle Goldman, Perry Link, and Su Wei

7. China Coast Identities: Regional, National, and Global   154
   Lynn White and Li Cheng

8. China as a Third World State: Foreign Policy and
   Official National Identity   194
   Peter Van Ness

9. China's Multiple Identities in East Asia: China as a
   Regional Force   215
   Robert A. Scalapino

10. Whither China's Quest for National Identity?   237
    Samuel S. Kim and Lowell Dittmer

    Index   291

Contributors

LOWELL DITTMER (Ph.D., Chicago) is professor of political science at University of California, Berkeley. He is the author of *Liu Shao-ch'i and the Chinese Cultural Revolution, China's Continuous Revolution, Sino-Soviet Normalization and Its International Implications,* and other works.

SAMUEL S. KIM (Ph.D., Columbia) teaches in the Woodrow Wilson School of Public and International Affairs, Princeton University. He is the author of *China, the United Nations, and World Order, The Quest for a Just World Order,* and other works. He is working on a book about Chinese perspectives on international relations.

MERLE GOLDMAN (Ph.D., Harvard) is professor of Chinese history at Boston University. She is the author of *Literary Dissent in Communist China, China's Intellectuals: Advise and Dissent,* and a number of edited works. She has completed a book tentatively titled *Sprouts of Democracy.*

MICHAEL H. HUNT (Ph.D., Yale) is professor of history at the University of North Carolina at Chapel Hill. His numerous publications range widely in U.S. and Chinese foreign relations. His most recent major works are *The Making of a Special Relationship* and *Ideology and U.S. Foreign Policy.* He is working on the foreign relations of the Chinese Communist party.

LI CHENG (Ph.D., Princeton) is assistant professor of government at Hamilton College. He has published articles, especially about the rise of Chinese technocracy, in *China Quarterly, Modern China, Asian Survey, World Politics,* and elsewhere.

PERRY LINK (Ph.D., Harvard) is professor of Chinese at Princeton University. He teaches modern Chinese language and literature, history of ideas, and popular culture. He has written and edited several books, most recently *Evening Chats in Beijing: Probing China's Predicament*.

MICHAEL NG-QUINN (Ph.D., Harvard) is associate professor of political science at the University of Redlands. He has written on Chinese foreign policy, Deng Xiaoping's political reform, the Chinese military, northeast Asian international relations, and the Hong Kong police. He is working on explaining the perpetuation of the Chinese state.

ROBERT A. SCALAPINO (Ph.D., Harvard) is Robson Research Professor of Government Emeritus, former director of the Institute of East Asian Studies, University of California, Berkeley, and editor of *Asian Survey*. He is a fellow of the American Academy of Arts and Sciences and has written or edited thirty-five books and over three hundred articles dealing with Asian domestic politics and international relations. His most recent book is *The Politics of Development: Perspectives on Twentieth Century Asia*.

SU WEI (M.A., UCLA) is a Chinese writer and literary critic who worked at the Institute of Literature of the Chinese Academy of Social Sciences from 1986 to 1989. From 1990 to 1992 he was a visiting scholar at Princeton University. He is author of *Distant Travellers* (fiction), *Words in the Western Mirror* (essays), and numerous other works of fiction and criticism.

PETER VAN NESS (Ph.D., Berkeley) is associate professor at the Graduate School of International Studies, University of Denver, and a senior research fellow in the department of International Relations at Australian National University. He is author of *Revolution and Chinese Foreign Policy* and editor of *Market Reforms in Socialist Societies: Comparing China and Hungary*.

JAMES L. WATSON (Ph.D., Berkeley) is Fairbank Professor of Chinese Society and Professor of Anthropology at Harvard University. His books include *Emigration and the Chinese Lineage* and the edited volumes *Asian and African Systems of Slavery, Kinship Organization in Late Imperial China, Class and Social Stratification in Post-Revolution China,* and *Death Ritual in Late Imperial and Modern China*.

LYNN WHITE (Ph.D., Berkeley) is teaching at Princeton University in the Woodrow Wilson School, Politics Department, and East Asian Studies

Program. He wrote *Policies of Chaos: The Organizational Causes of Violence in China's Cultural Revolution* and *Careers in Shanghai,* and edited *Political System and Change*. He does research often at the Centre of Asian Studies, University of Hong Kong, where some work on the chapter in this volume was done. He is writing a book about press, tax, and other reforms of the 1970s and 1980s in the People's Republic.

RICHARD W. WILSON (Ph.D., Princeton) is professor of political science at Rutgers University in New Brunswick. He is author of *Learning to Be Chinese, The Moral State,* and most recently, *Labyrinth: An Essay on the Political Psychology of Change*. He has coedited numerous volumes on modern China.

Preface

The weight of China's long and well-chronicled past has both fascinated and frustrated Western and Chinese observers concerned with what holds Chinese society together and what it means to be Chinese in a changing world. For the study of Chinese national identity, this rich legacy poses a genuine puzzle. On the one hand, that legacy has prepared the Chinese people for an interdependent modern world, providing them with an almost foolproof combination of pragmatic adaptability and bedrock security of identity as Zhongguoren (Chinese people), and resulting in a tremendous economic and intellectual flowering of ethnic Chinese throughout the Asian Pacific region (albeit more outside the People's Republic than within). On the other, this proud country has had enormous trouble finding a comfortable niche as a nation-state in the modern international system.

In trying to adjust to the post-Westphalian world of nation-states, China has succumbed to national identity "mood swings," rotating through a series of roles: self-sacrificing member of an international socialist community; self-reliant hermit, completely divorced from both camps in the global system; revolutionary vanguard tribunal on behalf of the global underdogs of the Third World; tacit conservative "partner" of NATO and favored recipient of largesse in the capitalist world system; and so forth. Given the travails of other states, from postrevolutionary France to the new nations of the Third World, we should not be surprised by China's difficulties. Yet China's search for a national identity has been unusually tumultuous, because of the vast gap between capabilities and commitments.

We conceived the idea of a study of Chinese national identity while we were engaged in our respective investigations of Chinese foreign policy. The need for a central reference point became clear to both of us—a reference point that incorporated not only "national interest" but recurring cultural themes. Much more than foreign policy was involved in the issues we were studying. Our interests converged during a research visit of Samuel Kim to the University of California at Berkeley in June through November 1988, when the MacArthur Group for International Security Studies at Berkeley supported Kim's appointment as a Distinguished Fellow of International Security Studies. Some of the ideas introduced in Chapter 1 had first been worked out by Lowell Dittmer under the auspices of a 1986–87 research fellowship, for which he thanks the Woodrow Wilson Center for International Studies of the Smithsonian Institution. The Center for Chinese Studies at Berkeley also contributed to the endeavor.

The second stage was inaugurated in a controversial, intellectually stimulating conference convened by the Center of International Studies (CIS) at Princeton University on January 25–27, 1990. Our largest debt is to the CIS, especially to then-director Henry S. Bienen (now dean of the Woodrow Wilson School of Public and International Affairs at Princeton). He has been more than a pro forma supporter; he has been, as always, an invaluable intellectual collaborator and an invisible contributor to the volume. Without his assistance, the book would not have been possible. For the financial wherewithal enabling us to hold the conference we are grateful to the Peter B. Lewis Fund of the CIS, and for indispensable logistic support to the helpful and hard-working CIS staff under the skillful administrative guidance of Geraldine Kavanaugh.

We express special appreciation not only to our contributors but also to Dru Gladney, Richard Kraus, Steven Levine, and Arthur Waldron for their learned contributions, which are committed to publication elsewhere, and to Jonathan Pollack for his ideas.

Finally, the manuscript that eventually resulted from this conference attracted two outstanding anonymous readings. Roger Haydon provided us with editorial advice from time to time.

Have we succeeded in setting the study of Chinese national identity on a new and more stable intellectual footing? We believe so, but time will tell. In any event, the project was an intellectually exciting one—a highly successful heuristic enterprise—from which we all learned a great deal.

The *pinyin* system, the official romanization system in the People's Republic of China, has been adopted by the United Nations and other international organizations. It has become the system most universally used in scholarship and journalism in the West. We use pinyin throughout this book, with some familiar exceptions for well-known place names and personal names that would be difficult to recognize in pinyin. Hong Kong, Tibet, and Taipei are retained in preference to Xianggang, Xizang, and Taibei, and Sun Yat-sen, Chiang Kai-shek, and Lee Teng-hui are used rather than Sun Zhongshan, Jiang Jieshi, and Li Denghui.

LOWELL DITTMER

Berkeley, California

SAMUEL S. KIM

Princeton, New Jersey

中
國 I

In Search of a Theory
of National Identity

Lowell Dittmer and Samuel S. Kim

The concept of "national identity," first introduced in the course of the so-called behavioral revolution in political science, has obvious relevance to the problems of development, integration, international relations, and a host of other issues.[1] Yet whereas other terms coined at that time have since sired abundant efforts at conceptual refinement and collateral research,[2] national identity has remained relatively barren. The reasons may derive to some degree from the concept's vagueness. Yet "charisma" and "political culture," at least equally troublesome, have nonetheless spawned a prolific literature. Nor can the concept's peripheral or epiphenomenal status be held responsible; for what could be more central than a nation's identity? The problem, we submit, has had rather more to do with the term's conceptualization, which did not point us in the direction of interesting research or specify the relevant variables precisely enough to conduct it. Meanwhile, in the "real world" of politics, issues of national identity

The authors are grateful to Richard Falk, Yale Ferguson, Michael Ng-Quinn, Susanne H. Rudolph, and Richard Wilson for their valuable comments and suggestions. Lowell Dittmer acknowledges the support of the MacArthur Group for International Security Studies at the University of California at Berkeley for research support; Samuel Kim acknowledges the support of much of his research and writing of this chapter by the Peter B. Lewis Fund of the Center of International Studies, Princeton University.

[1] See Leonard Binder et al., eds., *Crises and Sequences in Political Development* (Princeton: Princeton University Press, 1971).

[2] "Development," "participation," "distribution," and "integration," have, for example, all produced a vast monographic literature.

seemed eclipsed for the time being by the proselytizing fervor of rival transnational ideologies.

At no time, however, has the question of identity seemed more vital than in the 1980s, particularly in the former communist bloc states. Despite impressive and sustained improvements in national income, post-Mao China suddenly fell from the status of proud model of self-reliant socialist development to that of impoverished and underdeveloped power (and eager recipient of aid from international donor organizations), lagging far behind not only Japan but the small Confucian newly industrial economies (NIEs) on its periphery. Having overcome this sudden reality shock by a decade of highly successful economic reform, the Chinese Communist party (CCP) leadership turned violently against some of the sequelae of reform at Tiananmen, leaving the nation's future course and identity hanging in the air. The Soviet Union, a nation that had in the late 1970s arrived at "strategic parity" and appeared on the verge of claiming primacy in the superpower rivalry, suddenly became aware of its technological backwardness and economic stagnation and gave way to a crisis of confidence, relinquishing its hold on Eastern Europe and disavowing its old command economy with no feasible alternative at hand.[3] In all these countries the search for national identity has assumed great urgency since the sweeping repudiation of the Marxist-Leninist symbol system that had served to legitimate and unite the region. With the dissolution of the Marxist ideology that formerly cemented their ruling parties, Yugoslavia, the Soviet Union, and Czechoslovakia began to undergo an unraveling of national identity. Though less directly shaken by these epoch-making developments, even the West has been challenged to redefine old identities or alliances by the lack of any pressing threat to them. The United States has been promoted to the unusual (if perhaps fleeting) role of superpower in a unipolar world. But the issue of national identity is especially relevant to the case of China, given its abiding concern for cultural and political integrity.

National Identity Conceived and Applied

A satisfactory definition of "national identity" unfortunately presupposes an answer to the more fundamental question What is identity?

[3]In the late 1980s the USSR was third in GNP, slightly behind Japan, and projected to fall to fourth, behind China as well, by the year 2010. Commission on Integrated Long-Term Strategy, *Sources of Change in the Future Security Environment* (Washington, D.C.: Pentagon, April 1988).

Definitions, according to Erasmus, tend to be dangerous; Hegel called them arbitrary, and Wittgenstein said they were impossible. Still, they seem to be a necessary prerequisite to any systematic discussion. In contrast to the tendency of many philosophers to define identity as a logical equation between two distinct entities, as in "A is identical to B," Heidegger derives identity from the "Being" of things, a fundamental characteristic of which is unity within itself, a belonging together.[4] This is not inconsistent with standard lexical definitions, according to which identity is "absolute same-ness; individuality," "the state or fact of remaining the same one, as under varying aspects or conditions."[5] The term continues to inspire erudite disquisitions among philosophers.[6]

The concept was first imported from philosophy into the social sciences to deal with the problems of "psychosocial" identity. Erik H. Erikson, a post-Freudian whose own identity is interestingly ambiguous,[7] needed a term to reunify the "self" psychoanalysts had fragmented into ego, super-ego, id, object relations, and so forth. According to Erikson, a person's identity grows in the course of the life cycle—or it may degenerate, as in negative identity or identity diffusion.[8] The term quickly gained currency,

[4]Martin Heidegger, *Identity and Difference* (New York: Harper, 1969), p. 25.

[5]George Ostler, comp., *The Little Oxford Dictionary of Current English,* 3d ed. (Oxford: Clarendon, 1955), p. 248; C. L. Barnhart, ed., *The American College Dictionary* (New York: Random House, 1957), p. 599.

[6]See Milton Munitz, ed., *Identity and Individuation* (New York: New York University Press, 1971); Giuseppina Chiara Moneta, *On Identity* (The Hague: Nijhoff, 1976); Harold Noonan, *Objects and Identity* (The Hague: Nijhoff, 1980), and *Personal Identity* (London: Routledge and Kegan Paul, 1989); and Geoffrey Madell, *The Identity of the Self* (Edinburgh: Edinburgh University Press, 1981).

[7]Erikson was born of a German Jewish mother and a Danish father who abandoned his mother before his birth. He was later adopted by a German Jewish pediatrician named Homburger (he improvised the surname Erikson after immigration). Biographers have some-times accused him of seeking to evade his Jewish origins. See Marshall Berman, *The Politics of Authenticity: Radical Individualism and the Emergence of Modern Society* (New York: Atheneum, 1970); also Paul Roazen, *Erik H. Erikson: The Power and Limits of a Vision* (New York: Free Press, 1976), pp. 94–99.

[8]See Erik H. Erikson, "Ego Development and Historical Change," *Psychoanalytic Study of the Child* 2 (1946): 359–96; *Childhood and Society,* 2d ed. (New York: Norton, 1963); "The Problem of Ego Identity," *Journal of the American Psychoanalytic Association* 4 (1956):56–121; "Identity and the Life Cycle: Selected Papers by Erik H. Erikson," *Psychological Issues* 1 (1959): 1–171; *The Challenge of Youth* (Garden City, N.Y.: Doubleday, Anchor, 1965); "The Concept of Identity in Race Relations," *Daedalus* 95 (Winter 1966): 145–71; "Identity, Psychosocial," *International Encyclopedia of the Social Sciences* (New York: Free Press, 1968), 7:61–65; "Identity and Identity Diffusion," in Chad Gordon and Kenneth J. Gergen, eds., *The Self in Social Interaction* (New York: Wiley, 1968), pp. 197–205; *Dimensions of a New Identity* (New York: Norton, 1974); *Life History and the Historical Moment* (New York: Norton, 1975); and *The Life Cycle Completed* (New York: Norton, 1982).

particularly with reference to the possibility of an identity "crisis." In Erikson's theory, different forms of crisis occur at successive epigenetic stages in the life cycle. The first and most fateful crisis occurs in late pubescence–early adulthood, when a congeries of pivotal questions tend to converge—concerning choice of occupation, marital status and mate, lifestyle, and so on. Erikson never defines "crisis" explicitly, but his usage seems to coincide more with the Chinese [*weiji*] than with the English (or German, *Krise*) usage; for the Chinese term includes not only danger [*weixian*] but an opportunity [*jihui*] to be seized. It is also consistent with that of Jürgen Habermas, for whom "crisis" defines the limit beyond which a system can no longer resolve its problems without losing its identity.[9]

According to Erikson, identity "connotes both a persistent sameness within oneself (self-sameness) and a persistent sharing of some kind of essential character with others."[10] Erikson's definition is consistent with the implications of those cited earlier, but he goes on to supplement those in three respects: First, a person's solution to the riddle of identity has significant implications for subsequent psychological development, because without a successful resolution, further progress is somehow stunted. Second, personal identity has cultural resonance. This is true not only in the sense that the culture embodies the repertoire of possible identities available at any given time but also in the sense that the particular resolution selected may sometimes, as in the "great man phenomenon," reverberate throughout the culture. Erikson has made the latter case for Martin Luther, Mohandas Gandhi, and Adolf Hitler, among others.[11] Third, an identity is defined not in psychological terms, but as a *relationship* between self and others—and may hence be applied to any entity, individual or collective.

A collective identity thus may be said to have its own organizational needs and developmental propensities (if not a "life cycle," *pace* Oswald Spengler) beyond its function as a conceptual umbrella for its members. It is a logical corollary of the concept of personal identity: just as the self is defined in terms of its relationship to other selves, the group is defined in terms of its relationship to other groups. Some of these collectivities are mere conceptual categories to which members feel no particular sense of belonging, such as left-handed people, or people in a particular zip code or

[9]Jürgen Habermas, *Legitimation Crisis,* trans. Thomas McCarthy (Boston: Beacon, 1973).

[10]Erikson, "The Problem of Ego Identity," in Maurice R. Stein et al., *Identity and Anxiety* (Glencoe, Ill.: Free Press, 1960), p. 30.

[11]Erikson, *Young Man Luther: A Study in Psychoanalysis and History* (New York: Norton, 1958); *Gandhi's Truth: On the Origins of Militant Nonviolence* (New York: Norton, 1969), and "The Legend of Hitler's Childhood," in *Childhood and Society,* pp. 326–59.

tax bracket (although such groups may have significance for pollsters or direct-mail advertisers). There are also ascriptive groups that do inspire emotional attachment, such as those based on kinship, ethnoreligious origin, or minority nationality. Still others are "achieved" groups, which have to be joined and actively participated in, such as the Rotary Club, the Parent-Teachers Association, or the Communist Youth League. To underscore an admitted tautology, whether these collectivities are ascribed or achieved, they are focal points of identification to the extent that members "identify" with them; they become "reference groups" useful in defining the self ("I am a Rotarian"; "I am an Irish Catholic"; "I am a southpaw"). Why a person chooses to identify with one set of reference groups (or identifies with them intensely) rather than another set is, in a society in which such options are voluntary, a matter of ambition, mutual interests, even unconscious needs or fantasies (becoming a Madonna groupie or joining Earth First, the Jewish Defense League, or the American Nazi party).

It would of course be misleading to draw a direct analogy between personal and national identity—to anthropomorphize the nation-state— yet to assume that like other collective units a nation has a distinctive identity does not seem altogether farfetched. Indeed, to claim otherwise entails assuming that every decision is made fresh, on "facts," without consideration for enduring interests (for the very concept of "interests" presupposes an identifiable entity to which they can be attributed).[12] Erikson opined that the concept was indeed applicable to nations: "In nations, too, my concepts would lead me to concentrate on the conditions which heighten or endanger a national sense of identity rather than a static national character."[13]

Yet defining national identity is more problematic than defining individual or collective identity. It is sometimes defined, by logical extension, simply as the largest and most inclusive form of collective identity. There is, however, the complication that inclusion within the nation is not entirely voluntary—one cannot always exit without penalty (as the examples of Philip Nolan, Edward Everett Hale's "man without a country," and the current plight of the people of Hong Kong show), and in some cases one

[12]National identity may be educed from the geophysical attributes of the nation-state, as in Zbigniew Brzezinski, *Game Plan: A Geostrategic Framework for the Conduct of the US-Soviet Contest* (Boston: Atlantic Monthly, 1986). Although this process facilitates a systematic, long-term analysis of national interests, it uses a reductionist idea of national identity.

[13]Erikson, "Identity and Identity Diffusion," in Gordon and Gergen, *Self in Social Interaction* (see n. 8), p. 198.

also has precious little "voice"[14] (witness the fate of China's democracy activists since Tiananmen, as perceptively described in Chapter 6, by Goldman, Link, and Su). A nation is not merely a megacollectivity; it is a "nation-state," defined only partly by the dimensions of the group, partly also by the group's subordination to sovereign authority.

Whereas our own definition of national identity synthesizes both elements of the compound noun *nation-state,* most others tend to emphasize one or the other. The classic definition offered by Sidney Verba and Lucian Pye in the concluding volume of the Social Science Research Council series on comparative politics, for example, stresses the latter: national identity is the "set of individuals who fall within the decision-making scope of the state."[15] Accordingly, determining national identity becomes determining who is included and who is excluded by the national boundaries, however the state chooses to draw them. To be sure, boundaries may be social as well as physical, as there may be tourists, guest workers, even whole populations of alienated ethnic minorities (blacks in the ante-bellum South or the "homelands" of contemporary South Africa; Jews, homosexuals, communists, and Gypsies in the Third Reich), who are categorically excluded from a nation even though they are within its physical boundaries. In the case of expansionist powers or irredenta (often the distinction is unclear, as in the People's Republic of China's claims against the Spratley Islands or Hitler's on the Saarland or the Polish Corridor), the state may lay claim to areas beyond its current physical boundaries. In Verba's words, "If some members of the populace do not consider themselves as appropriately falling within the domain of the government or, conversely, feel that some other group not within that domain falls within it, one can talk of an identity problem."[16]

According to the Pye-Verba conceptualization, then, a nation's identity is normally circumscribed by its boundaries, whose dimensions tend to coincide with such objective criteria as common language, ethnic or racial origin, and political culture; but in the last analysis, boundaries are arbitrarily determined by the sovereign state carving out a precarious identity by force and guile in a competitive international environment. Given the crucial importance of boundaries, an identity crisis occurs when those boundaries blur, or are challenged at the margin. As Pye puts it, "In the

[14]See Albert O. Hirschman, *Exit, Voice, and Loyalty: Responses to Decline in Firms, Organizations, and States* (Cambridge: Harvard University Press, 1970).

[15]Sidney Verba, "Sequences and Development," in Binder, *Crises and Sequences* (see n. 1), pp. 283–316.

[16]Ibid., p. 299.

process of political development an identity crisis occurs when a community finds that what it had once unquestionably accepted as the physical and psychological definitions of its collective self are no longer acceptable under new historic conditions. In order for the political system to achieve a new level of performance . . . it is necessary for the participants in the system to redefine who they are and how they are different from all other political and social systems."[17] Accordingly Pye identifies four "fundamental forms" of national identity crisis, based on territory, class, ethnicity/nationality, and historical/cultural exclusiveness.[18] Though he disarmingly admits right after proposing it that he can think of no case in which "class" provides a basis for nationally exclusive identification, class does, of course, provide a basis for status rankings *within* a nation (even perhaps second-class citizenship in extreme cases, such as the homeless population).[19] Class could also be the basis for identification *transcending* the nation-state, although that has not yet happened decisively anywhere.[20] The other three are indeed typical criteria for inclusion in the nation-state.

[17]Lucian W. Pye, "Identity and the Political Culture," in Binder, *Crises and Sequences,* pp. 110–11.

[18]Ibid., pp. 101–34.

[19]Both Benjamin Disraeli and Richard Nixon were sufficiently exercised by this problem to refer to "two nations"—reflecting a form of national identity crisis—and to propose radical changes in the welfare system. See Charles A. Valentine, *Culture and Poverty* (Chicago: University of Chicago Press, 1968); and Daniel P. Moynihan, ed., *On Understanding Poverty* (New York: Basic Books, 1969).

[20]Of course the most famous instance is identification with the international working class, on which Karl Marx and his disciples capitalized. But the Second Communist International notoriously failed to mobilize this identification during World War I, and since that time it has been subverted by allegiance to one or another nation-state (either the host country or Moscow on behalf of the Left). Richard Kraus shows how this identification has been undermined in proletarian China itself on behalf of modernization and reform. See Richard C. Kraus, "China's Identity as a Proletarian State" (Paper presented at the Conference on China's Quest for National Identity, January 25–27, 1990, Princeton University). Political development theorists allude to the importance of identification with the international middle class, particularly in connection with the "international demonstration effect." See William Bloom, *Personal Identity, National Identity and International Relations* (Cambridge: Cambridge University Press, 1990), pp. 105–27. Student antiwar movements, or ecology movements, may, for instance, articulate an international middle-class ethic. Greenpeace, whose membership has doubled every two to three years since 1980, pursues transnational strategies for bringing about ecological well-being on the whole planet. Whether either of these class-based identities manages to supplant the nation-state as a focus of loyalty remains to be seen. According to a comprehensive cross-national survey conducted for "Images of the World in the Year 2000," the elimination of national boundaries and the setting up of a world government were among the five least popular alternatives related to peace (from a list of twenty-five). See Aleksandra Jasinska-Kania, "National Identity and Image of World Society: The Polish Case," *International Social Science Journal* 34 (1982): 93–112.

The Pye-Verba definition is not only coherent but simple to use, and empirical cases of identity problems of the type to which it refers are not lacking. According to one major empirical study, nationalist and ethnic conflict accounted for some 70 percent of 160 significant disputes with a probability of culminating in large-scale violence.[21] Thus postwar Italy experienced something of an identity crisis over the fate of Trieste, for example, and the difficulties in Cyprus, Francophone Canada, and Northern Ireland are notorious. Most common are cases of inconsistency among criteria for inclusion, as in the case when a significant compatriot population resides in an adjoining territory. Ernest Gellner speculates that there may be as many as eight hundred irredentist movements in the contemporary world.[22] The People's Republic of China (PRC) has had territorial disputes with practically every one of its contiguous neighbors.

In view of the difficulties posed by inconsistent criteria for inclusion within national boundaries, new states might rationally be expected to move early in their developmental sequence to rectify any glaring discrepancies. "Since the resolution of the identity crisis is so fundamental to the very establishment of the nation in the first instance, it is usually a crisis that occurs early in the sequence of developmental crises," as Pye puts it.[23] Only a few countries have retained their geographic identities over the course of their existence, while the rest have made some territorial realignments; but adjustments are usually made early and, once made, tend to remain surprisingly stable, as interests become vested in their maintenance.[24] Jeffrey Herbst points out that despite the widely recognized arbitrariness of the African "national" boundaries established by European colonialists, for example, there has not been "one significant boundary change in Africa since the dawn of the independence era in the late 1950s, and not one separatist movement has succeeded in establishing a new state."[25] Indeed, sovereignty for African leaders may be said to have become a sword with which to prevent internal secessionist threats and a shield with which to

[21]Steven Rosen, ed., *A Survey of World Conflicts* (Pittsburgh: University of Pittsburgh Center for International Studies, 1969).

[22]Ernest Gellner, *Nations and Nationalisms* (Ithaca: Cornell University Press, 1983), pp. 44–45.

[23]Pye, "Identity," in Binder, *Crises and Sequences,* p. 124. Whether a national identity crisis is limited to the early phases of development is of course an empirical question, investigated, in the Chinese case, in the following chapters.

[24]Dankwart A. Rustow, *A World of Nations: Problems of Political Modernization* (Washington, D.C.: Brookings Institution, 1967), p. 22.

[25]Jeffrey Herbst, "The Creation and Maintenance of National Boundaries in Africa," *International Organization* 43 (Summer 1989): 675–76.

ward off supranational threats so as to strengthen the weak national identities inherited by their respective states.

The question of identity typically arises early not only because the basic dimensions of a nation's existence are at stake but because identifying the membership of the nation-state is a necessary prerequisite for persuading that membership to pay taxes, fight for their country, and so forth. In short, Verba says, "Identity . . . directly affects the institutionalization of legitimacy, and legitimacy in turn affects penetration." As Anne Norton puts it in her thoughtful discussion, "The recognition of qualities that distinguish the polity from all others entails the propagation of abstract principles against which the conduct of the regime and constitution of the nation may henceforth be measured. The qualities definitive of the nation are abstracted from it and made objective. The citizens, having before them an objective principle of nationality, may therefore determine whether the regime, or the regime's actions, are appropriate to the nation. This is the beginning of legitimacy."[26]

Indeed, according to Habermas, a legitimacy crisis "is directly an identity crisis." Similarly, Gellner argues that nationalism "is a theory of political legitimacy, which requires that ethnic boundaries should not cut across political ones." Somewhat more cautiously, Ernst Haas deems national identity a necessary but not sufficient condition for legitimacy: "Legitimate authority under conditions of mass politics is tied up with successful nationalism; when the national identity is in doubt, one prop supporting legitimacy is knocked away."[27] Thus any new nation may naturally be expected to proceed expeditiously to survey its borders, conduct a census of the citizenry, dispatch a border guard and other representatives of the government to the far-flung corners of the realm, establish transportation and communication channels, promote a common language and educational curriculum, and otherwise consolidate its domain.

If contradictions among the criteria for inclusion tend to generate identity crises, then those nation-states with few or no contradictions might be supposed to have relatively "secure" national identities. Yet a superficial survey of the contemporary international system demonstrates that such

[26]Verba, "Sequences," p. 311; Anne Norton, *Reflections on Political Identity* (Baltimore: Johns Hopkins University Press, 1988), pp. 55–56.

[27]Habermas, *Legitimation Crisis,* p. 46—an assertion on which we reserve judgment: certainly a crisis of legitimacy may imply a crisis of national identity, but a crisis of identity need not imply a crisis of legitimacy, as our later discussion of subtypes of crises will show. Gellner, *Nations and Nationalisms,* p. 1; Ernst Haas, "What Is Nationalism and Why Should We Study It?" *International Organization* 40 (Summer 1986): 707–44.

states are indeed rare. To take for example the two criteria physical boundaries and ethnic/national group membership, Walker Connor found in a survey of 132 nation-states extant in 1971 that in only 12 (9.1 percent) did the two criteria fully coincide, while another 50 (37.9 percent) did at least have one major ethnic group that constituted more than three-quarters of the population. Of the remaining 70 states, 31 (23.5 percent) had a majority ethnic group accounting for only between one-half and three-quarters of the population, while in 39 (29.5 percent) the largest single ethnic community formed less than one-half of the total population. In other words, a majority (53 percent) of those contemporary nation-states had very large minority populations.[28]

Another pair of inclusion criteria to look at are physical boundaries and linguistic communities. The number of languages, not counting dialects, is estimated at around eight thousand. In most parts of the world, linguistic communities are either too large or too small to coincide with easily defensible or administrable national boundaries. In only two dozen or so countries do linguistic and national boundaries roughly coincide. In no less than half the countries of the world, less than 70 percent of the population speak the same language. If linguistic compatibility indeed provides a stable foundation for national identity in many European countries (though not in the Balkan, Danubian, or Baltic ares), the same cannot be said for various regions of the Third World.[29] In his thoroughgoing study of the relationship between language and national identity, John Edwards concludes: "Identities clearly survive language shifts and it is naive, ahistorical and, indeed, patronizing to think otherwise. The essence of group identity is individual identity and the essence of individual identity, ultimately, is survival, personal security and well-being. To the extent to which a language hinders these things, it will be deemed a negotiable commodity."[30]

Pye and Verba would hold that a contradiction among objective criteria

[28]Walker Connor, "A Nation Is a Nation, Is a State, Is an Ethnic Group, Is a . . . ," *Ethnic and Racial Studies* 1 (1978): 377–400. The People's Republic is among the happy few states with only part (about 8 percent) of its population consisting of minority nationalities, according to the last census. Yet of the more than four hundred ethnic/nationality groups that applied for recognition as official minority nationalities upon the founding of the People's Republic, only fifty-four succeeded in obtaining official recognition, and only one other group has been added since. On the CCP's nationality policy, see Walker Connor, *The National Question in Marxist-Leninist Theory and Strategy* (Princeton: Princeton University Press, 1984), pp. 67–100; also National Minorities Questions Editorial Panel, *Questions and Answers about China's Minority Nationalities* (Beijing: New World, 1985).

[29]Gellner, *Nations and Nationalisms,* p. 44.

[30]John Edwards, *Language, Society and Identity* (New York: Basil Blackwell, 1985), p. 85.

for inclusion within a nation-state is apt to provoke national identity problems of varying severity, ranging from border dispute to full-fledged identity crisis. Yet the foregoing list suggests that the objective criteria for inclusion need not coincide. Even more surprising than the coexistence of mutually incompatible criteria for inclusion is the fact that this condition does not necessarily precipitate a crisis. We would otherwise be bound to conclude that Switzerland, Belgium, or Canada, not to mention the ethnocultural melting pots India and the United States, are afflicted by insuperable identity crises—despite the fact that manifestations of intraethnic or other communal strife are either absent or normally contained. Dankwart Rustow finds it striking that "the talk about the nation has been loudest where the sense of nationality has remained weakest—among 19th century Germans and Italians and among 20th century Arabs, Asians, and Africans, rather than among English, Frenchmen, or Japanese."[31] We seem justified in concluding that mutually consistent criteria of inclusion is at best a sufficient but not a necessary condition for a secure national identity. Moreover, even having a national identity secure by objective inclusion criteria does not seem to ensure a country against identity problems or even crises. Such crises may under certain circumstances occur even relatively late in a nation's developmental trajectory, after World War II in Japan, for example.

The problem—or at least one of them—with the Pye-Verba conceptualization is that it consists of boundaries without contents. Its answer to the question Who (or what) is Switzerland is essentially that Switzerland consists of those people who are by consensus Swiss and who select a government in common to regulate public affairs in the land in which they all live. We have seen that these people are defined as Swiss not because they all speak the same language, for they do not, nor because they have the same religious affiliation, for they do not, nor because they stem from the same national or ethnic origins, for they do not. The land in which they live may be bounded by certain geophysical features that tend to impede invasion, such as the Alps in the south or the Rhine in the north, and thus become symbols in the national mythology; yet the exact demarcation of the borders is essentially arbitrary. These conventional answers to the question of identity seem almost to be missing the point. We do know that a sense of national identity must be important for people to be willing to sacrifice their own comfort or even their lives in order to render the level of cooperation necessary for this whole governmental arrangement to work,

---

[31]Rustow, *World of Nations,* p. 22.

but the Pye-Verba definition fails to explain *why;* or rather, it points to characteristics that turn out to have so many exceptions and qualifications that they make a very weak case.

The Pye-Verba definition is an *analytic* one, which defines the whole in terms of its parts: What is Bulgaria? Bulgaria is the Bulgarians, and the land that they live in. But in ordinary language, questions of identity do not normally elicit an analytic definition. Most people do not respond to the question Who are you? with a chorus of "Them Bones" or with a chemical analysis. The most likely answer would be a name, which might indicate family membership, ethnicity, and sometimes marital status. Probing further, one might elicit self-definitions based on gender,[32] behavioral criteria, status ranking, group affiliation, or age. Thus identity is a series of descriptions that define a person in terms of networks or categories of membership and location in the stream of time and human history. The point is that none of these answers are analytical definitions, but rather *synthetic* ones, which indicate the relation of the thing being identified to other things.[33] That is, a synthetic definition refers to the properties of the entity as a whole rather than simply breaking the entity down to its components.

Of course an analytic self-definition ("I am a 5-foot, 2-inch–tall heterosexual female with platinum blonde hair, near-sighted, weigh 140 pounds, walk pigeon toed, and speak with a slight lisp") is also possible and might also constitute a useful response. An analytical definition may capture a necessary dimension, but it is not sufficient. An analytic definition of national identity could not deal with those periods in a nation's history when there is pervasive uncertainty about national purpose unless that uncertainty happened to be focused on boundary questions, either geophysical demarcation of frontiers or inclusion of marginal subgroups. Thus the national socialist (or fascist) transformation of political systems in the 1930s and 1940s could be defined analytically as an identity crisis for Italy and Germany, where a readjustment of national boundaries was envisaged, but not for Spain, Argentina, or Brazil. The communist reorientation that followed revolutionary civil wars in Russia and China could be said to have evoked identity problems in China, which was forced to accept prolonged division into two states and two colonial outposts, but not in the Soviet

---

[32]We might assume gender has no parallel at the national level, but this is perhaps a premature conclusion. Russians refer to "Mother Russia," while Germans hail "das Vaterland." Gender politics of a more straightforward kind have become an issue with the rise of feminist and homosexual rights organizations; see, e.g., Shane Phelan, *Identity Politics: Lesbian Feminism and the Limits of Community* (Philadelphia: Temple University Press, 1989).

[33]Richard Robinson, *Definitions* (Oxford: Clarendon, 1950).

Union, which returned to prerevolutionary boundaries as soon as Versailles superseded the Treaty of Brest-Litovsk.

The Pye-Verba definition does capture an essential component and is empirically clear and methodologically workable. But it leaves out certain problematic phases in a nation's development when basic issues of national purpose are raised, issues to which the term *national identity* seems to apply better than any other. These problematic phases may have little or nothing to do with boundary delimitation or the inclusion or exclusion of marginal subgroups, and they may arise both early in a nation's self-definition, when boundary and inclusionary issues are typically at issue, and much later on. Such national watersheds as total defeat, revolution, or domestic bloodbath revive the issue of national identity. Involvement in a major war whose outcome did not involve boundary adjustment may just as easily precipitate a national identity crisis, as U.S. involvement in the Vietnam War illustrates only too well. Major boundary revisions may occur without perceptible sign of crisis, as in the American purchase of Alaska. In sum, the correspondence between boundaries and national identity, between blurred or revised boundaries and identity crisis, is only approximate. Without sacrificing the empirical precision of the existing paradigm, a more satisfactory definition could facilitate the investigation of identity problems that do not involve boundaries as well as those that do.

National Identity Reconceived

A serviceable definition requires substantive *content* as well as boundaries. When we ask "What is France?" we want to know not only that it is the area governed by the French government where French people live but also *why* those people identify with their country and their government and exactly *what* it is with which they identify. National identity should be understood as a predicate nominative rather than an abstract noun, as an ongoing process or journey rather than a fixed set of boundaries, a relationship rather than a free-standing entity or attribute. National identity is the relationship between nation and state that obtains when the people of that nation identify with the state. It is not a property or an aspect of either nation or state, which would force the differentiation between state identity and national identity, depriving the concept of the unity we have characterized as fundamental.

There are, to be sure, cases in which people identify with a state to some extent without being legal constituents of it. These range from purely sentimental identifications with states to which people trace their origins to espionage and fifth-column activity (suspected of German-Americans in World War I and of Japanese Nisei in World War II) or irredentism, when a foreign power chooses to activate an otherwise-latent nationalism. There are also cases in which people do not respond to claims for identification by the state with sovereignty over their political lives, in which instance that state lacks legitimacy. Both are pathological deformations that induce strain or even crisis: the former we might term "stateless nationalism" located in a nationality; the latter might be called "statism," and though it is difficult to envisage a nationless state, the Holy Roman Empire or the erstwhile Comintern in some ways approximate that condition.

There are two interdependent dimensions of national identity, one of which (the act of identification) ranges from strong to weak and might be measured on a scale of legitimacy (though an illegitimate system might continue to function in the absence of crisis).[34] The other dimension pertains to the substantive content with which people identify, namely the state itself. This in turn begs the question What is the state? The state may for our purpose be divided into two components: the state as defined by what it *does,* and the state as defined by what it *is.*

The state identifies itself most clearly by what it does as a collective unit. The state's performance is most visibly displayed in the international arena, where each state functions as an autonomous, unitary actor, engaging in behavior ranging from subtle demarches to waging major wars. Diachronically, national identity is the record of the zig-zag course of the ship of state through sometimes tempestuous international waters. To take this dimension into account is to provide the synthetic aspect of the definition, which defines the nation-state not in terms of its component parts but in terms of its relationship to other nation-states. Michael Ng-Quinn (Chap. 2) does so as he persuasively shows how the Chinese state, essentially through its foreign policy performance in response to various threats and opportunities during the formative Xia, Shang, and Zhou dynasties, defined itself as an entity with which its people (and indeed all succeeding Chinese people) could identify. Michael Hunt, in the next chapter, finds that this preoccupation with the state (particularly the *strong* state) as a focus of identification continued well into the twentieth century; in Chapter 9, Robert Scalapino demonstrates the relevance of this dimension national identity to China's role in contemporary East Asia.

[34]For a conceptualization of national identity that gives pride of place to the politics of identification, see Bloom, *Personal Identity.*

The total effect of state acts in relation to other states over a given period of time may be meaningfully characterized as a role played by the state. A national identity enacts itself by assuming various national roles. As Ng-Quinn puts it, a role is an identity fragment mobilized for a specific occasion. National roles, like their individual counterparts, perform the functions of mobilizing, testing, and validating an identity through interactions with other players in the same arena. In the case of China, Ng-Quinn shows how the elite selectively intensifies or moderates nationalism to secure domestic support for various roles on the international stage. In like manner, the German case illustrates how national roles can change over time. German nationalism quickly withered away after World War II, whereas previous defeats (1806 and 1918) had only fueled more radical nationalism. Harold James finds an explanation in the changing international milieu that molded national role expectations.[35]

Although some role theorists go so far as to contend that there is nothing beyond multiple roles,[36] most assume that underlying various changes of role there is a relatively stable design or purpose. This purpose, providing an intelligible "identity" to what might otherwise be considered random mutations, is empirically considered to be the result of integrating and ordering the roles designed to meet various social expectations and task environments. The national identity is, however, distinct from the sum of its roles: integral to the former is a sense of its uniqueness, which derives (in contrast to a role) from a perceived *incongruity* between role expectations and the sense of national integrity.[37]

According to symbolic interactionists, a role is formed by assimilating the judgments of significant others and then fashioning a specific "mask" in anticipation of such judgments; an identity is a repertoire of such roles.[38] The ensemble of significant others is called a "reference group," with whom frequent interaction is assumed to be functional and important. This reference group may be broken down into meaningful categories; for states,

[35]Harold James, *A German Identity, 1770–1990* (New York: Routledge Books, 1989).

[36]See, e.g., Erving Goffman, *Presentation of the Self in Everyday Life* (New York: Doubleday, 1959), or *Interaction Ritual* (Chicago: Aldine, 1967).

[37]Helen Merrell Lynd, *On Shame and the Search for Identity* (New York: Harcourt, Brace, 1958), pp. 210–58; see also Erikson, *Young Man Luther,* passim.

[38]See Anselm Strauss, *Mirrors and Masks: The Search for Identity* (Glencoe, Ill.: Free Press, 1959), p. 9; also George Herbert Mead, *Mind, Self, and Society* (Chicago: University of Chicago Press, 1934), pp. 337 passim. For a pioneering work on role theory in the study of foreign policy, see Stephen G. Walker, ed., *Role Theory and Foreign Policy Analysis* (Durham, N.C.: Duke University Press, 1987).

these might be bourgeois democracies, oil sheikdoms, NIEs, and developing countries. In addition to positive reference groups, with which a state desires to associate itself, there can be negative reference groups, whose opposition serves to dramatize the importance of defending the values of "us" against "them."

An international reference group contributes to national self-definition in two ways. First, it provides legitimacy. Discovering like-minded significant others allows a regime to maintain that its domestic social and political order has international validity. This is particularly important for revolutionary or freshly minted nation-states without ready resort to the sanction of a domestic tradition, which more established orders can rely on to bolster them. Second, it provides leadership. Once a state assumes an intimate ideological kinship with a chosen reference group, members will welcome its suggestions, even its vigorous leadership, in the pursuit of joint international objectives beyond realistic hope of attainment by one state alone.

In many, perhaps most, cases, both functions are served by the same international reference group. Thus for the Soviet Union, its position at the head of the international communist revolution has long provided both legitimacy and international leadership, reinforcing the leading role of the Communist party domestically. As for the United States, its self-appointed role as leader of the "free world" also serves both legitimating and leadership functions, though it is sometimes unclear what common values define this reference group (free in terms of markets or ballots?). India's erstwhile role as a leader of the Third World has served a similar legitimating function.[39] A forthcoming analysis of the Chinese case finds the People's Republic, in contrast, to be split between identification with the communist bloc, from which the regime derives its sense of historical mission, and with the Third World, on the basis of which it nurses its sense of grievance and "revolutionary" indignation.[40] Peter Van Ness, whose understanding of China's relations with other developing countries is second to none, provides in Chapter 8 a perceptive analysis of some of the strains that modernization and its attendant difficulties have imposed on that identity. He raises

[39]Ashis Banerjee, "The Ideology and Politics of India's National Identity," in Zoya Hasan, S. N. Jha, and Rasheeduddin Khan, eds., *The State, Political Processes and Identity: Reflections on Modern India* (Newbury Park, Calif.: Sage Publications, 1989), pp. 283–96.

[40]See Lowell Dittmer, *Sino-Soviet Normalization and Its International Implications, 1945–1990* (Seattle: University of Washington Press, 1992), chap. 4; see also Samuel Kim, *The Third World in Chinese World Policy* (Princeton: Princeton University, Center of International Studies, 1989).

the intriguing point that while Tiananmen reinforced identification with the Third World, at least for the hardline leadership faction that prevailed, this "official" identity is increasingly inconsonant with domestic conceptions of the "true," uniquely Chinese national identity. And while Tiananmen for similar reasons also reinforced identification with the communist bloc, the subsequent unraveling of that bloc (and many of its constituent members) has infused that identification with a sense of lonely paranoia.

Those nations whose size and resources do not permit them to exercise leadership over their reference groups still have several options open to them. First, they may reconcile themselves to the role of (sometimes reluctant or even nominal) followers and endeavor from this less salient position to persuade their reference group to adopt policies favorable to their interests, as in the cases of Mexico, Bulgaria, or postwar Japan. Second, they may attempt to usurp leadership, compensating for objective weakness with an especially compelling vision of a joint project or with a charismatic personal leader, as in the case of France under Charles de Gaulle or Fidel Castro's African exploits in the mid-1970s. Third, they may secede from their original reference group, as the Nicaraguans and Albanians have done. The need for an international reference group is so strong, however, that secession is usually followed by realignment with a new reference group, either by swinging to the opposite side, as in Castro's Cuba or Sadat's Egypt, or by attempting to assemble a totally new group, as in the nonaligned bloc organized by India, Yugoslavia, and others in the 1950s.

We have argued that the substantive content of national identity is the state and that the state defines itself by what roles it plays—by self-categorization in alignment with positive reference groups and in opposition to negative reference groups—by its performance in the international arena. But the state defines itself not only behaviorally but essentially—by what it "is" as well as what it "does." What the state is consists of the ensemble of symbols collected to represent the principles on which the group was founded and on the basis of which its members have contracted to live together. One of the distinctive properties of symbols is their connotative capacity, which goes beyond the denotative function of referring to empirical events to express and convey emotion.[41] The Japanese refer to this national symbol system (whose empirical referents of course

[41]Lowell Dittmer, "Political Culture and Political Symbolism: Toward a Theoretical Synthesis," *World Politics* 29 (July 1977): 552–84. The other distinctive property of symbols in their ability to designate multiple empirical referents, via metaphor, metonymy, and other figures of speech.

vary from case to case) as the *kokutai,* or "national essence" (roughly translated); the Chinese term, *guocui,* derives from the Japanese. This "essence" might consist of a canon of sacred texts. Thus the Jews are bound together by the Talmud, the Christians by the Bible, the Americans by their Constitution and Declaration of Independence, the English by the Magna Charta; the prewar Japanese were likewise bound by the Imperial Rescript. Beyond that, it might also include an oral tradition of myths and rituals— flags, holidays, national ceremonies of commemoration, inauguration, or even mourning; tales of national heroes, villains, battles, a foundation myth, and so forth.[42] In Chapter 4, James Watson shows how a sense of cultural identity was fostered in traditional China through a set of standard- ized rites and unifying symbols, focused for the most part around major life transitions (weddings, funerals). In the postrevolutionary period, he sees that cultural unity dividing into a rural culture, which still tends to be oriented around traditional symbolism, and an urban culture that has assimilated the new set of revolutionary symbols and rituals propagated by the regime.[43]

The national essence is, however, by no means fixed in the past, but subject to recurrent reinterpretation. The popular culture tends to spin out a medley of myths eulogizing the national symbol system even when the mass media are privately owned. A myth may be defined, in the words of Joan Bamberger, as "a part of a cultural history which provides justification for a present and perhaps permanent reality by giving an invented 'histor- ical' explanation of how this reality is created."[44] The national essence thus grows, stalagmitelike, by constant accretion. In Chapter 5, Richard Wilson shows how one central fixture of China's national essence, the filial ideal, has been reinterpreted in the course of modernization from an early par- ticularistic interpretation to a universalistic ethic—thus the ambit of "car- ing," for example, has shifted from an exclusive concern for one's "connec- tions" [*guanxi*] to a gradually increasing regard for equal rights, legally enforced. This change is demonstrated not on the basis of normative texts,

[42]See Steven I. Levine, "China and the Socialist Community: Symbolic Unity" (Paper presented at the Conference on China's Quest for National Identity) (see n. 20); also Claes Arvidsson and Lars Erik Blomquist, eds., *Symbols of Power: The Aesthetics of Political Legitima- tion in the Soviet Union and Eastern Europe* (Stockholm: Almqvist och Wiksell, 1987).

[43]See also James Watson, "The Renegotiation of Chinese Cultural Identity in the Post-Mao Era: An Anthropological Perspective" (Paper prepared for the Four Anniversaries China Conference, Annapolis, Md., September 11–15, 1989).

[44]Joan Bamberger, "The Myth of Matriarchy: Why Men Rule in Primitive Societies," in Michelle Zimbalist Rosaldo and Louise Lamphere, eds., *Woman, Culture, and Society* (Stan- ford: Stanford University Press, 1974), p. 267.

which are often too euphemistic to be empirically relevant, but through careful analysis of the court cases whereby norms are enforced—and preserved as precedents. Even certain facets of the Tiananmen crackdown, he points out, evinced a concern for legal norms.

The resulting structure of the *guocui* is like that of a nebula, in that it is clear at the core and increasingly hazy at the periphery. (Take the American symbol system for an example: it certainly includes the Federalist Papers, perhaps even Mark Twain, and has as its central focus an antinomian individualism somewhat alleviated by participation in voluntary associations and a vague ethic of civility—but does it include *Catch-22?*)[45] The People's Republic's *guocui* includes some of the Confucian and Daoist legacy as well as some selection of Mao's writings, with a central focus on filial piety and the qualified extrapolation of these principles to the political arena: the need for peace, harmony, and stability—underlined by the eruption of uncontrollable chaos when these values are jeopardized.[46] These traditions never reign unchallenged, and just as Americans are periodically afflicted by nostalgia for primary-group solidarity, the Chinese symbolic legacy has been even more directly confronted by the values of permanent revolution. Using the past to serve the present (and suppressing that part of the past deemed not to be useful) is standard operating procedure in China, as it perhaps is to some extent in all political systems, and what survives is a matter of time and context. In any case, all of these symbols, which may be easily shared among various ethnoreligious, linguistic, or nationality groupings within a given national culture, flesh out the content of what it means to be a Chinese—or a Pole, or a Pakistani. People define their national identities through *identification* with these symbols. If this proposition is correct, a comprehensive investigation of the national identity of a given nation-state should encompass not merely the categories by which inhabitants differentiate themselves but the nature and meaning of the symbol system with which they jointly identify.

In any arrangement of this kind, in which the group's identity is oriented

[45]See Alexis de Tocqueville, *Democracy in America,* 2 vols., trans. Henry Reeve (Rochelle, N.Y.: Arlington, 1956); Louis Hartz, *The Liberal Tradition in America: An Interpretation of American Political Thought since the Revolution* (New York: Harcourt, Brace, 1955); Sacvan Bercowitch, *The American Jeremiad* (Madison: University of Wisconsin Press, 1978); and Clive Jones, *A Dream of Reason: American Consciousness and Cultural Achievement from Independence to the Civil War* (London: Arnold, 1977).

[46]See Benjamin I. Schwartz, *China's Cultural Values,* Occasional Paper No. 18 (Tempe: Arizona State University, Center for Asian Studies, 1985); and Richard Solomon, *Mao's Revolution and the Chinese Political Culture* (Berkeley and Los Angeles: University of California Press, 1971).

around a core symbol system, there are apt to be winners and losers. Chief among the former would be the politicians and civil servants authorized to wield the powers and distribute the values for which the symbols stand, who are coincident beneficiaries of the whole process of identification that causes the group to cohere. Not only do they run the government, they have considerable power, even under the most pluralistic regimes, to manipulate the symbol system through which government activities are interpreted. Indeed they have the duty to do so; for they are in charge of guarding the *guocui* and ensuring that the day-to-day workings of the government coincide with the core symbols that define the system. Thus their duties coincide neatly with their interests. And, as they drape themselves in the flag, all their activities assume a magnified significance. Although the entire hierarchy stands to gain from this arrangement, the most conspicuous beneficiary is the symbolic leader chosen to represent the nation in the international arena. If that leader has the ability to capture the imagination of his or her people, the position of symbolic leadership can be enhanced to proportions tantamount to personally incarnating the national essence,[47] but the phenomenon of national incarnation is by no means limited to charismatic or authoritarian leaders.

Although political elites are the major beneficiaries of the *guocui,* their self-appointed role as its servitors and custodians is not unchallenged. Their major competitors for this responsibility in the modern age have been the intelligentsia, the secular priesthood of the national spirit, whose skills at symbol manipulation well qualify them to interpret the canonical texts, collectively meaningful experiences, and so forth. Although the Chinese Communist variant of "proletarian dictatorship" has, since liberation, guarded the CCP's monopoly over both the content of the national symbol system and the media through which it is routinely disseminated with unusual zeal, Chinese intellectuals have nonetheless still managed to interpolate their own construal of the principles for which the nation stands into its agenda. Ironically, suppression may have given them greater weight, by obliging them to express themselves obliquely through the entertainment media most accessible to popular consumption. Goldman, Link, and Su trace with

---

[47]Norton, *Reflections on Political Identity,* p. 122. Hans Mol points out that personal charisma may be a source of symbolic reintegration with the national essence rather than an innovative departure from it—prophets from Elijah through Malachi stood firmly in a tradition, for example, as do contemporary charismatics such as Khomeini or Pope John Paul II. This type of charisma "reinterprets catastrophic events as meaningful in the light of a tradition" (e.g., conquest, exile). Mol, *Identity and the Sacred: A Sketch and a New Social-Scientific Theory of Religion* (Oxford: Basil Blackwell, 1976).

considerably subtlety the evolution of Chinese intellectual thought over the course of Deng Xiaoping's reform era, from early support to increasingly explicit criticism and even resistance, in an approximation of the ancient model of Qu Yuan (338–278 B.C.), whose martyrdom has come to symbolize love of country combined with hatred of its current leadership.[48] In this they are eerily reminiscent of the politically engaged intellectuals depicted in the latter half of Hunt's chapter, who articulated an intellectual alternative to the old regime they spurned long before the organizational (or military) wherewithal was at hand to realize their plans. The relative positions of the actors in this national drama look familiar, though the ideological script has changed.

Why do people other than public servants and symbol manipulators identify with this symbolic artifact? The most conspicuous defendants of the national essence—the martyrs who give their lives for this symbol system (and very little else), the Lei Fengs and Jeanne d'Arcs of the world—are not necessarily among its leading beneficiaries. Generally speaking, there are both objective and subjective reasons for national identification with its essence. The objective reasons have to do with the powers and values that the symbol system represents. It is obvious that the nation-state as a whole can amass much more power than its disaggregated constitutents or even, under normal circumstances, any subgroup of them. The government monopolizes the instruments of violence (in most countries more effectively than in the United States), usually also wielding extensive power over transportation, communication, education, the public sector, and even varying portions of private life, such as abortion and possession of pornography. The core values of the national symbol system stipulate that this power will be used for the public weal and spell out the specific principles on the basis of which public weal is calculated. This vast power, utilized in the pursuit of what is consensually defined as the common good, naturally tends to inspire identification, sometimes even awe or worship.

The subjective reasons include the obvious but still important fact that people seem to have a universal psychological need to belong, which political systems are able to tap. Children thus undergo "political socialization," whereby they are taught to identify with the national symbol system.[49] Through the school system, various programmed political rituals

[48]See Laurence A. Schneider, *A Madman of Ch'u: The Chinese Myth of Loyalty and Dissent* (Berkeley and Los Angeles: University of California Press, 1980).

[49]Herbert Hyman coined this term with his book of the same name (New York: Free Press, 1959), which has since spawned a considerable literature, e.g., David Easton and Jack Dennis, *Children in the Political System: Origins of Political Legitimacy* (New York: McGraw-Hill, 1969).

(national holidays, anthems, the pledge of allegiance), and contact with local representatives of the government (the policeman, the court system, the school teacher), the child learns that the government is vast and powerful and that this power is used to defend the people and to promote something called the public interest. Throughout their lives, people are encouraged to identify with the national symbols and taught to be willing to fight and if necessary die for them. People learn that not only may they win plaudits for conspicuous defense of the *guocui,* but they may be shamed or even physically punished for refusal to show such deference. The vast power and imputed goodness of the government inspires various compensatory fantasies whose expression is not always permitted in personal identity formation; thus the national identity becomes the repository of the most cherished, sometimes even extravagant or demented, aspirations.

It must be conceded that despite this self-reinforcing feedback, identification with the national essence is to some extent a variable rather than a constant. Nor is it a completely one-way transaction: people do learn to identify with their state, but they also *project* their own aspirations onto it; and when those aspirations are not met, dismay is likely. People *do* sometimes burn flags, depose or even shoot their leaders, and overthrow their governments, despite all the risks and blame attached to such defiance. The typical justifications given for such opposition to the symbolically sanctified status quo is that the power and the values intended for realization of the national identity have been abused or corruptly distributed, that the politicians have confused their personal interests with the public weal. Aside from purely personal disappointments, a constant process of policy evaluation unfolds, based on two sets of criteria. First, a fact-value assessment: does the current formulation of policy accord with the ideals and principles set forth in the sacred documents of the *guocui,* making due allowance for the expedient need to maintain high economic growth, low unemployment, tolerable inflation rates, and so forth? Second, an assessment of the country's place in the world: does the state's role correspond to its national interests and ideal interests, making due allowance for its size and resources relative to the opportunities and risks inherent in the international milieu? The debate that forever preoccupies the public media is waged not according to Robert's rules of order but in euphemistic, self-serving rhetoric that distorts, sometimes outrageously, even while it illuminates the vital issues at stake. Indeed, the more fact diverges from value, the greater the confusion, as public officials engage in even more patriotic posturing than usual in an attempt to argue that any personnel change will have an adverse impact on the national essence, while opposition forces argue that all recent public policy should be reconstrued in terms of the selfish or partisan interests of incumbent politicians.

An unusually turbulent or refractory domestic or international environ-ment can cause a nation to have difficulties establishing a fully realized national identity, one that is realistically appropriate to its capabilities of power projection beyond its borders, that approximates the values of the *guocui,* and that meshes reasonably well with the ideal interests of its main ethnolinguistic groups. In those instances in which the dilemma resists resolution, owing perhaps to the correlation of forces supporting mutually incompatible ideal interests, a state may resort to "searching" behavior, such as experimenting with probationary roles, or to an overly ambitious, even "crazy," status drive.[50]

Finally, whereas much of this discussion has been focused on the "syn-thetic" dimension of identity missing from previous conceptualizations, the analytic dimension should by no means be discarded. Certainly the ethnic mix of the nation-state is vital to its identity, as is the national boundary and whom it includes and excludes. In this latter respect, it is interesting to note the identity-threatening paradox that the Chinese outside of the People's Republic are among the world's most wealthy and productive people, while those inside are among the world's poorest and least productive. As impor-tant as boundaries are to self-definition, they should perhaps not be concep-tualized in zero-sum terms, as White and Li make clear in Chapter 7. In a fascinating overview of Taiwan, Hong Kong, and South China, they depict the Chinese border as a permeable membrane, an interface with the outside world through which flow not only trade and people, but ideas. The whole center–periphery relationship seems to have shifted in the course of reform from one in which the center was the source of initiative and change to one in which the center is increasingly overtaken by developments along its periphery. As both Chapters 6 and 7 point out, this is symbolized in Su Xiaokang's 1988 *River Elegy* television documentary, which denigrates the historic Chinese symbols of the center—the Yellow River and the Great Wall—and heralds the Pacific Ocean as the symbol of innovation and progress. White and Li also show the impact that change in the function of China's littoral periphery has had on its natives, who have become far more cosmopolitan and open than their more centrally located compatriots.

[50]See Yehezkel Dror, *Crazy States: A Counterconventional Strategic Problem* (Lexington, Mass.: Heath, 1971). Dror's principal example of a "crazy state" is, of course, Nazi Germany— which, it is interesting to recall, deemed itself at the time to be a divided, emasculated nation.

Identity Relationships and Dynamics

Having just articulated a new conceptualization of national identity, we are not probably ready to attempt to formulate a fully fledged theory, but at least some of the areas where future research efforts seem most promising might be sketched out. One such is the relationships among different levels of identity. Harry Eckstein once proposed a theory of "congruence," according to which unless the various tiers of organization in a society (primary group, voluntary association, and national) are organized in the same pattern, "strain" will ensue.[51] National identity may be similarly conceived as the most stable and basic elements in a stratified hierarchy of self-defining political actions. Imagine an iceberglike arrangement, with the most visible and flexible at the top and the most invisible and invariant at the base. The iceberg should have at least five levels (beginning at the top): public opinion, policies, principles, a policy platform (what the Chinese would call the "basic line," valid for a period of 5–10 years), and at the base, the national identity. If the national identity is relatively stable and "mature," there will be "congruence" among all five levels; public opinion and policy will shift, of course, but it should remain possible to subsume the visible, variable levels to the more abstract subsurface levels. A sharp incongruity among levels might be expected to precipitate an "identity crisis." Any such crisis might be resolved either through appropriate adjustment of specific policies or, more momentously, through a redefinition of the national identity. Of course between these extremes lies a continuum from various compromises to ousting the incumbent leadership.

Whether this same model can be applied to the relationship between levels of identity within the polity is still unclear. Just what is the relationship between national identity and "national character"? Does China, (or Japan, or Panama) in its international comportment in any way reflect the culturally based role repertoire or set of expectations of the ideal-typical Chinese (Japanese, or Panamanian) citizen? As we have already indicated, any attempt to anthropomorphize the nation-state, or to assume an automatic equivalence between national identity and national character, is empirically untenable. More cautious hypotheses should not however be precluded. To the extent that foreign policy is conducted with an eye to

---

[51]Harry Eckstein, *The Natural History of Congruence Theory* (Denver: University of Denver, 1980). His most telling example is that of Weimar Germany, which consisted of authoritarian family patterns, authoritarian voluntary associations, and a highly democratic national political structure. The Weimar Republic was "odd man out" in this otherwise congruent arrangement, and it indeed proved vulnerable to pressure for congruence.

domestic popularity, there is an inducement to model the former after an idealized conception of the national character, and political leaders commonly do so, examples being Lyndon Johnson's frontier-style admonition to American forces to "bring home the coonskin" from Vietnam and George Bush's Rambo-style comportment in the Gulf War. Contrariwise, to the extent that foreign policy is visibly successful, there will be an inducement for the citizenry to identify with the nation-state and seek to embody its core values. Thus the incentives of leaders and masses for national identification are reciprocal but neither functionally equivalent nor necessarily oriented to the same policies for the same reasons.

The social environments of the nation-state and its constituent citizenry are quite different. Whereas the state operates in a decentralized system without central authority, the individual is constrained by political, moral, and legal sanctions. The result is that national identification elevates the citizen from moral constraint to the realm of raison d'état, tending to bring out the more primeval passions. At each level, the assumed identity must cope appropriately with challenges or opportunities in its respective environment, while at the same time attempting to maintain a meaningfully intelligible relationship to the other level; identity thus functions as a "bridging" concept.[52] The bridge consists of a complex form of psychocultural interdependency—national identity is not merely personal emotions writ large, as Harold Lasswell had it, but in some cases a compensatory device, serving a masking function. Thus where Chinese citizens are socialized to depend on others domestically (*guanxi*), in the international arena the People's Republic emphasizes self-reliance and independence; whereas the Chinese party-state is among the most intrusive in the world in the lives of its own citizenry, it vehemently denounces any intrusion by other states into its internal affairs. The authoritarian, aggressive national identity of Nazi Germany found its best match at the level of national character not in the self-assertive Superman that Nietzsche idolized but in the boot-licking toady. The types of interdependency that obtain between personal, domestic political, and foreign policy self-expression remain to be more fully investigated.

The relationship may also be expected to vary over time, as the national identity changes to reflect the changing fortunes of the state in the international arena, waxing and waning in its power to attract the identification of its citizenry. This may be expected to become ever more true with the

---

[52]See Andrew J. Weigert, J. Smith Teitge, and Dennis W. Teitge, *Society and Identity: Toward a Sociological Psychology* (Cambridge: Cambridge University Press, 1986), p. 2.

increasing dominance of electronic media and the growing forgetfulness of mass publics of history or "tradition." The situation of international enmity or threat seems to be particularly well suited to intense national identification, sometimes even leaving a lingering aura of nostalgia owing to these ancillary political benefits. Aside from enhancing solidarity, enmities can reflexively define the national purpose, the pace and direction of movement toward it, even the distribution of resources.[53] Aside from those nations forged in the furnace of war, such as Germany or the United States, are those whose identity was etched by early enmities—consider the role of the Holocaust in the formation of the state of Israel. Chinese "self-strengthing" in response to outside threats played a consistently significant role in the formation of modern China's national identity, as Hunt clearly demonstrates in Chapter 3.

A second question worth investigating is whether national identity formation has any "normal" career or developmental itinerary similar to the Eriksonian stages in the evolution of personal identity, each in reaction to a stage-specific dilemma. It would be interesting to determine in this regard (1) what stages the individual goes through in his or her identification with the nation-state and (2) whether the nation-state itself goes through various stages in the realization of a "mature" international identity. The first question has benefited from the findings of students of political socialization,[54] but the second seems not to have been systematically investigated. Why do nations at certain points conceive of a "mission" that must be fulfilled—a white man's burden, *mission civilisatrice,* or Manifest Destiny? Is it conceivable that the expansionist, imperialist drive to build an empire is specific to a particular stage in a nation's development? Was Japan's attempt to realize its East Asian Co-Prosperity Sphere simply out of phase with the high tide of imperialism in the eighteenth and nineteenth centuries when such ambitions were à la mode in the West? These are sweeping questions, of course, which those writing an introduction can more easily pose than serious scholars can responsibly answer. Still, other aspects of political development have been explored, and there is no a priori reason to rule these questions out of court.

In this spirit, we suggest some tentative hypotheses. First, if any nation surges rapidly ahead of others in economic, technological, or military

[53]Norton, *Reflections on Political Identity,* p. 56.

[54]E.g., cf. Gustav Jahoda, "The Development of Children's Ideas about Country and Nationality," *British Journal of Educational Psychology* 33 (February and June 1963): 46–60, 143–53; and Joseph Adelson and Robert P. O'Neill, "Growth of Political Ideas in Adolescence: The Sense of Community," *Journal of Personality and Social Psychology* 4 (September 1966): 295–306.

realms, there is a natural tendency to assimilate into the national identity a sense of expansive and sometimes aggressive self-confidence, as in the cases of England (the first industrialized country), Germany, the United States, and Japan. A nation newly emerging on the international scene in a position of economic and technological "underdevelopment" is, in contrast, apt to be afflicted with intense ambivalence, consisting of a sort of national inferiority complex, combined with envy of more advanced countries. This is particularly likely if the traditional status of that nation was in contrast very high (in the case of China, a "central kingdom," a recipient of foreign "tribute"). In this pattern of maturation, the emerging nation is apt to go through an initial phase of rebellion or revolution against its more advanced colonizer or patron, followed by a period of emulation and modeling (sometimes the sequence may be reversed, as in the Chinese pattern of subordination followed by rebellion against the Soviet embrace), before emerging as a truly autonomous national identity. Once this stage of "maturity" has been reached, identity issues tend to assume a lower profile as the citizenry becomes absorbed in issues of political economy—except in cases of unrealized identity, such as the divided nations. Under situations of national threat or major crisis, however, old issues of national identity are apt to resurface.[55]

Finally, the question of the nature and origin of identity threats, or crises in extreme cases, requires further analysis. We postulate two forms of such a crisis, the first of which is based on the analytic definition of national identity, which might be subtyped as "crises of inclusion," and the second, based on the synthetic definition, which might be called "crises of self-definition."

Crises of inclusion.   A crisis of inclusion is apt to occur when there is an extremely sharp or intractable discrepancy between sets of criteria for inclusion of populations or territory into the nation-state. After all, although boundaries are in a sense arbitrary, territory is essential: not all territorial states are nation-states, but all nation-states must be territorial. It is possible to have a national identity without a defined territory, but it is not possible to have a nation-state without territory, as demonstrated by the current predicament of the Palestinians.

There are three types of inclusion crises: border disputes over irredentas, secessionary conflicts and civil wars, and divided nations. An irredenta is an instance in which national or ethnic criteria provide grounds for a group's

[55]See Bloom, *Personal Identity*.

inclusion whereas legally constituted physical boundaries do not. Historically, Alsace-Lorraine was among the most notorious and explosive such
regions, shifting from French to German control for 1871 through 1917,
reverting to French sovereignty from 1917 to 1940, being reannexed by
Germany from 1940 to 1945, and thereafter being definitively ceded to
France. This type of crisis is not central to a nation's identity, but literally
peripheral, yet may fester for years—we have alluded to Israel's West Bank
issue. A border dispute over an irredenta may be resolved either by revising
the boundaries to include the disputed territory (as in the planned peaceful
retrocession of Hong Kong), by writing off the kindred national or ethnic
group (as in China's eventual decision to renounce claims on overseas
Chinese in Southeast Asia), or by some compromise between the two (as in
the 1975 partition of Trieste between Italy and Yugoslavia).

A war of secession may erupt when a group is included by physical
boundaries but is or feels excluded on the basis of ethnic or national criteria
and decides to secede. If the seceding group is relatively weak, a separatist
movement is likely, as in the case of the Basque separatists in Spain, the
Hungarians in Romania, the Bandangan minority in Uganda, or the Tibetan Buddhists or Xinjiang Moslem minorities in China. Given the imbalance of forces between central and minority governments, the prospects
of separatist movements are normally bleak, though a sudden collapse of
will at the center (as in the sudden repudiation of the hard line in Moscow
after the unsuccessful August 1991 coup) may open a window of opportunity for independence. To have a realistic chance of opting out and taking
a defensible chunk of territory with it, a seceding group must normally
constitute a sizable sector of the nation's population and military resources,
in which case, civil war ensues. Civil war elevates the crisis to a position of
such centrality in the nation's identity that bitter, sanguinary violence is
likely, whether the secession succeeds (as in the sundering of Bangladesh
from Pakistan) or fails (as in the American and Nigerian civil wars and the
strife between Sinhalese and Tamils in Sri Lanka).

The problem of a divided nation comprises elements of both the irredenta and the war of secession. As in an irredenta, a group that would have
normally been included on ethnonational grounds is excluded by territorial
boundaries. As in a civil war, this exclusion is defined (by both sides) as
central rather than peripheral to the nation's identity. Although this combination of factors creates a potentially explosive situation, the problem is
unique in the sense that the division coincides with a larger international
cleavage (the Cold War), making it impossible to bridge without complex
multilateral negotiations.

Nation-states will be susceptible to the types of inclusion crises consistent with their developmental status, the international environment, and other conditions. The first two subtypes seem to be endemic among less developed nations, while the third is an artifact of the international balance of power that involves nations on the basis of their strategic location without regard for their stage of development.

Crises of self-definition.   A crisis of self-definition may occur at any time in a nation's development when the consensually agreed-upon national developmental trajectory is thrown open to fundamental question. Inasmuch as less developed countries are apt to give development a higher priority than more technologically advanced countries, they may be more susceptible to such crises, though advanced countries are hardly invulnerable. Such a crisis is likely to erupt at three junctures: when the chosen developmental "road" conspicuously fails, when it succeeds beyond expectations, and when it is challenged by a convincing alternative. The reason failure can precipitate a national identity crisis is fairly obvious. Who we are depends on where we are going (particularly for Marxists), so if we have been moving toward a dead end, a fundamental rethinking seems called for. This seems to have been the case with regard to the Soviet Union since the death of Brezhnev.

Unexpected success can precipitate an identity crisis if it removes certain goals that hitherto provided the raison d'être for the regime's authority and popular legitimacy. Thus it is possible to argue, for example, that China was faced by such a crisis upon the unexpectedly swift completion of "socialization of the means of production" in 1956–57. If T. H. Rigby is correct in contending that communist systems are systemically different from constitutional democracies, aiming for "goal-rational" behavior rather than formal-legal procedural rationality, then communist systems may be vulnerable to identity crisis not only when they perpetually fail to achieve their proclaimed goals but when they achieve them with unexpected speed.[56]

The third subtype of crises of self-definition, which is precipitated by the confrontation of the nation-state with an apparently superior alternative approach to development, may but need not coincide with failure of the

[56]T. H. Rigby, "Introduction: Political Legitimacy, Weber, and Communist Mono-Organizational Systems," in Rigby et al., eds., *Political Legitimation in Communist States* (London: Macmillan, 1982), pp. 1–27. Western legal-rational bureaucracies, Rigby argues, are concerned with the application of abstract rules to particular cases, whereas socialist bureaucracies are oriented toward goal achievement rather than the application of rules and tend to disregard the violation of legal or administrative rules if the goal is achieved.

indigenous model (in the case of China's May Fourth movement it did, but in the People's Republic's more recent crisis of confidence about reform it did not). Two considerations seem to be important here: the relative objective levels of advancement or backwardness and the subjective awareness of this discrepancy, which depends essentially on the range of freedom and the penetration of the media. Inasmuch as media exposure is selective under even optimal conditions, such a crisis is likely to exacerbate tension not only between the native and the foreign (as in rustic xenophobia versus the cosmopolitan conviction that even the moon is rounder and brighter abroad) but between those exposed and those shielded from foreign media (urban elites versus backwater anti-intellectuals). Such a dual cleavage is apt to be so incapacitating that it results in compromise, for example, the "Western culture as technique, native culture as essence" formula that has had its heyday in Japan as well as China.

In sum, a serviceable definition of national identity would indeed include, in Verba's words, all those who "fall within the decision-making scope of the state," whether defined in territorial, ethnoreligious, linguistic, or cultural terms, in the sense that they are the ones who "identify." But a comprehensive definition should be synthetic as well as analytic, with a focus on what it is, exactly, that people identify with. We define this as a relationship of "identification" between nation and state. The state is of course an abstract noun, but its substantive content may be specified in both behavioral and essentialist terms. What the state does is engage in various exploits on behalf of the nation it represents, most visibly in foreign policy. These actions—supporting this, attacking that—make up a role, and the accumulated roles constitute an identity. What the state "is" is defined in a symbol system known as the national essence, which consists of the myths, rituals, ceremonies, and folklore that relate how the nation came to be and what it stands for. This symbol system bears the lasting imprint of the founding experience but nevertheless remains in some flux. Its evolution is the product of: (1) the projected aspirations and demands of the citizenry (both masses and elites); (2) domestic political history, particularly those epoch-making events (like Tiananmen) whose reverberations are felt by the population at large; and (3) foreign policy experience, as the ship of state navigates unpredictable international waters. Deciding just what the national identity is at any particular time is thus nearly always problematic, both in the sense that multiple considerations must be weighed and in the sense that the answer affects everyone. Finally, the national identity is defined vis-à-vis other identities in terms of its boundaries, and the integrity of those boundaries must be maintained at penalty of a crisis of inclusion. Yet boundaries are avenues of absorption as well as exclusion, a permeable membrane through which ideas as well as things and people flow.

Once reasonably securely established, a national identity may be expectd to provide a reasonable basis for expectations concerning that nation's future comportment, just as personal identity commonly provides a basis for predictions of individual behavior ("He stole it because he is a thief.").[57] And just as personal identity is by no means an infallible guide, neither is national identity: the "aggressive, have-not" Axis powers of World War II have since come to represent a quite different formula for national eminence,[58] though the suspicion attached to their previous identities lingers, as indicated by brouhahas over Japanese textbook revision. National identities may change, particularly in the wake of such major reshuffles of the international system as that precipitated by Yalta, or the no less profound transformation of Europe since 1989. At this writing, Europe aspires to synthesize a new supranational identity within the European Community, one superpower is searching for a new international role while the other is struggling desperately just to hold itself together, and China and Japan are both confronted by identity dilemmas of quite different types.

[57]See Glynis M. Breakwell, "Formulations and Searches," in Breakwell, ed., *Threatened Identities* (New York: 1983), pp. 3–29.

[58]See Richard Rosecrance, *The Rise of the Trading State: Commerce and Conquest in the Modern World* (New York: Basic Books, 1985).

中
國 **2**

National Identity in Premodern China: Formation and Role Enactment

Michael Ng-Quinn

In this chapter, I am concerned with "national identity" not as it relates to some ethnic community or social solidarity group but as it relates to the state. (I deal later with the terms *nation* and *state*.) The purpose of any identity is to regularize behavior so that uncertainties can be minimized and life rendered more manageable.[1] The function of a national identity is to sustain the state by unifying the population, at least psychologically. The state is important because it has historically proved to be the most effective unit of human organization to provide for the physical survival of a sizable population. Moreover, national symbols with which people identify arouse feelings, fulfilling primordial, affective needs. An emotional identity with the state as an embodiment of the combination of many common elements of the population also reinforces national distinctiveness, which justifies the perpetuation of the state.

A state is inanimate and has no consciousness, feelings, or self. Its identity is collectively constructed by its members. To the extent that only a small elite is actively involved in national and foreign affairs, national

Comments by Lowell Dittmer, Samuel S. Kim, Robert Scalapino, Arthur Waldron, Richard Wilson, and other participants in the conference, as well as those by two anonymous readers, are gratefully acknowledged.

[1]Kenneth R. Hoover, *A Politics of Identity: Liberation and the Natural Community* (Urbana: University of Illinois Press, 1975), pp. 116–17; Erik H. Erikson, *Childhood and Society,* 2d ed. (New York: Norton, 1963).

identity is usually mediated, if not dictated, by the elite. (The ability of the elite to transmit messages to the masses is assumed here.) But a nation-state's identity is a function of not only elite definition and domestic expectations but also the state's changing interaction with other states. Discrepancies between internal and external expectations and realities may cause identity confusion or even crises.

Such discrepancies can be adjusted by elite mediation, or "national role conception," as Kal Holsti calls it. As part of its definition of national identity, the elite can also define the state's status or position in the international system, thus determining what functions or roles the state should perform.[2] A "role" can be understood, says Peter du Preez, as "identity mobilized in a specific situation."[3] A firm identity can be flexibly mobilized in a variety of situations without confusion. A state can therefore play various roles in external circumstances beyond its control without having to alter its fundamental identity. Lacking a firm identity to begin with, or failing to establish a "national role conception," the state may have to constantly redefine its identity in reaction to changing external realities, causing uncertainty and instability. A firm national identity allows the elite to selectively and dynamically moderate or intensify nationalism to secure domestic support for various national roles. This elite mediation can be achieved through the manipulation of ideologies or other symbols.

In premodern China, national identity was characterized by a strong sense of unity of the state irrespective of internal (ethnic, local, factional, or individual) differences and conflicts and by a preference for differential interaction with other states on the basis of cultural compatibility. China managed to enact different roles as the state expanded, underwent disintegration at the hands of other states, or coexisted with them, never having to alter its fundamental national identity.

This broad and abstract topic and my interdisciplinary approach impose certain limitations. First, I treat historical information theoretically. Whereas historians may find many inadequacies in this chapter from their perspectives, any discussion of "national identity" must, however, involve abstraction, which by definition omits many empirical details. My generalizations are based on what I believe to be generally accepted historical data and physical evidence; but even this data and evidence—let alone all that

[2]Kal J. Holsti, "National Role Conceptions in the Study of Foreign Policy," *International Studies Quarterly* 14 (September 1970): 233–309.

[3]Peter du Preez, *The Politics of Identity: Ideology and the Human Image* (Oxford: Basil Blackwell, 1980), pp. 5–6.

which is not and cannot be included here—can of course be rearranged to support a totally different thesis. Any argument rests on assumptions, preconceptions, theories, and biases. A broad interpretation of history (as opposed to mere documentation of "facts") is therefore neither accurate nor inaccurate, only suggestive, persuasive, useful, or otherwise.

Second, my examples are drawn from premodern Chinese history, up through the Ming dynasty (A.D. 1368–1644). The Qing dynasty (A.D. 1644–1911), though I mention it, is not discussed in any detail because it marks the transition from premodern to modern history, and it involves massive contact with the West. Michael Hunt deals with some aspects of this difficult period in the next chapter.

Third, my purpose in this chapter is limited to hypothesis generating. Much more hypothesis testing is needed, not only against more extensive premodern data but also against data drawn from modern and contemporary China. This is an immense task that will take a great deal of time and work to accomplish. Meanwhile, I leave open the question of continuity or discontinuity, discussing briefly the implications of both possibilities in conclusion.

Finally, this chapter is about the formation and role enactment of state/national identity *as behavior*. Ideas and ideologies about the state are pertinent here only as devices used by the elite to justify state behavior. I am not particularly concerned here about the historical development of Chinese ideas of the state per se (which is the topic of my forthcoming study).

So much for disclaimers. Before turning to the claims, let me return to the terms *nation* and *state*. These two terms denote different entities. A cursory look at the literature suggests that a "nation" is only a community (ethnic, cultural, or social), whereas a "state" involves governmental institutions and sovereign control.[4] I take "sovereignty" to mean final and absolute authority and its acceptance by the people accomplished through identifying the claims of the state with the needs of the community.[5] Sovereignty as a criterion of differentiation between "nation" and "state" is unnecessary when the two in fact coincide, but it may be usefully applied to a multinational state (like the United States or China) or to a migrant or scattered "nation" without a state (such as the Jewish people before the founding of Israel).

As Hugh Seton-Watson has observed, "In the main European languages

[4]Hugh Seton-Watson, *Nations and States: An Enquiry into the Origins of Nations and the Politics of Nationalism* (Boulder, Colo.: Westview, 1977), p. 1; Louis L. Snyder, *The Meaning of Nationalism* (New Brunswick, N.J.: Rutgers University Press, 1954), p. 20.

[5]F. H. Hinsley, *Sovereignty,* 2d ed. (Cambridge: Cambridge University Press, 1986), pp. 86, 17–18.

the words 'international relations' and their equivalent are used to denote the relations between states."[6] I follow this common usage and treat "nation" and "state" and their derivatives as interchangeable. In place of "nation" to refer to a community, I use "ethnic group" (or *minzu* in Chinese). An ethnic group can be a clan, tribe, *narodnost* in Russian, or a minority group or "nationality" within a state. Race, however, is not necessarily a criterion; for instance, most of China's fifty-six component ethnic groups are Mongoloid in race.[7]

In this chapter, *nationalism* and *ethnonationalism* must be clearly distinguished. For our purposes, "nationalism" denotes an ultimate emotional identity with (and an ultimate loyalty to) the state. Additionally, one can have another, but not ultimate, emotional identity with one's own ethnic group, in one state or across many states. This is called "ethnonationalism,"[8] which must be understood here as a secondary sentiment: having it does not imply rejection of state sovereignty. Otherwise, it is better termed "separatism." Nationalism is the primary focus of this chapter.

Finally, I need to define "state" in clearer terms. The literature is full of suggestions and debates, which space does not allow me to introduce here.[9] Quite simply, by "state," I mean an organized, centralized, and stratified core population that occupies and has sovereign control over certain core territories. In this definition, allowances are made for (1) peripheral changes in population and territories (thus the absence of well-delineated boundaries), but not changes in the core; and (2) occasional but temporary disruption of sovereign control owing to internal disorder, regionalism, separatism, or foreign invasion.

Reasons of State

The state is important for at least three reasons: physical survival, national distinctiveness, and primacy.

Physical survival. Let me use the logic of the origins of state to illustrate its importance. We can agree that basic subsistence can be better fulfilled by

[6]Seton-Watson, *Nations and States,* p. 1.

[7]Yang Kun, "Some Problems in the Concept of 'Nation' and the Classification of Nations," *Social Sciences in China* 5 (June 1984): 161.

[8]Walker Connor, "Ethnonationalism," in Myron Weiner and Samuel Huntington, eds., *Understanding Political Development* (Boston: Little, Brown, 1987), pp. 196–220.

[9]For a review, see Gabriel A. Almond, "The Return to the State," *American Political Science Review* 82 (September 1988): 853–74.

collective action. The degree of collective action or the lack thereof is in part a function of interaction with the environment and the utility derived from such interaction. For instance, one may tend to be asocial if resources in the environment permit self-sufficiency, whereas one may be more inclined to cooperation if there is scarcity or predators.[10]

Collective behavior and interaction may also be prompted by sociability, which may arise from a primordial need for companionship and affection. Such a need helps explain the initial development of family. Otherwise, men and women would not stay together to form families after the fulfillment of their biologic needs (as in the prefamily stage where a woman may bear a child without knowing who the father is).

Another aspect of sociability is exercise of power. While the desire for power may be psychological, its exertion presupposes a social relationship: the power of one party makes a second party do what it otherwise would not.[11] A party may resist the exertion of power and a power struggle ensue. Another party may accept subordination to receive benefits or to fulfill a need to become dependent (and possibly supported, wanted, and protected). Since power can be used to allocate resources and values, it may be sought not only for psychological reasons but also for fulfilling material wants and needs.

The family is probably the first collective unit that fulfills both material and nonmaterial wants and needs. Because infants are physically (and most likely emotionally) dependent on their parents, parents can exert their natural power over infants. Even when parents have no particular desire to exert power, they may still have to exercise it in disciplining and training infants. This power relationship marks the beginning of "politics," into which people are born and gradually socialized. As infants become adults and have their own families, an originally nuclear family develops into a kinship group or lineage with its own genealogical power structure, corporate activities, and ways of conflict resolution.

Within an environmentally circumscribed area, initially there may be one or several families or kinship groups. Each may undergo segmentation under one or several of the following conditions: the elders die; intragroup conflicts arise; there is scarcity of resources; or the group becomes too large to be manageable under the existing power structure. Groups may merge to form one or more socially circumscribed populations. Mergence may be

[10]Roger D. Masters, "The Biological Nature of the State," *World Politics* 35 (January 1983): 161–93.

[11]See Robert A. Dahl, "The Concept of Power," *Behavioral Science* 2 (July 1957): 201–15.

facilitated by interlineage marriage (in part to avoid birth defects resulting from marriage among close relatives). Each population may also move into new environments to further segment, adventure, or look for resources and may run into other groups and populations in the process. Populations may merge, coexist, or engage in conflict. Through natural growth, mergence, or conquest, the size of each surviving population may increase.

Subsistence for a larger population involves greater tasks: production, collection and distribution of benefits, disaster relief, irrigation, defense, and trade. Performing these tasks requires a greater collective capacity and thus greater cooperation. A larger population also increases the number and complexity of power relationships. Contention for power breeds conflicts, which may lead to violence and destruction. Thus both cooperation for benefits and regulation of conflicts come to require a greater degree of role differentiation, managment, and organization.

The advantages of organization may or may not be clear to the whole population. Organization may be the outcome of deliberation or negotiation among segments of the population; or it may be superimposed from the beginning by individuals who already possess some power. Once in place, organization entails authority and hierarchy. An administrative elite and apparatus are created. The elite may subsequently be expanded through recruitment or co-option of those who have demonstrated managerial or administrative skills. The elite may use its power to allocate resources and values to give greater benefits to certain segments of the population (such as family members, kinship groups, followers, or effective performers). Social stratification based on power differentiation within family, kinship, or other smaller social groups is thus enlarged and institutionalized.[12] At this point, at least theoretically, a state—an organized, centralized, and stratified core population that occupies and has sovereign control over certain core territories—is born.

National distinctiveness.   For a state to come into existence, a population must first have been convinced by its own experience or reflection (or both) that only a state has the capacity to fulfill collective wants and needs, and there is no better choice. At this initial stage, state formation occurs, partly because of outside threats, possibly from other states. Eventually, though, it may be argued that these same collective wants and needs of this same population could conceivably be fulfilled as well or better by another

[12]See Jonathan Haas, *The Evolution of the Prehistoric State* (New York: Columbia University Press, 1982).

state—into which this particular state could be incorporated. If the original state is to remain and establish its legitimacy, its population must have distinctive wants and needs considered unfulfillable by another state.

"National distinctiveness" is not located in what is basic or merely material or organizational and thus usually transferable. For instance, in a pioneering work addressing why the Chinese state did not break up permanently into separate states like those of Europe, Mark Elvin has suggested that "the Chinese must on the whole have managed to keep one step ahead of their neighbours in the relevant technical skills, military, economic and organizational."[13] But such technical superiority is neither a natural given nor a constant and can be competitively acquired through innovation or diffusion. The same technology only creates a greater degree of sameness rather than difference. What is true of technology is also true of other transferable tools (such as ideology and political, social, and economic systems). And yet, to maintain autonomy and legitimacy, each state has to be distinctive.

National distinctiveness is likely to be centered initially around a common language, later around shared customs, values, religion, memories of history, and a concern for biologic and social perpetuation.[14] While some of these components may be separately transferable, the combination is difficult to duplicate. Moreover, what makes the whole incomparable and exclusive is the deep sentiment the population attaches to it as a result of habituation or socialization, as well as that population's receptiveness to the manipulation of symbols (reminders) by the elite. Once aroused, deep emotions and "we-feelings" are not easily transferable. These sentiments are so strong not merely because they fulfill primordial needs; they have also been evoked and reinforced by collective experiences and memories of actual benefits brought about by the state.[15] It is this nationalism—an ultimate, subjective, emotional identity with the state as an embodiment of the many common elements of the population—that augments the belief that this state is distinctive. Indeed, as Barbara Ward puts it, the essential nature of nationalism is "to leave other people out."[16]

[13]Mark Elvin, *The Pattern of the Chinese Past* (Stanford: Stanford University Press, 1973), 18–20.

[14]See Ping-ti Ho, "The Chinese Civilization: A Search for the Roots of Its Longevity," *Journal of Asian Studies* 35 (August 1976): 549–54.

[15]See William Bloom, *Personal Identity, National Identity and International Relations* (Cambridge: Cambridge University Press, 1990), p. 61.

[16]Barbara Ward, *Nationalism and Ideology* (New York: Norton, 1966), p. 56.

Primacy. Once formed, the state has to be maintained. This is the task of the government, which consists of an administrative elite operating through a set of hierarchical administrative institutions or bureaucratic offices. The relationship between the government and the population is hierarchical. Governmental power is differentiated from and supersedes all other kinds of power that may still operate in other interpersonal or social contexts within the state (such as family, church, social groups). At the government's disposal is the Weberian notion of a monopoly of the legitimate use of force or coercion.

The primary function of the government is to use its bureaucracy and coercive power to organize, protect, and sustain the state. Fulfilling collective wants and needs and sometimes having to exercise coercive power in the process are costly undertakings and have to be supported by resources extracted from the population. Ideally, to avoid overextraction (or imbalance between extraction and fulfillment of collective wants and needs), the government should minimize its overhead costs and power; yet it also has a vested interest in using some of the extracted resources to sustain and reproduce itself.[17] It must therefore find ways to induce the population to accept the indispensability not only of the state but also of the concomitant governmental costs and power. Invoking or even "creating"[18] nationalism may thus be how those in power attempt to arouse emotions as a means of "conning"[19] the population into accepting sacrifices.

That the government may have ulterior motives is a reasonable proposition. Bureaucrats and politicians are, however, citizens, too, and like the rest of the population, they need the state for more basic, functional fulfillment of collective wants and needs. The reproduction and power of the elite cannot be independent of the physical survival of the state. Therefore the forstering of nationalism can be justified on its own merit even though, secondarily, it has instrumental value to the elite in the promotion of its own interest.

The elite may also find nationalism dangerous. Once mobilized, mass emotions can get out of hand and strike at the elite and its policies.

[17]See Peter Evans, Dietrich Rueschemeyer, and Theda Skocpol, eds., *Bringing the State Back In* (Cambridge: Cambridge University Press, 1985); and Stephen D. Krasner, "Approaches to the State: Alternative Conceptions and Historical Dynamics," *Comparative Politics* 16 (January 1984): 223–46.

[18]See Arthur N. Waldron, "Theories of Nationalism and Historical Explanation," *World Politics* 37 (April 1985): 416–33.

[19]Du Preez, *Politics of Identity,* p. 73.

Moreover, nationalism can be triggered by forces beyond the control of the elite.[20] At the individual level, nationalism can also be seen as displacement of aggression and hostility onto outgroups, as a form of ego expansion, or as compensation for inferiority, insecurity, inadequacy, fear, or anxiety.[21] This instrumental use of nationalism to release of psychological tension can misdirect national policies and jeopardize the physical survival of both the state and those whose psychological tension needs releasing.

To ensure survival, then, the collectivity as a whole—both the elite and the population—must see the fostering of nationalism as a natural outgrowth of its own realization of the importance of the state. An unreflective elite or population may undergo repeated upheavals with survival at risk before it realizes that the primacy of the state outweighs other considerations.

Premodern Chinese National Identity

Are the three reasons of state only Western theory? Or do they represent a more universal statement that finds resonance in Chinese theory? Let us take a brief look at the evidence. Regarding state formation and physical survival, premodern Chinese theorists—including Xunzi, Guan Zhong, Han Feizi, Wang Fu, Lu Buwei, Huai Nanzi, Lu Jia, Dong Zhongshu, Ban Gu, Liezi, Ge Hong, Han Yu and Liu Zongyuan—made more or less the same arguments as I have. (One disagreement among them centered on whether the state had been formed as a result of the mandate of heaven or for the purpose of regulation of conflicts.) Textual evidence is buttressed by archaeological evidence supporting the hypotheses discussed earlier.[22]

Regarding primacy, there is, as Benjamin Schwartz says, evidence of a "conception of the supreme jurisdiction of the political order in all domains

[20]Bloom, *Personal Identity*, pp. 80–89.

[21]Snyder, *Meaning of Nationalism;* Herbert C. Kelman, ed., *International Behavior: A Social-Psychological Analysis* (New York: Holt, Rinehart, and Winston, 1965), particularly chaps. 2, 6, and 10.

[22]Kung-chuan Hsiao, *A History of Chinese Political Thought*, vol. 1, *From the Beginnings to the Sixth Century A.D.*, trans. by F. W. Mote (Princeton: Princeton University Press, 1979), pp. 184–85, 335–36, 390–92, 537–39, 562–63, 573–76, 650–56. This English translation stops at chap. 11; for chaps. 12–24, one has to turn to the original Chinese version (Taipei: Lian jing, 1982); see pp. 434, 436, and 446 n. 37. Much of the following discussion of Chinese political thought is drawn from this source. On archaeological evidence, see K. C. Chang, *Art, Myth, and Ritual: The Path to Political Authority in Ancient China* (Cambridge: Harvard University Press, 1983).

of social and cultural life." The state was symbolized by its monarch, who was sovereign.[23] Chinese theorists may have disagreed on whether and how the monarch should be elevated or constrained (by such devices as morality, aristocracy, bureaucracy, customs, law, the people and their natural wants and needs, and cosmic, natural, or supernatural forces). But they seldom challenged the institution of the monarchy and the state it symbolized. Even Mencius, whose emphasis on the people over the monarch (*min wei gui*) is well known, also preached "stability in unity" (*ding yu yi*) and "rectifying the monarch in order to stabilize the state" (*yi zheng jun er guo ding*). Dong Zhongshu made it clear that "the monarch constitutes the origin of the state" (*jun ren zhe guo zhi yuan*), and Mozi favored "agreement with the superior" (*shang tong*). Even the Daoists, preferring "spontaneity" or "inaction" (*wu wei*), advocated "a small state with few people" (*xiao guo gua min*) and "a monarch known to the people as simply being there" (*tai shang zhi you zhi*).

None suggested abandoning the monarchy until the appearance of such Neodaoists as Ruan Ji, Tao Qian, and Bao Jingyan of the Wei-Jin period (A.D. 220–420). Subsequent echoes can be found in such theorists as Wu Nengzi of the Tang dynasty (A.D. 618–907) and Fang Xiaoru, Wang Shouren (Yangming), Li Zhi, Huang Zongxi, Tang Zhen, Gu Yanwu, and Wang Fuzhi of the Ming-Qing period (A.D. 1368–1911). What these "later" (including Neodaoist and Neoconfucianist) theorists offered was a critique of the growing trend of authoritarianism (particularly since the Mongol rule). They instead emphasized elements of egalitarianism, naturalism, emancipation of thought, individualism, humanitarianism, localism or regionalism, people-oriented political doctrines, and nationalism on the basis of political-ethnic rather than cultural criteria. Influence of this group, however, was only at a "sprouting" stage (and the development of these ideas has continued into the modern and contemporary periods). According to Donald Munro and others, individual differences were seen in terms of distances from the common traits of the sages which were meant to be copied. Self-realization was to be completed in a communal setting, and often eremitism was resorted to only as a means of protection from power struggle or as a gesture of loyalty to a fallen monarch. In brief, individual-

[23]Benjamin I. Schwartz, "The Primacy of the Political Order in East Asian Societies: Some Preliminary Generalizations," in Stuart R. Schram, ed., *Foundations and Limits of State Power in China* (Hong Kong: Chinese University Press, 1987), pp. 1–10. On sovereignty, see Michael Loewe, "The Concept of Sovereignty," in Denis Twitchett and Michael Loewe, eds., *The Cambridge History of China*, vol. 1, *The Ch'in and Han Empires, 221 B.C.–A.D. 220* (Cambridge: Cambridge University Press, 1986), pp. 726–46.

ism was still checked by various forms of holism, including role fulfillment, social order, hierarchy, and harmony.[24] As the Ming loyalist Wang Fuzhi demonstrated, what he looked forward to in the end was an enlightened monarch who would "restore sovereignty to the country, accomplish its mission, stabilize its frontiers, and thereby guard the central territory and drive off the barbarians forever."[25] Despite Neodaoist and Neoconfucianist challenges, primacy of the state as symbolized by the institution of the monarchy remained the norm and reality in premodern China.

Regarding national distinctiveness, given the longevity of the Chinese state, the elements constituting national distinctiveness (along with the population and territories) have inevitably changed over time, but this does not mean that a cultural core cannot be identified. This distinctive core may not have been based on the origins of its component elements but on the materialization of a combination of different elements into one entity. Culture can be initially heterogeneous and yet distinctive. As K. C. Chang puts it, "If we trace the Chinese tradition backwards from Shang via writing evidence, there is no question of the Lung-shan and Yang-shao cultures being Chinese. But other cultures in neolithic China also bear more or less resemblance to the northern Chinese cultures . . . the historical Chinese civilization came to be formed from many sources—some main ones; others smaller tributaries."[26]

It is generally agreed that the formation of a Chinese state as well as the materialization of a distinctive Chinese core occurred during the period of the Three Dynasties of Xia, Shang, and Zhou, which may have been contemporaneous (ca. 2205–256 B.C.).[27] The core was initially centered around a common written language. Whether the archetypal Chinese script is "Sinitic," or genetically related to Tibetan and Burmese and other lan-

[24]Donald J. Munro, ed., *Individualism and Holism: Studies in Confucian and Taoist Values* (Ann Arbor: University of Michigan, Center for Chinese Studies, 1985). See also William Theodore de Bary, "Individualism and Humanitarianism in Late Ming Thought," in Theodore de Bary, ed., *Self and Society in Ming Thought* (New York: Columbia University Press, 1970), pp. 145–247.

[25]Quoted in Ian McMorran, "The Patriot and the Partisans: Wang Fu-chih's Involvement in the Politics of the Yung-li Court," in Jonathan D. Spence and John E. Wills, Jr., eds., *From Ming to Ch'ing: Conquest, Region, and Continuity in Seventeenth-Century China* (New Haven: Yale University Press, 1979), p. 161.

[26]K. C. Chang, "Chinese Archaeology since 1949," *Journal of Asian Studies* 36 (August 1977): 640.

[27]K. C. Chang, "Sandai Archaeology and the Formation of States in Ancient China: Processual Aspects of the Origins of Chinese Civilization," in David N. Keightley, ed., *The Origins of Chinese Civilization* (Berkeley and Los Angeles: University of California Press, 1983), pp. 495–521.

guages of that family, is irrelevant here.[28] The important point is that the Chinese used the language to record, spread, and canonize shared cultural values and norms (possibly of diverse origins), as reflected in the Confucian classics and other inscriptional materials. For our purposes here, we are concerned more about the existence of such a cultural core than about its precise content. (A full discussion of the content would include various modes of normative and analytic thought, language, national character, religion, literature, drama, opera, folklore, rituals, architecture, food, clothing, tools, and so on.)[29]

The Three Dynasties period provided an idealized model of Chinese national identity: Who was China? Despite its internal diversity, China was a unified state, had a core culture (while incorporating new and originally foreign elements at each stage of its development), and would differentially interact with other states on the basis of cultural compatibility. The term "Middle Kingdom" or "Middle State" (Zhongguo), first appearing during the Spring and Autumn and Warring States period (770–221 B.C.), did not refer to "the state in the middle," as usually understood, but, as Ying-shih Yu tells us, to "the cultural area of the *zhong yuan* (central plain) in the midst of a greater *tianxia* (all-under-heaven)."[30] This *tianxia* was the world known to the Chinese at that time. As the *Book of Odes* records, "Under the vast heaven, there is no land that is not the monarch's" (*pu tian zhi xia, mo fei wang tu*). Does it then mean that "state" and "world" coincided, forming some kind of a unipolar system?

At that early point, the Chinese evidently knew little of Mesopotamia, Egypt, Greece, or India, just as similar geographic constraints limited the world view of the other civilizations.[31] Yet, objectively, there were many

[28]For the "Sinitic" argument, see Ping-Ti Ho, *The Cradle of the East: An Inquiry into the Indigenous Origins of Techniques and Ideas of Neolithic and Early Historic China, 5000–1000 B.C.* (Chicago: University of Chicago Press, 1975); and Christopher I. Beckwith, *The Tibetan Empire in Central Asia* (Princeton: Princeton University Press, 1987), pp. 4–5. For the other view, see Edwin G. Pulleyblank's review of Ping-Ti Ho's book in *Journal of Asian Studies* 36 (August 1977): 716; and idem, "The Chinese and Their Neighbors in Prehistoric and Early Historic Times," in Keightley, *Origins of Chinese Civilization*, pp. 416–23.

[29]Chinese culture has been the focus of much scholarly attention in China lately. Multi-volume works have been produced at major centers such as Fudan University and Shenzhen University. Recent Chinese scholarship is too extensive to list here; see, e.g., Li Zonggui, *Zhongguo wenhua gailun* (A general discussion on Chinese culture) (Guangzhou: Zhongshan University Press, 1988). See also Benjamin I. Schwartz, *The World of Thought in Ancient China* (Cambridge: Harvard University Press, 1985).

[30]Ying-shih Yuh, *"Minzu yishi yu guojia guannian"* (Ethnonationalism and the idea of the state)," *Mingbao yuekan* (Mingbao 18 December 1983): 3–7.

[31]See Benjamin I. Schwartz, "The Chinese Perception of World Order, Past and Present,"

other states in that known world: Chinese interaction with the Yi, Man, Yue, Qiang, Rong, Di, and other peoples and states constituted a war-and-peace sort of international system. In fact, it is this competitive external environment that may have facilitated the formation of the Chinese state itself. Yet the Chinese perceived an overlapping between "state" and "world" both because the criterion of inclusion into the state was not race but culture[32] and because in their known world the Chinese did not encounter any equally established rival culture. Thus, perceptually at least, "state" and "world" and "culture" were meshed with one another, and there was no need for the Chinese to assert themselves as Zhongguoren (Chinese national), which is a modern term. Empirically, however, the Chinese state did interact with other states—albeit in a differential manner on the basis of cultural compatibility.

When a unified Zhou dynasty degenerated into the feudal, civil-war system of the Spring and Autumn and Warring States period, the traditional Chinese national identity based on unity and culture did not totally break down. Despite the fact that the feudal states interacted with each other as if they had gained sovereignty, each still nominally recognized Zhou as the symbolic, legitimate center. "Revere the Zhou monarch and reject the barbarians" (*zhuanwang rangyi*) was still the norm. Moreover, the feudal states did not see fragmentation as a permanent arrangement. Each wanted to "have the Zhou monarch in its power and order the vassals about in his name" (*xie tianzi yi ling zhuhou*). Each saw defeat of the others and restoration of the former territories of Zhou under its unified control as the end, which the Qin ultimately achieved. Moreover, maintaining culture as a criterion, the feudal states only viewed each other as equal; between Chinese feudal states and "barbarians," there was neither equality nor a "legal" war.[33]

Traditional Chinese national identity thus passed the test of disunity of this feudal period, and precisely because of the chaos and disruption, the elite began to see the need to adjust discrepancies between expectations and realities. The blooming of various ideologies in this (and subsequent)

---

in John K. Fairbank, ed., *The Chinese World Order: Traditional China's Foreign Relations* (Cambridge: Harvard University Press, 1968), p. 277.

[32]See Herrlee G. Creel, *The Origins of Statecraft in China*, vol. 1, *The Western Chou Empire* (Chicago: University of Chicago Press, 1970), p. 197; Hsiao, *History of Chinese Political Thought*, pp. 137–42; Ho, *Cradle of the East*, p. 344.

[33]Shih-tsai Chen, "The Equality of States in Ancient China," *American Journal of International Law* 35 (1941): 641–50. See also Richard L. Walker, *The Multi-State System of Ancient China* (Hamden, Conn.: Shoe String Press, 1953).

periods provided a pool of intellectual and emotive tools for the elite to selectively and dynamically moderate or intensify nationalism to secure domestic support for whatever national roles circumstances demanded. Let me turn now to three such patterns of role enactment.

Expansion and a Status Quo National Role

Why does state expansion occur? For numerous reasons, singular or in combination. Population growth may have exhausted existing resources; technological and production growth may require more raw materials and greater markets; both kinds of growth require expansion. Even if existing resources are sufficient, expansion may still be desired because more is preferred to less. Larger territories provide not only more resources but a greater margin of physical security. Space offers a cushion against foreign attacks (including nuclear ones in the modern age). Vast space leaves room for maneuver, retreat, relocation of capital and production facilities, regrouping, mobile defense, and protracted warfare. Expansion may also be triggered by the expansion of others. Finally, to an ambitious and adventurist elite, expansion also brings glory and more power. Expansion, then, depends on wants and needs, space available, and competitive conditions.

Justifying Chinese expansion would not have been difficult. The elite could define China's external position in "hard" Confucian terms, emphasizing hierarchy, status, authority, *da yi tong* (grand coordinating unity), and achieving *da tong* (great community). They could also invoke Xunzi's "realism" (that "human nature is evil"), the strategy of "balance of power" and alliances of the Zonghengjia (Vertical and Horizontal school), or the military doctrines of Sunzi. China could be portrayed as playing the role of "defender of the faith" (Confucianism), to use one of Holsti's labels.[34] Chinese national identity would not have been questioned.

Why then should expansion be constrained? There are at least two obvious reasons: costs and external resistance. When expansion is centralized and massive, costs incurred may outweigh benefits. Moreover, such expansion is likely to alarm or provoke competitors, adding to future defense costs. There are bureaucratic costs too. Militarily acquired territories need to be repeatedly pacified and effectively administered before they can be integrated into the core. Migration of colonists entails transportation, communication, and relocation costs. Such costs of a centralized and

[34]Holsti, "National Role Conceptions."

massive expansion, even if initially affordable under a particularly strong regime, may not be sustainable in subsequent periods under weaker regimes.[35]

To balance costs and benefits, the elite can manipulate national role conception. At the end of an initial, centralized and massive expansion, wants and needs have been fulfilled and further expansion is unnecessary. At this point, without altering the fundamental national identity, the elite can prescribe a status quo national role, and deliberately foster supporting philosophic or ideological notions and institute bureaucratic barriers against further militarism and expansionism. Once these notions and barriers are legitimized and institutionalized, they become cultural canons for subsequent periods.

In premodern China, initially private trade may have paved the way for the government to pursue an expansionist policy.[36] Once the centralized and massive expansion of the Qin-Han period (221 B.C.–A.D. 220) had taken place, however, Confucianism was endorsed as the official ideology. Despite its "harder" aspects referred to earlier, Confucianism was generally biased against militarism, trade, and external expansion.[37] This endorsement was in the national interest because it fostered primacy of the state by helping the state to refrain from overextension and maintain a cost-benefit balance. But it was also in the interest of the ruling elite because Confucianism prescribed submission to authority. The bureaucracy, influenced by Confucianism, likewise generally objected to any imperial interest or participation in overseas trade and affairs.[38]

Occasionally, these cultural canons were challenged by regimes who paid more attention to strategic and economic considerations and were more motivated by intellectual curiosity or an internationalist outlook.[39] For instance, centralized but far less massive expansion took place during the Tang and Ming periods, but disintegration ensued, supporting the propo-

[35]The same argument can be found in Paul Kennedy, *The Rise and Fall of the Great Powers* (New York: Random House, Vintage, 1987).

[36]Ying-shih Yu, *Trade and Expansion in Han China* (Berkeley and Los Angeles: University of California Press, 1967), p. 92.

[37]John K. Fairbank, "Introduction: Varieties of the Chinese Military Experience," in Frank A. Kierman, Jr., and John K. Fairbank, eds., *Chinese Ways in Warfare* (Cambridge: Harvard University Press, 1974), pp. 1–26.

[38]C. P. FitzGerald, *The Southern Expansion of the Chinese People* (New York: Praeger, 1972), p. 102 and chap. 6.

[39]S. A. M. Adshead, "China and Central Asia," in Nicholas Tarling, ed., *China and Its Place in the World* (Auckland: University of Auckland, 1967), pp. 11–25, and *China in World History* (London: Macmillan, 1988).

sition that the costs of centralized and massive expansion can outweigh its benefits. Likewise, in the Song period (A.D. 960–1279), trade actually flourished as a result of governmental participation and an elevation of the status of businessmen in Chinese society. This change also helped China become a sea power;[40] the Chinese fleet reached as far as Africa and western Asia in the fifteenth century.[41] This advancement in naval technology did not, however, bring about any centralized and massive expansion overseas. Thus the status quo national role and the cultural canons against expansionism, though challenged, remained strong and effective—unless and until change was necessitated by circumstances.

Of course expansion need not be centralized and massive. It can be less costly, more manageable and sustainable, and less alarming to competitors if it is decentralized, indirect, and incremental. Such expansion takes various forms. Sometimes areas may first be conquered by small local states before being conquered, along with those smaller states, by a larger state from outside. This was the case when some southern areas were first conquered by local tribal states such as Nanzhao and Dali before being conquered by a northern Chinese government.

Expansion takes another form when factions of a divided state independently expand in different directions, then bring their territories together upon reunification. In the competition among Chinese feudal states during the Spring and Autumn and Warring States period, for example, the Chu expanded toward the south; the Wu expanded toward present-day Zhejiang; and the Yan expanded into southern Manchuria and northern Korea. Likewise, Chinese expansion came about as a southern regime competed with the north in a civil-war situation or as "barbarians" invaded, as in the respective cases of the Wu in the Three Kingdoms period (A.D. 220–285) and the southern dynasties after the collapse of the Jin in the fourth century.

Domestic turmoil or foreign invasion can cause massive migration to the peripheries, which in turn helps integrate the peripheries into the core, yet without the state incurring extra migration costs. This sort of expansion

[40]See Jung-pang Lo's three essays: "The Emergence of China as a Seapower during the Late Sung and Early Yuan Periods," *Far Eastern Quarterly* 14 (August 1955): 489–503; "The Decline of the Early Ming Navy," *Oriens Extremus* 5 (December 1958): 149–68; and "Maritime Commerce and Its Relation to the Sung Navy," *Journal of Economic and Social History of the Orient* 12 (January 1969): 57–101.

[41]Su Chung-jen, "Places in South-East Asia, the Middle East and Africa Visited by Cheng Ho and His Companions, A.D. 1405–1433," in F. S. Drake, ed., *Symposium on Historical, Archaeological and Linguistic Studies on Southern China, South-East Asia and the Hong Kong Region* (Hong Kong: Hong Kong University Press, 1967), pp. 198–211.

occurred during the civil wars at the beginning of the Han dynasty, the "barbarian" invasions of the north in the fourth through the sixth centuries, the Huangchao Rebellion of the nineth century, the Taiping Rebellion of the nineteenth century, and the transition from the Song to the Yuan dynasties and from Ming to Qing.

In still another form of expansion, one state is conquered by a second state, only to launch a successful revolt against that second state, taking over its territories. Thus did the Mongols conquer the Chinese Song dynasty, only to be overthrown by the Chinese Ming; and the Manchus conquered the Ming and were then overthrown by the Chinese Republic.

In all the above examples, the massive expansion of the Chinese state is not attributable to the expansionist intent of a centralized Chinese elite. Without a firm national identity, confusion might have arisen as events beyond centralized Chinese control attempted to bestow an expansionist role that China had not appropriated.[42] With a firm national identity, however, the occurrence of decentralized, indirect, and incremental expansion as an unintended consequence did not necessarily preclude the maintenance of a status quo national role in centralized and intentional foreign policy. Having expanded unintentionally, but without being confused by the expansion, the Chinese state was able to keep itself from becoming overextended.

In addition to costs, external resistance also constrained Chinese expansion (partly by making it even more costly). The nature of such resistance and how China dealt with it determined not only the extent of Chinese expansion but also the extent of the disintegration of China by other states and the extent of coexistence between China and other states. Generally, if resistance is centered around another state of approximately equal strength, coexistence is the likely result. A prime example is how Chinese expansion in the north and northwest during the Han period was checked by the equally strong Xiongnu.

External resistance can also come from a group of secondary states already engaged in competition. Even if there is no coalition among them, their regularized interaction can generate enough competitive pressure to resist intrusion from outside; for fighting or making friends with one of them can lead to an unintended but costly involvement in a web of intermingling relationships, eventually bringing the original intrusion to a halt. Two examples will suffice: (1) In the northeast, Chinese expansion was

[42]On negotiations of identities, see Andrew J. Weigert, J. Smith Teitge, and Dennis W. Teitge, *Society and Identity: Toward a Sociological Psychology* (Cambridge: Cambridge University Press, 1986), p. 31.

checked by a preexisting multiactor competitive system consisting first of the Koguryo, Puyo, Okcho, Yemaek, Yilou, and Sam Han tribes, later of the three kingdoms of Koguryo, Paekche, and Silla. In addition, there were third actors competing with the Chinese for control and influence over the Korean peninsula, including various Xianbei tribes in the fourth century; the Japanese Yamato state in the fourth through the seventh centuries; and the Qidan (Khitan), the Jurched (Sushen), and the Mongols in the tenth through the thirteenth centuries.[43] In Southeast Asia, Chinese expansion was similarly checked by a preexisting multiactor competitive system. Relations among these Indianized states were based on a conception of war which made prestige and proof of superiority, not material or territorial gain, its major goal. The actors involved were numerous, their definitions of boundaries unclear, and their conception of the distribution of international power in the form of concentric circles was such that the closest neighbor was taken to be the primary enemy. The net results were a high frequency of wars and an unstable system of international relations.[44] Intruding into this system meant involvement in a web of intermingling relationships and constant warfare. Thus, so long as Chinese interests in Vietnam (colonized by China during the Qin-Han expansion) were not threatened, China's goals in the region, consistent with its more general status quo national role conception, were those of promoting trade, imposing suzerainty and gaining prestige. In pursuing these goals, China's policy was one of limited intervention and maintenance of an impartial posture (which was different from Holsti's roles of "mediator-integrator" or "regional-subsystem collaborator").[45] When Vietnam revolted against China in the tenth and the fifteenth centuries, Chinese expansion in this region was finally brought to an end.[46]

Disintegration and a Complacent National Role

A multiactor competitive system can also cause disintegration. When competition is with another state of approximately equal strength, it is

[43]Michael Ng-Quinn, "The Internationalization of the Region: The Case of Northeast Asian International Relations," *Review of International Studies* 12 (April 1986): 107–25.

[44]G. Coedes, *The Indianized States of Southeast Asia,* ed. Walter F. Vella and trans. Susan Brown Cowing (Honolulu: University of Hawaii Press, 1968).

[45]Holsti, "National Role Conceptions."

[46]FitzGerald, *Southern Expansion,* p. 97; Wang Gungwu, "China and South-East Asia 1402–1424," in Jerome Ch'en and Nicholas Tarling, eds., *Social History of China and South-East Asia* (Cambridge: Cambridge University Press, 1970), and "Early Ming Relations with Southeast Asia: A Background Essay," in Fairbank, *Chinese World Order,* pp. 50–54; Jung-pang Lo,

usually prominent and intense, preventing either side from becoming lax or negligent. If, however, external competition comes from a group of secondary states that are also competing with each other, the larger state may view it as less intense and too decentralized to be alarming. The complacency thus generated may form a national role conception for the larger state. If internal disintegration of the larger state occurs at this point, the decentralized expansion of the secondary states vis-à-vis both each other and the larger state will drive them toward further disintegrating the internally weakened larger state.

After a long period of stability and prosperity, a state (or its elite) may have become lax and excessively confident about its external competitiveness. This is especially the case when the state has gone through a pacific cultural transformation and adopted a status quo national role. If not carefully monitored and controlled, this indulgence can generate complacency or a false sense of security, which in turn can lead to negligence of, or failure in responding to, challenges to the status quo.

A prime example in Chinese history is the Song dynasty. Because traditional Chinese national identity was based on unity and culture, the Song elite responded to internal disintegration by becoming preoccupied with internal consolidation and restoration. Instead of focusing on an external competitor, the Qitan, the founder of the Song was preoccupied with subjugating the rest of the Ten Kingdoms that had declared independence in the preceding Five Dynasties period. By the time the decisive battle of Gaoliang River was fought between the Song and the Qitan, Song forces had become exhausted and were defeated.[47]

Though the Song dynasty was militarily weak, conforming to tradition, it was still culturally complacent, which in turn led to missed opportunities. Despite its defeat by the Xixia, another external competitor, the Song continued to view the Xixia as barbarians, even inferior to the Qitan.[48] Otherwise, the dynasty might have taken the suggestion of a few of its officials and collaborated with the Xixia against the Qitan.[49]

"Intervention in Vietnam: A Case Study of the Foreign Policy of the Early Ming Government," *Tsing Hua Journal of Chinese Studies* 8 (1970); and A. B. Woodside, "Early Ming Expansionism, 1406–1427: China's Abortive Conquest of Vietnam," in *Papers on China*, vol. 17 (Cambridge: Harvard University Press, 1963).

[47]Xie Yizheng, *Song zhi waijiao* (Foreign relations of the Song) (Shanghai, Dadong shuju 1935); Jing-sheng Tao, "Yu Ching and Sung Policies toward Liao and Hsia, 1042–1044," *Journal of Asian History* 6 (1972).

[48]Jing-sheng Tao, "Barbarians or Northerners: Northern Sung Images of the Khitans," in Morris Rossabi, ed., *China among Equals* (Berkeley and Los Angeles: University of California Press, 1983), pp. 78–79.

[49]Xie, *Song zhi waijiao,* pp. 25–31; Tao, "Yu Ching and Sung Policies . . ."

The Song was physically separated from the Jurched by the Qitan,[50] but contact was not impossible because the Jurched had paid tribute to the Song (in 961). At this early point, the Song could have forged an alliance with the still weaker Jurched against the Qitan. This would have been consistent with the traditional doctrine of "make friends with those afar and attack those nearby" (*yuanjiao jingong*). Instead, a complacent Song showed little interest in the remotely situated Jurched. When the Jurched became stronger and attacked the Qitan (in 1114), the Song's preoccupation with its previous competition with the Qitan precluded any alliance between the two against the Jurched. Still concerned about unity and hoping to reclaim the sixteen prefectures of Yan and Yun lost to the Qitan earlier, the Song (in 1120) belatedly allied with the Jurched, who by this time had turned into a rising and expansionist power stronger than the Song.[51]

The Jurched defeated the Qitan and forced the Song to move to the south. This time, the Southern Song was blocked by the Jurched from contact with the remotely situated but weaker Mongols. The Mongols then became stronger and attacked the Jurched. The Southern Song, preoccupied with its previous competition with the now-adjacent Jurched, made the same mistake of belatedly allying with the Mongols, who by this time had also become a rising and expansionist power stronger than Southern Song. The Mongols eventually defeated both the Jurched and Southern Song.[52]

Another aspect of a complacent national role conception is a lack of internal preparedness for external contingencies. Rigid hierarchy and settledness tend to produce inertia. Secondary states, in contrast, tend to be more capable of effective and efficient mobilization because they are less burdened by heavy bureaucratic costs and constraints. Secondary states may also be more competitive because they face a dual threat: from larger or stronger states and from each other. Their participation in further disintegrating an internally weakened larger state becomes a necessity when a chain of competitive reaction is sparked by the intrusion of one of them into the peripheries of the larger state.

Most of the secondary states surrounding China were populated by

[50]Wang Gungwu, "The Rhetoric of a Lesser Empire: Early Sung Relations with Its Neighbors," in Rossabi, *China among Equals,* p. 61.

[51]Tao, "Barbarians or Northerners" p. 71, and *The Jurched in Twelfth-Century China: A Study of Sinicization* (Seattle: University of Washington Press, 1976).

[52]Charles A. Peterson, "Old Illusions and New Realities: Sung Foreign Policy, 1217–1234," in Rossabi, *China among Equals,* pp. 204–39, and "First Sung Reactions to the Mongol Invasion of the North, 1211–17," in John Winthrop Haeger, ed., *Crisis and Prosperity in Sung China* (Tucson: University of Arizona Press, 1975), pp. 215–52.

nomads. Even nomads could form states because their movement from pasture to pasture took place within certain core territories. Their mode of subsistence and economic organization could adjust to a prolonged period of instability and warfare without causing any structural dislocation.[53] Let us take the Tibetans during the fourth through the sixth centuries as an example. They were competing with other nomadic federations such as the Xiongnu, Xianbei, and Tuoba (Toba) over the territories of Jin China. With a sheep-breeding economy, the Tibetans were confined to high altitudes, making it difficult for them to have large political units within an integrated political structure. Thus they were usually unable to initiate large-scale warfare or expansion. Yet their small groups could easily be converted into military units under a centralized command once war was forced upon them. Moreover, their mainly infantry units could easily incorporate non-nomadic elements. These characteristics made them competitive and enabled them to set up the state of Former Qin (under Fu Jian) in the north.[54]

But underlying China's complacent national role conception with all its disadvantages was a firm national identity, which would eventually allow China to reintegrate. To sustain identity under adverse conditions, the Chinese elite could turn to the "softer" side of Confucianism by emphasizing humanness, inner morality, virtue, righteousness, faith, self-cultivation, yielding, contentment, humility, and magnanimity. Mencius's differentiation between *wangdao* (way of true or benevolent kingship) and *badao* (way of hegemony) could justify weakness and the enemy's dominance. Following the Daoists, one could claim to be natural and refrain from war and instead find satisfaction in *wuwei* (spontaneity or inaction), *xiaoyao* (unfettered bliss), and *zaiyou* (letting the world alone). Passivity or defensiveness could take a Mohist disguise as *feigong* (pacifism), *jianai* (universal love), or *huli* (mutual benefit). Or withdrawal from worldly affairs could pass for a retreat into the harmony of Buddhism. The purpose of this manipulation of ideologies is to make adverse conditions tolerable and keep the national identity unbroken; the function of national identity is to sustain the state by unifying the population, at least psychologically.

Chances of physical reunification may meanwhile be enhanced by the continued competition among the intruding secondary states. Such competition creates multiple checks and cross-pressures and thus prevents these states from achieving a total conquest, leaving room for the disintegrated

---

[53]Owen Lattimore, *Inner Asian Frontiers of China* (Boston: Beacon, 1962), pp. 66–76, 545–46.

[54]Wolfram Eberhard, *Conquerors and Rulers: Social Forces in Medieval China* (Leiden: Brill, 1965), pp. 115–24.

larger state to regroup. In the Jin China example, the secondary states continued to compete with each other in a decentralized manner: Former Yan and Dai were adjacent to and competing with each other and were thus unwilling to form an alliance against Former Qin, a common adversary to their southwest. When there was polarization between east and west in the case of Later Yan against Later Qin, they consolidated their positions within their immediate regions rather than make alliances across regional lines. Previous tribal competition between the Xianbei (Later Yan) and the Xiongnu (Western Qin) precluded an alliance between them, even though both shared a common interest in containing Northern Wei or Later Qin.[55] As a result of this fragmentation of the intruders, remnants of Jin China (in the form of the Eastern Jin regime in the south) gained breathing space to regroup.

Coexistence and a Regulatory National Role

When there is neither expansion nor disintegration, a state is in coexistence with others. Competition under coexistence does not lead to disruption of each other's core domestic structures. To maintain coexistence and avoid disintegration, a state must regulate its conflicts with others. Playing a regulatory role means playing no fixed role but, rather, whatever role is required at any given time to regulate conflicts. A regulatory role is not based exclusively on expansionism, the status quo, or complacency but on some combination, flexibly, dynamically, and suitably applied to changing circumstances.[56] The emphasis is on pragmatic tactics rather than dogmatic ideologies. For premodern China, playing a regulatory national role required a more cosmopolitan orientation that broadened the base of cultural compatibility in interaction with other states.

Contrary to the static Sinocentric approach usually taken in the literature on premodern Chinese foreign relations, China demonstrated a capacity for highly skillful and imaginative diplomacy when it played a regulatory role, especially under the Tang dynasty (A.D. 618–907). Tang China did expand but not on the same massive scale as Qin and Han China. Generally, the Tang dynasty coexisted with its competitors in a multiactor environment. In the west and northwest, there were various groups of Turks

[55]Michael C. Rogers, *The Chronicle of Fu Chien: A Case of Exemplar History* (Berkeley and Los Angeles: University of California Press, 1968).

[56]It means playing, at one time or another, any or all of the roles Holsti discusses in "National Role Conceptions."

(including the Tujue, who were divided into the eastern and western halves; the Tielei; the Uighurs; and the Shatuo); the Tuyuhun (a Tibetanized branch of the Xianbei around the Qinghai Lake); the Qiang tribes, such as the Tangut (Dangxiang) and Tibetans (Tufan); and other more remote actors in the far west (such as the Hephtalites or Bactria, the Arabs, and the Persians). In the south, there were Nanzhao, other smaller tribal states, and the southeast Asian states. In the northeast, there were the Qitan, Xi, Shiwei, Jurched, Yilou, Mohe, Wuji, Yemaek, Okcho, Parhae, Puyo, and the Korean kingdoms and tribal states.

The Tang avoided a multiple-front war by setting priorities and dealing with multiple conflicts in sequence. This policy entailed playing different roles with different actors at any one time, being harsher on some, more friendly toward others. The Tang concentrated on the more turbulent northwest and west and used only limited force in the northeast and south. Tang China first defeated the Eastern Turks, using the help of the Western Turks and the Uighurs. Then it pushed the Western Turks further westward. It continued to use the Uighurs to fight the Syr-Tardush (a tribe of the Tielei) and the Tibetans and to suppress the revolt of Anlushan in 757, despite the Uighurs' occasional rebellions.[57]

The Tang balanced its roles, exercising restraint lest preoccupation with one conflict exhaust available resources. A case in point is its military action over the Korean peninsula in the seventh century. Having helped Silla defeat the Koguryo-Paekche-Yamato coalition, the Tang did not expand this particular role (Holsti's "regional protector")[58] by attempting to impose control over Silla or invade Japan. Otherwise, the Tang's other roles and defense on the fronts facing the Turks and the Tibetans might have been weakened.

Facing multiple actors and conflicts, the Tang manipulated multilateral alliances to maximize its own capabilities. Forming alliances with "cultural inferiors" was not generally practiced by other Chinese regimes, for doing so could have shaken traditional Chinese national identity based on culture. To avoid this kind of identity crisis, the Tang broadened the base of cultural compatability by adopting a more cosmopolitan orientation (as reflected by its very cosmopolitan capital, Changan). This was a pragmatic response to the "barbarians": they had transformed the Chinese doctrine of "use bar-

---

[57]Edwin G. Pulleyblank, *The Background of the Rebellion of An Lu-shan* (New York: Oxford University Press, 1955); Cen Zhungmian, *Tujue ji shi* (A collected history of the Tujue) (Beijing: Zhonghua shuju 1958); Ma Changshou, *Tujueren he Tujue hanguo* (People and kingdom of the Tujue) (Shanghai: Shanghai renmin chubanshe 1957).

[58]Holsti, "National Role Conceptions."

barians to check barbarians" (*yiyi zhiyi*) into "use barbarians to check China." For instance, from 747 to 751, the Tang faced multilateral opposition in the west among remnants of the Western Turks, the Arabs, and the Tibetans. Tibetan expansion culminated in the 763 raid on Changan. In that battle, the Tibetan armies consisted of contingents of Tangut, Tuyuhun, Di, and Qiang. In another battle, the Tibetans were joined by the Uighurs, Tuyuhun, and Tangut.[59] The Tang responded by forming multilateral alliances of its own. In 765, it formed an alliance with the Uighurs, whose interests in the west were also threatened by the growing strength of the Tibetans. In 776, the Tang attacked the Tibetans by allying with the Turks, Tuyuhun, Di, Man Qiang, and Tangut. In the south, the Tang also succeeded in allying with Nanzhao against the Tibetans.[60]

Coexisting with competing factions of a divided state sometimes requires a balancer's role enacted through shifting alliances. For instance, when the Xiongnu were divided into the northern and southern halves, Han China (206 B.C.–A.D. 220) used the southern half to check the northern half and allowed the southern half to settle along the Chinese peripheries. At the same time, the Han accepted hostages and tributes from the northern half. When the southern half got suspicious, the Han rejected peace initiatives from the northern half (as in 51). Yet when the northern half became too powerful, the Han concluded a treaty with it to keep it within bounds (as in 84). At other times, the Han launched fierce attacks on the northern half.[61]

Coexistence can sometimes be enhanced if conflicts can be avoided in the first place. Conflict avoidance is possible if the same needs can be fulfilled by different means, or if exchanges leading to the mutual fulfillment of disparate needs can be arranged. Let us take the suzerain-tributary system as an example. A suzerain received its vassal in ceremonial audiences, and a vassal paid tributes to and received investitures from its suzerain.[62] The Chinese need to play the role of suzerain was more psychological than material:

[59]Ren Yucai, *Tufan yu Tangchao guanxi zhi yanjiu* (Research on relations between Tufan and the Tang Dynasty) (Taichung, Taiwan: Zili chubanshe, 1971), pp. 41–47; Li Futong, *Bianjiang lishi* (Frontier history) (Taipei: Mengzang Weiyuanhui 1962), pp. 124–26.

[60]Ren, *Tufan yu Tangchao guanxi*, pp. 52–78; Liu Yitang, *Zhongguo bianjiang minzu shi* (A history of the frontier ethnic groups of China) (Taipei: Zhonghua shuju, 1969), pp. 434–40.

[61]Yu, *Trade and Expansion in Han China,* chap. 4 and p. 101; William M. McGovern, *The Early Empires of Central Asia* (Chapel Hill: University of North Carolina Press, 1939), pp. 187–88, 192–204, 256–97.

[62]Klaus Mading, "Suzerainty over Annam: A Legal Discussion of China's Traditional Concept," in Drake, *Historical, Archaeological and Linguistic Studies,* pp. 150–52; William L. Tung, *International Law in an Organizing World* (New York: Thomas Y. Crowell 1968), pp. 45–46; Woodside, "Early Ming Expansionism" (see n. 46), pp. 3, 5–6.

Chinese national identity was based on culture and an extension of hier-archical social relationships to foreign relations. A vassal's submission may have been the result of Chinese military pressure only in the first instance; thereafter, the suzerain's prestige and cultural influence might be sufficient to maintain its political influence. While suzerainty necessarily involved tributes, tributes alone did not necessarily imply suzerainty. As private trade usually preceded and accompanied tributary relations, many "vassals" were simply motivated by economic or commercial interests, entering a "tributary relationship" to regularize private trade. In this sense, a "tribu-tary relationship" was but a means of communication and stabilization of interaction. Given this framework, the same needs (a means of communica-tion and stability) were fulfilled by different means (a formal tributary system to the suzerain and profitable trade to the tributary). Alternatively, the arrangement can be seen as exchanges of official tributes for profitable trade leading to the mutual fulfillment of disparate needs (psychological versus material).

Expressing a desire for conflict avoidance can give a wrong signal of weakness. States do, however, vary in tangible resources and capabilities and thus in absolute or physical margins of safety. A state that enjoys a greater margin of safety (or controlled complacency) is in a better position to initiate mutually desirable alternatives to conflicts. Such a state can afford to make mistakes and may not feel compelled to make preemptive moves; unnecessary tension and distrust can thus be minimized.

Given its vast territories and resources, China generally enjoyed the greater margin of safety and could therefore afford to play the role of initiator. An example is China's letting surrendered external competitors, such as the Xiongnu, Turks, and Mongols, settle along its peripheries. With their settlement needs fulfilled, they became more cooperative and acted as buffers against China's more remote adversaries, fulfilling in turn China's security needs. Another example is China's willingness to protect a tribu-tary, as when it fought Japan to protect Korea in the seventh, sixteenth, and nineteenth centuries, despite Korea's unwillingness to reciprocate by join-ing China to fight the Qitan, Jurched, and Mongols in the tenth through the thirteenth centuries. In return, China enjoyed a prolonged suzerain-tributary relationship with Korea, fulfilling China's own psychological or legitimizing need. Finally, China's *heqin* policy of initiating matrimonial alliances and sending of gifts served as another means of exchanging sym-bolic and material rewards for strategic cooperation, enlarging the base of cultural compatibility in the process. This approach was first adopted by the Han dynasty in dealing with the Xiongnu and the Wusun; subsequently, it was also practised by the Northern Wei, Northern Qi, Northern Zhou, and Tang.[63]

Even with the greater margin of safety, a state may choose not to play the role of initiator; for it may deem conflict avoidance unnecessary when the costs are not high. In the absence of prior or ongoing acute conflicts, a state may not give a high priority to the anticipation and control of costs. For example, in the absence of any prior or ongoing acute conflict with Japan since the seventh century, Ming China saw little reason to use trade as an exchange for Japan's cooperation. Meanwhile, the Ming's ineffective handling of the piracy problem confirmed Japan's suspicion of the Ming's impotence. These misreadings may have been one cause of the Hideyoshi invasion of Korea in the sixteenth century. That trade could have been used as an exchange for Japan's cooperation is suggested by part of the peace conditions Hideyoshi offered to Ming envoys in 1593, which demanded that Japanese trade ships be allowed to enter Chinese ports freely.[64]

Finally, playing the role of initiator does not mean offering benefits or rewards indiscriminately or unilaterally. Any effective initiation of the substitution of exchanges for conflicts must be based on an offer of benefits or rewards appropriate to the particular instance and leading to mutual fulfillment. Otherwise, conflicts may not be avoided. An example in point is Song China's foreign trade. Despite the Song's active promotion of trade with foreigners in all directions,[65] the needs of Song's northern neighbors were nor primarily commercial. As a result, conflicts in the north were not channeled into trade. Likewise, in the case of Qing China (A.D. 1644–1911), while an earlier failure to meet trade demands from the West bred conflicts with the West, later appeasement policies only invited further disintegration of China.

I have argued that in premodern China an idealized national identity based on unity and culture had existed since the period of Xia, Shang, and Zhou. This national identity offered stability and helped sustain the Chi-

---

[63]Zhaqi Siqin, *Beiya youmu minzu yu zhongyuan nongye minzu jian de heping zhanzheng yu maoyi zhi guanxi* (Peace, war, and trade relations between the nomads of northern Asia and the farmers of the central plain) (Taipei: Zheng zhong shuju, 1973), pp. 183–248.

[64]Giuliana Stramigioli, "Hideyoshi's Expansionist Policy on the Asiatic Mainland," *Transactions of the Asiatic Society of Japan*, 3 ser. (December 1954): 97, 102–6; Yi-t'ung Wang, *Official Relations between China and Japan, 1368–1549* (Cambridge: Harvard University Press, 1953); Kwan-wai So, *Japanese Piracy in Ming China during the Sixteenth Century* (East Lansing: Michigan State University Press, 1975).

[65]Shiba Yoshinobu, "Sung Foreign Trade: Its Scope and Organization," in Rossabi, *China among Equals,* pp. 89–115.

nese state regardless of circumstances by unifying the population, at least psychologically. That the Chinese state has physically perpetuated itself testifies to the importance of that identity.

Through the manipulation of ideologies and other symbols, the Chinese elite selectively and dynamically moderated or intensified nationalism to secure domestic support for various national roles, a role being understood as identity mobilized in a specific situation. While my analysis emphasizes culture, it also shares a basic "rational-choice" assumption—that patterns of behavior can be explained, in the words of Daniel Little, "as the aggregate outcome of the goal-directed choices of large numbers of rational agents."[66] But I am not suggesting that role enactment was a mechanical process. Options were not automatically available. Circumstances were sometimes forced on the Chinese elite. Decision making undoubtedly involved human errors and failures. Disintegration of China did occur. But none of these contingencies necessarily negated the existence of a firm Chinese national identity. The absence of confusion at this critical, psychological level provided stability and direction and sharpened perception and reflection. Uncertainties and flux became more manageable. Repeated instances spanning millennia demonstrate how the perpetuation of the Chinese state was enhanced by its ability to optimize expansion (or limit centralized and massive expansion), minimize disintegration, and maximize coexistence. Physical perpetuation and national identity thus reinforced each other.

Although this chapter deals with "national identity" as it is affected by, and contributes to, the state, there are, of course, other possible levels-of-analysis. For instance, one could look at dialectal, local, provincial, or regional identities,[67] let alone individual, factional, or group identities at various levels (including inner/outer court differences, identities of ethnic minorities and religious groups, views of individual theorists and statesmen, and so on). To the extent that these identities and views did not have an impact massive or critical enough to lead to the effective rejection of sovereignty claimed by the state, they remained secondary. However, separatism (as well as internal disorder, regionalism, and foreign invasion) did occasionally disrupt Chinese unity: the fact that unity was eventually re-

[66]Daniel Little, "Rational-Choice Models and Asian Studies," *Journal of Asian Studies* 50 (February 1991): 35.

[67]See, e.g., Joseph R. Levenson, "The Province, the Nation, and the World: The Problem of Chinese Identity," in Albert Feuerwerker, Rhoads Murphey, and Mary C. Wright, eds., *Approaches to Modern Chinese History* (Berkeley and Los Angeles: University of California Press, 1967), pp. 268–88.

stored without exception suggests that the state must have been a stronger force.

I have assumed only a small elite was actively involved in national and foreign affairs and in a position to mediate, dictate, and manipulate national identity at the state level and transmit messages to the masses. I shall leave aside the perennial question of cultural integration and differentiation between the "great tradition" and the "little traditions."[68] Suffice it to say here that linkages were provided by such institutions as the examination system, the bureaucracy, markets, religious activities, rituals, story telling, theater, and so on. Consequently, "being Chinese" in the late traditional period, as Myron Cohen has suggested, was linked to "a firm consciousness of participating in a nationwide system of political, social, religious, and symbolic relationships, with even localisms being transformed into state-ments of such relationships."[69] From this perspective, Chinese culture (both great and little traditions) may have been peripherally transformed and substantively enriched, even made more cosmopolitan and hetero-geneous at certain points (such as the incorporation of Buddhism, Islam, influences from central Asia, as well as Marxism and capitalism in the modern period), but the integrity of its core seems to have remained intact.

It is beyond the scope of this chapter to link the Chinese past to the present or future. Given the present state of our knowledge, it does not seem likely that any historiography or social science theory can provide a satisfactory answer to the question of continuity and discontinuity, as demonstrated by the lively debate on Chinese foreign relations.[70] Given our definition of a "state," it may be difficult to deny the remarkable continuity between premodern and contemporary China: both comprising the same organized, centralized, and stratified core population that has occupied and had sovereign control over the same core territories (despite

[68]P. Steven Sangren, "Great Tradition and Little Traditions Reconsidered," *Journal of Chinese Studies* 1 (February 1984): 1–24.

[69]Myron L. Cohen, "Being Chinese: The Peripheralization of Traditional Identity," *Proceedings of the American Academy of Arts and Sciences* 120 (Spring 1991): 123. See also Benjamin A. Elman, "Political, Social, and Cultural Reproduction via Civil Service Examinations in Late Imperial China," *Journal of Asian Studies* 50 (February 1991): 7–28.

[70]On continuity, see Mark Mancall, "The Persistence of Tradition in Chinese Foreign Policy," *Annals of the American Academy of Political and Social Science* 349 (September 1963): 14–26. On discontinuity, see Albert Feuerwerker, "Chinese History and the Foreign Relations of Contemporary China," ibid., 402 (July 1972): 1–14. See also Yen-p'ing Hao and Erh-min Wang, "Changing Chinese Views of Western Relations, 1840–95," in John K. Fairbank and Kwang-ching Liu, eds., *The Cambridge History of China*, vol. 11, *Late Ch'ing, 1800–1911*, pt. 2 (Cambridge: Cambridge University Press, 1980), pp. 142–201.

peripheral changes in population and territories and occasional disruption of sovereignty owing to internal or external factors). In Kang Youwei's conception of the political ideal of *da tong* (great community) and Sun Yat-sen's *tianxia weigong* (a public spirit for everything under heaven), one can find the same traditional assumption of a cultural *tianxia,* despite the fact that the real worlds each faced consisted of heterogeneous and sovereign nation-states. In contemporary Chinese politics, unity seems to have remained a central value: the ruling elites on both sides of the Taiwan Straits have taken reunification as the ultimate goal (as had the warlords in the Republican period); and Hong Kong and Macau are scheduled to be reintegrated with greater China. As Stuart Schram puts it, "Neither in the realm of organization nor in that of ideology and culture would Mao and his successors have striven so hard to promote uniformity if the unitary nature of state and society had not been accepted, on the whole, in the Chinese tradition, for the past two thousand years, as both natural and right."[71] Beneath a communist or capitalist veneer, traits of traditional culture seem to have survived China's passage to modernity.

But in an age when even the Soviet empire has collapsed, possibilities of discontinuity are very much alive. Iconoclastic critique can be found from the May Fourth movement to the *River Elegy* television series. Ideas about federalism have been discussed by intellectuals from Hu Shi to Yan Jiaqi.[72] According to Schram, even Mao himself may have entertained such ideas in the 1930s and 1940s.[73] In some circles, independence of Taiwan and Tibet is seriously advocated. Others consider multiple or alternative identities as substitutes for an obsolescent, singular national identity. China thus faces two distinctly modern challenges. First, to maintain unity of a physically large entity, acceptance of certain degrees of hierarchy and authority is required. Individual sacrifices must be made in the interest of the collectivity. But the current prevailing ideology—of those states where the largest number of visiting Chinese students and professionals can be found—is Western liberalism, which emphasizes precisely the opposite values of freedom, individualism, and pluralism. Under such an ideology, the maintenance of unity is not only less important in theory but also more costly in practice, requiring an infrastructure—mass education and literacy, demo-

[71]Stuart R. Schram, ed., *The Scope of State Power in China* (Hong Kong: Chinese University Press, 1985), p. xi.

[72]Arthur Waldron, "Warlordism versus Federalism: The Revival of a Debate?" *China Quarterly* 121 (March 1990): 116–28.

[73]See Stuart R. Schram, "Decentralization in a Unitary State: Theory and Practice, 1940–1984," in Schram, *Scope of State Power,* pp. 81–83.

cratic tradition and practice, economic development, means of communications, and so on—that China currently lacks. The tension between individualism and holism is likely to increase as China continues to interact with the West. Second, culture helps make a state distinctive, whereas technology and a capitalist world economy have had a homogenizing effect across state boundaries. Materialism and efficacy have subjected dignity and pride to critical reevaluation and redefinition. Given these two challenges, it remains an open question whether a Chinese national identity based on unity and culture will be able to move forward in its long journey toward "maturity."

中
國 3

Chinese National Identity and the Strong State: The Late Qing–Republican Crisis

Michael H. Hunt

An important, perhaps even dominant feature of Chinese national identity has been a preoccupation with creating and maintaining a strong centralized state. During the crisis of the late nineteenth and early twentieth centuries, this preoccupation reached proportions that an outside observer might characterize as obsessive. But there were good reasons for this intense concern. For about three thousand years of recorded and remembered history, the state had played an important role both in fact and myth. It had come to be associated with China's glories and especially the cultural achievements and territorial conquests that put China far in advance of premodern Europe. Moreover, had no statist tradition existed, the woes afflicting China in this era would in any case have moved politically engaged intellectuals toward the conviction that bringing an end to the crisis of the state was the precondition for lifting China out of danger and building a modern China.

By examining the persistent concerns and the evolving programs of the late Qing and early Republican period, we learn about identity in a dual sense—about how a politically influential group, long oriented to state service, saw their own role (as servitors and saviors of the state) and about how they put state building at the very center of the nationalist agenda. In both guises the statist imperative did much to give Chinese politics an identity that helps to distinguish it from the experience of other nations in this century that have struggled against the twin evils of internal weakness and foreign domination.

Nationalism, the term usually favored to describe the process of cultural consolidation and state building in the modern era, may not be the best term to apply to the Chinese case. The term itself translates uneasily into Chinese. Keenly aware of the conceptual importance of nationalism in the West, Chinese intellectuals have long searched for a Chinese equivalent. *Guojia, guomin,* and *minzu* have each had their proponents. But the search for the right term has become politically charged and intellectually tangled, thus rendering all three suspect.[1] To get around this problem, Chinese historians have recently begun to give greater attention to patriotism (*aiguo zhuyi*).[2] They have done so on the basis of compelling textual evidence that suggests that term enjoyed wide currency across political lines over the decades treated here (no less than in more recent times).

This point is important to our quest for identity; for the way the term itself was and is used suggests a conception of China which is state centered. By professing *aiguo,* Chinese usually expressed loyalty to and a desire to serve the state, either as it was or as it would be in its renovated form. *Aiguo* also highlights the old and indigenous nature of this seemingly "modern" and "Western" phenomenon and thus helps us guard against reducing Chinese nationalism to Western terms.[3] For all these reasons, this essay substitutes patriotism for nationalism, and it is hoped that even readers not entirely persuaded by this choice will nonetheless be impressed by the peculiarities of the Chinese search for national identity.

What follows is a sketch of how successive generations sought to think their way out of the downward spiral of defeat and weakness in which China had become caught. The response to developments in foreign relations appears prominently in this sketch because much of the impetus for patriotic reflection on China's plight came from the repeated blows struck

---

[1]The origins and evolution of these terms in Chinese political discourse—and the related ones for "people," "race," and "ethnicity"—is a tangle that badly needs sorting out.

[2]Particularly noteworthy is Yu Danchu's "Zhonguo jindai aiguo zhuyi de 'wangguo shijian' chugao" (A preliminary examination of the "historical warnings from perished countries" in modern Chinese patriotism), *Shijie lishi* (World history), 1984, no. 1:23–31, and "Meiguo dulishi zai jindai Zhongguo de jieshao he yingxiang" (The introduction and impact of the history of American independence on modern China), ibid., 1987, no. 2:60–81.

[3]The wisdom of this solution is confirmed by Huỳnh Kim Khánh's sensitive treatment of Vietnamese revolutionaries, whose preoccupations were strikingly similar to the generations of Chinese under consideration here; see *Vietnamese Communism, 1925–1945* (Ithaca: Cornell University Press, 1982), pp. 26–34.

by foreign powers. Each new imposition or humiliation set off a wave of alarm among patriots by revealing afresh China's vulnerability and the inadequacy of previous efforts to reverse the crisis. Strategies for saving the state shifted rapidly, as patriots of various persuasions experimented with different mixes of state ideology, political recruitment, and popular mobilization, and were couched in ever more sweeping and radical terms.

The patriotic response dates back to the nineteenth century. Two decades of struggle climaxed by military defeat and the occupation of the capital in 1860 gave rise to a broad concern with state renovation. The Tongzhi restoration of the 1860s devoted itself to a program of self-strengthening and reform. It sought to promote "men of talent" (meaning those with demonstrated ability in political affairs as well as moral cultivation); train specialists in Western techniques; launch military, economic, and diplomatic projects that would add muscle to the state; and experiment with institutional innovations such as a rudimentary foreign office.

These initiatives were sponsored by leaders with a "statecraft" (*jingshi*) approach to government affairs. They gave the writings of Wei Yuan, an earlier advocate of that approach, a privileged place in their thinking. Already an expert on inner Asia, Wei had in the 1830s looked to the maritime frontier, where he discovered that the penetration of Western and especially British naval power into Southeast Asia posed a geopolitical threat to China, which combined with Muslim unrest in the deep interior constituted an unprecedented danger. In response he had recommended borrowing from foreigners to develop a navy, and he advocated making common cause with both China's southeast Asian dependencies and Britain's rivals to check the British advance.[4] The events of the subsequent two decades had vindicated Wei's fears and made more timely his call for urgent action to direct scholarship to the pressing practical problem of arresting the decline of state power, preserving China's territory, and restoring her glory.

Feng Guifen, a prominent exponent of the restorationist philosophy and adviser to the prominent statesman Li Hongzhang, offers insight into the

[4]Jane Kate Leonard, *Wei Yuan and China's Rediscovery of the Maritime World* (Cambridge: Harvard University Council on East Asian Studies, 1984); and the treatment of Wei Yuan by Susan Mann Jones and Philip Kuhn in *The Cambridge History of China* (hereafter *CHC*), gen. ed. Denis Twitchett and John K. Fairbank (Cambridge: Cambridge University Press, 1978–), 10:150–51, 154–55. See also Fred W. Drake, *China Charts the World: Hsu Chi-yu and His Geography of 1848* (Cambridge: Harvard University East Asian Research Center, 1975), on another influential scholar-official of the statecraft persuasion, who shared Wei's practical commitment to understanding the maritime threat.

patriotic premises of the post-1860 effort. His overriding concern was to "restore our original strength, redeem ourselves from further humiliations, and maintain the integrity of our vast territory." But if China was to reach this goal and in time surpass the foreigners and become "the leading power in the world," then the emperor would have to "set us in the right direction," and the very foreigners who subjected China to humiliation would, for a time at least, have to be taken as teachers and models.[5]

The Tianjin settlement and reverses suffered during the Sino-French struggle dealt a fresh blow to patriots' hopes and evoked militant attacks on the misplaced and ineffective attempts at self-strengthening and on the meek accommodation to the disruptive missionary presence and the insatiable and unreasonable demands of the Westerners. The critics bemoaned the neglect of the popular and moral foundations of the state and called for a program of ideological revitalization, stressing the links between the throne and the people. A strong policy and restored prestige were possible only if high officials listened to the will of the people and turned its enormous potential against the foreign danger. In pursuing this course Beijing would have to be prepared to sanction popular violence and where necessary embrace warlike measures. An enlightened and virtuous ruler sensitive to the will of his subjects and open to the views of his orthodox officials could lead a united and aroused country to victory.[6]

Defeat by Japan and the ensuing assault by the powers hammered home the inadequacy of this program put forward by the populist patriots of the 1870s and 1880s. While Chinese divided in their response to these most recent setbacks, their reactions revealed an emerging point of agreement on the importance of "the people." One important tendency in the 1890s took up and extended the self-strengthening program of institutional reform but supplemented it with an emphasis on the popular base of the state that echoed the views of the militants.[7]

A group of marginal intellectuals which included Wang Tao had helped

[5]Quotation from Feng in William Theodore de Bary et al., eds., *Sources of Chinese Tradition* (New York: Columbia University Press, 1960), pp. 708–10.

[6]John E. Schrecker, *Imperialism and Chinese Nationalism: Germany in Shantung* (Cambridge: Harvard University Press, 1971), chap. 2, contains a description of the militant point of view.

[7]John E. Schrecker suggests that the militants of the 1870s and 1880s took an increasing interest in reform, eventually emerging as supporters of it in the late 1890s. Schrecker, "The Reform Movement of 1898 and the *Ch'ing-I* Reform as Opposition," in Paul A. Cohen and Schrecker, eds., *Reform in Nineteenth-Century China* (Cambridge: Harvard University, East Asian Research Center, 1976), pp. 289–305. This idea is further developed by Mary Backus Rankin, "'Public Opinion' and Political Power: *Qingyi* in Late Nineteenth Century China," *Journal of Asian Studies* 41 (May 1982): 453–84.

to pull these two elements together. They articulated the familiar and fundamental concern with catching up with the power of the Western states so that China could compete effectively. But they also warned that the self-strengtheners had not gone far enough in winning popular support for government policy. "Of all the great evils in the world," Wang had written in 1893, "the greatest is when the people lack confidence in their rulers." China suffered from precisely that evil—"the failure of communication between ruler and ruled and the distance separating the sovereign and the people." To bring the two together would require institutional changes anathema to the militants but essential to opening avenues of expression for the bureaucracy and even for broad sectors of the politically minded public.[8]

Writing against the backdrop of an almost feverish search for new policies, Kang Youwei skillfully drew these new ideas together in lengthy memorials intended for the emperor himself: "Your official has heard that all the countries in the world today which have held to old ways have without exception been partitioned or put in great danger." With China helpless to stem the rush of foreign demands, it was evident that the state would have to undergo extensive renovation. China would have "to dismantle the building and build anew if we want something strong and dependable." The Meiji reforms in Japan offered one example of what vigorous action could achieve. Turkey and Poland, both helpless and exploited, were warnings of the disasters inaction would bring. Kang's proposals moved well beyond the more modest changes advocated by the earlier self-strengtheners to include a thorough shake-up of the bureaucracy, a top-to-bottom revision of economic and educational policy, higher taxes, a popular army equipped with the most advanced equipment, the removal of the capital to a more defensible position inland, and the development of an extensive railway system. Though all these proposals were intended to make the state stronger, Kang had not lost sight of the people: "If we cannot think how to foster those people, then we ourselves destroy our own foundation."[9]

The other tendency in foreign policy in the late 1890s was to downplay reform and to follow the line of the earlier militants. Li's defeat in 1895 once

---

[8]Quotation from Wang Tao in Paul A. Cohen, *Between Tradition and Modernity: Wang T'ao and Reform in Late Ch'ing China* (Cambridge: Harvard University Press, 1974), pp. 227, 229.

[9] Quotation from Huang Zhangjian, *Kang Youwei wuxu zhenzouyi* (Kang Youwei's authentic 1898 memorials) (Taipei: Zhongyang yanjiuyuan lishi yuyan yanjiusuo, 1974), p. 507; and Jonathan D. Spence, *The Gate of Heavenly Peace: The Chinese and Their Revolution, 1895–1980* (New York: Viking, 1981), pp. 39, 49; see also pp. 30, 36–40, 47, 49, 61–62.

again revealed the bankruptcy of self-strengthening and inspired demands for his execution. The militant prescription gained powerful adherents through the late 1890s and finally was taken up by the court in 1900. Supported by such influentials at court as Ronglu and Kangyi, the empress dowager Cixi decided to test the claim that a united and determined China could turn away repeated and demeaning foreign demands and withstand even a strong invader. To official objections that the Boxers were a weak reed for Beijing to lean on and that their claims to immunity from firearms were laughable, Cixi responded in the language of the militants: "If we cannot rely on the supernatural formulae, can we not rely upon the hearts of the people? China has been extremely weak, the only thing we can rely on is the hearts of the people."[10]

The foreign occupation of north China and the crisis in the northeast (Manchuria) culminating in the Russo-Japanese conflict once again galvanized patriots. While militant populists fell silent, official policy began again to move along the lines earlier advocated by Kang and others. The result was a flurry of activity intended to strengthen the state, restrict foreign privileges, and lay the basis for a constitutional monarchy.[11] Backing this ambitious program was a coalition that harnessed the heirs of Li Hongzhang, who were more interested in immediate gains in state power, together with former militants such as Zhang Zhidong and Xiliang, who gave priority to popular mobilization.

Some Chinese were, however, beginning to entertain doubts about whether the Qing state was an adequate foundation for renovation. A weak foreign policy did much to nurture if not create those doubts. The first widespread signs of disaffection were evident among students, after the Qing's failure to recover the northeast from Russia and the Qing's betrayal of the anti-American boycott movement. Between 1903 and 1905, protesters made markedly patriotic appeals intended to mobilize popular support deemed essential to saving China and the Chinese people.[12]

From the last decade of the Qing, the revolutionary persuasion would win growing numbers of converts. But patriots that embraced the revolu-

---

[10]Quotation from Immanuel Hsu in *CHC* 11:122.

[11]Mary C. Wright emphasizes the impetus foreign policy reverses gave to domestic political developments in this period. Wright, "The Rising Tide of Change," in Wright, ed., *China in Revolution: The First Phase, 1900–1913* (New Haven: Yale University Press, 1968), pp. 1–63.

[12]Yang Tianshi and Wang Xuezhuang, comps., *Ju E yundong, 1901–1905* (The movement to expel the Russians, 1901–1905) (Beijing: Zhongguo shehui kexue, 1979); and Michael H. Hunt, *The Making of a Special Relationship: The United States and China to 1914* (New York: Columbia University Press, 1983), pp. 230–41.

tion as the only solution to China's crisis were to divide among themselves over whether the clearing operation that would have to precede the raising of the new state would be political only or include sweeping social change as well. Among the radical statists some such as Sun Yat-sen held that political renovation would be sufficient. Alienation from Manchu rule created growing support for a political clean sweep. Constitutional monarchy was not enough; only a republic purged of all traces of the self-serving and inept Manchus could make the state strong and realize their patriotic goals—"to rescue the ancestral country" (as Qiu Jin phrased it) or (in the more chauvinistic language of Song Jiaoren) to live up to "the mightly accomplishments of our ancestors over the past five thousand years—in conquest, administration, expansion of our national territory, and the elevation of our national prestige."[13]

The 1911 revolution did not yield the hoped-for results. New political arrangements failed to bring unity and order, not to mention legitimacy. Representative government degenerated rapidly into an autocracy hostile to popular participation and ineffective in foreign policy. Japanese encroachment intensified, taking advantage of the World War and the weakness of the Beijing government to secure new territorial concessions in 1914 and to press a long list of new demands in 1915. Though China joined in the war effort, there was no reward from the victorious Allies. The Versailles settlement leaving in Japan's hands the German possessions in Shandong brought frustrations over these difficulties in domestic and foreign affairs to a pitch.

Like earlier "foreign shocks," Versailles dealt a blow to patriotic hopes while forcing a reappraisal of past strategies. It deepened the division among the ranks of radical statists. Sun held the Nationalist party to the task of political revolution. His successor, Chiang Kai-shek [Jiang Jieshi], kept to that course. As a patriot, he wanted a state strong enough to restore unity and order, end foreign humiliation, abolish unequal treaties, regain lost territory, and ultimately restore China's lost grandeur. But the chief means Chiang was to rely on was to be military might; moral homilies and half-hearted efforts at popular mobilization were to supplement the main military effort.

For some among the students who took to the streets on May 4, 1919, and for their intellectual mentors, political revolution seemed less and less

[13]Quotations from Mary Backus Rankin, *Early Chinese Revolutionaries: Radical Intellectuals in Shanghai and Chekiang, 1902–1911* (Cambridge: Harvard University Press, 1971), p. 46; and Don Price, *Russia and the Roots of the Chinese Revolution, 1896–1911* (Cambridge: Harvard University Press, 1974), p. 181.

adequate to encompass China's salvation. The continued decline of the state and widespread popular apathy over China's future convinced them that only a China thoroughly made over could be expected to function effectively in international affairs, perhaps even to survive at all. The idea of a revolution that would (in the phrase of the intellectual and reformer Liang Qichao) "make the people new" by effecting fundamental social and economic changes gradually gained converts.

This outlook had been gaining adherents since the last decade of the Qing. Anarchists and socialist had already, then, begun to listen to foreign authorities on those subjects, filtered for the most part through Japanese translations. The New Culture movement initiated in the midteens extended and popularized a socially critical outlook and added to the urge of intellectuals to explore iconoclastic foreign "isms."

The result was to push patriots into positions that seem paradoxical. To save China meant destroying important parts of it. The state would have to be torn down, and a society filled with pernicious practices and feudal attitudes would have to be uprooted. Only on a firm political and a fresh social foundation was it possible to build a new China. To save China also required patriots to put their faith in Russia, a country that only recently had been one of China's most dangerous tormentors. But the Bolshevik revolution seemed to offer the only successful model of social revolution and state building, and the Soviet Union was the only power that appeared sympathetic to the aspirations of radical Chinese patriots. Finally, to save China required breaking down what little political order and unity was left in the name of anarchism, federalism, or revolutionary base building. While the resulting division and disruption might facilitate foreign meddling and impose hardship on the people, destruction of the old political and social system was the painful but unavoidable path to unity and order and ultimate renewal.

These most radical of patriots had by the early 1920s wandered far indeed in search of the cure for their state in crisis. But they had done so for good reason. They had become increasingly sensitive to the complex matrix in which that state functioned. On the domestic side, the network of ties between state and society seemed to doom simple political reform. The state, it seemed, could be transformed only if the program of transformation extended outward into the society. The state's ideology, its personnel recruitment, and its relations to the people and the elite would have to be rethought. But predictably, those patterns of thought and interest tied to the state as it was would inspire resistance, and because the state's social entanglements were so extensive and at points deep, revolutionaries could expect the resistance to be widespread and stubborn. The growing realization of the power of this resistance to genuine revolution would in turn become the justification for ever more radical measures, further intensifying the conflict over the revolutionary road to China's salvation.

On the international side, much the same problem confronted the patriot. China was entangled in a global system whose dominant powers would fiercely resist revolutionary changes that threatened long-nurtured foreign interests. The strength of those powers was by itself formidable, and it was augmented by the support of Chinese tied to foreigners economically, culturally, and diplomatically. To succeed, a revolution would need allies abroad as well as popular support at home.

Out of the May Fourth generation came the founding members of the Communist party. Some would survive the grim winnowing of the 1920s and 1930s. Out of those that were not lost to execution, assassination, exhaustion, or disillusionment would emerge the leaders who would found a new state meant to realize long-nurtured patriotic aspirations. An examination of their road to social revolution helps us to see from yet another angle the importance of patriotic concerns and the way that foreign crisis sharpened and radicalized them.

For the two leaders instrumental in the founding of the Chinese Communist party, Li Dazhao and Chen Duxiu, patriotic concerns gave urgency to their thinking about China's future. Wrestling with the problem of how to shake the elite out its pessimism and the people out of their passivity ultimately carried both Li and Chen from their early studies in the classical curriculum to Marxism and a faith in the power of social revolution and an alliance with the Soviet Union to retore greatness to China.

Patriotism was a particularly stark concern in Chen's thinking. He had been shaken in his youth, in the late 1890s, by the assault on China and had then called for the government to act "to avoid the ruin of our nation" and for the people to awaken and "care about the fate of the country." As a student in Japan, he had reacted angrily to the Qing failure in the northeast, and on his return home in 1903 he had helped prepare a charter for a patriotic society, whose goals were to "develop patriotic thought and stir up a martial spirit, so people will grab their weapons to protect their country and restore our basic national sovereignty."[14]

Chen was also driven by a realization that China's society was rotten. The

[14]Quotation from Lee Feigon, *Chen Duxiu: Founder of the Chinese Communist Party* (Princeton: Princeton University Press, 1983), pp. 33, 41.

imperial examination was bankrupt, and to prepare for it, he recalled, was a torture. The exam itself, he remembered from his own experience in Nanjing in 1897, was "just like an animal exhibition of monkeys and bears performing every few years; and then I pondered whether this system was not as defective as every other system in the nation."[15] To pass the exam and become an official was to launch oneself on a career of swindling and aggrandizement that might honor ancestors and benefit family but not save the nation. By 1903, Chen had extended his critique to the Chinese people, who passively watched their country's humiliation and accepted its backwardness. He would never forgive the popular indifference to the patriotic imperatives that gripped him.

Chen's search for a way out brought him first under the spell of the moderate reformers Kang Youwei and Liang Qichao. Western constitutional models and popular education became the key to China's salvation. By December 1919, Chen had turned against the Anglo-American model of progress and democracy, stressing instead the danger that capitalism and imperialism posed.[16] He now turned to Marxism, which offered an appealing critique of both evils and, even more important, a program for moving China toward a more just social order and toward a higher level of political and economic development.

Even Li Dazhao, known for his internationalist loyalties, demonstrates how a broader vista could evolve out of and yet continue to rest on a concern with China's regeneration. Like Chen, Li followed a tortuous path as he sought a solution to China's crisis. He too took an early interest in constitutional reform leavened with a conviction that society required reforming if China were to become strong and prosperous. In 1913 while in Japan he threw his support to Sun Yatsen's revolutionary program.

The Japanese menace caused Li to suffer great shame over China's decline from past heights and to fear the prospect of his country's extinction, and it drove him to contemplate a more radical program. Responding to Chen's sharp attack on the culture and people, Li pleaded, "We ought not to stop thinking about our country and refuse to love it because the country has deficiencies." He urged "patriots" (including even the minority peoples) to

[15]Quotation from Richard C. Kagan, "Chen Tu-hsiu's Unfinished Autobiography," *China Quarterly* 50 (April–June 1972): 314.

[16]Deng Ye, "Shilun wusi shiqi Chen Duxiu shijieguan de zhuanbian" (An exploration into the changes in Chen Duxiu's world view late in the May Fourth period), in Wang Shudi et al., eds., *Chen Duxiu pinglun xuanbian* (A selection of critical essays on Chen Duxiu), 2 vols. (N.p.: Henan renmin, 1982), 1:381.

feel confidence that the Chinese, like the people of any other nation, could transform their condition and restore "the springtime of our nation."[17] While calling for unity at home, Li also sought to promote unity with other Asians also threatened by Japanese Pan-Asianism.

The Bolshevik revolution and the Versailles settlement soon led Li to subordinate this vision of popular and regional unity in favor of social revolution and a more far-reaching internationalism. Li reaffirmed that China, caught in a "robbers' world," required for its survival both popular resistance at home and friends abroad. He found hope in the Chinese people, who had ever since the Opium War (1839–42) fought back ever more vigorously against foreign aggression. He also found hope in the October Revolution in Russia, "the revolution of the twentieth-century type" that would sweep all before it.[18] China's struggle, already well underway, should not proceed in isolation but rather join with other peoples similarly oppressed and exploited in the irresistible march toward a liberated, socialist future for all.

The case of Zhang Guotao, who was to find his way into the Communist party as a disciple of Li Dazhao, nicely illustrates once again the way foreign aggression spurred patriots on. Zhang himself is quite explicit on his patriotic beginnings and his persistent search for the key to saving China:

> In the very beginning I was a passionate patriot; and like the ambitious youths of the time, I looked forward wholeheartedly to China's becoming rich and powerful. Then I became more radical by supporting the New Culture Movement, opposing the old influences, and advocating social reform and national salvation through revolution. Finally, I became enthusiastic about the Communist movement, studied Marxism, and looked up to the example of the Russian Revolution, believing it to be the panacea for national salvation and the guide to revolution.[19]

[17]Quotation from Maurice Meisner, *Li Dazhao and the Origins of Chinese Marxism* (Cambridge: Harvard University Press, 1967), p. 27.

[18]Quotation from Li's "Bolshevism de shengli" (The victory of Bolshevism), December 1918, in Yuan Qian et al., *Li Dazhao wenji* (Collected works of Li Dazhao), 2 vols. (Beijing: Renmin, 1984), 1:602. For Li's angry reaction to the Shandong settlement, see "Mimi waijiao yu qiangdao shijie" (Secret diplomacy and the robbers' world), May 18, 1919, in ibid., 2:1–3. For Li's views on the tradition of popular resistance, see Zhu Jianhua and He Rongdi, "Shilun Li Dazhao de fandi sixiang" (An exploration of Li Dazhao's anti-imperialist thought), in Han Yide and Wang Shudi, eds., *Li Dazhao yanjiu lunwenji* (A collection of research papers on Li Dazhao), 2 vols. (Shijiazhuang: Hebei renmin, 1984), 2:527.

[19]Quotations here and in the next paragraph from Chang Kuo-t'ao [Zhang Guotao], *The Rise of the Chinese Communist Party, 1921–1927* (Lawrence, Kan.: University Press of Kansas, 1971), pp. 32, 87.

The burgeoning Japanese ambitions in China between 1914 and 1919 had served to focus Zhang's interest in public affairs. Now "a zealous patriot," he "began to pore over the modern history of China and accounts of how India and Korea had lost their sovereignty. Many were the discussions I had with teachers and friends about how to save our country." May Fourth intensified Zhang's concerns and turned him into a political activist. He sought to reach out to his countrymen beyond the narrow circle of his Peking University friends. But preaching on the street, he soon realized, would not redeem China. So he took the only step that seemed to offer the slightest ray of hope. Giving up on Sun Yatsen's narrow political ambitions and his aloofness from the masses, Zhang embraced Marxism, turned to the Soviet Union as China's only international friend, and helped organize the Chinese Communist party.

Mao Zedong was also shaped by the May Fourth patriotic spirit of desperate searching. Writing in 1952, Mao located the origins of the Chinese revolution in the popular resistance to the British invaders during the Opium War and flatly stated that "China's modern revolutionary struggle has for its goal, first and foremost, the opposition against the invasion of imperialism."[20] Mao's own early years reflect this symbiotic relationship between patriotic concerns and the turn toward radical social and political programs.

Mao's politics were powerfully conditioned by an anxiety over the peril facing China and the need to save it. He entertained an ever more imposing picture of foreign power and an ever more alarming vision of China's vulnerability in an international order governed by amoral struggle. Within his own lifetime he had seen the loss of Korea and Taiwan, the occupation of Beijing, the repeated payment of indemnities to foreign powers, and the informal partition of the northeast. Sometime around 1910 or 1911, Mao picked up an 1896 pamphlet on China's imminent dismemberment which so impressed him that years later he could still recall its opening line ("Alas, China will be subjugated") and his own feeling of depression "about the future of my country" and the dawning realization "that it was the duty of all people to help save it."[21]

Mao's early political views underwent an almost kaleidoscopic set of changes. He moved rapidly and, from all appearances, unsystematically

---

[20] Michael Y. M. Kau and John K. Leung, *The Writings of Mao Zedong* (Armonk, N.Y.: M. E. Sharpe, 1986–), 1:268.

[21] Edgar Snow, *Red Star over China* (1938; reprint, New York: Grove, 1961), p. 131.

through "Western learning," the works of the late nineteenth-century self-strengtheners, and the writings of the early twentieth-century reformers, including Yan Fu's translations of Western writings and Kang Youwei's and Liang Qichao's commentaries. In 1917 and 1918, after much worry "over the coming destruction of our country," Mao had become convinced it could be averted, but "what I am not yet clear on are the ways in which changes can be successfully brought about. I incline to believe that a [complete] reconstruction is needed."[22] He had by now arrived at a strong faith in concentrated state power, firmly if not ruthlessly exercised, as the key to the livelihood of the people and China's survival. "The first and foremost need," Mao is supposed to have asserted at that time, "is for a strong and powerful government! Once that is established, the people could be organized!"[23]

Mao's patriotism was tinged with a strong populist faith. "If all the hearts in the realm are moved, is there anything which cannot be achieved? And . . . how, then, can the state fail to be rich, powerful, and happy?" Writing in 1919, Mao could praise the Chinese people for their "great inherent capacities": "The more profound the oppression, the greater its resistance. . . . [O]ne day, the reform of the Chinese people will be more profound than that of any other people, and the society of the Chinese people will be more radiant than that of any other people. . . . We must all exert ourselves! We must all advance with the utmost strength! Our golden age, our age of glory and splendour, lies before us."[24]

In 1920, in the wake of the May Fourth movement, Mao (then aged twenty-seven) found himself drawn to Marxism. The Bolshevik revolution pointed to the future. Russia, he concluded, "is the number one civilized country in the world."[25] Along with his admiration for the Soviet revolution, he also shared widespread hopes for a new international order. It was understandable, he observed, for Chinese to direct their effort into the

[22]Mao's detailed commentary penned in a translation of F. Paulsen's *A System of Ethics,* in Takeuchi Minoru, ed., *Mao Zedong ji bujuan* (Supplements to the collected writings of Mao Zedong), 9 vols. (Tokyo: Sōsōsha, 1983–85), 9:19–47. Translated excerpts (incorrectly dated) in Jerome Chen, *Mao and the Chinese Revolution* (London: Oxford University Press, 1965), 44–45.

[23]Hsiao Yü [Siao-yu], *Mao Tse-tung and I Were Beggars* (Syracuse: Syracuse University Press, 1959), pp. 138, 139 (quotation), 193–94. Mao later recalled that his views after his arrival in Beijing in September 1918 were "a curious mixture of liberalism, democratic reformism, and Utopian Socialism. I had somewhat vague passions about 'nineteenth century democracy,' Utopianism and old fashioned liberalism." Snow, *Red Star,* pp. 147–48. Anarchism was yet another part of the mixture.

[24]Quotation from Stuart R. Schram in *CHC* 13:794, 799.

[25]Ibid., *CHC* 13:802.

reconstruction of their own country. China was their home, and it was "relative to other places around the world more immature and corrupt." But the Chinese should broaden their vision of their field of work to include other countries and not just China: "We should make it a point that some should work in China and some should work in the world. Helping the USSR in the completion of its socialist revolution, helping Korea to its independence, helping Southeast Asia to its independence, and helping Mongolia, Tibet, and Qinghai toward self-governing autonomy are all important."[26] For Mao as for others, patriotism led to revolution and internationalism.

Zhou Enlai, only twenty-one years old when the May Fourth movement began, brought a polished, cool, well-schooled intelligence to his patriotic concerns that distinguished him from the others treated here. World War I and the disillusioning outcome of the peacemaking had stirred him no less than his classmates in Nankai to a consciousness of China's vulnerability and the urgency of action to bring it out of its backwardness. He quickly developed the internationalist preoccupations that others were also then cultivating. In August 1919 he appealed to Japanese students to overthrow their own warlords, bring an end to the aggressive spirit directed against China, and then unite China and Japan in one "national social movement." His decision to leave for study in Europe would not only carry him to a commitment to the Communist party but also provide an opportunity to think about China's future in an international context and a comparative perspective. Writing from London at the very beginning of his four-and-a-half years in Europe, Zhou reported that he was impressed by the Russian revolution's swift, insurrectionary assault, which was "effective in thoroughly cleaning out old abuses. If as in the case of China where long-standing abuses are so deep the French and Russian type of revolution is not followed, then it will not be easy to make effective changes."[27]

[26]Mao to Cai Hesen et al., December 1, 1920, in Zhonggong zhongyang wenxian yanjiushi, comp., *Mao Zedong shuxin xuanji* (A selection of Mao Zedong letters) 2(Beijing: Renmin, 1983), pp. 2–3. Robert A. Scalapino deals in detail with this phase of Mao's life. Scalapino, "The Evolution of a Young Revolutionary: Mao Zedong in 1919–1921," *Journal of Asian Studies* 42 (November 1982): 29–61.

[27] Quotations from Zhongguo geming bowuguan, comp., *Shou Enlai tongzhi lu Ou wenji xubian* (An addition to the collected writings from Comrade Zhou Enlai's European stay) (Beijing: Wenwu, 1982), p. 71. This letter was but the first of an outpouring of commentary on and analysis of the European scene and international relations that would foreshadow Zhou's later diplomatic career. These materials are in Huai En, comp., *Zhou zongli gingshaonian shidai shiwenshuxinji* (A collection of writings from Premier Zhou's youth), 2 vols. (Chengdu: Sichuan renmin, 1979–80). For treatment of the early Zhou years, see Huai En, *Zhou zongli shengping dashiji* (A chronicle of events in Premier Zhou's life) (Chengdu: Sichuan renmin,

The preoccupation with state power stood—and still stands—as one of the signal features of modern Chinese national identity. Looking to the past to define the new China, political activists in the late Qing and the early Republican periods took as a fundamental point of departure in their thinking the conviction that establishing a strong state was essential if China were to be saved. These figures from the decades around the turn of the century, important in their own right, were also to be important as "ancestors" for later generations of politically engaged intellectuals. The editor of a "liberal" journal in the late 1940s, when continuing destruction gave good reason for despair, would invoke their spirit as a source of courage: "Friends, we should . . . remain determined in our loyalty to the nation. If today one method does not work, then tomorrow use another and continue the effort."[28] Patriotism remains even today a vital tradition. Chinese still searching for the right road continue to echo the plaints and aspirations of these ancestors.

While the nationalist preoccupation with the state is striking, we should not lose sight of its complexity. The patriots' concerns about the welfare of the state and China's greatness were not expressed in a fixed formula. Politically engaged intellectuals did disagree among themselves and continually reformulated their views. Indeed, patriots advanced a striking and rapidly changing assortment of specific diagnoses and remedies for China's illness. The differences that developed among patriots turned largely on three issues, each essential to the proper functioning of the state and to any scheme to resuscitate it.

First, what ideology would shore up the state and give its operation legitimacy and direction? Could the state crisis be resolved within the framework of the existing imperial value system or some alternative indigenous system, or did it require the importing of some new, foreign-derived ideology?

Second, where were the cadres that were to manage the bureaucracy and to occupy the leadership positions to come from and what rules were to govern their behavior? Here too the imperial system with its exams and elaborate rules of official behavior offered a foundation for reform. But as this system fell into disfavor, proponents of change would look elsewhere for ways to recruit and control political activists—to the secret societies, the Western parliamentary system, or the Leninist party model.

1986), and the richly documented volume by Jin Chongji, *Zhou Enlai zhuan, 1898–1949* (A biography of Zhou Enlai, 1898–1949) (Beijing: Zhongyong wenxian, 1989), chaps. 1–6.

[28] Chu Anping writing in *Guancha* in July 1948, quoted in Suzanne Pepper, *Civil War in China: The Political Struggle, 1945–1949* (Berkeley and Los Angeles: University of California Press, 1978), pp. 194–95.

Third, who were the "people" and what was the proper basis for their relationship to the state? Though the people were always regarded as in some sense the foundation of the state, the precise identity of the people, the degree of popular involvement in saving the state, and the values that the "people" were to be mobilized on behalf of were all the sources of considerable disagreement.

Nor should our attention to these politically engaged intellectuals suggest that they were the only group with a conception of what China should be. Nations are not unitary, whatever the nationalist mythmakers may say to the contrary. They are, rather, divided by region, class, and ethnicity—to list but some of the most salient cleavages that can make the construction of a national identity the source of considerable contention. Merchants, peasants, warlords, overseas Chinese, and those with strong provincial loyalties brought their own perspectives to China's national crisis, and we should by no means assume that their perspectives neatly coincided with the intellectuals discussed above.

The treatment here linking foreign relations with elite thinking on identity highlights some of the inadequacies of the analytic Social Science Research Council (SSRC) definition of identity treated in Chapter 1 of this volume, and it supports the effort to formulate a less rigid, more synthetic definition pursued in that chapter.

The developments treated in this chapter fit uncomfortably within the framework of the SSRC definition. A mounting foreign threat triggered an intellectual crisis. Convinced that a strong state was essential, indeed the prerequisite for a secure and revitalized China, patriots found to their great chagrin that somehow their efforts and the talents of the Chinese people fell short of what was required to realize their dreams. This disparity between the ideal and the sad conditions they faced domestically and internationally led them in turn to explore increasingly radical roads out of the impasse. These roads included, not least, transcending the national identity problem by locating China in a broader, international community (the transnational community of the oppressed and the revolutionary) and by making the complete overhaul of the society the precondition for China's political restoration (the continuing revolution that at times would undercut the state). In effect, challenges from the foreign "other" played off and forced an increasingly radical rethinking of the Chinese "us" and, by extension, of the state itself as a structure of authority, along with its functional relationships to society.

This prolonged crisis cannot, to begin with, be easily understood in terms of an objective set of boundaries central to the SSRC definition of identity. Rather, the national crisis has to be understood essentially in terms of states of mind. To be sure, boundaries came into the picture but not as indicators of who the Chinese were. Boundaries might be better seen here as psychological trip wires. As foreigners time and again crossed those lines at a wide variety of points, pressing in ever more deeply, those incursions steadily fed and deepened the intellectual crisis.

Boundaries in this Chinese case played a second role not envisioned in the SSRC conception. The boundaries handed down from the high point of imperial expansion contained peoples of diverse cultures, a diversity that made difficult the assimilation of Western models of nationalism with their emphasis on uniformity of language, history, and outlook. With so much of China's vulnerable inner-Asian territory occupied by non-Chinese (that is, non-Han), Chinese intellectuals would have undermined their own dream of empire if they had couched identity in narrow, explicitly Han terms. But if they were to include non-Han in the nation and thereby preserve the integrity of the empire, then finding the national essence would become exceedingly problematic.

By suggesting that nations and empires might in objective terms be equivalent, the formulators of the SSRC notion of identity may have been exercising their sense of paradox on the sly; even so, the suggested equivalence seems neither plausible nor analytically fruitful. If, however, we consider the relations between empire and nation in subjective terms, then we put ourselves in the framework in which the patriots discussed here thought of identity, and we realize that a nation could be an empire if the dominant group saw the imperial holdings as an essential part of their heritage. Paradox plays out better in the subjective than in the objective realm!

The other weakness in the SSRC definition revealed by this case is the stress in that definition on identity as the product of crisis early in the formation of the nation. Not only does the crisis treated here come well after the formation of identity, but the very sturdiness of the identity and the pervasiveness of its acceptance would appear to have exacerbated the crisis and made a way out more difficult to find. Indeed, in thinking about the Chinese case, one wonders if an alternative to the SSRC argument might be more plausible: that the construction of identity is a gradual process often climaxed by a conflict with a dominant power or group obstructing the expression of the emergent identity. The most severe crisis may not come at the point of consolidation but later, when identity has become deeply rooted and tightly integrated. If those challenged have a strong sense of identity, they may be hobbled by a repertoire of responses that are either limited or inappropriate to the occasion.

There is much to be said in favor of the attempt in the introduction of this collection to think about national identity as something consciously constructed, the object of contestation. This approach is consistent with the prevailing trend in cultural studies to see meaning as created and dynamic. The case develped in this chapter not only fits nicely this general characterization but also seems tailor made for one of the specific types of crisis characterized in the introduction—the crisis of self-definition brought on by the dual challenge of external models and external intrusion. China during the late Qing and early Republican periods illustrates how discrediting identity by example and by force could precipitate uncertainties that are arguably still playing themselves out in Chinese politics and intellectual life.

But this notion of a constructed identity may deserve to be taken a step farther so that national self-conceptions are linked to the social and economic formations that generate and sustain them. It would seem particularly important to look at the ways battles, between or within groups, for power and preeminence may shape identity. The politically engaged intellectuals of this chapter, it should be remembered, were a group intent on promoting and defending definitions of identity consistent with their own self-image and interests, while resisting alternative conceptions. The most bitter aspects of this battle occurred within the group—between generations and within generations with divergent backgrounds, educations, and social experiences. These intellectuals may have shared a self-conscious commitment to their roles both as custodians of the culture out of which identity was to arise and as servants of the state that would establish, promote, and defend the identity of the political collective. But at the same time, deep divisions did exist. An understanding of those divisions and their relation to patterns of privilege and power in Chinese society is as important as the re-creation of the visions they shared. This chapter has sought to bring those visions back to life and identify the critical points of division; it remains for others to explore the social reality behind those visions and thereby deepen our understanding of Chinese national identity in this period.

中
國 4

Rites or Beliefs? The
Construction of a Unified
Culture in Late Imperial China

James L. Watson

In recent decades anthropologists have stopped talking about "national identity," a topic they associate with the now-discredited culture and personality school of comparative ethnography.[1] Today the leading journals of our discipline compete to publish essays on the origin and development of cultural traditions, past and present. Those not initiated into the mysteries of anthropological jargon would be hard pressed to determine where "national identity" ends and "cultural identity" begins, but for anthropologists, the distinction is an important one.

In this chapter, I demonstrate how a shared sense of cultural identity predates (and, thus, conditioned) the establishment of a national identity in China. National identity presupposes the formation of a modern, media-conscious state system and the promotion of an ideology of nationalism among common citizens. As the editors of this volume note in their intro-duction, national identity does not grow "naturally" in any society; it has to be created, nurtured, and carefully promoted by state authorities.[2] The

I thank the Fairbank Center, Harvard University, for its support during the writing of this chapter. Earlier versions were presented as public lectures at Marlboro College, Vermont, and at the Premodern China Seminar, Harvard University. The chapter was also discussed at the Institute for Culture and Communication, East West Center, Honolulu.

[1] Summarized in Victor Barnouw, *Culture and Personality* (Homewood, Ill.: Dorsey, 1973), pp. 91–235.

[2] See also Benedict Anderson, *Imagined Communities: Reflections on the Origin and Spread of Nationalism* (London: Verso, 1983).

process I outline here is similar, yet different in one important respect: It is my argument that ordinary people (not just state authorities) played a central role in the promotion and perpetuation of a shared sense of cultural identity. In China, nationalism—and with it, *national* identity—came later.

I begin with a question that has preoccupied Western observers since the early Jesuits first began to write about the Central Kingdom: What held Chinese society together for so many centuries? Put another way, how was it possible for a country of continental dimensions, inhabited by people who speak mutually unintelligible languages and exhibit an amazing array of ethnic differences, to be molded into a unified culture? What was it about China that made it so very different from Europe or, for that matter, South Asia?

Solutions to the puzzle are legion: Some have stressed the role of an ideographic (that is, nonphonetic) script that cuts across speech communities, thereby allowing educated people from different regions to share in a common literary and philosophic tradition.[3] Others have argued that it was the autocratic power of the Chinese state, projected through a complex bureaucracy, that held this society together.[4] Still others point to China's elaborate hierarchy of commercial centers and marketing communities as the key to cultural unity.[5] All of these explanations are, of course, correct. One cannot conceive of "China," or the abstraction we call Chinese culture, without a common script, a centralized state, and a complex hierarchy of central places. Other factors, such as a standardized educational system,[6] might be added to the equation, but these are basically derivative of the first two components.

I propose to examine the problem of cultural unity from yet another perspective, one that emphasizes the role of ritual in the lives of ordinary people. Culture in this context is not a reflection (exclusively) of literati pursuits. It is an ever-changing entity that must be recreated by each new generation. It is not something that is preordained or immutable; nor is it a set of traits that people inherit passively from ancestors, as earlier Tylorian notions would lead us to expect. Rather, culture has to be negotiated,

---

[3]See, e.g., Ping-Ti Ho, "The Chinese Civilization: A Search for the Roots of Its Longevity," *Journal of Asian Studies* 35, (1976): 547–54.

[4]Karl Wittfogel, *Oriental Despotism: A Comparative Study in Total Power* (New Haven: Yale University Press, 1957).

[5]G. William Skinner, "The Structure of Chinese History," *Journal of Asian Studies* 44 (1985): 271–92.

[6]Evelyn S. Rawski, "Economic and Social Foundations of Late Imperial Culture," in David G. Johnson, Andrew J. Nathan, and Rawski, eds., *Popular Culture in Late Imperial China* (Berkeley and Los Angeles: University of California Press, 1985), pp. 29–32.

transacted, and achieved. My approach thus stresses the active participation of people who cooperate (some willingly, some not) to "construct" a unified culture.[7]

Earlier attempts to explain China's remarkable record of unity focused, inevitably perhaps, on the superelite of scholar-bureaucrats (degree holders and government servants) who are most visible in the historical record. Many of these men obviously saw themselves as primary movers responsible for directing the course of history.[8] It is not my aim to downgrade the role of China's educated elite; as in all societies the intervention of key individuals did indeed affect the outcome of historical events. But, I would argue, it is not to this rarefied stratum of society alone that one should turn for an answer to the puzzle of cultural unity. One must also consider the role of ordinary people: farmers, artisans, shopkeepers, midwives, silk reelers, and laborers—both male and female—of every conceivable description. It is these people, together with local elites, scholar-bureaucrats, and even the emperor himself, who were engaged in the construction of a unified culture. The focus of attention thus shifts from the passive to the active mode; people at all stations in life are perceived as actors rather than reactors. In this view, peasants are not, as some have claimed, "easy material for ideological molding";[9] they are leading actors in the performance that we have come to call Chinese culture.

My discussion focuses on the late imperial era of Chinese history, a period dating roughly from 1500 to 1940. There is considerable debate among China specialists regarding the definition of "late imperial," but the cultural system under investigation appears to have crystallized during the mid-Ming and dominated social life throughout the Chinese-speaking world until the Pacific War.[10] The 1940 cut-off date is arbitrary in the sense

---

[7]The construction of culture approach is, by now, one of the dominant themes in American anthropology; it draws on the work of Clifford Geertz, *Negara: The Theatre State in Nineteenth Century Bali* (Princeton: Princeton University Press, 1980); Marshall Sahlins, *Culture and Practical Reason* (Chicago: University of Chicago Press, 1976); and David Schneider, *American Kinship: A Cultural Account,* 2d ed. (Chicago: University of Chicago Press, 1980); see also Allan Hansen, "The Making of the Maori: Cultural Invention and Its Logic," *American Anthropologist* 91 (1989): 890–902; and Jocelyn Linnekin, "Defining Tradition: Variations on the Hawaiian Identity," *American Ethnologist* 10 (1983): 241–52.

[8]Although there were some important (and well-known) exceptions, the vast majority of people in this category were male. The role of women as culture constructors among the superelite remains relatively unexplored.

[9]Kung-chuan Hsiao, *Rural China: Imperial Control in the Nineteenth Century* (Seattle: University of Washington Press, 1960), p. 225.

[10] See, e.g., Patricia B. Ebrey, "The Early Stages in the Development of Descent Group Organization," in Ebrey and James L. Watson, eds., *Kinship Organization in Late Imperial*

that late imperial culture—particularly in the form of religious and ritual activities—is still very much in evidence in Taiwan, Hong Kong, Singapore, and rural sectors of the People's Republic. In respect to culture, therefore, the late imperial label has little to do with the demise of the last dynasty (1911) or the establishment of successor governments, first the Republic (1912) and later the People's Republic (1949). What is intriguing about the Chinese case is that key elements of cultural construction (such as rites associated with birth, marriage, and death) have not, as yet, taken on new, modern forms distinct from late imperial models. This is true in the communist as well as noncommunist Chinese world. More will be said about the issue of culture change in the postscript to this paper.

In selecting from the many ways to approach the problem of cultural unity, one must begin by acknowledging that not all social systems have a high degree of cultural uniformity; the pluralistic states of colonial Southeast Asia spring immediately to mind.[11] In pluralistic systems it is the state, often but not exclusively managed by a colonial elite, that holds the society together. My chapter deals with a very different problem, one in which the outward signs of cultural unity appear to be more salient than the power of the state.[12]

In societies that exhibit a high degree of internal integration, two modes of explanation can account for this development: in some contexts, people actively construct a unified culture by nurturing a system of shared beliefs; in other circumstances, cultural unity is maintained (and initiated?) by following a set of shared practices or rites. These two approaches are, of course, closely interrelated; it is impossible to isolate beliefs from practices in real societies. All unified cultures must, by definition, have a set of shared beliefs that underpin collective rites. Nevertheless, for the purposes of argument, I choose here to build on the admittedly arbitrary distinction between belief and practice.

China (Berkeley and Los Angeles: University of California Press, 1986); and Rawski, "Economic and Social Foundations."

[11] John S. Furnivall, *Netherlands India: A Study of Plural Society* (Cambridge: Cambridge University Press, 1944).

[12] The decline of state power during the nineteenth century is a major preoccupation for historians of Qing China; see, e.g., Chu T'ung-tsu, *Local Government in China under the Ch'ing* (Stanford: Stanford University Press, 1962); Philip A. Kuhn, *Rebellion and Its Enemies in Late Imperial China* (Cambridge: Harvard University Press, 1970); and Frederic Wakeman, Jr., *Strangers at the Gate: Social Disorder in South China, 1839–1861* (Berkeley and Los Angeles: University of California Press, 1966). This decline, however, did not appear to affect the cultural unity of the Chinese people; they continued to identify themselves as representatives of a grand civilization, irrespective of political developments.

This dual approach to cultural unity is hardly original, drawing as it does on the work of Emile Durkheim, Robertson Smith, and a host of anthropological ancestors. The problem only becomes interesting when one compares societies. Certain cultures appear to be heavily weighted toward shared beliefs while others lean toward collective rites. Societies of the latter type place primary emphasis on what anthropologists would call the performative domain.[13] It would appear that the construction of a unified culture in China depended primarily on nurturing and maintaining a system of shared rites; there was, by contrast, relatively less emphasis on common beliefs.

This is not to say that the Chinese lacked a set of shared beliefs. Obviously they did have such a system as Maurice Freedman proposed in a discussion of Chinese religion: "The religious ideas and practices of the Chinese are not a congeries of haphazardly assembled elements, all appearances and the greater part of the extensive literature to the contrary. . . . Behind the superficial variety there is order of some sort. That order might be expressed . . . both at the level of ideas (beliefs, representations, classifying principles . . .) and at that of practice and organization (ritual, grouping, hierarchy, etc.)."[14] Steven Sangren's recent work might also be cited to support the view that a coherent set of beliefs underscored Chinese ritual practices.[15]

While granting that key elements of a unified belief system did indeed exist in late imperial China, it is my contention that orthopraxy (correct practice) reigned over orthodoxy (correct belief) as the principal means of attaining and maintaining cultural unity. Two sets of ethnographic data illustrate this point: The first relates to the structure and performance of funerary rites. The second deals with the standardization of temple cults and efforts by state authorities to control local religion. It is important to note that marriage ritual could just as easily substitute for funerary ritual in this analysis; both were subject to the standardizing processes outlined below, and both were key elements in defining Chinese orthopraxy.[16]

[13]See, e.g., Stanley J. Tambiah, "A Performative Approach to Ritual," *Proceedings of the British Academy (1979)* 65 (1981): 113–69.

[14]Maurice Freedman, "On the Sociological Study of Chinese Religion," in Arthur P. Wolf, ed., *Religion and Ritual in Chinese Society* (Stanford: Stanford University Press, 1974), p. 20.

[15]Steven P. Sangren, *History and Magical Power in a Chinese Community* (Stanford: Stanford University Press, 1987).

[16]See, e.g., Maurice Freedman, "Ritual Aspects of Chinese Kinship and Marriage," in Freedman, ed., *Family and Kinship in Chinese Society* (Stanford: Stanford University Press, 1970); Susan Naquin, "Marriage in North China: The Role of Ritual" (Paper delivered at the Chinese Death Ritual Conference, Oracal, Arizona, 1988); and Rubie S. Watson, "Afterward,"

Critical readers will note that the choice of data is likely to affect the outcome of the analysis. Fieldworking anthropologists have a special—some would say restricted—perspective on society: We work from the bottom up, not the top down as do most specialists on Chinese society. This means that we talk mostly to villagers, shopkeepers, workers, and retired people (with heavy emphasis on the latter, given that the elderly have more time to chat with inquisitive outsiders). With rare exceptions, anthropologists seldom focus on members of the elite, intellectual or otherwise. Most of my field contacts are barely literate, and those who are educated have narrow ranges of reading and writing competence. They are, in other words, a far cry from the sophisticated elites David Johnson has called "the classically educated/legally privileged."[17]

Like many anthropologists my representation of Chinese society derives from having lived in villages, in this case two Cantonese communities in Hong Kong's New Territories for periods totaling nearly three years, plus briefer stays in Guangdong's Pearl River Delta. The Hong Kong field sites are lineage-based communities, meaning that all males, save for a handful of shopkeepers, are descendants of pioneer ancestors. The lineages in question (surname Man and Teng) have existed in the New Territories region for four hundred and six hundred years respectively.[18] In recent decades these communities have changed a great deal owing to influences emanating from Hong Kong's urban areas. Nonetheless, key elements of late imperial culture have been maintained and revitalized by local villagers. These include the ancestor worship cult, temple organizations, and the complex rites associated with birth, marriage, and death. Life for these Cantonese villagers is punctuated by ritual, and hence my personal vision of Chinese culture is conditioned by constant exposure to and discussions of ritual.

Another way to address the problem of cultural unity in China is to ask the question What makes Chinese culture "Chinese"? What, in other words, are the basic elements of the cultural equation that allows some

---

in R. S. Watson and Patricia B. Buckley, eds., *Marriage and Inequality in Chinese Society* (Berkeley and Los Angeles: University of California Press, 1991). See Judith A. Berling, "Orthopraxy," in Mircea Eliade, ed., *The Encyclopedia of Religion,* vol. 11 (New York: Macmillan, 1987).

[17]David G. Johnson, "Communication, Class, and Consciousness in Late Imperial China," in Johnson et al., eds., *Popular Culture in Late Imperial China* (Berkeley and Los Angeles: University of California Press, 1985), pp. 56–58.

[18]James L. Watson, *Emigration and the Chinese Lineage: The Mans in Hong Kong and London* (Berkeley and Los Angeles: University of California Press, 1975); Rubie S. Watson, *Inequality among Brothers: Class and Kinship in South China* (Cambridge: Cambridge University Press, 1985).

residents of that vast country to call themselves Chinese (*han*) and be accepted as such while other peoples are labeled "barbarian" (*fan,* or more politely *xiao shu min zu,* minority peoples)? The set of cultural attributes that makes one Chinese appears to have little to do with beliefs, attitudes, or a shared creed. There was never a unified religious hierarchy or church in China charged with the responsibility of dispensing truth, as in Christendom. The notion of truth, in fact, may very well be a culture-bound concept that only has meaning in Western discourse.[19] The closest parallel to the Western church hierarchy in China was the imperial bureaucracy, but Chinese officials were relatively few in number and preoccupied with good governance, not religious beliefs.

In examining the processes of cultural construction, it is perhaps best to begin with the distinction between Han and non-Han. Chinese ordinarily present this as a straightforward dichotomy: One either is or is not Han. The key diagnostic feature here is whether a set of people are deemed to have *wen,* variously translated as civilization, learning, or elegance. In English this dichotomy might be rendered as civilized versus uncivilized; Han Chinese by definition perceived themselves as civilized whereas they viewed non-Han peoples (such as the Miao, Yao, and Zhuang) as uncivilized.[20] In historical terms, however, the distinction between Han and non-Han was never so simple, particularly in the south.[21] Over the centuries, whole populations, on the order of European states, have made the transformation from non-Han to Han.[22] More recently, in the wake of post-Mao reforms, certain groups who had been recognized as Han are seeking to reclaim their non-Han identities.[23] These labels, therefore, are purely cultural and are not racial or biological in any obvious sense.

To be Chinese in this context meant that one played by the rules of the

[19]See Chad Hansen, "Chinese Language, Chinese Philosophy, and 'Truth,'" *Journal of Asian Studies* 44 (1985): 491–519; Mark Hobart, "Anthropos through the Looking Glass: Or How to Teach the Balinese to Bark," in Joanna Overing, ed., *Reason and Morality* (London: Tavistock, 1985); and Rodney Needham, *Belief, Language, and Experience* (Oxford: Basil Blackwell, 1972).

[20]In recent decades, central authorities have discouraged the use of terms such as barbarian (*fan*) and uncivilized (*meiwenhuade, weikaihuade, yemande*) when speaking of non-Han. One nonetheless still hears these terms in Taiwan and in many parts of the People's Republic.

[21]On Han/Yao interactions in south China, see David Faure, "The Lineage as a Cultural Invention: The Case of the Pearl River Delta," *Modern China* 15 (1989): 4–36.

[22]Wolfram Eberhard, *China's Minorities: Yesterday and Today* (Belmont, Calif.: Wadsworth, 1982), pp. 105–47; Herold J. Wiens, *Han Chinese Expansion in South China* (Hamden, Conn.: Shoestring Press, 1954), pp. 130–226.

[23]David Y. H. Wu, "Minority or Chinese? Ethnicity and Culture Change among the Bai of Yunnan, China," *Human Organization* 49 (1990): 1–13.

dominant culture and was judged to be a good performer by those who took it upon themselves to make such judgments—neighbors, local leaders, or imperial officials. What, then, were the rules of the game? How did one *become* Chinese and maintain one's "Chineseness"? From the perspective of ordinary people, to be Chinese was to understand and accept the view that there was a correct way to perform key rituals associated with the life cycle, namely, the rites of birth, marriage, death, and ancestorhood. Correct performance of these rites was one clear and unambiguous method of distinguishing the civilized from the uncivilized or, when considering marginal peoples, the cooked from the uncooked.[24] Put another way, practice rather than belief was what made one Chinese.

Funeral Ritual: Variation within Unity

Considerable anthropological research has focused on Chinese ancestor worship and related mortuary practices.[25] In my own field experience, I have attended nearly twenty funerals and witnessed hundreds of rituals associated with death. In writing up this material, I began, like all ethnographers, to compare what I had seen among the Cantonese with descriptions of funerals in other parts of China (spanning the late imperial era). It became clear that the basic form of funeral rites is similar throughout the empire. There are, of course, interesting regional variations, but in general, all Chinese—from the poorest farmer to the emperor himself—perform the same sequence of ritual acts as funerals.[26] This sequence of acts might be called the elementary structure of Chinese funerary ritual. Poring over ethnographic descriptions, it is possible to isolate nine specific acts that must be performed for a funeral to be judged proper. These nine acts are what distinguish civilized from uncivilized rites. There can be no ambiguity: a funeral either is or is not performed according to Chinese ritual sequence.

[24]The metaphor of cooking is frequently employed by ordinary Chinese when discussing non-Han communities; see, e.g., Susan Naquin and Evelyn S. Rawski, *Chinese Society in the Eighteenth Century* (New Haven: Yale University Press, 1987), pp. 127–28. The dichotomy between "cooked" and "uncooked" is still common in today's Taiwan and is used to designate the degree to which Taiwan's original inhabitants have been assimilated into Han culture.

[25]For a survey, see James L. Watson, "The Structure of Chinese Funerary Rites: Elementary Forms, Ritual Sequence, and the Primacy of Performance," in James L. Watson and Evelyn S. Rawski, eds., *Death Ritual in Late Imperial and Modern China* (Berkeley and Los Angeles: University of California Press, 1988).

[26]On imperial rites, see Evelyn S. Rawski, "The Imperial Way of Death," in J. L. Watson and Rawski, *Death Ritual*.

Briefly summarized, these nine acts are: (1) ritual wailing to announce the death, usually but not exclusively performed by women; (2) wearing hempen garb and associated symbols of mourning; (3) ritualized bathing of the corpse; (4) transfer of food, mock money, and goods to the deceased, often through the medium of fire; (5) preparation of a soul tablet in written characters (which means that the deceased must have a Chinese name); (6) use of copper and silver coins in ritualized contexts; (7) performance of high-pitched piping and percussion to mark transitions in the rites; (8) sealing the corpse in a wooden coffin; and (9) expulsion of the coffin from the community, accompanied by a formal procession. Some of these acts may well be performed by non-Han peoples, but it is the package of rites, the unique combination, that makes a funeral Chinese.[27]

It is the last two acts that are of most interest when considering the processes of cultural unification. One of the requirements of a Chinese funeral is that the corpse must be sealed in an air-tight coffin prior to evacuation from the community. The act of closing the coffin is perhaps the most dramatic in the series; it is accomplished by hammering nails into the lid. When the coffin is carried beyond the boundaries of the community (usually symbolized by gates or walls), the required sequence of ritual acts has been accomplished. It matters little what one believes about death or the afterlife as long as the rites are properly performed. Cynics, agnostics, and active nonbelievers participate in these rites along with those who profess strong faith in the efficacy of the acts. Those who refuse to follow accepted procedure are consciously isolating themselves from the community and hence withdrawing from the dominant culture. It is interesting in this regard that many Cantonese Christians manage to perform the rites according to accepted sequence, even though the oral and textual part of the funeral conforms to Christian expectations.

Key elements of this sequence are indeed supported by an underlying belief system that the majority of Chinese no doubt shared. One of the professed goals of funerary rites is to keep corpse and soul together; separation before ritualized expulsion from the community is thought, by many, to bring disaster. The rites are also deemed to have a controlling and placating effect on the deceased's soul, which is portrayed as volatile and disoriented—potentially dangerous to the living. Closely associated with these beliefs is the idea that living and dead are linked in a network of exchange, as symbolized by the transfer of food, money, and goods to the

---

[27]For more on the ritual elements, see Watson, "Structure of Chinese Funerary Rites."

otherworld. In return, the living expect to receive benefits in this world, including luck, wealth, and progeny.

Important as these beliefs are, in the discourse of ordinary people it is anxiety over the practice of the rites, in the correct sequence, that takes precedence over discussions of meaning or symbolism. This does not mean, however, that there is no variation in performance. As long as the acts are accomplished in the approved sequence, there is room for infinite variety in ritual expression. For instance, the bathing of the corpse and the sealing of the coffin were performed very differently in the two Cantonese villages I have studied, although the overall structure of the rites was identical.

Herein lies the genius of the Chinese approach to cultural integration: the system allowed for a high degree of variation within an overarching structure of unity. The rites associated with the final disposal of the corpse constitute an excellent example of this principle. Once the sealed coffin is removed from the community in the accepted fashion, mourners are free to dispose of the corpse according to local custom. There is no elementary structure of disposal applying to China as a whole.

Research on Chinese burial customs is surprisingly underdeveloped; most of our information derives from the south, notably the provinces of Guangdong, Fujian, and Taiwan. It is intriguing to see how people in these areas, who practice secondary burial, have accommodated to the standardized funeral rites. Chinese secondary burial involves an initial burial in a coffin for approximately seven to ten years, followed by an exhumation of bones, which are placed in a large pot and eventually reburied in a permanent tomb.[28] The fundamental requirement of Chinese funeral ritual that the corpse be preserved in an airtight coffin, which is often of very substantial construction, is diametrically opposed to the requirements of secondary burial, which puts a premium on the rapid decomposition of flesh— thereby allowing for the retrieval and reburial of unpolluted bones.

Peasants in south China have no difficulty following the standard funeral rites, given that the prescribed actions of a proper funeral ended when the coffin left the community. In northern Taiwan, villagers sometimes bash in

[28]Emily M. Ahern, *The Cult of the Dead in a Chinese Village* (Stanford: Stanford University Press, 1973), pp. 163–219; Ling Xunsheng, "Dongnanyade xiguzang qi qihuan taipingyangde fenbu" (The bone-washing burial custom of Southeast Asia and its circum-Pacific distribution), *Zhongguo minzuxuebao* (Bulletin of the Ethnological Society of China) (Taiwan) 1 (1955): 25–42; Stuart E. Thompson, "Death, Food, and Fertility," in J. L. Watson and Rawski, *Death Ritual;* James L. Watson, "Of Flesh and Bones: The Management of Death Pollution in Cantonese Society," in Maurice Bloch and Jonathan Parry, eds., *Death and the Regeneration of Life* (Cambridge: Cambridge University Press, 1982).

one end of the coffin with an axe just before burial; in another part of Taiwan, a ritual specialist is hired to drill holes in the coffin at the grave-side.[29] Among the Cantonese and Hakka of Guangdong (including Hong Kong), the seal around the coffin lid is often broken before interment. All these practices are designed, of course, to hasten the decomposition of the flesh; the coffin thus becomes a convenient receptacle for the bones rather than a final resting place.

In north China, secondary burial was not practiced during the late imperial era; in fact northerners are often revolted when they learn about southern customs. On numerous occasions I have witnessed northern cadres recoil in absolute horror when the purpose of Cantonese bone pots is explained to them. But northerners do things that shock southerners, such as storing coffins above ground, sometimes for decades, awaiting the death of a spouse or parent, thereby allowing family reconstitution by simultaneous burial.[30]

In the borderlands of Sichuan, people who claim to be Han do not bury their dead at all. Instead, coffins are left in hillside caves that serve as family vaults.[31] In Shanxi province, many villagers continue to bury their dead in the traditional manner: a huge pit is dug in the loess and a niche is carved in the north wall; the coffin is then placed in the niche and the pit is covered with earth; the procedure takes ten days and involves elaborate rituals.[32] It is obvious even from this brief survey that there are no uniform rites of disposal.

The secondary burial complex found among the southern Han peoples (Cantonese, Hakka, Hokkien, for example) tells us something important about the construction of a sense of shared cultural identity among Chinese. There can be little doubt that the custom is historically linked to close interactions with non-Han (or more precisely pre-Han) cultures of the region. The pattern of burial and reburial, which plays on the distinction between flesh and bones, is found throughout the highlands of Southeast

[29]Personal communications with (and photographs by) Emily Martin and Stuart Thompson respectively, 1988.

[30]Patricia B. Ebrey, "State Response to Popular Funeral Practices in Sung China," in Patricia Buckley Ebrey and Peter S. Gregory, eds., *Religion and Society in T'ang and Sung China* (Honolulu: University of Hawaii Press, forthcoming); Susan Naquin, "Funerals in North China: Uniformity and Variation," in J. L. Watson and Rawski, *Death Ritual.*

[31]Shi Zhongqian, "Sichuan xuan guan zang" (Sichuan hanging burials), *Minzuxue yenjiu* (Ethnological research) 4 (1982): 100–118.

[32]This procedure is followed in parts of rural Shanxi (personal communication with Xu Xiaomin, University of Pittsburgh, 1988).

Asia and extends down the peninsula into Borneo and New Guinea.[33] Somehow, during the long history of Sinicization in south China, indigenous burial practices appear to have been transformed and incorporated into the local versions of Han culture.[34] This is not to say that secondary burial is simply a survival from an earlier era of interethnic exchange. Mortuary rites are deeply embedded in the political economy of local subcultures throughout China; they are, for instance, intimately related to notions of property and landownership. Accordingly, changes in burial practices automatically implied a threat to the legitimacy of regional power structures.

Given their political centrality, it is surely significant that rites of disposal were never subject to renegotiation and modification in the pursuit of cultural unity. The exclusion of burial rites from the roster of prescribed death rituals can thus be seen as an implicit concession to ethnic and regional sensitivities. This may well have been the consequence of a conscious policy by imperial officials and educated elites, given that any attempt to control burial practices would have been disastrously expensive and impossible to enforce—as Communist authorities were to discover during the 1950s and 1960s. Following the standard funeral sequence, by contrast, did not impinge substantially on the structure of power relationships; the rites were easily adapted to suit special needs (as the Christian modifications of the modern era demonstrate). Those who chose not to perform funerals according to the standard procedure were marked as non-Han or, worse, dangerous sectarians.

The Chinese cultural system thus allowed for the free expression of what outsiders might perceive to be chaotic local diversity. The domain of ritual, in particular, gave great scope to regional and subethnic cultural displays. The system was so flexible that those who called themselves Chinese could participate in a unified, centrally organized culture while at the same time celebrating their local or regional distinctiveness.

[33]See, e.g., Robert Hertz, *Death and the Right Hand* (1907; reprint, New York: Free Press, 1960); and Peter Metcalf, *A Borneo Journey into Death: Berawan Eschatology from Its Rituals* (Philadelphia: University of Pennsylvania Press, 1982).

[34]It is obvious that the burial practices of the modern Cantonese and Hokkien are not mere duplications of pre-Han forms. The Chinese pattern of secondary burial has no doubt changed over the past thousand years—just as modern non-Han cultures have. One cannot, in other words, expect to find Cantonese-style pot burials among extant minority peoples in Guangdong. For the origins of this burial complex one must look to the pre- and proto-Han cultures that fostered both modern populations. W. L. Ballard proposes a similar line of analysis for understanding the origins of southern Chinese dialects. Ballard, "Aspects of the Linguistic History of South China," *Asian Perspectives* 24 (1981): 163–85.

The imperial state was of course intimately involved in the standardization of funerary ritual, but it would never have been possible to impose a uniform structure of rites on a society of such vast size and complexity. More subtle means were required. There is good evidence that imperial officials were engaged in the promotion of a standardized set of funeral and mourning customs throughout the empire;[35] the same is true for marriage rites.[36] Accepted norms were enshrined in manuals available in even the smallest towns of the realm.[37] Given what we know about the distribution of power in late imperial China, it is probable that local elites subscribed to the accepted customs and encouraged a kind of ritual orthopraxy in the communities under their control: they led by example. Unacceptable practices were gradually suppressed or modified to conform to centralized models.[38]

This may have been the mechanism for the superimposition of a standard ritual structure, but we still know little about the process of acceptance. Is the standardization we now perceive a consequence of government-sponsored social engineering carried out over centuries or is it the result of voluntary adoption by the general populace? Need we assume that these processes are mutually exclusive? Obviously there must have been strong incentives for people of all classes and regional backgrounds to cooperate in the cultural construction of a standardized set of rites. Much more work needs to be done before we can answer these questions with any certainty. What is clear, however, is that the preoccupation with ritual practice, rather than beliefs, made it possible for imperial authorities, local elites, and ordinary peasants to agree on the proper form for the conduct of funerals.

[35] See Ebrey, "Early Stages" (see n. 10); and Evelyn S. Rawski, "A Historians Approach to Chinese Death Ritual," in J. L. Watson and Rawski, *Death Ritual*.

[36] R. S. Watson and Ebrey, *Marriage and Inequality*.

[37] See for example the list of ritual handbooks discovered in Hong Kong bookshops by James Hayes, "The Popular Culture of Late Ch'ing and Early Twentieth Century China: Book Lists Prepared from Collecting in Hong Kong," in Johnson *Popular Culture*, p. 174. Most of these texts were published during the late Qing and early Republican periods. Handbooks of this nature were often modeled on a famous text called *Family Ritual* (Jiali), usually attributed to the Neoconfucian scholar Zhuxi (1130–1200); on this text see Patricia B. Ebrey, "Education Through Ritual: The Formulation of Family Rituals in the Sung Dynasty," in John Chaffee and William Theodore de Bary, eds., *Neoconfucian Education: The Formative Stage* (Berkeley and Los Angeles: University of California Press, 1990). Written guidelines for proper funeral and mourning rites have a long history in China, beginning with the *Book of Rites* (Liji), produced between the fifth and second centuries B.C. and the writings of Xunzi, dating from the third century B.C. See also Naquin, "Funerals in North China," pp. 63–65, on the wide availability of funeral manuals.

[38] See Naquin, "Funerals in North China," on the standardizing role of ritual specialists.

Thus the process of becoming Chinese involved no conversion to a received dogma, no professions of belief in a creed or a set of ideas. One became Chinese, in essence, by acting Chinese, by behaving like Chinese; and perhaps the clearest indicator that this cultural transformation had been accomplished was the performance of key rituals in the accepted manner.

The stakes of playing the game of culture according to Chinese rules were very great indeed. It made the difference between being treated as a subject of the imperial state or as simply a victim. State authorities have always harbored deep suspicions toward those who remained culturally separate. The most common means of imperial expansion was the Sinicization of non-Han peoples. Depending on historical circumstances, this process took the form of gradual absorption through intermarriage or enforced assimilation through political domination.[39] In the south, non-Han peoples offered little resistance, and over a thousand-year period, the vast majority have been Sinicized or eliminated. The picture is very different, however, in the north and west. Here, in the steppes and the highlands, Chinese culture met its match, and even today the non-Han peoples of borders are fiercely resisting assimilation into Han society.

Vietnam and Korea are also relevant to this discussion, particularly as the funeral rites of these two societies closely parallel the Chinese sequence of nine acts.[40] Performing the rites according to Sinitic norms made the Vietnamese and the Koreans "civilized" in Chinese eyes, but neither group could be categorized as Han Chinese while living outside the boundaries of the Central Kingdom. Geographic origin is thus an important criterion when determining who is and who is not fully Chinese; many overseas Chinese are careful to maintain traditional rites, thereby distinguishing themselves from nonsinitic neighbors. Definitions of Chineseness also depend on point of view: During certain periods, Vietnam and Korea were linked to China as vassal states that paid homage, in the form of tribute, to the Chinese emperor. Thus Chinese officials may well have treated Vietnamese and Koreans as Chinese subjects, albeit second class ones, for political reasons;[41] it is quite another matter what the Vietnamese and

[39]Eberhard, *China's Minorities*, pp. 105–47.

[40]See, e.g., Paul C. Dredge, "Korean Funerals: Ritual as Process," in Laurel Kendall and Griffin Dix, eds., *Religion and Ritual in Korean Society* (Berkeley: University of California Center for Korean Studies, 1987); Gerald C. Hickey, *Village in Vietnam* (New Haven: Yale University Press, 1964), pp. 123–32; and Phan Ke Bihn, *Viet Nam Phong Tuc* (Vietnamese Customs) (Saigon: N.p., 1915), pp. 42–52.

[41]Alexander B. Woodside, *Vietnam and the Chinese Model* (Cambridge: Harvard University Press, 1971).

Koreans thought (and continue to think) of themselves.[42] Nevertheless, the fact that funerary rites in these two societies are fundamentally Sinitic in a striking testimony to the hegemonic power of Chinese culture.

Action versus Belief: The Standardization of Religious Practice

Even those people who were unambiguously Han Chinese had to play by the rules of the dominant culture. In particular, ordinary people were wary of involvement with heterodox cults or fringe religions not sanctioned by imperial officials. Dabbling in sectarianism could easily lead to the extermination or exile of one's entire patriline.[43]

What was interesting about the Chinese state's policy toward sectarian religions was that it stressed action rather than belief. Beliefs that were not translated into political action (in the form of cult organizations, pilgrimages, and festivals) were not of immediate concern. In comparison to their European counterparts, therefore, Chinese officials spent relatively little time investigating the belief systems of fringe religions; it was the behavior of adherents, especially antistate behavior, that drew the wrath of the emperor. As C. K. Yang observes, "There is an abundance of empirical facts to show that it was not philosophical or theological objection but practical political consideration that was the leading motivation for the traditional antagonism toward heterodoxy. One may say that purely religious arguments between Confucianism and other doctrines or faiths did not exist in Chinese classical literature."[44] David Johnson, in a recent study of ritual opera, argues the point even more strongly: "For officials, the most infallible signs of heresy were not doctrinal but behavioral; if worshippers became ecstatic or frenzied, if powerful emotions were being summoned up, if people were exhibiting signs of extraordinary devotion, then [state] officials were likely to step in."[45]

---

[42]I am grateful to Hue-Tam Ho Tai for discussions concerning these matters and for Vietnamese references to funeral ritual, including the Phan book cited in n. 40. She is not of course responsible for my arguments.

[43]See, e.g., Susan Naquin, "Two Descent Groups in North China: The Wangs of Yung-p'ing Prefecture, 1500–1800," in Ebrey and J. L. Watson, *Kinship Organization*, pp. 238–39.

[44]C. K. Yang, *Religion in Chinese Society* (Berkeley and Los Angeles: University of California Press, 1961), p. 193.

[45]David G. Johnson, "Actions Speak Louder than Words: The Cultural Significance of Chinese Ritual Opera," in Johnson, ed., *Ritual Opera, Operatic Ritual: "Mu-lien Rescues His Mother" in Chinese Popular Culture* (Berkeley: Chinese Popular Culture Project, 1989), p. 25.

Ordinary villagers could play it safe by following the received models of marriage and funeral rites and by building temples to deities sanctioned by the imperial court. Most of the temples one sees today in Hong Kong and the Pearl River Delta are dedicated to these approved goddesses and gods. During the late imperial era it was risky to pay too much attention to deities outside the imperial pantheon.[46] Favored deities, meaning those deemed to have rendered service to the court, were given imperial titles and promotions, much like living officials.

One of the most popular deities in south China is Tianhou (Tin-hau in Cantonese), usually translated as "Empress of Heaven." The goddess's name is in fact an illustrious title conferred on her by the Qianlong emperor in 1737, as a reward for suppressing pirates and assisting imperial officials.[47] In Taiwan she is known as Mazu and is widely accepted as a symbol of Taiwanese cultural nationalism.[48] The Tianhou cult spread along the Chinese coast from Hainan in the south to Weihaiwei in the north; the goddess came to be associated with protection at sea and security on shore. District magistrates actively promoted her cult as a physical manifestation of state control and encouraged the suppression of rival deities that were not part of the imperial pantheon. By the 1850s, Tianhou, along with a handful of other state-approved deities, had effectively superseded thousands of parochial gods and goddesses known only to local communities. This process of religious standardization has been described in detail elsewhere.[49]

The essential point to note about Chinese religion is that the imperial state did not try to legislate beliefs. Officials were concerned primarily with the proper practice of worship, reflected most directly in temple building and festival observations. As long as people worshipped in approved temples, they were free to believe anything they wished about the deities housed there. Rural Cantonese, for instance, held a confusing and often contradictory array of beliefs regarding Tianhou: for local officials she was a symbol of civilized—that is, passified, state-approved—behavior; for the landlord-merchant class she was a guardian of social order; for free-holding

[46]C. K. Yang, *Religion in Chinese Society,* pp. 144–65.

[47]On Tianhou's titles, see Judith M. Boltz, "In Homage to T'ien-fei," *Journal of the American Oriental Society* 106 (1986): 211–32; and Von Bodo Wiethoff, "Der Staatliche Ma-tsu Kult," *Zeitschrift der deutschen morgenlandischen Gesellschaft* 116 (1966): 311–57.

[48]Donald R. DeGlopper, "Religion and Ritual in Lukang," in Wolf, *Religion and Ritual* (see n. 14).

[49]Prasenjit Duara, "Superscribing Symbols: The Myth of Guandi, Chinese God of War," *Journal of Asian Studies* 47 (1988): 778–95; James L. Watson, "Standardizing the Gods: The Promotion of T'ien-hou ('Empress of Heaven') along the South China Coast, 960–1960," in Johnson, *Popular Culture.*

farmers she was a champion of lineage hegemony; for subservient tenants she was a protector of the disadvantaged; for boat people and pirates she promised to quell dangerous seas; for women of all classes she was a fertility goddess who conferred male offspring. These are but a few of Tianhou's collective representations; documentary sources reveal many other identities during the late imperial era, some of which verged on the heterodox.[50] But state officials were not concerned with these mental constructs; what mattered was which deities people chose to worship, not what they believed about them. The state stressed form rather than content. There was never any attempt to foster a standardized set of beliefs in Chinese religion.

This seems a good point to consider some cross-cultural comparisons. By one reading, the history of Christian Europe is very largely a history of changing beliefs or, more precisely, a history of fragmentation resulting from disagreements over correct belief. This is, of course, a simplistic view of the Reformation and its aftermath, but in general there seems always to have been a heavy premium on correct belief in European society and relatively less concern with ritual form.[51] This is a matter of emphasis; obviously orthopraxy played an important role in the spread and maintenance of Christianity. Nonetheless, there is a clear contrast between the Chinese system of religion, which stressed ritual form to the near exclusion of standardized belief, and the European religious system, which emphasized both (at different times), with heavy emphasis on truth and the eradication of heresy.

The never-ending debate about the Christian Eucharist is a good case in point. Disagreements dwell on the meaning of the acts, which in turn reflects differing beliefs.[52] There is nothing comparable among the Chinese. Discussions regarding sacrifices in China, conducted by farmers and imperial officials alike, focus on the proper form of the rites, rarely on their internal meaning or signification.[53] What was important in the Chinese context was that it be done correctly.

The Hindu religious tradition presents another interesting contrast.

[50]Discussed in J. L. Watson, "Standardizing the Gods."

[51]See, e.g., Talal Asad, "Medieval Heresay: An Anthropological View," *Social History* 11 (1986): 345–62.

[52]See, e.g., Rudolf Bultmann, *Theology of the New Testament,* vol. 1 (London: SCM Press, 1952); Charles Gore, *The Body of Christ: An Inquiry into the Institution and Doctrine of Holy Communion* (London:Murry, 1901); and A. M. O'Neill, *The Mystery of the Eucharist* (Dublin: M. H. Gill, 1933).

[53]There are, of course, exceptions, most notably among Buddhist clergy, a point Robert Weller makes in his study of Taiwanese religion, *Unities and Diversities in Chinese Religion* (Seattle: University of Washington Press, 1987), pp. 110–24. It is significant, however, that the Buddhist professionals he studied did not attempt to impose their interpretations of ritual acts on laypeople.

Before the British Raj, South Asia was not dominated by a centralized state system; indeed, according to David Washbrook, the very notion of "India" as a political and cultural entity did not emerge until relatively late in the colonial era.[54] It was fostered first by the British and later by Western-educated South Asians who were interested in nation building.[55] In China, by contrast, the political reality of state power was reflected in the acceptance of Zhongguo, the Central Kingdom, as a meaningful concept by everyone who lived within the boundaries of that state from a very early (and much debated) date. The Chinese peasantry did not need modernizing elites to remind them that they shared a grand cultural tradition and were subjects of a centralized state.

This difference in national identities is reflected in ritual. Unlike China, the Indian subcontinent does not have a standardized set of rites to mark important life crises. Even if one restricts the analysis to the Hindu population, the contrast with China is striking. In funerary ritual, for instance, Hindu performances do not follow a standard set of acts that distinguishes this tradition from other ethnic or religious traditions. There is, in other words, no elementary structure of Hindu rites; various communities (*jati*, subcastes) perform funerals in different ways, and there are more differences than similarities.[56] The same, apparently, is true of marriage rites.

Thus it is not orthopraxy that holds Hindu India together as a unified culture. What, then, of orthodoxy? Here too there are serious questions, given that the subcontinent has not had a standardized set of religious beliefs nor a uniform creed. There is, of course, a generally recognized assemblage—as opposed to state-regulated pantheon—of goddesses and gods worshipped in various ways by Hindus.[57] But beliefs regarding these deities are diverse in the extreme; furthermore, no state apparatus is charged with the responsibility of regulating belief.

Louis Dumont and his followers have proposed that the unity of Indian

[54]David Washbrook, "Gandhi and the Creation of 'India'" (Paper presented at Fairbank Center, Harvard University, 1987).

[55]See also Bernard S. Cohn, "Representing Authority in Victorian India," in Eric Hobsbawm and Terrence Ranger, eds., *The Invention of Tradition* (Cambridge: Cambridge University Press, 1983).

[56]These observations are based on discussions with Chris Fuller, Jonathan Parry, Stanley Tambiah, David Washbrook, and others. A search of ethnographies on Hindu communities confirms the point; this is in striking contrast to evidence contained in Chinese ethnographic sources, as discussed in J. L. Watson, "Structure of Chinese Funerary Rites."

[57]See, e.g., C. J. Fuller, "The Hindu Pantheon and the Legitimation of Hierarchy," *Man* 23 (1988): 19–39; McKim Marriott, "Little Communities in an Indigenous Civilization," in Marriott, ed., *Village India: Studies in the Little Community* (Chicago: University of Chicago Press, 1955); and M. N. Srinivas, *Religion and Society among the Coorgs in South India* (Oxford: Clarendon, 1952).

society is to be found in the realm of ideas and values, specifically those relating to the ideology of pollution, purity, and social hierarchy.[58] The first issues of *Contributions to Indian Sociology* carried a by now famous exchange on this question: Dumont and David Pocock argued that the unity of India is evident in "the existence of castes from one end of the country to the other, and nowhere else." Furthermore, "the very existence, and influence, of the higher, sanskritic, civilisation demonstrates without question the unity of India."[59] F. G. Bailey replied that it was not, in his view, the task of sociologists and anthropologists "to make sense of the 'flagrant contradictions in popular thought' by abstracting out consistent elements" in search of an underlying structure of unity, as Dumont and Pocock had advocated.[60] Thus for Bailey, and a host of other critics,[61] the ideology of caste is not the universal glue that holds Indian society together. Viewing this debate from the perspective of China, we are left with the conclusion that India may have the formal apparatus of a modern state, but it lacks the essential ingredients of a unified culture.

What Held China Together?

In concluding, I return to my original question: What held China together for so many centuries? One unifying factor was the power and resilience of the state; the very idea of China implies a complex bureaucracy and an imperial center. Another element was the superimposition of a common written script that allowed educated speakers of different Han dialects to communicate and thus participate in a national culture. Equally important was the rise of a centralized monetary system and a national market in key commodities. All of these components were crucial but they were not in themselves sufficient to generate and maintain a unified cultural tradition. How did the Chinese know they were "Chinese"? What, in other words, were the social processes that led to the construction of an integrated culture in late imperial China?

[58]Louis Dumont, *Homo Hierarchicus: The Caste System and Its Implications* (Chicago: University of Chicago Press, 1970).

[59]Louis Dumont and David Pocock, "For a Sociology of India," *Contributions to Indian Sociology* 1 (1957): 9.

[60]F. G. Bailey, "For a Sociology of India?" *Contributions to Indian Sociology* 3 (1959): 90.

[61]See, e.g., Steve Barrett et al., "Hierarchy Purified: Notes on Dumont and His Critics," *Journal of Asian Studies* 35 (1976): 627–46; Richard Burghart, "Renunciation in the Religious Traditions of South Asia," *Man* 18 (1983): 635–53; and Pauline Kolenda, "Seven Kinds of Hierarchy in *Homo Hierarchicus*," *Journal of Asian Studies* 35 (1976): 581–96.

In my view it was just that—a *construction,* a social and ideological fabrication. What we call Chinese culture was an illusion, a facade consisting of forms and practices that had very little content as such. "Content" in this context is what many in the West take to be a uniform and internally consistent set of beliefs and attitudes. "Form" is what most of us have in mind when we speak of outward appearance—represented by public demeanor, collective behavior, and standardized ritual. In the European tradition it is fashionable to denigrate form and dwell on content, especially belief, as the true test of cultural integration. For most Westerners what is "inside" is what counts. This is obviously a Eurocentric view of culture and national identity.

One can find the origins of what I take to be the unique Chinese approach to cultural integration as far back as the Confucian *Analects,* and perhaps earlier.[62] By many interpretations, the central theme of Confucianism is harmony in thought and action; correct ideas follow from proper behavior.[63] In this sense, orthopraxy is primary to, and takes precedence over, orthodoxy. At the core of Confucian notions of order is the principle of *li,* defined by Benjamin Schwartz as "all those 'objective' prescriptions of behavior, whether involving rite, ceremony, manners, or general deportment."[64] The Confucian approach to *li* is relevant to cultural construction: following correct forms ensures that one is playing the game of culture by civilized rules and, in so doing, one becomes Chinese.

It will come as no surprise that the vision of Chinese culture presented here derives from Cantonese villagers. My cultural instructors know little of the formal teachings of Confucius or Zhuxi, but they know a great deal about *li,* or *laih* as it is pronounced in colloquial Cantonese. Villagers use the term in ordinary speech; one hears it dozens of times each day. To them it is not an abstract, philosophic concept but, rather, an ordinary, mundane idea that has concrete associations. Constant references are made to funeral *li,* wedding *li,* and the *li* of ancestral rites; the term permeates their discourse on social activities. One of the worst things to be said of someone is that she or he is "without *li*" (*mouh laih* [*meiyou li*]), meaning oblivious to proper behavior, impolite, and uncivilized.

---

[62]K. C. Chang, *Art, Myth, and Ritual: The Path to Political Authority in Ancient China* (Cambridge: Harvard University Press, 1983), pp. 101, 108; David N. Keightley, "Archaeology and Mentality: The Making of China," *Representations* 18 (1987): 166.

[63]For a development of this argument, see Herbert Fingarette, *Confucius: The Secular as Sacred* (New York: Harper and Row, 1972).

[64]Benjamin I. Schwartz, *The World of Thought in Ancient China* (Cambridge: Harvard University Press, 1985), p. 67.

In the Cantonese village context, *li* (*laih*) is best translated as "proper form," associated closely with correct performance. To perform a ritual properly, in the local view, is to follow its *li*. A funeral or a wedding has a recognized form (*li*), and deviations from that form cause great concern. Older people often stand on the sidelines of funerals, watching like hawks to make certain proper form is followed. They do not hesitate to shout advice or dissent when they see what they perceive to be departures from standard ritual practice. Cantonese funeral priests are choreographers of public ritual; they tell people where to stand, how to sit, when to wail, what to eat, who to greet, when to leave.[65] If the ritual goes wrong or is not completed in the appointed time, disaster is certain to follow, not just for the bereaved but for the entire community.

Thus the villagers' concern for proper form (*li*) is not simply a matter of aesthetics or personal predilections. It is the glue that holds the cosmos together. Without *li* there would be chaos (*luan*), another concept that has concrete associations for most ordinary Chinese. Among rural Cantonese, *luan* conjures up visions of banditry, famine, and that ultimate symbol of social breakdown, cannibalism. Villagers in the Pearl River Delta have a rich corpus of folklore focusing on mythic massacres carried out by imperial troops who intervene to reestablish order when local society collapses.[66] The message is clear: those who depart from accepted norms of ritual and action invite retribution of the most terrifying kind.

But this is not to say that Cantonese villagers are social automatons, performing by rote rituals over which they have no control and little understanding. Nor should they be seen as puppets dancing on strings of convention held by agents of the state. Stressing orthopraxy rather than orthodoxy had profound consequences for all social classes. It allowed China to attain a level of cultural unity that was never possible in other, large-scale agrarian societies. The processes of cultural construction I have outlined involved the active participation of all Chinese, not just scholar-bureaucrats but farmers, artisans, merchants, and workers. There is evidence, for instance, that imperial officials were forced to accept, adapt, and co-opt mortuary customs that first emerged among the peasantry.[67] The

[65]James L. Watson, "Funeral Specialists in Cantonese Society," in J. L. Watson and Rawski, *Death Ritual*.

[66]James L. Watson, "Waking the Dragon: Visions of the Chinese Imperial State in Local Myth," in Hugh Baker and Stephan Feuchtwang, eds., *An Old State in New Settings: Studies in the Social Anthropology of China in Memory of Maurice Freedman* (Oxford: Journal of the Anthropological Society of Oxford, 1991).

[67]See Ebrey, "Early Stages" (see n. 10), pp. 20–29.

standard Chinese funeral one sees today appears to be timeless but is, in fact, an amalgamation of ancient and modern rites.[68] Ordinary people, such as the ancestors of my Cantonese consultants, had as much to do with creating and promoting this amalgamation as anyone else in the realm, including the emperor himself.

Postscript: Ritual Form and Cultural Unity in Socialist China

As those who have followed developments in post-1949 China well know, traditional rituals of the sort discussed in this chapter were rigorously attacked by Communist party officials during the late 1950s (Great Leap Forward) and the late 1960s (Cultural Revolution). Funeral and burial rites were obvious targets of social engineering, especially in south China, where activists objected to the "feudal" implications of the ancestral cult. There were also attempts to introduce a new set of socialist rituals, based roughly on Soviet models,[69] as replacements for traditional Chinese rites.[70] Although field research on this problem has yet to be done, it would appear that these new rites have had most influence in the larger cities, among professional classes. There is considerable evidence that late imperial–style funerals and burials are still common in the Chinese countryside and that the recent economic reforms have fueled a resurgence in ritual activities.[71] Martin Whyte has argued that there is a growing divide between urban and rural life-styles in post-Mao China, reflected most clearly in funeral and wedding rites.[72] Interviews with Chinese students

[68]Rawski, "Historians Approach" (see n. 35).

[69]Christopher A. Binns, "The Changing Face of Power: Revolution and Accommodation in the Development of the Soviet Ceremonial System," pt. 2, *Man* 15 (1980): 180; Cristel Lane, *The Rites of Rulers: Ritual in Industrial Society—The Soviet Union* (Cambridge: Cambridge University Press, 1981).

[70]See, e.g., Donald E. MacInnis, *Religious Policy and Practice in Communist China* (New York: Macmillan, 1972), pp. 333–34; and William L. Parish and Martin K. Whyte, *Village and Family in Contemporary China* (Chicago: University of Chicago Press, 1968), pp. 264–65.

[71]Based on ethnographic surveys I conducted in Guangdong, Jiangsu, and Shandong (1985–90); see also Parish and Whyte, *Village and Family*, pp. 265–66; and William R. Jankowiak, "The Soul of Lao Yu," *Natural History* 97 (1988): 4–11. Myron Cohen (personal communication) reports that late imperial–style funerals were performed in rural Hebei during his field research in 1986–87. David Wu (personal communication) observed a traditional funeral, complete with full mourning garb, in Zhejiang, summer 1987, as did Yan Yunxiang (personal communication and photographs) in Heilongjiang, 1991.

[72]Martin K. Whyte, "Death Ritual in the People's Republic of China," in J. L. Watson and Rawski, *Death Ritual*.

studying in the United States confirm Whyte's view: urbanites aged thirty-five and under rarely have any direct experience with traditional wedding or funeral rites, and they consider such performances to be "feudal" (even humorous) vestiges of a rural past.[73]

This chapter ends as it began, with a question: Does the fact that China no longer has an agreed upon set of rites mean that it no longer has a unified culture? In the past, well into the 1950s, one of the central experiences of life was that people of all social stations—rich and poor, rural and urban, official and commoner—performed funerals and weddings according to the same basic form. The disappearance of a unified cultural tradition is something that concerns many Chinese, particularly of the older genera-tion. The physical destruction of the "four olds"[74] during the Cultural Revolution is paralleled by an erosion in knowledge about the past. Thus, the bifurcation of ritual into rural and urban forms may well be part of a general trend toward cultural reformation in China. Will a new culture, based on a new set of rites and unifying symbols, emerge from the old? Or have the Chinese people changed the ground rules of cultural construction and begun to emphasize internal beliefs and attitudes rather than external form and ritual?

It is possible to interpret the Cultural Revolution as a state-sponsored movement in that direction, from orthopraxy to orthodoxy. The political campaigns of that era were designed to break the traditional mold, in a shift from form to content. Primary emphasis was placed on inner beliefs ("Red-ness"); Red Guards and other activists did not allow people to fall back on ritual form or standardized behavior. The new approach required public confession, conversion, and whole-hearted acceptance of Maoist doctrine. Richard Madsen calls this a system based on "rituals of struggle," constitut-ing a radical departure from older notions of ritual as a means of main-taining community cohesion.[75] No one, in effect, knew how to act during the early years of the Cultural Revolution. By the 1970s, routinization

[73]Interviews carried out at the University of Pittsburgh, 1984–88.

[74]Old thought, old customs, old culture, and old morals. During the Cultural Revolution, Red Guards destroyed many historical monuments, including graves and tombs; see, e.g., Anita Chan, Richard Madsen, and Jonathan Unger, *Chen Village: The Recent History of a Peasant Community in Mao's China* (Berkeley and Los Angeles: University of California Press, 1984), p. 118; and Gao Yuan, *Born Red: A Chronicle of the Cultural Revolution* (Stanford: Stanford University Press, 1987), p. 218.

[75]Richard Madsen, *Morality and Power in a Chinese Village* (Berkeley and Los Angeles: University of California Press, 1984), pp. 22–26.

began to set in and people learned techniques of distancing, thereby re-ritualizing political activity.[76]

The results of the Maoist preoccupation with orthodoxy are by now universally recognized: disruption, disintegration, and anomie on a massive scale. It would appear that the pursuit of unity through the imposition of a centrally controlled ideology was an unmitigated disaster for China. One is led to conclude that such efforts run against the grain of Chinese culture, defying the very principles that held this vast society together for so many centuries.

[76]See Martin K. Whyte, *Small Groups and Political Rituals in China* (Berkeley and Los Angeles: University of California Press, 1974); and David Zweig, *Agrarian Radicalism in China, 1968–1981* (Cambridge: Harvard University Press, 1989).

中
國 5

Change and Continuity
in Chinese Cultural Identity:
The Filial Ideal and the
Transformation of an Ethic

Richard W. Wilson

National identity is in large part cultural identity. Cultural meanings structure perceptions of social life and provide a framework for understanding others. More than this, they serve as guideposts for behavior. Cultural meanings are thus the operational core of identity; they are the basis for distinctive patterns of individual and societal conduct. Societies vary in the cultural meanings they honor, and cultural meanings vary over time within societies. If, as I contend, cultural meanings in China are shifting from a stress on particular obligations to an emphasis on universal rights, we need to examine how Chinese understandings of right and obligation have changed.

In traditional China the most important injunctions governing relationships clustered under the rubric of filial piety. How Chinese cultural meanings are evolving, therefore, is revealed by the changes taking place in the idea of filial piety, from a view of social life in which status inequalities obliged different duties to one in which others are seen as equals who have commensurate rights that are (or should be) impartially protected by law. This shift, I maintain, underlies a profound change in national identity. Yet the subversion of an essentially antidemocratic traditional culture does not

I am most grateful for the assistance given me by Professor Yu Xingzhong of the Northwest Institute of Political Science and Law, who at the time of writing was a visiting scholar at the Center for Chinese Legal Studies, Columbia Law School.

imply the birth of a modern civil one of the highly individualistic liberal-democratic type found in Western societies. Rather, the transformation has gone hand-in-hand with the persistence of a strong communitarian ethic.

A Piagetian approach to determining cultural meanings is better suited for an examination of this shift than the traditional surveys, interviews, and observations used to measure the cognitions, feelings, and evaluation schemes people acquire during socialization. The latter techniques, still widely used, clearly have their purposes, but the aggregated data are often rife with inconsistency and lack stability over time. Concern over these deficiencies has prompted revisions in the way culture is conceptualized, beginning with the work of Lowell Dittmer and continuing in a different theoretical mode with that of Shawn Rosenberg and Stephen Chilton.[1] These efforts point away from the traditional social-determinist model rooted in a social learning perspective and toward a model that takes cognitive psychological factors into account.

Cognitive development psychologists work in the tradition of Jean Piaget, who held that the way people think changes with age in a stage sequence. Given that the purpose of thought is to integrate and make understandable the complexity of reality, cognitive development is a process in which increasingly inclusive and abstract models (or structures of reasoning) evolve in order to make sense of the world. The way people organize their thoughts varies, therefore, with ontogeny, age, and experience, thus defying simple aggregation of survey responses as a method of determining cultural meanings. Individual meanings and cultural meanings are not homologous.

What, then, are cultural meanings? Economists suggest that there is a ubiquitous human propensity to exchange and that for exchanges to take place in a stable manner, there must be rules governing cooperation and competition. In the cultural domain, exchangeable items must be conceived of in the broadest terms, encompassing such "goods" as favors and deference as well as material goods, with the most important social contexts of exchange being the family and the workplace, with formal politics secondary. The rules that coordinate exchange are independent of any individual yet come into being as the consequence of interactions among people. Because of this link to individuals, the cultural meanings embedded in rules have structure in the same sense that an individual's reasoning does (for

[1] Lowell Dittmer, "Political Culture and Political Symbolism: Toward a Theoretical Synthesis," *World Politics* 29 (July 1977): 552–84; Shawn W. Rosenberg, *Reason, Ideology and Politics* (Princeton: Princeton University Press, 1988); Stephen Chilton, *Defining Political Development* (Boulder, Colo.: Rienner, 1988).

they are rooted in a comprehensive explanatory framework), but that structure need not correspond with that of any given person. As individuals interact, they interpret the meaning of behavioral rules. From this process of discourse there emerges the possibility (albeit often retarded by conservative influences) of a transformation of explanatory frameworks at both individual and social levels.

Cultural meanings can be typed structurally in terms of their inclusivity and abstractness, for example, particularistic face-to-face rules that govern patron-client relations and property rules embedded in general laws of contract. But cultural meanings also coordinate behavior through what Piagetians call "content." Content differs from structure in that it is the idiosyncratic agglomeration of beliefs and expectations that characterize a society in any given period and that frame the ways people are expected to orient themselves one to another. Content is interwoven with particular moral and ethical precepts that justify social stratification in a way that sustains solidarity. Cultural meanings, therefore, partake of two characteristics. They have content that defines appropriate orientations toward others through specific injunctions and structure that reveals the sophistication of underlying explanations of social reality.

Is content limitless in form or are there constraints on this aspect of cultural meanings? Granted that cultural meanings are never entirely consistent in any society, it is nevertheless possible to ascertain dominant patterns, which appear to be related to the ways that care and autonomy are differentially stressed as social ideals.[2] When care as an ideal is emphasized, role relationships are infused with concern, human feeling, and responsibility; the stress is on the community and solidarity. When autonomy as an ideal is emphasized, role relationships are founded on justice considerations, contract, and the right of individuals to be free from interference. Western psychologists have tended to favor autonomy as the end point of preference in human development, but love of humanity is certainly just as reasonable. And, indeed, historically most societies have tended to favor communitarian values over those associated with individualism.

Although transformations in structure result in profound discontinuities in the explanatory frameworks underlying cultural meanings, these changes occur in ways that conserve intergenerational solidarity through the maintenance of communitarian or individualistic orientations. Thus it is important to note which content ideal predominantly informs cultural meanings;

---

[2]Carol Gilligan, *In a Different Voice: Psychological Theory and Women's Development* (Cambridge: Harvard University Press, 1982), p. 100.

for this ideal tends to persist even while the ways that social relationships are understood are being transformed. In examining changes in cultural meanings in a society like China, therefore, it is as important to track the continuities of content as it is to understand the structural transformations.

Norms of reciprocity help in all societies to regulate exchange by answering the question Who is entitled to what and in what manner? Of importance is not merely the content of the exchange relationship (care versus autonomy) but how reciprocity is conceptualized. As cultural meanings become structurally more sophisticated, the concept of reciprocity becomes largely neutral with regard to situational and particularistic criteria. (In Piagetian terms, reciprocity is increasingly legitimized by abstract criteria that hold equally in all instances regardless of which side of a relationship is referenced.

As in all societies, traditional Chinese conceptions of reciprocity were delimited by particularistic criteria; care, human feeling, and responsibility were nevertheless articulated in universal terms that were developmentally advanced. Unlike many cultures, the Chinese developed a set of concepts that defined desirable behavior independent of the context of any particular instance of exchange. Such virtues as *ren* (human heartedness), *yi* (righteousness), *zhong* (conscientiousness), *shu* (altruism), and *li* (propriety) were not restricted in their application to a particular societal stratum (as was the code of chivalry in Europe), although it was assumed that the *junzi* (gentleman) was the true bearer of these qualities.

These nondifferential virtues, which were at the center of Chinese moral life, were, however, interwoven with differential ones such as *xiao* (filial piety), which established the process by which the moral order was made realizable, especially for those considered natural inferiors, for example. In fulfilling *xiao,* emphasis was placed on particular status obligations; meeting these was then presumed to reveal the nondifferential virtues that define a moral being. By carrying out particular duties, a person ideally exhibited qualities that served to harmonize the groups of which that person was a member, from the family up through society as a whole and also backward through preceding generations, knitting together in a total moral community both the living and the dead.

Confucius, it is said, when asked to define filial piety, remarked, "While [the parents] are living, serve them with *li;* when they die, bury them with *li;* sacrifice to them with *li.*" "Filiality," he said, "is the root of virtue, and that from which civilization derives . . . [it] begins with the serving of our parents, continues with the serving of our prince, and is completed with the establishing of our own character." "There are," he said, "three thousand [offenses] meriting the five punishments, but there is no crime greater than unfiliality."

As *The Great Learning,* the work of followers of Confucius, makes clear, obligations in traditional China were mutual only in the sense that they were relational ("Whenever the conduct of a person above me is wicked, I will not employ the same conduct when dealing with those below me"). As Cheng Zhongying notes, "A person does not do for others by abstract considerations, but from the feeling of a concrete 'relationship of assigned position in social intercourse.'"[3] While reciprocity, therefore, ideally depended on every person acting in such a way as to reveal the universal qualities of moral virtue, the actual behavior associated with filial piety stressed service by subordinates—women, children and subjects—while leaving parents and rulers far less fettered.

This stress on duty led at times to great tragedy. In "A peacock southeast flew," a poem written nearly two thousand years ago at the close of the Han dynasty, the story tells of a double suicide brought about by the dismissal of a beloved wife by her mother-in-law on the charge of lacking a sense of decorum. The son remonstrated with his mother, but she angrily replied:

> My son, have you no respect?
> How dare you speak in your wife's defense!
> I have lost all feeling for you,
> On no account will I let you disobey me![4]

His filiality was thus placed in opposition to his love. Unable to be reunited without violating filiality (but violating it nonetheless by committing suicide), the couple then ended their lives.

Law, Obligation, and Traditional Filial Piety

How can structural changes in cultural meanings be empirically validated? I propose that they can best be ascertained from laws that adjudicate relations among individuals (with surveys supplying supplementary data for determining content). In examining changes in the meanings associated with filial piety, therefore, it is primarily to legal decisions that I looked for

[3]Cheng Zhongying, "On Confucian Filial Piety and Its Modernization: Duties, Rights, and Moral Conduct," *Chinese Studies in Philosophy* (Winter 1988–89): 57–58, 69–71.

[4]Anne Birrell, trans., *New Songs from a Jade Terrace: An Anthology of Early Chinese Love Poetry* (London: Allen and Unwin, 1982), pp. 53–62.

evidence. "Each society," says Roberto Unger, "reveals through its law the inner-most secrets of the manner in which it holds men together."[5] The law addresses conflicts, and areas of potential conflict, and through adjudication teaches what a society does and does not value. It is that social instrument which specifies rules of behavior when questions of appropriateness arise. Law is "obligation imposing," to use H. L. A. Hart's term, and comes into being only in communities concerned with the moral issues involved with obligations.[6]

What is law? At one level it can be thought of as authoritative rules. At another it is also the processes and institutions that carry out and enforce these rules with the avowed function of settling disputes and imposing punishments. Law accomplishes these functions by defining what obligations are owed among broad classifications of persons (classes, guilds, families, and so on) and among different roles (parents and children, for example, or husbands and wives). It acts like a kind of rationing board that tells people what they can and cannot do by setting forth their rights and duties in respect to one another; it confers benefits and takes them away and enforces its own rulings. Law articulates cultural meanings in that it serves ideally as the enforcer of community standards. At the same time, it is a framework for discourse about the structural adequacy of cultural meanings. As law evolves, structural and content changes in cultural conceptions of rights and duties are revealed.

Law has different forms. Even in a society that denigrates law per se, prescriptions that are binding must exist to regulate behavior. Thus law may be customary, defining long-held expectations of obligation. Or it may be bureaucratic or regulatory, establishing and enforcing explicit rules. The way in which law is administered also affects the ways obligations are defined. Procedural law imposes conditions on the processes by which obligations are determined. Substantive law governs the outcome of decisions regarding obligations. Here the moral ends of community life are directly articulated as criteria that are to regulate conduct.

Law developed very early in China. Chinese rules of law, unlike those in much of the ancient world, were not tightly intertwined with religious norms. Nor did there develop a Chinese legal profession distinct from policy makers, like the *juris prudentes* (those wise in the law) of ancient

[5]Roberto Mangabeira Unger, *Law in Modern Society: Toward a Criticism of Social Theory* (New York: Free Press, 1976), p. 47.

[6]David Lyons, *Ethics and the Rule of Law* (Cambridge: Cambridge University Press, 1984), pp. 69–70. The Hart citation is from p. 43.

Rome. There was also no third estate as in Europe or strong ecclesiastical body to promote the idea of law as universal principles of divine will which govern the adjudicating of interests independently of role and status. Instead, from very early on, bureaucratic law was paramount. While there were rules of process, they existed in an intellectual framework that stressed knowable virtue and definable obligations.

Although the strictness, minuteness, and frightening qualities of Legalist doctrine were softened over time by Confucian ethics (Han Fei Zi, the Legalist, believed that there was a political, and hence legal, implication in just about anything that anybody did), ancient Chinese law nevertheless developed in its bureaucratic form (*fa*) with little dichotomy between commands and law and with greater or lesser degrees of particularity as rulers themselves required. For ordinary people the cardinal virtue was absolute obedience. These laws were supplemented by injunctions regarding *li* (propriety) which established the etiquette required in interactions among people of different status. The legal conception of reciprocity depended on a clear definition of status and the precise articulation of particular forms of obligation as rules of conduct. Both bureaucratic law and the rules of propriety, which became part of law as it became Confucianized, were structured in accordance with this vision.

Thus, in determining culpability, the law tended to emphasize derelictions of obligations as required by *li* above the actual nature of a transgression. In the Tang period (A.D. 618–906), for instance, a law that had first been introduced in Wei times (A.D. 200–65) stipulated that sons and grandsons who registered separately and divided family property while the grandparents and parents were still living could be transported for three years.[7] Whatever the ultimate purpose of this law, it is clear that the conception of wrongdoing did not lie in the commission of certain acts (for dividing property would in other circumstances have been permissible) but in the violation of the obligations associated with filiality.

The law, in fact, nicely reveals the degree to which circumstances are of secondary importance to issues of obligation. Consider a case from the year 1812 in which a father-in-law had a piece of his lip bitten off while attempting to rape his daughter-in-law. In finding fault the provincial authorities ruled against the woman and sentenced her to be decapitated, a decision ultimately reversed by Emperor Jaiqing. This precedent, an important one, was of only marginal help for another daughter-in-law who, in 1830, injured

---

[7]David G. Johnson, *The Medieval Chinese Oligarchy* (Boulder, Colo.: Westview, 1977), p. 112.

and caused the death of her father-in-law while he, too, was attempting rape. She was sentenced by the governor to be dismembered, and her punishment also was reduced—to detention in prison and beheading.[8]

Under Ming and Qing law (A.D. 1368–1643, 1644–1910) a similar act could be judged differently depending on degrees of obligation. A law permitting a person to conceal the crime of a close relative was amended by supplementary statute in 1789 as follows: if a mother killed a father and the son attempted to conceal the crime, he was punishable with eighty or one hundred strokes depending on the circumstances surrounding the reporting of the offense; if, however, it was the father who killed the mother, then the son was allowed to conceal the crime.[9]

During the early years of the Republic, Chinese intellectuals took a lively interest in family reform, and some of their ideas were incorporated in the civil code put into effect in 1929. As several scholars have pointed out, however, the provisions of this code were far less revolutionary than the rhetoric surrounding them, despite significant departures from the traditional format. While the code established monogamy, for instance, it did little to alter the lineaments of the patrilineal and patriarchal family.

A tendency to recognize status distinctions of some sort has continued in Taiwan. In the *Laws of the Republic of China,* for example, Article 1123 declares that every house shall have a head; that this headship will fall, failing an election, on the person who is highest in rank or, where ranks are equal, on the one who is senior in age (Article 1124); that the affairs of a house are to be managed by its head (Article 1125); and that the head may order an adult member or a married minor separated from the house for good cause (Article 1128).[10] By and large, Chinese people under the Republic have continued to view family obligations in ways tinged with custom.

The flavor of traditional ideas about obligation was caught by Michael J. Moser, who witnessed a divorce mediation hearing in the Xinzhu District Court (Taiwan) in 1975. A petition for divorce was brought by a young woman, age twenty-three, against her thirty-year-old farmer husband, whom she accused of neglect, adultery, and physical abuse. She had run away on several occasions and stated that her mother-in-law had told her that she would kill her (once threatening her with a meat cleaver) if she did

---

[8]Qu Tongzu, "The Qing Law: An Analysis of Continuity and Change," *Social Sciences in China* 1 (September 1980): 110.

[9]Ibid., p. 109.

[10]*Laws of the Republic of China: First Series—Major Laws* (Taipei, December 1961), pp. 331–32.

so again. After hearing mutual recriminations between the wife and husband, the judge broke in, saying:

> Now, wait a minute. It seems to me that both of you have been in the wrong here. [To the wife] The duties of a wife are not easy, but this is our fate and you must struggle with it. Divorce will not solve these problems, but only create more troubles. You have a duty to your children, and to their grandmother, to care for them—isn't this the glory of being a mother and daughter-in-law? You cannot let every little trouble provide you with an excuse to run off. That is selfish. You have special responsibilities in your husband's family. The good wife knows how to cultivate forebearance—this is why the Chinese family system has endured for thousands of years. Westerners don't care about things like this and that is why today their families are dying. You shouldn't act like a person who has no face at all! [To the husband] But these problems are not your wife's alone. . . . You must share the blame for—(at this point the husband interjected).[11]

Reciprocity as Rights

The study of rights is extensive and complex, beset with multiple definitions and too often infused with polemical assertions. Suffice it to say here that rights as such—entitlements that inhere in persons—is largely a modern construct. As an underpinning for definitions of reciprocity, the idea of rights represents a major structural shift in cultural meanings. Whereas reciprocity as a series of obligations focuses on rules of conduct constrained by status definitions, rights are both analytically more abstract and more inclusive in that they define reciprocity in terms of entitlements that are universally shared. They are, thus, a more sophisticated way to conceptualize reciprocity than emphasizing obligation alone. Obligations, of course, do not vanish, but in their dyadic relationship to rights, they too are structurally transformed: into duties that, like rights, are not constrained by status rules.

Rights, in their simplest and clearest definition, are divided into those that are positive (permitting a person to participate in social life and to have a fair share of social rewards) and those that are negative (protecting a person from undue interference from others, especially from authority). To the degree that societies adhere in their ideals more to one type of right than the other, they betray a major bias in the content of their cultural meanings. A disposition toward positive or negative rights derives from the linkage of

[11]Michael J. Moser, *Law and Social Change in a Chinese Community: A Case Study from Rural Taiwan* (Dobbs Ferry, N.Y.: Oceana, 1982), pp. 136–38.

these rights with the ethics of care or autonomy. The ethic of care, because it promotes concern for the welfare of others, underlies a dedication to positive rights. The ethic of autonomy, by its promotion of privacy and individualism, underlies negative rights.

Just such a transformation in the structure of cultural meanings in China is revealed in the shift away from a historical content in which the ethic of care was realized by fulfilling differential obligations depending on status and toward an emphasis on care achieved by honoring equally held rights. Elwyn Thomas, for example, reports (for Singapore) a shift "from a more esoteric and absolute view of filiality to one which is pragmatic, and truly interpersonal,"[12] a finding fully consistent with data from mainland China. There are interesting reports of radical changes in family roles, especially that of the father, toward a role that is less absolutistic and more affectional.[13] Cheng Zhongying, in setting forth the qualities of this modernized ethic of filial piety, notes that "the relational morality between parents and children . . . [places] . . . equal and reciprocal demands . . . [on] . . . parents' and children's duties."[14]

Some interesting work by Godwin Chu also indicates a shift, especially in gender roles, away from traditional ideas of filial piety. Chu found, for example, that of eighteen traditional Chinese values, respondents still felt positively, in descending order, about loyalty to the state, benevolent father and filial son, submission to authority, harmony, and tolerance and deference, whereas they felt negatively, in ascending order, about chastity of women, glory to ancestors, a house full of sons and grandsons, pleasing superiors, and treating men and women differently. Various comparative studies make clear, however, that this shift is taking place firmly within a persistent communitarian orientation. Fritz Gaenslen, for instance, shows how the Chinese, in comparison to Americans, put far more emphasis on the public realm and on the importance of upholding the social order and its values. George Domino, in a study of children from Guangzhou and Phoenix, found that the most common response for American children is individualism (getting the greatest reward for oneself), followed by competition (getting a greater reward than the other child), whereas for Chinese children the most common response is equality (an equal division of

---

[12]Elwyn Thomas, "Filial Piety and Adolescence in a Changing Society," in *Proceedings of CCU-ICP International Conference: Moral Values and Moral Reasoning in Chinese Societies* (Taipei: Chinese Culture University, 1990), p. 159.

[13]David Y. F. Ho, "Fatherhood in Chinese Culture," in M. E. Lamb, ed., *The Father's Role: Cross Cultural Perspectives* (Hillsdale, N.J.: Erlbaum, 1987), p. 236.

[14]Cheng, "On Confucian Filial Piety," p. 85.

rewards), followed by group enhancement (getting the greatest joint reward).[15] These responses point clearly to content differences between the two societies along the dimensions of the ethic of autonomy/negative rights for Americans and the ethic of care/positive rights for Chinese.

Law and Rights in the People's Republic

As Sir Henry Maine observed in 1861, there is a pattern of growth in legal systems from law based on status to law based on contract. This shift reveals changes in the way people think of themselves and in the way that society is organized. In the first thirty years of Communist rule on mainland China, relations between the government and the people continued to stress status in class relations and citizen obligations. The top officials of this centralized bureaucratic state sought maximum leeway for their own instrumental rationality and the power to limit the scope and opportunities of other groups. There was an extensive economic growth strategy linked organizationally to a very old conception of leaders as models of appropriate behavior. At lower levels, as Richard Madsen has pointed out, a good leader was not a democrat but a patriarchal figure. Conversely, as a writer in *Tansuo* (Exploration) put it in 1979, "The common people in China in general did not dare to put any hope in the law; they could only hope that the people carrying it out would uphold justice."[16]

During the period from 1958 to 1978, rights were generally disregarded. This was especially the case for negative rights in that there were no explicit guarantees against torture or degrading treatment, while arrest and detention, although carried out in accordance with law, could be arbitrary and unreasonable. Nor was there equality before the law, with all citizens possessing uninfringeable basic rights. Indeed, as articulated by China's rulers, rights are benefits granted by society—privileges that are subordinate to definitions and modifications of the law. In that sense, rights of assembly and association, though they have been articulated, are weakly protected. Andrew Nathan cites comments about rights in *Hongqi* in 1979:

[15]Godwin Chu, "Change in China: Where Have You Gone Mao Zedong?" *Centerviews* 7 (July–August 1989): 7; Fritz Gaenslen, "Culture and Decision Making in China, Japan, Russia, and the United States," *World Politics* 39 (October 1986): 91–92; George Domino, "Social Values: A Comparison of Chinese and American Children," in *Proceedings of CCU-ICP International Conference*, p. 790.

[16]Richard Madsen, *Morality and Power in a Chinese Village* (Berkeley and Los Angeles: University of California Press, 1984), p. 79. *Tansuo* writer quoted in Donald C. Clarke, "Political Power and Authority in Recent Chinese Literature," *China Quarterly* 102 (June 1985): 240.

"Human rights are not 'heaven-given'; they are given and regulated by the state and by law; they are not universal but have a clear class nature; they are not abstract but concrete; they are not absolute but limited by law and morality; they are not eternally fixed and unchanging but change their nature and proper scope in accordance with changes in the functions and position of people in the midst of shifting conditions of material production."[17] Nor does the Communist party have any intention of giving away its power over the legal system that defines rights. Yu Shutong, professor of law, vice-president of the China Law Society, and director of both the Department of Education and the Bureau of International Judicial Assistance of the Ministry of Justice, was emphatic in declaring in 1988 that the party had no intention of giving up its control over legal matters nor should it.

Part of the reason for the trauma of change in the People's Republic of China has been the extraordinary emphasis (by comparison to any modern Chinese society) on obligation, now, however, directed unambiguously toward the party and the state. Into this obligation-centered political environment, a conception of rights has begun to intrude. In 1979 political and civil rights were restored to landlords and rich peasants, groups that for thirty years had been labeled "enemies of the people." Equality for all citizens was recognized in the 1982 constitution, which also included a provision (Article 38) that the personal dignity of citizens is inviolable. There has been too a heightened emphasis on law that is at least partly in accordance with the conception of the rule of law as a restraint on evil power and as a resource to be harnessed in the service of society. However frail this rule still is in China, it is undeniable that there has been a great increase in the number of law institutes and law students, of statements about educating the Chinese public about the nation's laws and legal system, and in injunctions to cadres to subject themselves to the limits of law and to recognize that they have no special entitlement to ride roughshod over legal requirements. Lawyers, however, are still enjoined to foster a harmony of interests between state and citizen. As *The Laws of the People's Republic of China* state, lawyers are to "protect the interests of the state and collectives as well as the lawful rights and interests of citizens."[18]

The flavor of a new conception of reciprocity is nowhere more apparent

[17]Andrew J. Nathan, "Sources of Chinese Rights Thinking," in R. Randle Edwards, Louis Henkin, and Andrew J. Nathan, *Human Rights in Contemporary China* (New York: Columbia University Press, 1986), p. 130.

[18]Article 1, The Task and Rights of Lawyers, in *The Laws of the People's Republic of China 1979–1982* (Beijing: Foreign Languages Press, 1987), p. 177.

than in family relations. Here the law is less directly fettered by political considerations and more in keeping with the party's own ideals of its progressive mission. That a move toward greater rights in this crucial area might ultimately affect wider cultural meanings seems not to be fully recognized.

Marriage laws still reflect older conceptions of obligation, but now with equal emphasis on all parties concerned. There is heavy stress on the duty of parents to rear their children properly and, should they be deceased, for this responsibility to be borne by grandparents or older siblings. When parents have lost the ability to work, children, in turn, are legally responsible to heed demands from parents for support. The laws give spouses equal status in the home, with each having the right to work and to be able to demand support and assistance from the other. Each can inherit the other's property, and each may also appeal directly to a people's court for divorce (although this is rarely done). Property settlements in divorce cases are to be made by agreement between the two parties.[19] Obviously, great changes have taken place in conceptions of family rights and obligations.

In an inheritance case tried in Fujian Province and reported on in 1986, a woman, Wu Jia, brought suit to be included as an heir, along with her two brothers, to the estate of her dead parents. According to the two brothers, "Wu Jia was no longer a member of the Wu's since her marriage and what was more, since her marriage Wu Jia did not provide for their parents, although Wu Jia's financial situation was good." Wu Jia countered, "Now that there is equality between man and woman, a daughter has the same right to inherit as a son does." The court held that "Wu Jia had the same right as her brothers to inherit the legacy and that this right shall not be deprived of on the ground that she was married."[20]

In a proceeding reported on in 1980 and heard by the Beijing Appeal Court, a woman, Zhou Hui Xie, a thirty-year-old cashier in a bank, sued for divorce from Han Fa Li, thirty-six, a truck driver. Zhou claimed that she had been beaten seven times, once resulting in a miscarriage. The judge partly excused Han on the grounds that he was a victim of the old tradition of feudal thinking in China. The wife's representative, an official from her bank, disagreed, saying, "The superstition is deep-rooted that a wife is subordinate to a husband, so this husband thinks that the wife is his

---

[19]*The Marriage Law of the People's Republic of China* (Beijing: Foreign Languages Press, 1982), pp. 8–10, 12–14, 16.

[20]Translated from Fujian Province Department of Justice, ed., *Jiu Fa Yi Li' An Li Xuan Xi* (Cases on nine laws and one regulation) (Fuzhou: Fujian People's Publishing, 1986).

property. She should be treated as an equal. After all, both work very hard. The relationship should be on an equal footing."[21]

Another case reported in 1980 concerned a dispute between a mother-in-law and a daughter-in-law over the property of their son and husband, killed four months earlier in an industrial accident at the age of thirty-seven, leaving his wife, a four-month-old baby, and his mother. The courtroom was packed, as workers had been given time off to see the trial. Of principal interest here is how the status of daughters-in-law has been redefined. According to the lawyer for the plaintiff (the daughter-in-law),

> The defendant [the mother-in-law] is a retired worker and she gets her pension and she also works in the street committee and gets some financial assistance, in addition. So, compared with plaintiff her financial condition is fairly good. Also, her sons and daughters work and have the right [obligation?] to take care of their mother. So the life of the old lady is quite guaranteed by her family. But for the young lady, the monthly income compared with the mother is less. In fact, the mother-in-law is already taking part of the insurance money from the factory where the husband [her son] worked. So the mother's rights must come after the daughter-in-law's. In speaking of the distribution of the property, the wife and child and defendant all have rights of succession, but they aren't equal. It must be done according to law and the specific conditions of the two families."[22]

The Political Implications of Change in Cultural Meanings

As Godwin Chu has indicated, the Chinese people today overwhelmingly endorse, above all other propositions, the greatness of China's heritage.[23] Yet when they express pride in this tradition, they do so from a world view now removed from the central value of that tradition. An understanding of the particular obligations associated with status is no longer the pillar of interpersonal relations, and the result is a profound change in how the Chinese see themselves. The world is no longer a succession of nested "middle kingdoms," each "kingdom" demanding def-

[21] "Divorce Court Offers Glimpse of Legal Philosophy in China," *Los Angeles Daily Journal*, February 14, 1980, p. 4.

[22] Emily Jane Goodman, "The People's Court Hears a People's Problem," *National Law Journal*, August 18, 1980, pp. 13, 18, 19.

[23] Chu, "Change in China," p. 7.

erence and the performance of appropriate duties from those of lower status. China's national identity remains collectivist, to be sure, linked in this manner with its past, but composed now of beings who, in some areas of their lives, are being challenged to see themselves as equals with the right to advance equal claims.

The process of change is fitful, uneven, only barely underway in many areas of life, and fraught, especially in the eyes of elites, with possibilities for unintended consequences. Clearly, change in cultural meanings has been brought about partly through such political activities as organized struggle sessions against former status superiors. Other pressures, for example, the need to justify novel roles in new forms of organizational life and new ideas from abroad, have also been important. But ultimately, giving force to all the reasons for change, through a continuous process of interaction, are individual interpretations of reality, linked to a moral dimension, and revealed through discourse.

How traditional meanings have been altered by new conceptions of relationships is highlighted by a particular form of discourse, namely, acts of dissidence. Here the usually placid process of discourse becomes active confrontation, in which two visions are vividly contrasted. In China this drama is nowhere clearer than in a comparison of the way appeals to authority have been framed in the late nineteenth century and now.

As the nineteenth century drew to a close, China's weakness, paired with the threat of partition, loomed ever larger. For ten years after defeat by the French in 1885, a movement for reform had been gathering momentum but with heightened urgency after military humiliation at the hands of the Japanese in 1895. The self-strengthening movement had failed, but the need for extensive reform was widely recognized up to the throne itself. Three separate possibilities presented themselves, two being conservative, involving limited administrative reorganization combined with the adoption of some Western techniques. The third, and more radical, possibility was advocated by Kang Youwei, an idealistic scholar, and involved sweeping institutional change. The proposals were set forth in a series of memorials to the throne phrased, by the standards of that day, in forthright, blunt language. What followed, after Kang's proposal had secured the emperor's approval, came to be known as the Hundred-Day Reform, lasting from June 11, 1898, to September 20 of the same year. All told, some forty or fifty reform decrees were issued dealing with such matters as international cultural exchange, government administration, industry, and education.

Although Kang Youwei's rhetoric seemed blunt to his contemporaries, he took care to delineate status differences clearly and to expose his powerlessness and insignificance in the face of imperial wrath. As a loyal subordinate he made no pretense whatever that he had any rights vis-à-vis superior authority. This care is obvious in the opening and closing lines of a memorial he wrote in 1897. Kang began with "K'ang Yu-wei, your humble servant presently serving in the Ministry of Public Works, respectfully reports to Your Majesty as follows," then discussed the possible partition of China and proposals for reform before concluding:

> If Your Majesty chooses to heed some of the words in this memorial and proceed with reforms so as to preserve this nation, all of his subjects will be most gratified. When that happens, your humble servant would have no regret even if he were punished by death on account of his outspoken and impudent remarks. The alternative is one disaster after another until the nation ceases to exist. Your humble servant, as Your Majesty's most loyal subject, cannot bear to see a repetition of the Coal Mountain incident [when the last Ming emperor, upon the overthrow of the dynasty, hung himself]. Looking at Your Majesty's residence in the distance, how can any loyal subject not be occupied with worry and concern? The eyes are dry, since there are no more tears to shed; the veins are empty, as there is no more blood to be let. Since he may have offended Your Majesty with his candid statements, your humble servant is presenting this petition with trepidation.[24]

Although retired, the empress dowager still held the reins of power. She was not opposed to reform, indeed, had supported the self-strengthening movement; but her inclinations were for conservative change. What she sensed in the Hundred-Day Reform was a plan to wrest power from her, and she reacted vigorously, with strong support from conservative officials. By the end of September the emperor was in detention on a small island in the imperial garden (his incarceration was justified by a statement that he had fallen ill), and Kang was in flight. Prominent reformers seized by the government were executed, and most of the reform measures were reversed. Needless to say, parts of this scenario have an eerie familiarity.

The year 1988 saw rioting in Lhasa which had to be quelled by force. The turn of the new year, however, did not see an end to troubles. Low productivity in urban enterprises continued to burden the national economy, although economic development on the whole was satisfactory. In 1988, for example, the gross national product increased 11.2 percent over 1987, with even sharper gains in industrial output (20.7 percent) and in total investment in fixed assets (18.5 percent). Unfortunately, retail prices also

[24]Dun J. Li, trans., *Modern China: From Mandarin to Commissar* (New York: Scribner's, 1978), pp. 83, 93.

rose sharply, to 18.5 percent above 1987 overall, while general living costs skyrocketed upward by 20.7 percent.[25] These difficulties were compounded by a 14 percent increase in the crime rate in the first three months of 1989 alone, and the crimes included numerous cases of graft, corruption, and bribery by party members or their relatives.[26] In the second half of 1988, for example, more than twenty-four thousand party and government officials, including seventeen at ministerial and provincial levels, were reported for committing crimes.[27] All was not well. Surveys revealed a deep resentment of official corruption which fueled, in some quarters, existing dispositions toward political reform in the direction of greater democracy.

The death of former party secretary general Hu Yaobang on April 15, 1989, was a signal to students in Beijing to commemorate Hu by organizing a campaign for political reform. Carefully showing support for the party, the police, and socialism, the students on April 18 offered a list of seven demands encompassing dialogue, a free press, the publication of the private assets of leaders, a crackdown on corruption, an increase in education funds, and a rescinding of regulations on demonstrations. Two of the demands (the first two presented) clearly pertained to political issues. The first asked for a reassessment of Hu Yaobang's merits and demerits and an affirmation of democracy, freedom, magnanimity, and harmony; the second asked for an open clarification of the nature of the movements against "spiritual pollution" (meaning bourgeois liberal tendencies) and "liberalization" and a redressing of cases in which people in these movements had been treated unjustly.[28]

A revised set of seven demands issued on May 2 echoed the first set in most respects but also asked for the punishment of police officers accused of attacking student demonstrators and for sanctions against leaders who had committed errors leading to inflation. And other groups were joining in submitting demands. Forty-two prominent intellectuals sent an open letter to senior party officials urging them to meet with students and release political prisoners. At the end of April an unknown workers' group in Beijing had called for increased wages, stabilization of prices, and the publication of the incomes of party and government officials. In early May journalists asked for an end to censorship and for independence of the media.

[25] State Statistical Bureau of the People's Republic of China, "Statistics for 1988 Socio-Economic Development," *Beijing Review,* May 29, 1989, pp. i–viii.

[26] "Criminal Cases on the Rise," ibid., May 22, 1989, p. 12.

[27] "24,000 Officials Reported for Irregularities," ibid., January 30, 1989, p. 9.

[28] Stefan R. Landsberger, "The 1989 Student Demonstrations in Beijing: A Chronology of Events," *China Information* 4 (Summer 1989): 37–55.

The demands, reflecting to some extent the experiences of the Cultural Revolution, were phrased quite differently from those of earlier reformers. Gone were the obsequious deference and the phrasing that highlighted the obligation expected of inferiors. There remained loyalty, a commitment to the state, and a deep sense of communitarianism. But new were the requests for negative rights in the form of press freedom and the right to demonstrate, although neither request exalted individualism as such, being framed, rather, as policy changes that would benefit society. Two points stand out. One was the desire, expressed by a student spokesman, for "a legal guarantee for such things as the rights of citizens."[29] The second was the aspiration to dialogue between the students and the government "on the basis of full equality between the two parties" with the spokesmen of both sides enjoying "equal rights" and with the "personal and political safety of representatives of both sides [to be] guaranteed."[30] However naïve this hope may seem in retrospect, it shows clearly the belief held by China's young intellectuals that relations among people and between the people and government must be based on the recognition of a right to equal treatment.

Surprisingly, a close look at the responses of those in power also reveals a shift in perceptions of rights and obligations, although full account must be taken of the fact that the confrontation between government leaders and students was generational as well as political. Not all the official rhetoric in the preceding years about law and rights had been cynical bombast, despite the severity of the repression ultimately visited on the students. At the same time, of course, there remained at the core of the government's argument, particularly in comments by the octogenarian Deng Xiaoping, an emphasis on avoiding the "chaos" and antiparty activity the *Renmin ribao* (People's daily) branded as a "planned conspiracy against the socialist state."[31] As early as April 26, at a meeting between Deng and Premier Li Peng, Deng is reported to have said that the student unrest should be quashed "by any means." Here, in modern form, is a response worthy of the empress dowager, to uphold at all costs an obligation-centered political order.

Yet Chinese leaders did not, as they might have earlier, move immediately, when the demonstrations began, to brand the students as rightists and counterrevolutionaries and to have them seized, humiliated, and pun-

[29]Willy Wo-Lap Lam and Seth Faison, "Students Organize Strike," *South China Morning Post* (Hong Kong), in *Foreign Broadcast Information Service* (hereafter *FBIS*), April 21, 1989, p. 21.

[30]"'Full Text' of Petition" (in Chinese), *Xinhua* (New China), May 3, 1989, in *FBIS*, May 3, 1989, p. 25.

[31]Patrick Lescot, "Students Issue Strike Order," in *FBIS,* in April 26, 1989, p. 19.

ished forthwith, legal niceties aside. Granted that serious factional infighting was also taking place among the leaders, with party secretary general Zhao Ziyang increasingly moving to support the student demonstration for his own political ends. A debate about rights was taking place within the government itself as well as between the government and the students, with the outcome of the latter debate depending to a great extent on the outcome of the former.

In the beginning, in response to a question from *Newsweek,* Li Peng had said, "The Chinese government attaches great importance to the question of human rights. Since the end of the 'Cultural Revolution' the basic rights of citizens have been guaranteed. We continue to make improvements in this regard." Through April and into early May, the government stressed keeping mourning activities for Hu Yaobang organized and orderly and avoiding trouble or sabotage. Rights were not ignored, but they were defined in the context of acceptable activity. As official statements expressed it in late April, "It is imperative to firmly stop any acts that use any excuse to infringe upon the rights and interests of legitimate organizations of students," and "it is necessary to protect the just rights of students to study in class." On May 3, State Council spokesman Yuan Mu proclaimed, "We respect the democratic rights of the vast numbers of young students."[32]

By mid-May the factional debate within the government and the nature of the government's ultimate response to the students were both near resolution. Li Peng met with representatives of the striking students on May 18, saying, at the close of the meeting, "You have gone too far." On the same day, at a meeting at Deng Xiaoping's house, Zhao Ziyang expressed disagreement with a proposal put forth by Deng to implement martial law. On the next day, Li called for powerful measures to curb turmoil, telling government representatives that martial law for parts of Beijing had been approved and would be in force at 10:00 A.M. the next day. Zhao, now in eclipse, claimed ill health and did not attend. Martial law went into effect, but rallies and demonstrations continued, including the dramatic May 30 unveiling of the Goddess of Liberty statue, which stood twenty-seven feet high in central Tiananmen Square.

It is of some interest that the government was at pains to justify its actions as complying with the law and its provisions regarding rights. On May 26, for example, Peng Zhen, chairman of the Standing Committee of

---

[32]Yang Xiaobin and Li Rongxia, "Premier Li on Internal, External Policies," *Beijing Review,* April 17, 1989, p. 12; "Beijing Notice on Unrest" (in Mandarin), April 20, 1989, in *FBIS,* April 21, 1989, p. 19; Editorial (in Mandarin), *"Renmin ribao,* April 25, 1989, in *FBIS,* same day, p. 24; "Yuan Mu Holds News Conference 3 May" (in Mandarin), in *FBIS,* May 3, 1989, p. 23.

the National People's Congress, set forth at the request of the central authorities the gist of this justification. In a lengthy speech about the constitution and other statutory provisions, he pointed out that the former provides that the country is to be led by the working class, not the bourgeoisie, and that promoting bourgeois liberalization runs counter to the interests of the people and, significantly, of the party as well. "Unity of thinking," he reminded his listeners, "is the general principle." Next there followed a lengthy discussion of how Article 35 of the constitution permits demonstrations, but Article 51 provides that in the exercise of freedoms and rights, citizens may not infringe on the interests of the state, society, or collective or "upon the lawful freedoms and rights of other citizens." To make this point perfectly clear, Peng then added that Articles 2, 158, and 159 of the criminal law provide that nobody may use any means he wishes "to disturb the social order . . . or the people's daily life." Thus, in upholding the legality of martial law, Peng asserted that "the decision of the State Council to impose martial law in some parts of Beijing for the sake of upholding the dignity of the Constitution and preserving the social order, the order of production, work, education, scientific research, and the daily life of people in the capital is entirely lawful, necessary, and proper." Peng concluded by saying, "Some people only pay lip service to rule by law. In practice, not only have they themselves trampled underfoot the Constitution and the law, but they have also instigated other people to go against the Constitution and the law. Students and people of all walks of life: Please heighten your vigilance."[33]

It is, then, ironic that the government appealed for support in the name of the law and justified its bloody suppression of the students on June 4, 1989, by the same criteria. There were, of course, more primitive motives at work as well. Deng Xiaoping spoke to military commanders on June 9, noting that student activity had developed from "turmoil" to "counter-revolutionary rebellion" with the goal of overthrowing the Communist party and establishing "a bourgeois republic entirely dependent on the West." Toward enemies, he said, "we should not have an iota of forgiveness."[34] Yet in the context of China's historical development, these autocratic words must be placed side-by-side with the emphasis by the government

[33] "Peng's 26 May Speech" (in Chinese), *Renmin ribao*, May 30, 1989, p. 1, in *FBIS*, same day, pp. 24, 25.

[34] "Deng's Talks on Quelling Rebellion in Beijing," in *Massacre in Beijing: The Events of 3–4 June 1989 and Their Aftermath*, App. E (Report prepared by the International League for Human Rights and the Ad Hoc Study Group on Human Rights in China, New York, August 4, 1989), pp. 14, 15.

on legality, however self-servingly the legal cloak has been used. For to talk of law and rights at all, to feel a need to justify actions by these criteria, is to reveal a profound shift in cultural meanings. It is also, in the end, likely to be the basis for the transformation of the absolutist political system.

Against the reality of an entrenched authoritarian political system, young Chinese are increasingly articulating ideas about political equality and a more open political process. Somewhat paradoxically, and not necessarily from the same motives, the government itself has been placing greater emphasis on legality; citizens are being exhorted to view social relations as governed by principles embodied in law and independent of role and status. Across the spectrum of Chinese society, therefore, changes are clearly evident in the way people perceive themselves and their relations with others. A new sense of national identity, based on equality of persons combined with communitarian ideals, is emerging. As these ideals become manifest, a transformed Chinese national identity will come into being.

中國 6

China's Intellectuals in the Deng Era: Loss of Identity with the State

Merle Goldman, Perry Link, and Su Wei

One of the slogans held aloft during the Tiananmen demonstrations in April and May 1989 read: "We love our country, but we hate our government." This slogan reveals the radical change in outlook of China's student and intellectual community since the end of the Cultural Revolution. Love of country but disillusionment with government and leaders was repeatedly expressed during those heady seven weeks of protest. For a large portion of the urban population, patriotism had come to be defined as loyalty to one's society and country as distinguished from loyalty to the party-state and its leadership. Intellectuals especially were changing their understandings of their identification with the party-state and of their own proper relationship to it. By intellectuals, we mean mostly "higher" intellectuals (*gaoji zhishifenzi*)—professionals, academics, scientists, engineers, writers, and artists—but the views they express extend beyond "higher" or even intellectual circles.

Until the post-Mao period, state and society were regarded as virtually the same, or as Benjamin Schwartz has pointed out, the line between them was blurred.[1] The traditional Chinese view was that individual interests were inseparable from those of society, and society, at least theoretically, was indistinguishable from the state. Since the ruler's intentions were regarded as good and in harmony with the people, the relationship between

---

[1] Benjamin I. Schwartz, *China's Cultural Values*, Occasional Paper No. 18 (Tempe: Arizona State University, Center for Asian Studies, 1985).

the state and the society was not seen as one of confrontation and opposition as it was in the West, but as one of unity. When a principled literatus remonstrated with an abusive ruler or official, he hoped to persuade him to rectify his actions so he could rule more effectively. Thus, to criticize a ruler or official was to express one's true loyalty to the ruler and state because the criticism was meant to improve governance and, therefore, society. Although the literatus theoretically carried out the highest ideals of Confucianism, in reality he could suffer serious consequences, even death, for his courage and independence.

Whereas it was possible in imperial times to express one's loyalty to the leader and government by remonstrance, it was virtually impossible to do so in the Mao period. While a traditional literatus could be regarded as more loyal when he opposed unjust rule than when he pledged unquestioning loyalty, the exercise of individual conscience was virtually impossible in the People's Republic of China. The Mao regime, emulating the Soviet model, completely subordinated the individual, economy, society, culture, and academia to the needs of the party-state. When the Chinese Communist party became the state in 1949, service to the party was regarded as service to the state, which in turn was regarded as service to society. Consequently to serve the party's needs was to carry out one's patriotic duty.

The Chinese intellectual tradition of dedication to serving *tianxia* ("all under heaven, the world"), specifically by means of offering ideas to the rulers of the state, is well known and in many respects has survived into the period of the People's Republic.[2] Consciously or unconsciously, Chinese intellectuals, almost without exception, have wanted to be of service to their country and have had difficulty conceiving their ultimate vocations in any other terms. This self-conception has led them to want a certain "identity" with the communist state, notwithstanding the cruel treatment that the state has repeatedly dealt them.

In addition, the intellectuals wholeheartedly supported the party-state in the early years of the regime because they believed the party would finally achieve the goal that China had been searching for since the late nineteenth century: to make China "rich and powerful." Equally important, they expected the party to create a more just and equal society. Like the literati,

---

[2] See Yu Ying-shih, *Shi yu Zhongguo wenhua* (The literatus and Chinese culture) (Shanghai: Shanghai renmin chubanshe, 1987); on survival into the People's Republic years, see Perry Link, "Intellectuals and Cultural Policy after Mao," in A. Doak Barnett and Ralph N. Clough, eds., *Modernizing China: Post-Mao Reform and Development* (Boulder, Colo.: Westview, 1986), pp. 81–102.

they assumed a fundamental harmony of interests of all groups and individuals with the party-state. Should there be any conflicts, the intellectuals expected to help moderate and resolve them as they had done throughout Chinese history. Also like their literari predecessors, they expected the party-state and its leadership to be responsive to the wishes of the people, as articulated by the intellectuals.

In the 1950s they believed that it was unnecessary to impose any external restraints on the party and its leaders. On the contrary, they believed it was necessary that the leadership be unrestrained in order to achieve modernization as quickly as possible. In their view, the single-party state represented a unified Chinese society and expressed the wishes of all the people. Unlike the Western and Russian intellectuals, who considered moral autonomy to be independent of official power, the intellectuals in the People's Republic, like their literati predecessors, regarded themselves as establishment intellectuals and assumed that moral and political authority converged and were the same. Even when the party launched campaigns against intellectuals who refused to subordinate themselves completely to the party, such as the writer Hu Feng and his disciplines, and even against those who basically did conform, such as those who spoke out during the Hundred Flowers movement as Mao had asked, virtually all those not themselves under attack participated actively in the campaigns against their colleagues. They feared that if they did not participate they and their families would also be punished. Most important, they truly believed that the critics had acted unpatriotically and had disunited the nation at a time when it should have remained unified behind the party's efforts to build a new society.

But as these campaigns became more widespread and more intensive, culminating in the Great Leap Forward with more than thirty million dead and the Cultural Revolution with over a hundred million persecuted, the bonds between the intellectuals and the party-state were slowly broken. The Deng Xiaoping regime that came to power in late 1978 tried to retie the bonds by promising never again to carry out campaigns like those of the Mao era. But as the campaigns and persecution continued, albeit less violently under Deng, the intellectuals' belief that serving the party-state was a moral, patriotic duty waned. By the time of the June 4, 1989, crackdown, the intellectuals, like their Soviet counterparts, had come to see themselves more in conflict with the party-state and its leader than as participants in it. To China's politically engaged intellectual elite, patriotism no longer meant upholding and rectifying the prevailing regime but fundamentally changing it. They were influenced by Western ideas and the

happenings in the Soviet Union and in Eastern Europe, but their arrival at
this relatively radical view was determined more by their own bitter experience in China than by outside influences.

The movement of the politically engaged intellectual elite from being
supporters to opponents of the political leadership was very gradual. In
fact, they initially supported the Deng regime as enthusiastically as they had
supported the Mao regime in 1949. They believed that, this time, there
would be genuine reform. Even when Deng repressed the Democracy Wall
movement in 1979 and imprisoned its leaders, they did not protest. They
feared they might lose the stature they had finally won and did not want to
jeopardize privileges issuing from the Deng leadership. Moreover, many of
them did not agree with the most outspoken activist of the movement, Wei
Jingsheng, who had rejected Marxism-Leninism as inappropriate for China
and had charged that Deng was as much a dictator as Mao. Equally
important, they wanted to cooperate with the Deng regime to revitalize the
nation after the disasters of the Mao period.

Like the principled literati and the intellectuals who had spoken out in
the Mao period, they saw themselves as the intermediaries who interpreted
the "murmurings" of the people to the government. If the rulers listened to
the voice of the people as interpreted by them and responded, then they
believed that the relationship between the rulers and the ruled would be
strengthened and the leadership would govern more effectively. Consequently when victims of the Anti-Rightist Campaign (1957–59) and the
Cultural Revolution were exonerated by Hu Yaobang at the end of the
1970s, many of them resumed where they had left off in the Mao period, by
"appealing on behalf of the people" to the government. In exposing the
abuses of the leaders so they could be corrected, intellectuals believed they
were serving both the leaders and the led. Thus they regarded themselves as
loyal and patriotic citizens. As the 1980s progressed, however, China's
intellectuals became more and more radically alienated from the party-
state; their alienation occurred in three stages.

Returning to "Normal": 1978 through 1981

For all Chinese intellectuals save the very youngest, the entire "decade of
opening and reform" should be viewed in the penumbra of the Cultural
Revolution. From the Democracy Wall and "scar literature" in the late
1970s, to the growing despair of the mid-1980s to the protests of 1989,
Chinese intellectuals attempted to forge a post–Cultural Revolution iden-

tity for themselves. The fact that these efforts have been marked by fits and starts, and twists and turns, only underscores the strong implicit consensus that, whatever it may be, *some* new way, *some* alternative to the Mao and Cultural Revolution model, had to be discovered. During the Cultural Revolution it was impossible for intellectuals to "identify"—except falsely and superficially—with the state or its leaders.[3] They might have tried, on an abstract level, to identify with the official ideology, but that was hardly more congenial. The shrill puffery of Maoism's "most, most, most . . ." ("most great . . . most correct . . . most beautiful . . .") only helped to instill spiritual and moral disillusionment in intellectuals. What might be called an identity crisis of great depth and scope is captured in the phrase "three belief crises" (*sanxin weiji*) that circulated among intellectuals at the end of the Cultural Revolution: crisis of belief (*xinyang*) in Marxism, crisis in faith (*xinxin*) in socialism, and crisis in trust (*xinren*) of the Communist party. A line from China's most famous young poet, Bei Dao, which was widely repeated among young intellectuals because it so well captured their acute anguish and mood of defiance, said: "I do not believe."[4]

Nevertheless, after the death of Mao, when the opportunity came to restore faith of some kind, intellectuals of all generations tended, in their somewhat separate ways, toward a kind of restorationism. They wanted China to return to "correct" socialism, vaguely conceived as that of the early 1950s. The phrases that circulated at the time attest to this spirit of seeking change based on continued identification with the Communist party: *Zhengben qingyuan* ("thoroughly overhaul the system") sought a return to the socialist system in its original and "pure" form. *Boluan fanzheng* called for fixing (*bo*) the chaos (*luan*) of the Gang of Four's "false socialism" and returning (*fan*) to the true path (*zheng*) of the revolution. Most telling, perhaps, were the phrases *butian* ("repair heaven") and *chaitian* ("dismantle heaven") describing two attitudes intellectuals had toward the party and state. The word *tian* carries important traditional connotations of the intellectual's duty toward *tianxia* and the heavenly authority (*tianzi*) that rules the state. (The phrase "repair heaven" also recalls the mythical *nüwa*, "repairer of heaven.") In the late 1970s, most intellectuals were *butianpai*, or would-be "rebuilders" of the state.

In emerging from the catastrophe of the Cultural Revolution, there

[3] See Anne F. Thurston, *Enemies of the People: The Ordeal of the Intellectuals in China's Great Cultural Revolution* (New York: Knopf, 1987).

[4] From a poem called "Answer" (Huida), originally published in *Jintian* (Today) (Beijing), no. 1, pp. 28–29; trans. in Bonnie S. McDougall, *Notes from the City of the Sun: Poems by Bei Dao* (Ithaca: Cornell University, China-Japan Program, 1983), p. 38.

seemed scarcely an alternative; people who might have thought of alternatives had strong incentives not to discuss them in public. Thus the few (such as Wei Jingsheng) who dared to be *chaitianpai,* or would-be "dismantlers" of the state, faced not only the lonely intellectual challenge of how to articulate an alternative but the fearsome prospect of opposing virtually alone a state whose ruthless violence was all too vivid in recent memory. This helps to explain why Wei Jingsheng was not more widely supported in 1979, even though what he advocated—for example, that democracy should be the "fifth modernization"—was hardly radical by the standards of the 1989 democracy movement or even what was being said in the official press in spring of 1989.

Two important expressions of the basically "restorationist" temper of the 1978–81 years were: (1) the discussion of "practice is the sole criterion for testing truth" and (2) the literature of the post-Mao thaw, including both the so-called scar literature and the "reflective literature" (*fansi wenxue*) that followed. The "sole criterion" debate was a major, nationwide political campaign aimed at countering the power of the remnant Maoists within the leadership (Hua Guofeng, Wang Dongxing, Chen Xilian, Wu De, and others). The fundamental principles of this group lay in the so-called two whatevers: whatever Mao Zedong said should be followed and whatever Mao ordered should be carried out. To argue that "practice" was the "sole criterion" of truth was, by clear implication, to rule out the sanctity of received wisdom, be it from Mao or any other source. In restrospect, Chinese intellectuals have realized the theoretical shallowness of the sole criterion argument. But this shallowness was, and is, beside the point. The sole criterion debate was not, despite its clothing, serious epistemology; it was pure politics, and politics that Chinese intellectuals overwhelmingly supported, because of the implicit liberation from Maoist policies. But the effort was still restorationist in that most people knew that the sole criterion slogan was backed by Deng Xiaoping and other non-Maoists in the Communist establishment.[5] To support the slogan was to support the "enlightened" group in the leadership, notably including people who had had power in the pre–Cultural Revolution years.

The great tide of post-Mao thaw literature shows a basic restorationism even more clearly. Many of these works were essentially duets on the themes of the horrors of the Cultural Revolution and idealized memories of the "golden age" of the 1950s. Many leading writers (Wang Meng, Liu

[5]See Michael Schoenhals, "The 1978 Truth Criterion Controversy," *China Quarterly* (June 1990): 243–68.

Binyan, Zhang Xianliang, and Cong Weixi, for example) also stood as personal symbols of the change from the early 1950s to the late 1970s: revolutionary enthusiasts in 1949, they were attacked as "rightists" in 1957, had suffered for about twenty years, and now, with the post-Mao thaw, were relatively free again. The general stance adopted by this group of writers was captured in the oft-cited formula that likens the relationship of party and intellectuals to that between mother and child. A mother might spank a child incorrectly, and indeed excessively, but a child does not for that reason reject the mother. The mother basically still loves the child. This formula gets almost verbatim expression in the film *The Herdsman's Story,* based on a story by Zhang Xianliang,[6] when the narrator says, referring to the case of a persecuted intellectual, "A child does not find its mother too ugly."

A more richly illustrative example is Wang Meng's novella *Bolshevik Salute,*[7] which uses stream of consciousness technique to produce frequent, sharply contrasting juxtapositions of scenes of mindless chaos during the Cultural Revolution and the author's rosy recollections of the early 1950s. In the story a "young Bolshevik" (presumably Wang Meng himself) is sent into hard labor during the Cultural Revolution, all the while wishing he could deliver a "Bolshevik salute" to protest his innocence and the "mistake" of his punishment. As he suffers, he still sings Russian songs and reads Soviet novels he had learned to love in the 1950s. His pride in this identity leads him to a self-protecting device reminiscent of Lu Xun's famous character Ah Q and his famous dictum "We used to be so much better off than you."[8] It also leads him to intense frustration: "There's nothing wrong with the *sutras,* but the monks are chanting them wrong."

The Chinese intellectuals' sense of identification with the state, as of the late 1970s, can be summarized in the formula "Return XXX (history, truth, realism, and so on) to its original form" (huan XXX de benlai mianmu). Few really inquired into the value of the "original forms" themselves. It was not easy to make such inquiries publicly; and one could assume that the original forms would at least be a big improvement over the Cultural

[6]The film is *Mumaren,* adapted by Li Zhun from Zhang Xianliang's story *Ling yu rou* (Spirit and flesh), directed by Xie Jin and produced by Shanghai Film Studios, 1982.

[7]Wang Meng, *Buli* (Bolshevik salute), in *Wang Meng zhongpian xiaoshuo xuan* (A selection of the novellas of Wang Meng) (Fujian: Haixia chubanshe, 1984); trans. Wendy Larson as *Bolshevik Salute* (Seattle: University of Washington Press, 1989). Wang Meng served as minister of culture from 1986 until he was removed for declining to praise the June 4, 1989, massacre.

[8]"Women xianqian—bi ni kuo de duo la!" Lu Xun, *A Q zhengzhuan* (The true story of A Q) (Beijing: People's Literature Publishing, 1976), p. 8 (chap. 2, par. 2).

Revolution. But this unexamined assumption about original forms was gradually undermined between 1979 and 1981, as both of the major liberating breakthroughs of the period—the sole criterion slogan and thaw literature—were negated by policy decisions from the top. As these reversals emerged, intellectuals began to doubt and reappraise their identification with the idea of return to original forms.

In late March 1979, at an important "meeting to discuss theoretical guidelines," Deng Xiaoping introduced the Four Cardinal Principles (the leadership of the Communist party, the dictatorship of the proletariat, Marxism-Leninism–Mao Zedong-thought, and the socialist system), which were supposed to consolidate party dictatorship and were later written into the preamble to the Chinese constitution. In the ensuing months, these principles were used to oppose the sole criterion theory and its accompanying "emancipation of thought" slogan that had preceded the Third Plenum in December 1978. The much-feared slogan "Never forget class struggle!" reappeared.[9] Some of the people who had been prominent in supporting the sole criterion idea were subsequently purged or demoted.[10] In late 1979 and early 1980, as Deng Xiaoping emerged with his power consolidated anew, he moved to suppress the Democracy Wall movement and arrest Wei Jingsheng and other of its activists. This turn in policy was especially significant because Deng had personally supported the emergence of Democracy Wall and even manipulated to a certain degree the content of its posters for his own political benefit.

The termination of thaw literature was decisively accomplished in 1981 with the national campaign against "bourgeois liberalization," focusing on criticism of Bai Hua's filmscript "Unrequited Love".[11] The writer Bai Hua had joined the Red Army in the 1940s to fight against the Guomindang and help bring the Communists to power. He first remonstrated in the Hundred Flowers movement, in which he urged officials to interfere less in the work of younger writers. For his advice he was designated a rightist. Although this designation was lifted in 1961, he had trouble publishing his works, and in May 1966, he lost his freedom again. For seven years, he was

---

[9]Wu Jiang and Sun Changjiang, "Hu Yaobang yu zhenli biaozhun de taolun" (Hu Yaobang and the criterion-of-truth debate), reprinted in *Xinhua wenzhai* (New China digest) 6 (1989): 7.

[10]For example, Guo Luoji, a teacher in the Philosophy Department at Beijing Univeristy, was, on behest from the top, reassigned from Beijing to Nanjing; Ruan Ming, of the Central Party Academy, was stripped of his party membership; and Li Honglin, a senior party theorist, retreated to Fujian.

[11]Bai Hua and Peng Ning, "Kulian" (Unrequited love), *Shiyue* (October) 3 (1979).

unable to visit or correspond with his wife and child. Although free again in 1974, he was unable to publish until the fall of the Gang of Four.

Bai Hua saw himself in the tradition of Qu Yuan, one of the first principled literati in Chinese history, who, when his remonstrances with the ruler over prevailing policies were ignored, killed himself in protest in 278 B.C. Qu Yuan was a symbol of the politically engaged intellectual willing to take a stand against unjust policies for the good of society. Bai Hua continued his tradition of standing up to unjust leaders and pointing out their misdeeds in several plays he produced in the early years of the Deng regime, arousing official consternation. But the work that provoked the first official campaign of the Deng era was "Unrequited Love." Although the script was published in *Shiyue* (October) in September 1979, it was not until April 1981 that Bai Hua was singled out by name for criticism in the army press. He was still a member of the army, which was much less enthusiastic about reform than the intellectuals and Deng's reformist protégés Hu Yaobang and Zhao Ziyang. One of the major charges against Bai Hua in the series of unsigned "special commentator" articles in *Jiefangjun bao* (Liberation Army daily) was that "Unrequited Love" lacked a sense of patriotism.

It was the story of an intellectual who had devoted himself to his country because of a strong sense of patriotism that had been requited only by repression and cruelty. The intellectual protagonist, an artist, is forced to leave China in the 1940s because of the Japanese occupation and flees to the West, where he becomes famous and wealthy. Yet he is drawn by the 1949 revolution to return to China, because of his love for his country and his desire to help it modernize. But very quickly, his love of country is distorted into the worship of an individual. This distortion is described symbolically in a scene in which the artist, as a child, is taken to visit a Chan Buddhist Temple, where he asks, "Why is this Buddhist statue so black?" The reply is "The incense smoke of many good men and pious women has blackened it."[12] The implication is that it is not only the ruler and the party who have created this blackened idol, because the people themselves have done so willingly. Their patriotism has degenerated into the deification of one man.

Despite repeated persecution, the artist continues to love his country even during the Cultural Revolution when he is attacked by Red Guards. When his daughter tells him of her plan to marry an overseas Chinese and live abroad, he objects. But his daughter replies, "Papa, you love this nation

[12]Trans. in Michael Duke, *Blooming and Contending* (Bloomington: Indiana University Press, 1985), p. 137.

of ours. . . . But does this nation love you?" Michael Duke has pointed out that throughout this scenario, Bai Hua has used the term *zuguo* to describe the artist's reason for returning from the United States. *Zuguo* means the Chinese people, the motherland, and the country, but not necessarily the state, government, or political party. The only significant departure from this usage appears in this particular dialogue with his daughter, which instead uses *guojia*, which means government or state as well as a geographic unit.[13] Bai Hua himself has confirmed that his use of these two different terms was to distinguish the country and society the intellectuals love from the government and its policies that had persecuted them.[14]

Shortly after this conversation with his daughter, the artist dies, fleeing from a band of Red Guards. The film ends with the artist falling and dying in the snow, his body forming a large question mark, as if asking whether the artist's life of "unrequited love" for his country had been worthwhile. Unlike her father, forced to flee from China before the revolution, his daughter willingly flees during the revolution, suggesting that life under the Guomindang, difficult as it was, might have been better than under the Communists.

Why were "Unrequited Love" and Bai Hua made the targets of a campaign? After all, the movie had been seen by only a small, select group of higher military and party officials. Many other works were more well known and controversial. As in all campaigns, there were personal and factional reasons. The fact that Bai Hua was in the army and that high army officers were upset with the reforms, and particularly with the criticism of Mao, may explain the choice. The charges against Bai Hua also reveal that his view of patriotism—as a loyalty to one's country which does not include loyalty to the party, the government, or its leaders—was equally important. Not only the army but the more conservative party elders, the veteran revolutionaries who had made the Long March with Deng Xiaoping, were upset with this view. *Beijing Daily,* whose editors were allied with the more conservative party officials, charged that Bai Hua had confused persecution by the Gang of Four with the way the party had treated the intellectuals. He had made no distinction between what happened to intellectuals before and after the Cultural Revolution. He was also criticized for not distinguishing between the Gang on one hand and Mao on the other. A *Liberation Army Daily* article explained that the use of *guojia* rather than *zuguo* in the daughter's question meant that Bai Hua was saying that *guojia* is "no longer

---

[13]Ibid., p. 144.
[14]Personal conversation with Bai Hua in Shanghai in July 1986. Also explained in Duke, *Blooming and Contending*.

the people's country and is dominated by the Gang."[15] The film was termed "antiparty" and "antisocialist" as well as "antipatriotic," as if all these terms were synonymous.

Although Hu Yaobang tried to stop the attacks on Bai Hua and bring the campaign to an end, Deng revitalized it in August 1981 by using the terms *bourgeois liberalization* and *opposition to party leadership* to characterize Bai Hua's lack of patriotism. Although Hu Yaobang acknowledged weakness of the party secretariat in dealing with the "erroneous tendencies" expressed in "Unrequited Love," he did not use the expression *bourgeois liberalization* to describe it. Nevertheless, Deng's criticism sparked a resurgence of criticism against Bai Hua. A long article written by two deputy editors of *Wenyibao* repeated the assertions of the army newspaper, principally that "the patriotism of today is inalienable from love for the party and love for socialism." Moreover, the authors explained that Mao was worshipped not just because of the personality cult or because of blind superstition, as Bai Hua had implied, but because his "prestige is interrelated with his vital contribution to the revolution over the years." That this worship became fanatic was due to Lin Biao and Jiang Qing, not to Mao. They charged that Bai Hua had used "a ridiculous allegory to negate totally the leadership of the party and mock and belittle the masses."[16]

Unlike intellectuals who were attacked and ostracized in the Mao era, Bai Hua received over a thousand letters of appreciation. Wall posters were put up at Beijing University and Fudan University defending him. Nevertheless, despite this open support and Hu Yaobang's efforts to limit the campaign, Bai Hua was again separated from his family, just as he had been in the Mao era. He was put under house arrest in Wuhan, where he was stationed, and forced to make a self-criticism. His son said, "For other people the Cultural Revolution has ended, but for our family it continues."[17] Thus Bai Hua's experience proved to him and his family that there was little difference between what happened to him in the Cultural Revolution and before or after the Cultural Revolution. The campaign finally ended with the November 1981 publication, in *Liberation Army Daily* and *Wenyibao,* of his self-criticism, in which he apologized for failing to recognize the power of the party to reform itself.

With the closing of the Democracy Wall, the stifling of thaw literature,

[15] Zhang Chenghuan, "The issues and lessons of 'Bitter Love'" (in Chinese), *Jiefangjun bao* (Liberation Army daily), May 17, 1981, in *Foreign Broadcast Information Service* (hereafter *FBIS*), May 29, 1981, p. K5.

[16] Tang Yin and Tang Dacheng, "On the erroneous tendencies of 'Bitter Love'" (in Chinese), *Wenyibao* (Literary gazette), 19 (August 1981), in *FBIS,* October 14, 1981, pp. K4, 5, 6.

[17] Personal conversation in Shanghai in July 1986.

the opposition to the sole criterion theory, and finally the Bai Hua campaign, Chinese intellectuals began to doubt their assumptions about "repairing the state" (*butian*). Originally wanting to "fix the chaos and return to the true path," they now found that some of the "chaos" was rooted in the "true path" itself. This conclusion brought troubling implications for their identity as restorationists, not only because of the uneasiness that doubt brings but because of the loneliness that results from not being able to discuss it openly.

"Irreversible" Reform within the System: 1982 to 1988

During the years 1982 to 1988, beneath the surface fluctuation in authoritarian controls on expression (tightened in 1983, loosened in 1986, tightened in 1987, loosened in 1988), Chinese intellectuals asked questions of increasing breadth and depth about their country's system. If the original "true path" was flawed, then how should the system be altered? Public discussion was made easier by the fact that the regime promoted the word *reform* and pursued its own reform agenda. Mikhail Gorbachev's bold political reforms were also a stimulus, not necessarily as a model to be emulated but because they demonstrated the possibility of reforming a Marxist-Leninist system.

The agenda of the intellectual debate after 1981 was conditioned by the authoritarian style of the Deng Xiaoping regime and its resonance with traditional Chinese despotism. The Communist formula "one-ism, one party, one leader," whose extreme case had been definitively supplied by Mao, drew on the traditional concepts of "unity of heaven and man" (*tianren heyi*) and "unity of governance and religion" (*zhengjiao heyi*). Deng's version of the formula, asserted through his insistence on the Four Cardinal Principles, amounted to the claim that "the party *is* the country (or: the emperor *is* tianxia). That Deng took the trouble to dress up his authoritarianism in the clothes of modern democracy (for example, by writing his Four Cardinal Principles into China's constitution) did not lessen the frustrations of intellectuals whose efforts to find a new path for China seemed repeatedly blocked by old forms and old patterns of thought.

The Discussion on Alienation

It is in this context that the discussion on alienation, which had begun in the late 1970s, reached a climax in 1983. Wang Ruoshui, who was then deputy editor-in-chief of *Renmin ribao* (People's Daily), was the major exponent of the view that alienation can exist in a socialist as well as a capitalist society. This view implied a distinction between, on the one hand, the party and the government and, on the other, the society and the country. Wang's views on alienation were influenced by his reading of Western and Eastern European Marxists whom he began studying in the early 1960s when, under Zhou Yang's leadership, he had become a member of a small group of philosophers and theorists who read this Marxist literature in order to criticize revisionism. At that time, Wang and his associates had rejected "alienation" as a concept inappropriate for China and had accepted the orthodox interpretation that Marx's use of the concept applied only to the proletariat in a capitalist system. But Wang's experiences in the Cultural Revolution made him more responsive to the view of alienation held by some European Marxists. Basing their thinking on Marx's early writings, they had concluded that alienation can exist in any system that produces forces that oppress citizens.

Wang's disillusionment was all the greater because he had been such an enthusiastic supporter of the revolution, the party, and Mao. In the 1940s he had studied philosophy at Beijing University, where he had joined left-wing organizations, written wall posters, and participated in students' strikes and demonstrations that helped bring the communists to power. In an interview with a Hong Kong journal, he talked of his excitement in 1949 as "indescribable." He worked in the theory section of *People's Daily,* and in the beginning of the Cultural Revolution he participated actively, believing it to be "a democratic mass movement." He said, "I thought I was emancipated, but actually I was deeply mired in the personality cult without being conscious of it."[18] When he supported Zhou Enlai's call in 1972 to criticize "ultraleftist trends," Wang provoked the anger of the Gang of Four. Trusting in Mao's good judgment, he lodged a complaint with Mao against the Gang, but to his surprise, Mao sided with the Gang, and Zhou Enlai was either unable or failed to protect him from their wrath. He became one of the persecuted rather than one of the persecutors. Wang and his mentor, the editor Hu Jiwei, were condemned and denounced as representatives of "an evil trend" and were subjected to brutal punishment.[19]

Thus when Wang was rehabilitated in the late 1970s, he adopted the interpretation of alienation which his group had rejected in 1963 and 1964 and argued that the system of socialism that had developed in China since

---

[18]*Jing bao* (Mirror), May 1985, in *Joint Publication Research Service* (hereafter *JPRS*), no. 85-083, August 16, 1985, p. 148.
[19]Ibid., p. 149.

1949 had produced the opposite of what had been intended. Instead of enhancing human worth, it had diminished it. Specifically, it had caused alienation because of (1) the cult of the personality around Mao, (2) irrational economic policies such as the Great Leap Forward and the emphasis on heavy industry, and (3) party cadres leaders. Supposedly "It is highly necessary to prevent these servants of the people transforming themselves into masters of the people." Just to overthrow the Gang and guard against another Cultural Revolution was not enough, he claimed, to end this alienation. "At the least, we should eliminate the leaders' privileges."[20] Like his literati predecessors, he advocated an ideological change to counter this repressive, dehumanizing society that he had helped to produce. He called for a revival of humanism, whose principles, he said, could be found in Marxism. Through reinterpreting and humanizing Marxism, he and his associates sought to help it regain the legitimacy it had lost in the Mao era.

Wang continued to believe in socialism, but not the model established in China or the Soviet Union. In a speech made soon after his rehabilitation, he rejected an orthodox view of socialism imposed by a government leader or any other country: "For many years we were not used to thinking for ourselves; we used to wait for the central government and Mao to say something, and then we would do whatever Mao told us to do. Now we cannot rely on them any more," because, he explained, "there are no ready-made answers." More important, the leaders do not necessarily represent the people they lead; "not every word and deed of the leaders absolutely and undoubtedly conforms to the people's interests," because, "leaders sometimes can make mistakes." Until the present, Wang said, the Chinese people had always thought the leaders listened to their cries and responded, but since that was no longer true, he recommended that the people act for themselves—through general elections; for "we cannot expect upright officials to do all this for us. We have to rely on ourselves."[21]

Unlike most party intellectuals at the time, who regarded democracy as a means to an end, Wang regarded it as both a means and an end. Nevertheless, even though he mentioned as early as 1979 the need to restrict official power by means of genuine democracy and a legal system, his emphasis for most of the 1980s, like that of his fellow intellectuals, was on ideological rather than institutional change. It was only after repeated rebuffs and attacks in his efforts to humanize and relegitimize Marxism that his em-

[20]Wang Ruoshui speech, August 15, 1979, published in his collected essays, *Wei rendaozhuyi bianhu* (In defense of humanism) (Beijing: Sanlian shudian, 1986); quotations from p. 16.
    [21]Ibid., pp. 8, 13, 16.

phasis shifted by the late 1980s to institutional means of restraining the leadership and bringing it closer to the people. In the early years of the Deng regime (1979–83), there appeared more than six hundred articles discussing the concept of alienation. The debate evoked a wide and profound response among intellectuals.

In May 1982, Zhou Yang, who had apparently come to a similar conclusion on alienation after his own persecution in the Cultural Revolution, made a speech in which he repeated Wang's views. Since Zhou was a much higher official and had been the cultural czar during much of the Mao era, his reinterpretation of alienation caused consternation in official circles. No major party newspaper would publish his speech, until March 1983, when China again moved into a more relaxed intellectual climate. At a meeting commemorating the centennial of Marx's death, Zhou presented a version of his 1982 speech. The conservative ideologue Hu Qiaomu suggested that the speech be published in the scholarly journal *Zhexue yanjiu* (Philosophical research), which had a small circulation; but Wang Ruoshui had it published in *People's Daily* on March 16, 1983, giving it a large circulation and the imprimatur of the party.

By the spring of 1983, the conservative officials and their ideologues began organizing to stop the discussion of alienation. Hu Qiaomu's ally, Deng Liqun, then head of the Propaganda Department, led the way in a talk given on June 4, 1983, at the Central Party Academy headed by the conservative official Wang Zhen. Deng Liqun observed that a small group of people, including a few party members, under the pretext of "emancipating the mind," a phrase associated with Hu Yaobang, were opposing the socialist system and the party's leadership. For the first time, the phrase "spiritual pollution" was used to describe the effect of the concept of alienation in literature, art, and theory. And at the Second Plenum of the Twelfth Central Committee in October 1983, Deng Xiaoping similarly denounced "spiritual pollution on the ideological front," explaining that it was due to contacts with the outside world, especially in literary and art circles. He again decried the laxness in the ideological field and expressed concern that Marxism was being challenged with "erroneous" views, specifically the view that alienation exists under socialism. Restating the orthodox view, Deng declared that the concept was applicable only to a capitalist society.

Immediately after his speech, a campaign against spiritual pollution began and spread quickly, indicating the conservatives were ready to strike. Meetings were held nationwide and articles were published in all the major newspapers, interpreting spiritual pollution as spreading not only the concept of alienation but also other concepts of bourgeois liberalization, such as modernism, individualism, Freudianism, and existentialism. People who espoused these concepts were associated with those who wanted to undermine the orthodox ideology with "degenerate" Western ideas. The reform leaders, Hu Yaobang and Zhao Ziyang, assuming the campaign was directed against them and their reforms, attempted to bring it to a quick end. With the crucial help of Deng Xiaoping, who feared the campaign would undermine his economic reforms, they were able to wind it down by late 1983. Before it was concluded, however, Wang Ruoshui and Zhou Yang were made public targets. Several others, among them Bai Hua, Hu Jiwei, and Liu Binyan were privately criticized.

The spiritual pollution campaign was directed at several provocative Western ideas and styles, but its main target was the idea that alienation can exist under socialism, because this belief implicitly attacked the existing system and its political leadership. As the party theoretical journal, *Hongqi* (Red flag), explained, "Some derive pleasure from talking about alienation in socialist society . . . and attribute certain malpractices and defects in socialist society to alienation peculiar to the socialist system itself." This "reflects a loss of confidence in socialism." Such an approach, *Red Flag* asserted, "leads people to criticize, doubt, and negate socialism and lose faith in communism," even to the point of rejecting party leadership.[22]

Although this was the most widespread campaign since the end of the Mao era and many intellectuals had feared it presaged another Cultural Revolution, it was limited to a few public targets. Its scope was contained by the reform leaders. Although members of the Central Advisory Commission, of which Zhou Yang was a member, severely criticized him, Zhou in his self-criticism only criticized his "rash manner" and his greater concern with leftist trends than with bourgeois ideas from abroad. It was a superficial confession that did not condemn the concept of alienation itself. More important, despite tremendous pressure on him, Wang Ruoshui refused to make a self-criticism. Some famous intellectuals, such as the writers Ding Ling and Wang Meng, publicly denounced the concept of alienation, but what was most significant about this movement was that the majority of China's prominent intellectuals did not participate publicly. Even though the campaign lingered on until early 1984 in literary and theoretical circles, it was virtually brought to an end in a period of three or four months not only because the reform leaders limited it but also because people refused to participate.

[22]"Pollution Takes on Many Forms," *China Daily* (Beijing), October 23, 1983, p. 4.

The Second Kind of Loyalty

Controversy over the concept of alienation of the individual and society from the party and its leaders exploded again in 1985 when Liu Binyan published his work of reportage called *Di'er zhong zhongcheng* (The second kind of loyalty).[23] This piece contrasted the loyalty of the party's icon Lei Feng, who unquestioningly did everything the party and Mao ordered, with two protagonists who dissented from the party and Mao and sided with society against the leadership when their consciences led them to believe that the leadership and its policies were wrong.

Liu distinguished between loyalty to one's country, society, and even the party from loyalty to the party leadership and its shifting political line. People from all over the country came to tell Liu about their grievances in the hope that he would write about them and win them redress and justice. In the absence of a free press and an independent judiciary, Liu, through his reportage, became a sort of national ombudsman. The two protagonists of Liu's piece—Chen Shizhong, a mechanical engineer, and Ni Yuxian, a former People's Liberation Army soldier—despite great personal risk had challenged the party and Mao's policies because they believed those policies were harmful to the Chinese people. In the manner of their literati predecessors, they wrote "remonstrances" to the leaders, pointing out where the leaders' actions had diverged from their doctrine and ideals.

Returning to China in 1963 after studying mechanical engineering in the Soviet Union, Chen was upset by the leftist policies being carried out. He wrote letters to Mao and Khrushchev urging them to join together to reform their countries. Two months later, he was jailed for breaking into the Soviet Embassy in order to deliver the letter to Khrushchev. In jail he wrote another letter, this time "admonishing the party" for not realizing what a serious mistake it was making promoting blind faith in Mao. Although he had to spend eight years in prison because of his admonition, when he was released, he continued to remonstrate, this time against a case of injustice that had occurred in prison. A prison inmate had been shot and left to die of his wounds without medical help for inadvertently walking across a security boundary. Chen sought compensation for his widow and child.

Like Chen, Ni Yuxian remonstrated with the leadership when he found its policies in conflict with his principles. At the age of eighteen, he had written to Mao pointing out that, contrary to party propaganda, the

[23]*Kaituo* (Explorer), March 1985.

destructiveness associated with the Great Leap Forward policies was caused by men rather than natural disasters, and he had suggested various agricultural reforms. Because of his impudence, he was discharged from the army. He entered the Shanghai College of Marine Transport, where he put up posters during the Cultural Revolution attacking associates of the Gang of Four. He also published with his own funds ten thousand copies of selected quotations from Lenin in order to demonstrate that Mao's ideas differed from orthodox Marxist-Leninist doctrine. Even though Ni was then expelled from the college, he continued to protest against the Gang in wall posters, even proposing that Deng Xiaoping be returned to power. He was imprisoned and was sentenced to death a month after Deng was restored to power. A letter of appeal he wrote from death row to Ye Jianying (the former Long Marcher who had led the effort to overthrow the Gang in 1976) postponed his execution, and he was released with other political prisoners in 1979. He returned to the college, where he criticized the party branch secretary. Even though that leader of the revolutionary rebels in the Cultural Revolution had brought tragedy to many individuals and their families, he continued in his post. When Liu Binyan's piece was published, the college threatened to bring suit against Liu. Shortly thereafter, Ni went into exile in the United States.[24]

Both of Liu's protagonists, like their literati predecessors, affirmed their loyalty to the country and its ideology. Writing in the language and style of their predecessors they remonstrated with their leaders for carrying out policies that could lead the country to disaster. Chen's admonition declared: "For the last time I give you most sincere advice . . . I think the Central Committee . . . has committed a series of mistakes, and many of them are mistakes in principle. . . . The main one is the worship of the individual or what is called the cult of the individual." Then, addressing Mao, he said, "You do not permit others to criticize your shortcomings and mistakes. If there is some criticism of your principles that is a little sharp, you immediately turn hostile and carry out ruthless struggle and attacks." Prophetically, he warned that "in the course of time, those who will be left around you will be a group of villains holding sway . . . I am extremely worried about the destiny of the party and state. With feelings of utmost sincerity . . . I hope you will distance yourself from petty men and bring men of noble character close to yourself."[25] Chen pointed out that it would

---

[24]See the biography of Ni Yuxian in Anne F. Thurston, *A Chinese Odyssey* (New York: Scribners, 1991).

[25]*Zhongguo baokan* (China Journal), February 18, 1985, in *JPRS,* No. 86-004, January 15, 1986, p. 36.

be dangerous to have a nation of Lei Fengs. Because of Lei Feng's blind obedience "never does it occur to him to say 'no' to a wrong decision from his superior."[26] Like their literati predecessors, Chen and Ni took great personal risks to try to persuade their leaders to reform their ways and replace bad officials with officials of integrity. They believed that such changes would resolve China's problem.

In "The Second Kind of Loyalty," Liu Binyan intended to show that people with independent character, who had the courage to criticize the political leadership, were truer, more genuine patriots than the Lei Feng types who never questioned their leaders' judgment. People of individual conscience like Chen and Ni are the real patriots, whereas "yes" men merely strengthen the repressive system. Liu held that when the government and its leaders do not correct injustices and continue their abuses, then politically engaged intellectuals, such as Chen Shizhong and Ni Yuxian, must continue to speak for those who are being abused. Despite the criticism and repression of its editors, Liu's piece had a tremendous impact, especially among the middle and older generations of intellectuals and students. Even a high official like Wan Li, a reformer, said in his important speech on the soft sciences in the summer of 1986 that China needs not only the first kind of loyalty, epitomized by Lei Feng, but also the second kind, represented by Liu Binyan and his protagonists.

The Appearance of "Culture Fever"

In the 1980s, Chinese intellectuals began increasingly to view their country's political problems as stemming from elements in China's historical tradition. As a consequence, they became consciously and intensely interested in Chinese "culture." This trend, which began in 1983 and reached full maturity in 1985 and 1986, was popularly called "culture fever" (or in the literary realm, "searching-for-roots fever"). It had two basic themes: criticism of traditional Chinese culture and criticism of Chinese national character. The underlying rationale and inspiration for both was a need to discover "new" cultural concepts and ideals of character.

This kind of questioning echoed that of the May Fourth movement, notwithstanding major differences in the contexts of the two times. Another similarity with May Fourth was the hasty snatching of ideas from the West, as ways to suggest possible alternatives for China, or at least to serve as intellectual foils against which to measure perceived "deficiencies" in

[26]Ibid., p. 42.

Chinese culture. The list of Western names and -isms that found followings in Chinese intellectual circles during these years, in philosophy, literature, art, and social sciences, is mind boggling: from Nietzsche, Freud, Weber, Kafka, and Sartre to Benjamin, Marcuse, Lacan, and Derrida; from the Latin American writer García Márquez to the French "new fiction" writer Robbe-Grillet; from stream-of-consciousness, modernism, futurism, and surrealism to New Criticism, structuralism, semiotics, poststructuralism, postmodernism, and reception theory; also analytic philosophy, linguistic philosophy, abnormal psychology, information theory, systems theory, and control theory. The whole scene was as stimulating as it was superficial; a gaggle of Western thinkers from various periods, traditions, and viewpoints donned new vestments to climb up on a Chinese stage to sing again together, if not in harmony.

At the same time, a great variety of associations, discussion groups, and "salons" sprang up. Editorial groups produced some new book series, the most important of which were the *Culture: China and the World* series and the *Advancing to the Future* series.[27] Out of the general ferment, what were called "clusters of brilliance" (*jingyingqun*) emerged, the most notable of which were the Fifth Generation (of film directors, literary critics, and such); the group associated with the journal *Dushu* (Reading); and the Zhao Ziyang brain trust, centered in the Research Institute for System Reform (Tizhi Gaige Yanjiusuo). Among prominent individual intellectuals, the so-called Three Lius and One Li represented in a general way the somewhat differing attitudes of three generations: Liu Binyan, for the senior generation; Liu Zaifu, literary theoretician, and Li Zehou, aesthetician and intellectual historian, for the forties-to-fifties generation; and Liu Xiaobo, literary and cultural critic, for the younger generation. Fang Lizhi, emerging from the realm of the natural sciences with his "shining light" of universal democracy, appealed across generations, but especially among the young.

Whatever their myriad internal groupings, interests, and approaches, Chinese intellectuals during the mid-1980s were virtually unanimous in two underlying assumptions: that the basic direction of Chinese reforms was correct and that this trend "could not" (meaning "absolutely must not") be reversed. These assumptions initially implied a substantial continuing identity with the state, because the state itself was largely supporting reform. Agricultural reform was a demonstrable success; urban reform began in 1984; Communist leaders Hu Yaobang and Zhao Ziyang were backing

[27]*Wenhua: Zhongguo yu shijie congshu* and *Zou xiang weilai congshu.*

reform; in 1985, Hu Qili, politburo member in charge of ideology and culture, gave a ringing endorsement of "freedom of creation"; and the novelist Wang Meng in 1986 was elevated to minister of culture, concretely symbolizing state respect for intellectuals. Most intellectuals still took pride in such connections to *tian* (the state), despite bumps in the road such as the 1981 campaign against Bai Hua and the 1983 Spiritual Pollution Campaign. Most were willing to identify with the period's spirit of "pluralist directions" (*duoyuan quxiang,* in Li Zehou's phrase),[28] and most, in their various spheres, persisted in the faith that "reform is irreversible" (*gaige quxiang buke nizhuan*).

In January 1987, the abrupt purge of Hu Yaobang; the expulsion from the party of Liu Binyan, Fang Lizhi, and the Shanghai writer Wang Ruowang; and the ensuing campaign to "oppose bourgeois liberalization"[29] again led intellectuals to the question that had originally led them to culture fever: How much is the weight of Chinese tradition frustrating China's reform? The prominence of this question helps explain the great stir that surrounded the appearance of the six-part television series called *River Elegy* (*He shang*) in summer 1988.[30] Since "river" in the title stands for the Yellow River, regarded as a standard symbol for China, the title nearly amounts to "mourning the nation." As the logical culmination of culture fever, *River Elegy* traces virtually all China's contemporary problems to Chinese tradition, sidestepping problems of more recent origin (notably the systemic problems of Marxist states) and consciously praising China's reform leaders. (There are a dozen or so favorable references to "reformers" such as Deng Xiaoping and Zhao Ziyang.) At the same time, the series as a whole presents a great parable on the past, present, and future of China, arguing, along with many Westernized intellectuals, that China must emerge from the constrained, inward focus of "Yellow River civilization" and head out into the open "azure ocean civilization."

[28]Li Zehou, "Ershi shiji Zhongguo wenyi yi du" (A view of twentieth-century Chinese literature and art), in *Zhongguo xiandai sixiang shi lun* (Essays on modern Chinese intellectual history) (Beijing: Dongfang chubanshe, 1987), p. 255.

[29]These events were abrupt from the standpoint of intellectuals because many were still steeped in the heady atmosphere of late 1986. Student demonstrations had occurred and not been punished, and on December 30, a "poetry reading session" of unprecedented size, and attended by Minister of Culture Wang Meng and other establishment figures, had taken place at the Capital Gymnasium in Beijing. As intellectuals basked briefly in the glory of speaking in a huge forum with the apparent approval of the state, state leaders in other quarters were even then planning the major purges soon to follow.

[30]For a transcript of the narration that accompanies *He shang,* as well as some commentary on the series, see Cui Wenhua, ed., *He shang lun* (On 'River Elegy') (Beijing: Culture and Art Publishing, 1988).

Partly because of its boldness, and partly because it was shown on national television, *River Elegy* delivered a jolt to the whole of China. The leadership group, led by Vice-President Wang Zhen, saw it as wholesale Westernization and thus as a threat to the leadership's vested power and proceeded to criticize it (October 1988), ban it (November 1988), and finally root out copies to crush beneath steamrollers (summer 1989). For ordinary viewers, never much exposed to intellectual debates over such questions, *River Elegy* was like a great bolt of lightning that ignited little blazes everywhere. Popular response was generally positive, despite a common complaint that the work "forgot the ancestors" (took insufficient pride in Chinese tradition). Among intellectuals, *River Elegy* generally garnered praise for raising important questions and reaching the larger populace with them, but it was also widely criticized for historical inaccuracies and an excessively slanted interpretation of Chinese tradition.

For the question of intellectuals' identity, the *River Elegy* phenomenon had a deeper significance. Not only was it the culmination of several years of culture fever, meaning the effort to find the roots of China's problems in tradition, but also, essentially, the end of that fever. After *River Elegy*, Chinese intellectuals were less inclined to view traditional culture as the nub of China's contemporary problems. Official complaints about wholesale Westernization as well as popular complaints about forgetting the ancestors could both be explained and basically set aside, but for many intellectuals the comprehensiveness of *River Elegy*'s indictment of tradition, magnified by its sentimental, moralizing tone, made the tradition-is-everything theory seem too simple. In March 1989, Li Zehou, who had been one of the original movers in the culture fever debate, sought to dissociate himself from the radical opposition to tradition urged by *River Elegy* and to indicate a new direction for China's search for the root of its problems:

> I do not believe that the key problem, as of now, is so-called culture or "enlightenment," but reform of the political-economic system. Those people who oppose "tradition" so vehemently have covered up precisely this point. The implication of their excessive criticism of "culture" is to say that the fault lies equally with all of us. This, in turn, tends to exonerate those who really should bear responsibility. There is no way I can believe that the fault lies more with us than with them. The problem before us is how to reform our extremely irrational, feudalistic, and copiously flawed system.[31]

[31]Li Zehou, "Wusi de shishifeifei" (This and that on May Fourth), *Wenhuibao* (Wenhui daily) (Shanghai), March 28, 1989, p. 4.

From Reform *within* to Reform *of* the System: 1988 and Beyond

By the summer of 1988, Chinese intellectuals were asking questions about their country and its system that went far beyond the questions of the scar literature, alienation, and traditional culture of the Deng era. Was socialism, worldwide, simply a failed experiment? Was the 1940s faith in a peasant-led revolution fundamentally misguided? Were the anti-intellectual campaigns of the 1950s just the historical negation of the enlightenment of May Fourth?

This radical questioning, which outflanked and eventually engulfed the debate over *River Elegy,* though partly provoked by Gorbachev's dismantling of the Soviet system, had its roots in the 1987 purge of Hu Yaobang and other prominent intellectuals.[32] Until then, intellectuals and the party had accommodated their relationship through a working compromise: The party had played down its traditional demand that intellectuals regard the party and country as one, thus allowing intellectuals to identify with the country under such banners as "The Four Modernizations" and "Opening and Reform." For their part, most intellectuals had downplayed their demand for an entirely independent status that would recognize individual interests over collective ones. Thus both the party and the intellectuals had taken a step backward to allow "the country" to have top priority and to serve as a link between them. This compromise had left intellectuals in a position they had often had in Chinese tradition: standing separately, but not entirely separately; stating criticisms, but also cooperating, as in Liu Binyan's second kind of loyalty. Despite swings of the political pendulum, the compromise embodied in the three-part structure of party-country-intellectuals, with country at the center, had proved stable enough to remain workable throughout the early and mid-1980s.

It could not, however, withstand the jolt of 1987. If there were any two figures whose attitudes had best symbolized the working compromise and whose active participation most supported it, they were Hu Yaobang (for the party) and Liu Binyan (for the intellectuals). The inglorious purge of these two and others, against a background of worsening social problems of corruption, inflation, and decline of public civility, led Chinese intellectuals for the first time, in large numbers, to face squarely and directly the question of the "original face" of China's Marxist system.

[32]In addition to Liu Binyan, Fang Lizhi, and Wang Ruowang, who were named publicly, Wu Zuguang, Su Shaozhi, Zhang Xianyang, and others were also relieved of their party membership.

Such questioning was of course dangerous and could not be done in public. Even in secure confidence, there was often a nagging reluctance to state matters directly. In the fall of 1988, the brief flirtation of some Chinese intellectuals with New Authoritarianism, which called for an "enlightened dictator" such as Singapore's Lee Kuan-yew, exemplified the temptation to backslide to a safer, less confrontational stance toward the state. That New Authoritarianism, in spite of its support by Zhao Ziyang and other top leaders, seemed to have influenced only a small number of young Chinese intellectuals is evidence of the depth of the intellectuals' alienation.

The more radically alienated stance of intellectuals is well illustrated by the three petitions of February and March 1989, which came in the wake of Fang Lizhi's open letter of January 6 to Deng Xiaoping calling for a general amnesty and release of political prisoners including Wei Jingsheng. The intellectuals' petitions somewhat resembled those of the Donglin party in the late Ming period and the Civil Service Candidates' Petition and Ten-Thousand-Word Memorial of the late Qing period, through which Chinese scholars as a group, out of concern for the Chinese state, remonstrated with Chinese emperors. But the 1989 petitions also had modern overtones, most notably in their implicit assertion of the independence of modern intellectuals and their demands for human rights and civil liberties. The Ming and Qing petitions were—in terms of "dismantling heaven" (*chaitian*) and "repairing heaven" (*butian*)—clearly efforts to "repair"; the signatories were offering their loyal advice to the state, hoping to improve it—an approach not so clear-cut among the 1989 petitioners.

The petitioners were, first of all, an interesting mix of people. The first petition, which bore thirty-three names, was organized by young, non-establishment intellectuals, including the poets Bei Dao, Lao Mu, and Mang Ke, who had published primarily in unofficial journals and who, despite the considerable international fame of Bei Dao, remained, from the official viewpoint, marginal figures. But the petition was also signed by figures with weighty establishment credentials, such as senior writers Bing Xin and Wu Zuxiang, middle-aged writers Zhang Jie and Shao Yanxiang, and distinguished scholars Tang Yijie and Li Zehou. These people, however they may have spoken out in the past, were basically repair-heaven types. Yet in this petition, now, they were joined with marginal intellectuals and echoed Fang Lizhi—who had moved from a "repair" to a "dismantle" position during the 1980s—in his call for release of Wei Jingsheng, who was an out-and-out dismantler. The first petition, moreover, was followed by a second bearing forty-two names of natural scientists, many very distinguished, and nearly all of whom had never ventured into public political expression before. Then came a third petition, signed by forty-three young and middle-aged social scientists who likewise were emerging from scholarly work to venture into public protest for the first time.

Such a public and concerned challenge to the highest political authority was unprecedented in the People's Republic. It is not clear what glue held the new coalition together or what new sense of identity underlay it, but it does seem that the petitions transcended the conceptual framework of *butian* versus *chaitian*—both of which terms, after all, are defined by a person's attitude toward *tian*. The petitioners seem to have been speaking in considerable measure from a sense of their own integrity as intellectuals, which they sometimes consciously distinguished from a sense of duty either to support or oppose the state. Part of the debate over the significance of the May Fourth anniversary was over this question of a modern intellectual's independent integrity, which was perceived as a valuable kind of identity that had flourished in China briefly in the 1920s, then lost in the intervening years. A full account of what caused the events of spring 1989 is beyond our present scope, but for intellectuals, this problem of how to regain independent integrity was clearly a major factor.

Patriotism after June 4, 1989

The post–June 4 regime, established by the party octogenarians and their middle-aged assistants, Premier Li Peng and General Secretary Jiang Zemin, blamed the April and May demonstrations in part on the fact that Hu Yaobang and Zhao Ziyang had been unwilling to promote ideological indoctrination. Consequently, students as well as intellectuals no longer regarded their love of country as inseparable from the love of the party, the leadership, and the socialist system. A *Guangming ribao* commentator article on August 3 pointed out that those who have practiced bourgeois liberalization "negate the civilization and culture of several thousand years . . . and the brilliant achievements made by the Chinese nation under the leadership of the party in the last several decades." Their purpose was "radically to change the leadership of the party and the socialist system and make the Chinese nation forever lie prostrate at the feet of Western capitalist nations."[33] The fact that some of the participants in the demonstration had fled abroad and that Fang Lizhi and his wife, the physicist Li Shuxian had sought refuge in the American Embassy before going abroad was cited

---

[33]*Guangming ribao* (Guangming daily), August 3, 1989, p. 1, in *FBIS,* August 18, 1989, pp. 20, 21.

as proof that the participants and "manipulators" of the demonstration were unpatriotic.

In contrast to these "traitors," *Qiushi* (Seeking truth—the replacement for *Red Flag* as the party's theoretical journal), pointed out "that the people love the party and support the socialist system." Even though a small group of "turmoil creators" claimed that their actions had been based on their love of country, *Qiushi* declared, their definition of patriotism was wrong; for patriotism means "one must uphold and safeguard the Four Cardinal Principles, inscribed in the constitution, and especially the party leaders and the socialist system, because this is the foundation for the establishment of the state." Invoking the phrase Sun Yat-sen had used to justify the need for a period of political tutelage before the establishment of democracy, *Qiushi* continued: "Without the party as the leadership core, China would disintegrate and fall apart like a sheet of sand."[34]

The regime blamed one of the causes of the turmoil on the distinction the intellectuals had made between the party and the people. In addition to Liu Binyan, the concept of alienation, and *River Elegy,* the regime particularly blamed journalists as represented by Hu Jiwei, who since the late 1970s had asserted that when there was a conflict between the demands of the party and the demands of the people, one must side with the people. This view, the party insisted, separated the party from the people and set the two against each other; moreover, "those calling for freedom of the press want to oppose the central authorities and their important policy decisions" and "instigate the overthrow of the legitimate government." In calling for newspapers to supervise the party on behalf of the people, journalists were claiming that "the party cannot represent the people and only the newspapers can." Such people, particularly Hu Jiwei, "can only create anarchy." Nevertheless, the regime assured the people, "The way the counterrevolutionary rebellion was quelled had made people realize that the real representatives of the people are the Central Committee and the proletarian revolutionaries of the older generation, represented by Deng Xiaoping."[35]

A *People's Daily* article further explained that "apart from the interests of the people, the party has no other special interests of its own. In this sense, the party spirit is essentially identical with the people's spirit." Moreover, "the party spirit of the Communists refers to putting interests of the party above everything else."[36] But not only had the 1989 demonstrations re-

[34]Zhou Zuochun, "How should we view the nature of the disturbances?" (in Chinese), *Qiushi,* July 16, 1989, pp. 16–24, in *FBIS,* August 14, 1989, pp. 39, 41.

[35]*Xinhua* (New China), August 5, 1989, in *FBIS,* August 7, 1989, pp. 20, 21.

[36]*Renmin ribao* (People's daily), October 27, 1989, p. 6.

vealed that the party's interests did not represent the people's; more important, the crackdown had revealed that the party put its interests—specifically, the interests of the octogenarians—above the interests of society.

Some of the intellectuals who had signed the petitions in early 1989 also participated in the spring demonstrations. This was the first time in the People's Republic that elite intellectuals had joined a demonstration. More significant, for the first time they had come to see themselves as in the opposition and questioned whether their previous efforts to persuade the regime to reform had, in fact, been counterproductive. Although most of them had not agreed with Fang Lizhi's advice to students in the autumn 1986 to go out and get their own rights because the government would not give them, in the aftermath of the June 4 crackdown, these same intellectuals moved closer to Fang's position. They finally concluded that they could no longer rely on the good intentions of a political leadership that did not represent the people. Few of them any longer believed that significant reform was possible under the existing political system and political leadership.

This general view had been advocated for some years by a literary critic and radical political thinker, Liu Xiaobo, at Beijing Normal University. He had also produced a penetrating critique of his fellow intellectuals, which intellectuals themselves were only coming around to after the crackdown. In an article in the Hong Kong journal *Zhengming* (Contending), he charged that the reason China continued to have a despotic government was because China's intellectuals had acted like their traditional predecessors: "In both modern and ancient times, there were people who were not afraid of brutal suppression, but they all wanted to oppose only the muddle-headed rulers and corrupt officials and not the system of despotism." He specifically cited Liu Binyan as an example of an intellectual who could not, for all his courageous expression, fundamentally break with the existing system: "Even Liu Binyan . . . an unbending personality and twice expelled from the party, still expresses loyalty to socialism and Marxism-Leninism." Liu Xiaobo explained that Liu Binyan and others chose this approach not only because they were confronted with a brutal, despotic regime and had no other choice but also because "this loyalty was regarded as one of the highest virtues in ancient China, and still is in modern China." Thus some who have been rehabilitated and allowed to reenter the party "are very proud, as if they have become national heroes, and are extremely grateful to their benefactors. . . . Yet, the fact that despots alone can rehabilitate those persecuted under a despotic system is itself despotic. Why can't the persecuted rise in rebellion on their own, instead of waiting for rehabilitation by the despots who almost destroyed them in the first place? Why can't intellectuals rehabilitate themselves by other independent means? [Actually,] rehabilitation would not change the nature of the despotic system." With utter disdain, Liu Xiaobo declared, "Not only are Chinese intellectuals mistreated politically, but they are torturing themselves with their 'loyalty.'"[37] Even though persecuted and humiliated in the Anti-Rightist Campaign and the Cultural Revolution, intellectuals still "spoke bluntly out of loyalty" and remain as faithful as ever.[38]

Liu Xiaobo rejected Liu Binyan's concept of the second kind of loyalty by arguing that it is just this kind of loyalty that makes possible the continuation of the prevailing oppressive system. It "only strengthens the unequal master-slave relationship," when what is necessary is "to abolish this despotic system, not advise it at the risk of one's own life"; intellectuals should be loyal and social-minded but "not be loyal to political power at any level."[39] Rather, Liu Xiaobo said, they should be loyal to their own beliefs, the law, academic freedom, and freedom of speech and religion. Foremost, they should be loyal to each one's own rights, which means participation in government and political affairs. A society is democratic when loyalty is not to the ruler or the head of the state but to the law, whereas "in China power is more important than national interests." Liu Binyan and the intellectuals Liu Xiaobo was attacking had made this same argument, but whereas they had tried reform from within, he advocated action from without: "In the autocratic society where the law of the party is higher than the law of the state and where the party members are higher than citizens, the intellectual's place is not to offer advice loyally to those in power at the risk of their lives, but to resist them." To his fellow intellectuals persecuted for their efforts to reform the system from within, he said, "You should not complain at all for being persecuted. You asked for it."[40] Liu lived by his beliefs. He returned from a visit to the United States in the spring of 1989 to participate in the Tiananmen demonstrations and was arrested in the crackdown.

Since June 4, many intellectuals who had been loyal to the system despite decades of repression have finally moved closer to Liu Xiaobo's and Fang Lizhi's position. Especially after seeing the subsequent demonstrations in Eastern Europe, they began to ask themselves if instead of begging the regime to reform itself and trying to work within the established political

[37]Liu Xiaobo, "Contemporary Chinese Intellectuals and Politics," pt. 2, *Zhengming,* April 1989, pp. 78–81, *JPRS,* No. 89-088, p. 11.
[38]Ibid., p. 12.
[39]Ibid.
[40]Ibid., p. 13.

order, they might have been more loyal to their countrymen by going into the opposition. For the first time, a segment of China's intellectuals, like their Soviet and East European counterparts, are beginning to identify with the opposition and not the prevailing regime and system. Although these views have been expressed by only a small number of intellectuals who have escaped abroad, in the context of Chinese history, this line of thinking, if it continues and spreads, would be a radical, even revolutionary, change in the intellectuals' view of their relationship with the state. Chinese intellectuals might no longer conceive of themselves as intermediaries between the government and the people and move completely over to the side of the people and act in opposition to the government. Their loyalty to the people would no longer necessarily imply loyalty to the government, its leadership, and the prevailing political system. This shift, if it develops, will have been stimulated by outside ideas and events but be a consequence primarily of the intellectuals' profound disillusionment with a regime and a system they had once wholeheartedly supported.

What are the consequences for Chinese intellectuals' conceptions of the identity of their state and their own relationship to it? Although it is still too early to answer this question, we can observe that over the decade of the 1980s, Chinese intellectuals came increasingly to draw distinctions among "party," "state," and "nation" (or "people") instead of regarding all three as aspects of the same thing. Under the emotional need to preserve patriotism while rejecting a government, China's identity had split into at least two or three. This disaggregation of the components of national identity has forced the question of which component is primary, and hence the most deserving object of the intellectual's loyalty. Chinese intellectuals have, moreover, come increasingly to challenge the Communist party's long-standing claim not only to be the exclusive representative of "state" and "nation" but also to be the "mother" on whom all citizens depended for everything they have had. Fang Lizhi's stated opinion that the party-state should be based on the support of the people, not the other way around, has found a considerable following, especially among the young.

Yet the traditional concept of a political center (or "heavenly authority")—which is implicitly "higher" than the people, on which the people are dependent, and to which it is the highest calling of the scholar to offer advice and service—remains deeply embedded in China's political culture. If, as seems likely, the 1980s eventually emerge as a turning point in the thinking of Chinese intellectuals about the nature of the state and their proper relation to it, the contribution will be more in raising questions than in solving them.

中
國 7

China Coast Identities:
Regional, National, and Global

Lynn White and Li Cheng

Identity is a notion useful to politics only if it remains flexible. The governing elites of nation-states levy taxes and armies, and they have substantial reasons to promote popular identification with groups they can control. Loyal identity is a resource. It inspires group action; so governments tend to try for as full a monopoly of it as they can arrange. China is no different from other modern states in this respect. Yet that country's traditions provide many options in how people think of themselves—and national elites are not the only entrepreneurs in this field.

Mencius taught that each person could harmonize identifications with family, friends, ministers, and a sovereign—presuming all knew how to perform their roles properly.[1] This Confucian approach does not exhaust traditional Chinese views of identity, but Mencius offers a framework that long enjoyed official sponsorship. In recent times, as foreign incursions rose, modern Chinese writers proposed "to establish Confucianism as the national religion . . . to protect the national essence."[2] To mobilize China's

The authors thank Professors Robert A. Scalapino, Samuel Kim, and Lowell Dittmer for their helpful comments, and Princeton's Center of International Studies for sponsoring the conference that led to this volume.

[1]A brief translation of Mencius's scheme is in Franz Schurmann and Orville Schell, eds., *Imperial China* (New York: Random House, 1967), p. 17; or William Theodore de Bary, ed., *Sources of Chinese Tradition*, vol. 1 (New York: Columbia University Press, 1960), p. 92.

[2]Quoted in Joseph R. Levenson, *Confucian China and Its Modern Fate: The Problem of Monarchical Decay*, vol. 2 (Berkeley and Los Angeles: University of California Press, 1964), p. 17, from a 1917 writing of Wang Xiejia.

people for development, bureaucrats increasingly sponsored rigid frame-works of identification that required a loyalty to the nation-state separate from that to other kinds of collectives, such as families. The orthodox terms of political debate among China's leaders were affected by this change. Military incursions by Japanese and other foreigners during the twentieth century nationalized the identities of local elites in many parts of China.[3] Policies of the early 1950s can be linked to the success of the new govern-ment in changing the range of groups with which Chinese people tended to identify.[4]

Coastal Chinese have multiple identities, which evolved because each of their self-concepts has been useful in specific events, both historical and current. There is no one "China coast identity" from which to make deductions about behavior. We can only point to the options or preferences groups have deployed, and we can exemplify a method for approaching the subject by looking at three cathartic events that have given rise to new ideas about identity in Guangdong, Taiwan, and Hong Kong.

An Operational Definition of Identity

Identification is a process. It occurs on many levels and has been used conceptually in several kinds of discourse, each of which has left an imprint on the ways it can be conceived. These levels need to be evaluated before we can approach the subject of identity in particular places, as along the China coast. The dimensions of the concept reflect its several past "identity crises."

Individual or Collective?

It has become almost mandatory when writing about identity to cite Erik Erikson. China coast authors sometimes begin their cogitations about their own identities by referring to him.[5] This psychologist studied personality

[3] See Chalmers A. Johnson, *Peasant Nationalism and Communist Power* (Stanford: Stanford University Press, 1962). Some comparisons with a slower, less foreign-induced change may be seen in Eugen Weber, *Peasants into Frenchmen* (Stanford: Stanford University Press, 1976).

[4] An effort to show this link among urban Chinese is Lynn White, "Changing Concepts of Corruption in Communist China: Early 1950s vs. Early 1980s," in Yu-ming Shaw, ed., *Changes and Continuities in Chinese Communism* (Boulder, Colo.: Westview, 1988), pp. 316–53.

[5] Yin Zhangyi, "Taiwan de rentong weiji ji qi fazhan shi" (Taiwan's identity crisis and the history of its development), in *Jindai Taiwan de shehui fazhan yu minzu yishi* (Social develop-ment and national consciousness in contemporary Taiwan) (Hong Kong: Hong Kong Chi-nese University Extramural Department, 1987), p. 263.

development, used identity as a technical term, and strove to diagnose individuals on the basis of individual growth. He did not aim to explain any sameness in groups.[6] He described personality as if it were like an onion: something that grows, layer on layer. He noticed that each human being goes through a specifiable series of problems in life, and the experiences of trying to solve these in succession leave imprints on personality.[7] Since he wrote, the notion of identity has been put to so many social purposes, it sometimes seems to be a word in search of a definition.[8] Other usages nonetheless involve individual group members' memories of their experiences, at least in a collective. Charles Westin writes that "identity is seen as a process founded in consciousness and time."[9]

There has also been some air of mystery about the word—it means something deep, "primordial," best fathomed by Austrian doctors. This mystique has not made for much clear analysis, though it rightly suggests identity is important. Particular identities, either personal or collective, may be impossible to describe separate from the experiences that shaped them. For any group or person, such a history need not be homogeneous; it has stages, which leave different (often inconsistent) memories. This is the strongest logical similarity between the ways identities have been attributed to groups and to individuals. Erikson calls one of the eight "ages of man," which occurs during adolescence, "identity vs. role confusion." But his theory, right or wrong, explains individuals more than it gives reasons for social facts.[10]

Many psychological approaches to personality development require

[6]Identity as a "distinctive sameness" is discussed in the many essays in Anita Jacobson-Widding, ed., *Identity: Personal and Socio-Cultural* (Stockholm: Almqvist och Wiksell, 1983), e.g., p. 13.

[7]Erikson distinguishes eight such passages that each individual makes: communicating (at first with the mother), controlling basic bodily functions, muscle skills such as walking, learning in school, choosing an "identity" in social and occupational roles, marrying, parenting, and facing death. See his *Childhood and Society,* 2d ed. (New York: Norton, 1963), chap. 7.

[8]The same comment is made of another term in Harry Eckstein, "The Idea of Political Development: From Dignity to Efficiency," in Ikuô Kabashima and Lynn White, eds., *Political System and Change* (Princeton: Princeton University Press, 1985), pp. 311–46.

[9]Charles Westin, "Self-Reference, Consciousness, and Time," in Jacobson-Widding, *Identity,* p. 108.

[10]The Erikson psychobiography of Martin Luther argues that the German reformer's creativity arose from an unusually vivid personal response to the main crisis everyone confronts in adolescence. When Luther "found himself" in this psychological process, he also found styles that had many echoes in Renaissance German society (but this last was a social not personal matter). See *Young Man Luther: A Study in Psychoanalysis and History* (New York: Norton, 1958). Erikson is not among the psychologists who suggest that personality development stops at a young age. On one man's response to death in terms of immortal things, see Erikson, *Gandhi's Truth: On the Origins of Militant Nonviolence* (New York: Norton, 1969).

heroic assumptions, and their utility for understanding groups remains moot.[11] Nonetheless, as Andrew Weigert and his colleagues point out, sociologists "knew of Erikson's work and quickly adopted his term. . . . Identity was 'in the air' by the 1960s and on everyone's tongue by the 1970s." This was an era when new nation-states were being challenged or threatened by "primordial" identities. Talcott Parsons, the great guru of functionalist sociology, frankly admitted, "Identity has become a fashionable term." He linked an interest in this concept to a new scientific approach to old issues of free will and human dignity. He thought a growth of wisdom about identity was possible—indeed, vital to the completeness of a "codified knowledge that can lead to changes in the human condition."[12] Parsons's whole sociology was strung along two dimensions: the need to deal with both factual situations and human norms, and the need to be serious about both collectives and individuals.[13] To explore the personal pole of this second dimension, he spent much effort working with psychologists. It would be sanguine to say his vision of a unified social science has yet found any consensus on methods to show why the contributions of personalities, as such, sometimes flourish in social contexts but at other times are merely odd there.

Chinese analysts, such as Wang Bin, have also theorized that identity has two aspects: individual (*ziwo*) and common (*tongyi*).[14] The best means to link these two remains obscure. Collectivizing individual identity has run

[11]This is not the place to try a full evaluation of Erikson, of psychobiographers' use of historical data, or of their method's relevance to social questions. The middle "ages of man," including "identity vs. role confusion," could surely be subjected, for instance, to contemporary feminist critiques; and the number of stages may be somewhat arbitrary. Also, this Eriksonian framework may well say as much about the settings that produced it as about the objects to which it has been applied. In discussing Erikson we have chosen to emphasize the naturalness of passage through life stages and to downplay many Freudian premises that are (at the least) acquired tastes. A relatively robust aspect of the theory is, however, the one we stress here: that personality is a diverse thing, an accumulation from different, often inconsistent, layers of experience in time.

[12]Andrew J. Weigert, J. Smith Teitge, and Dennis W. Teitge, *Society and Identity: Toward a Sociological Psychology* (Cambridge: Cambridge University Press, 1986), p. 1. Talcott Parsons, "The Position of Identity in the General Theory of Action," in Chad Gordon and Kenneth J. Gergen, eds., *The Self in Social Interaction* (New York: Wiley, 1968), pp. 11, 22.

[13]Parsons encouraged exploration of the frontier between "the social system" and psychological/individual variables, and he published a collection of essays entitled *Social Structure and Personality* (New York: Free Press, 1964). For more on the generation of his four main "subsystems" by the two dimensions mentioned above, see Lynn White, *Policies of Chaos: The Organizational Causes of Violence in China's Cultural Revolution* (Princeton: Princeton University Press, 1989), p. 44, and "Shanghai's Polity in Cultural Revolution," in John W. Lewis, ed., *The City in Communist China* (Stanford: Stanford University Press, 1971), p. 363.

[14]*Guangzhou yanjiu* (Canton research) (hereafter *GZYJ*) 6 (1988): 35.

into snags. The notion that layers of experience accumulate over time has survived well, but there has been scant progress in showing the links between personal and group identities.

Primordial, Contextual, Political, or Multiple?

Many treatments of layers of experience stress modernization. Nonstate identities are sometimes deemed detrimental to progress. The Committee on Comparative Politics of the Social Science Research Council listed "six crises that may be met in different sequences but all of which must be successfully dealt with for a society to become a modern nation-state." The "first and most fundamental," called the "identity crisis," arises because citizens "must feel as individuals that their personal identities are in part defined by their identification with their territorially delimited country. . . . The identity crisis also involves the resolution of the problem of traditional heritage and modern practices, the dilemma of parochial sentiments and cosmopolitan practices. . . . As long as people feel pulled between two worlds and without roots in any society, they cannot have the firm sense of identity necessary for building a stable, modern nation-state."[15] This approach to identity treats it as a factor within individuals for the construction of modern government.

Such a concept can organize some data, but it also gives rise to questions about the ultimate value of modern states. As Robert Bellah writes, making the short jump from the governmentalist idea of identity to that of "nation," "The problem with the word 'nation' is that it contains a profound ambiguity. On the one hand, it designates a people with a shared history and a shared identity. On the other hand, it designates a modern nation-state. In the former sense, cultural memory, continuity, and integrity is of the essence. In the latter sense, the economic, political, and military power of the nation-state is of the essence. The 'nation' in the latter sense has often subordinated, manipulated, and exploited the 'nation' in the former sense."[16] Modernizers' approaches to identity retain the idea that it accumulates by strata, in response to problems, while discarding the psychologists' suggestion that the time order for facing such problems is regular in each case.

[15]Lucian W. Pye, *Aspects of Political Development* (Boston: Little, Brown, 1966), p. 63. The other crises are of legitimacy, penetration, participation, integration, and distribution.

[16]Robert N. Bellah, "Cultural Identity and Asian Modernization," in Institute for Japanese Culture and Classics, *Cultural Identity and Modernization in Asian Countries: Proceedings of the Kokugakuin University Centennial Symposium* (Tokyo: Kokugakuin University, 1983), p. 17.

Chinese publications of the 1980s similarly moot a specifically modern "identity crisis" (*rentong weiji*), and they often reach conclusions like Bellah's. Guangzhou analyst Wang Bin writes that faults in official policy or modern culture can cause people to sacrifice their individual identities too mindlessly, for the sake of the collective, as if only the group exists. This is opposite to the mid-1960s SSRC view of the problem. Jin Yaoji, a Taiwanese author writing in Hong Kong, treats "world culture" (*shijie wenhua*) as an ideal for China. But Wang Bin disagrees, hoping for a modern Chinese solution to the old difficulty of reconciling identifications with different sizes of collectivity.[17]

Anthropologists' work on ethnicity has also influenced both Chinese and Western discussions of identity. Two decades ago, Clifford Geertz stressed the power of "primordial" ethnic sentiments to ruin "new" states: "Civil discontent finds its natural outlet in the seizing, legally or illegally, of the state apparatus. Primordial discontent strives more deeply and is satisfied less easily [than other policy disputes]. If severe enough, it wants not just Sukarno's or Nehru's or Moulay Hasan's head, it wants Indonesia's or India's or Morocco's." Cynthia Enloe agreed with this assessment but was happier about it: "Nation-states are not the sole realities. Other political entities are capable of choice and innovation. . . . It is one thing to acknowledge the existence of national polities; it is quite another to assume that they are the logical goal of all political development."[18]

Crawford Young suggests that identity is less primordial than contextual. Many traits (for example, language, kinship, citizenship, race, religion, caste, region) are possible bases for ethnic divisions, but each individual shares many of these traits simultaneously.[19] People can often choose to stress or ignore diverse aspects of their own identities, depending on the situation and the behavior of others. Young proclaims "that processes of integration and disintegration and crystallization of identity are dynamic; that the definition and boundaries of cultural groups are fluid rather than static; that the secular trend is toward broader patterns of incorporation, both at the national and subnational level." He considers "the political

[17]Wang Bin in *GZYJ* 6 (1988): 35–36.
[18]Clifford Geertz, *The Interpretation of Cultures* (New York: Basic Books, 1973), p. 261; Cynthia Enloe, *Ethnic Conflict and Political Development* (Boston: Little, Brown, 1973), p. 11.
[19]Geertz, in his famous "Notes on the Balinese Cockfight" (*Interpretation of Cultures,* esp. p. 452), suggests that another essay could be written about the Brahmana ordination ceremony, which is a quieter and very different symbol—but just as "like Bali," because the people there enjoy various inconsistent cultural options. This Geertz meshes better with recent approaches to cultural pluralism than did the Geertz who stressed "primordial sentiments."

arena an independent variable." "Cultural entrepreneurs," including states and their elites, try to organize groups in conflict so as to benefit themselves. Similarly, Zhou Gucheng of Fudan University has written that culture "isn't a single piece of iron" but comes in many forms. Tan Qirang, from the same institution, writes about the need to deal with Chinese culture in terms of different periods and regions. He thinks most writers about China are indiscriminate, ignoring variation among the country's eras and places. No consistent, unchanging idea of culture comprehends China's long history or whole geography.[20]

Supranational or world identities, just like nationalist or ethnic ones, can be useful options for cultural entrepreneurs. These leaders are often easier to distinguish by their interest in using identity than by the specific content of their identification. In the Sudan, for example, Young says that "the aspirant young Fur can achieve identity as an Arab. . . . It is the very Fur who is most readily incorporated [as Arab] who, if frustrated, might be most disposed to organize the cultural mobilization of the [Fur] ethnic group."[21] Friedrich Meineke, in *Cosmopolitanism and the National State* (1907) points out that "cosmopolitanism did not merely sink to the ground, pale and exhausted; and the new national idea did not then spring up in its place, unimpeded and victorious. Cosmopolitanism and nationalism stood side by side in a close, living relationship for a long time." As the Germanist Harold James has recently put it, "There are always, in any society, not one but several storytellers in the invention of nationality, who usually cannot agree even about the general structure of the narrative."[22]

Modernization can exacerbate conflicts between clearly identified groups.[23] People have died in this process; so it may not be enough simply to report that identities can have primordial, contextual, political-entrepreneurial, and multiple aspects. Some political scientists, including Donald Horowitz, have explored certain kinds of modernization, such as

[20]Crawford Young, *The Politics of Cultural Pluralism* (Madison: University of Wisconsin Press, 1976), p. 11; Zhou Gucheng in *Xinhua wenzhai* (New China digest) 9 (1986): 186; Tan Qirang in *Fudan xuebao: Shehui kexue ban* (Fudan journal: Social science ed.) 2 (1986): 4–13.

[21]Young, *Politics of Cultural Pluralism,* p. 109. The classic revisionist functional ethnography on choice of identities is Edmund Leach, *The Political Systems of Highland Burma* (Boston: Beacon, 1965), describing two ethnicities—involving different religions, modes of raising food, and so forth—either of which individuals can choose.

[22]Harold James, *A German Identity, 1770–1990* (New York: Routledge Books, 1989), p. 12 (Meineke quotation), 8.

[23]See Robert Melson and Howard Wolpe, "Modernization and the Politics of Communalism: A Theoretical Perspective," *American Political Science Review* 64 (December 1970): 1112–30.

the rise of more representative state institutions, which can reduce ethnic strife. After offering hundreds of detailed case histories on modern communal conflicts around the world, Horowitz holds that "there is no case to be made for the futility of democracy or the inevitability of uncontrolled conflict. Even in the most severely divided society, ties of blood do not lead ineluctably to rivers of blood."[24] Cosmopolitan, nationally ambiguous, and democratic identity often coexists with more particular patriotic commitments. National leaders of both the narrow and universalist kinds have often come from peripheries: Napoleon was from Corsica, Hitler from Austria, Stalin from Georgia, Nehru from Kashmir, and Sun Yat-sen from an overseas Chinese community many of whose leaders had departed Guangdong.

As all these dimensions of the subject suggest, it would be dubious to seek a single China coast identity that could be taken as a consistent premise for making valid deductions. Identity offers people choices. Otherwise, it becomes too uninteresting and inflexible to adapt in many contexts. Official states and anti-official movements often *use* such options for their own ends. The political, instrumental value of identities is basic in explaining their slow rise or fall. Each person's or group's multiple identifications are like concrete resources—for them, and for others who wish to influence them. The study of identity in peripheral regions can make a big contribution to the topic as a whole, because these zones where different identities interface bring out both the instrumental and the primordial sides of identity.

Wang Gungwu presents a nuanced view of "multiple identities" among Chinese in Southeast Asia, who are shaped by their kinship, politics, culture, and even economic class. These "are not situational identities, or alternative identities which one can switch around or switch on and off, [but they show] the simultaneous presence of many kinds of identities, e.g., ethnic, national (local), cultural and class identities."[25] These traits are primordial because they cannot quickly be changed, situational because

[24]Donald Horowitz, *Ethnic Groups in Conflict* (Berkeley and Los Angeles: University of California Press, 1985), p. 684.

[25]Wang Gungwu, "The Study of Chinese Identities in Southeast Asia," in Jennifer Cushman and Wang Gungwu, eds., *The Changing Identities of Chinese in Southeast Asia* (Hong Kong: Hong Kong University Press, 1988), p. 17. Wang Gungwu discusses Beijing's and others' policies toward Chinese outside the People's Republic in "External China as a New Policy Area," *Pacific Affairs* 58 (Spring 1985): 28–43. The allowance, available in Wang's scheme, that class or occupation can be a source of identity (as much as birth, culture, or national citizenship can) permits a link to much research that has been done on the "ethnicity of the poor" in countries such as the United States.

individuals can sometimes choose to stress one or another, political because such choices have purposes, *and* multiple because they coexist. The point is not just that all these approaches are valid; it is that their variety reflects their uses.

Identity cannot, in this operational definition, ever be final for any person or group. It is not changeable completely at will, but it is also no fixed or consistent set of characteristics. It is based on ethnic, state, cultural, and socioeconomic traits that emerge over time as results of events. An observer mainly sees the effects of identity. (The notion of "mass" in physics may be like this, though natural science has an easier explanatory task because its concepts can be linked to contexts more predictably.) Identity is not completely determinable; it is a moving and multiplex target. Specific data may suggest that identities are changing in response to new conditions, but it is in practice impossible to know *all* the conditions that might be relevant to such change.

Identity's contextual and multiple aspects alone fail to explain why people make particular choices in large groups, although the interests of political entrepreneurs often suggest a great deal about that. Identity, in any short run, is a resource that elites try to use in dialectical arguments with each other.[26] A treatment of identity should therefore show:

1. The basic layers of historical experience that have created "primordial" or "subethnic" groups there,
2. The more recent "situational" layers of historical experience that have given these groups further preferences of identification, and
3. The way they are led actually to choose or alter their options, in instrumental attempts to meet or redefine their current needs.

Complete coverage of these strata of identity is too much for a chapter; we can only begin to illustrate the approach especially for the most variable component, the third one above. The first must be largely omitted here, not because it is unimportant but because the reader may already have some familiarity with relevant historical facts. A change in identity can be more reliably detailed than its whole development; but with this understanding, it is still possible to treat the subject as an historical accretion.

It is easy to justify treating China's south coast in such a study. Identity often emerges by contrasts with alternative identities, and this coast has had contact with outsiders for centuries. The material here comes from a Peo-

---

[26]See Charles F. Keyes, "Introduction: The Dialectics of Ethnic Change," in Keyes, ed., *Ethnic Change* (Seattle: University of Washington Press, 1981).

ple's Republic of China (PRC) province, from an island under a separate Chinese regime, and from a city-state scheduled to become a "special autonomous region" (SAR). *The focus is on identity in each area after a specific event—respectively, the rise of extensive commodity markets in 1978, the U.S. derecognition of Taiwan in 1979 and 1980, and the Tiananmen events in spring and summer of 1989.* Other regions of China, north of these, could be analyzed by the same method.[27] Our purpose is to exhibit changes in the three regions, which are important in their own right, and to study changes of "identity" by a procedure that takes account of the dimensions along which that concept has evolved in past treatments of it.

Many kinds of data are relevant in such research. In each of the three cases, statements are available from China coast writers about changes in their own groups' identities. The magazine literature on local identity has proliferated more than Western scholars have noted, and this interest is itself an important datum. Attitude surveys, despite the severe methodological problems they entail, can also be useful in gathering information about reactions in these places to the identity-altering events we examine. Finally, behavioral information suggesting identity change can also be used, despite the methodological difficulties of attributing observed acts to apparent attitudes.

A Province, a Separated Island, and a Proto-SAR

Guangdong and the Commodity Economy after 1978

Regional identity.   In Guangdong, local identity has been strong for many centuries. Geographic and linguistic reasons are clear; but Cantonese

---

[27]The north, even in its port cities, has had less recent contact with outsiders and more with the PRC government than have the areas we chose. Special research opportunities are worth mentioning for Wenzhou, in south Zhejiang, where isolated geography, bad communications, and proximity to Taiwan made quasi-liberal identities safe by the mid-1980s. See Wang Wence, ed., *Wenzhou qiye dachuan, 1986* (Compendium of Wenzhou enterprises, 1986) (Wenzhou: Wenzhou shi qiye guanli xiehui and Wenzhou shi gongye pucha bangong shi, 1986); Pan Shangeng, ed., *Wenzhou shiyan qu* (The Wenzhou experimental zone) (Beijing: Nengyuan chubanshe, 1988); Lin Bai et al., eds., *Wenzhou moshi de lilun tansuo* (Theoretical exploration of the Wenzhou model) (Nanning: Guangxi renmin chubanshe, 1987); Yuan Enzhen et al., *Wenzhou moshi yu fuyu zhi lu* (The Wenzhou model and the road to affluence) (Shanghai: Shanghai shehui kexue yuan chubanshe, 1987); and more. But there is no way here to do justice to Wenzhou or many other distinctive China coast identities further north. We would not so briefly try to tackle the most complex and largest case, which is Shanghai.

separatism has also been justified ideologically, by Mencius's old concept of political space centering on the emperor.[28] The exemplary imperial influence was thought to decrease with distance from the throne. The traditional ecumene's borders could be bands, not lines.[29] Buffer areas, notably Guangdong, allowed the state to absorb ideas from across the ocean while keeping invaders far from the capital. Guangdong has long served the Chinese state as a place for dealing safely with problems of interface.

This old role leads to some official recognition of a Cantonese identity. It encourages uniqueness in coastal areas. Recent PRC authors note that modern Chinese identity can be divided in several ways: between Han and minority areas, between north and south, and (most important here) between coast and inland. Within the coastal areas, authors list differences between "Guangdong-Fujian culture," more local "special zone culture" (in Shenzhen, Zhuhai, and Xiamen), "Jiangsu-Zhejiang culture," more local "Shanghai culture," "Shandong culture," "Beijing-Tianjin culture," "Taiwan culture," and "Hong Kong–Macau culture."[30] This can all be seen as hairsplitting, until politics makes the differences meaningful. Other PRC authors say the distinction of coastal cultures is economic. They put the current special trade zones in a first "layer," fourteen coastal cities and Hainan in a second, rich parts of coastal deltas in a third, then adjacent areas further inland.

Such geographic taxonomies reflect both current political tensions and old stereotypes of regions.[31] Cantonese competition with northern areas remains explicit in recent PRC publications. One historian said that Guangzhou rather than Shanghai should become the "New York of China," because of the far-south city's prowess in commerce. As a Cantonese author put it, "Guangzhou should be the cradle of China's new culture," defining this culture as a superstructure appropriate for the development of a "commodity economy."[32] The Cantonese region has been seen as having a good "competitive consciousness," creativity, and a free exchange of information.

---

[28]See n. 1.

[29]Borders-as-lines, rather than bands, is in some tension with moralistic legitimacies for state power; but linear borders have become formalized, especially by the Treaty of Westphalia. For related ideas, see Ishwer C. Ojha, *Chinese Foreign Policy in an Age of Transition: The Diplomacy of Cultural Despair* (Boston: Beacon, 1971), pp. 146ff.

[30]"Guangdong-Fujian culture" is *Lingnan wenhua;* "Shandong culture," *Qilu wenhua;* and "Beijing-Tianjin culture," *Jingjin wenhua.* See Wang Shida and Tao Yajing, *Shehui kexue* (Social science) 8 (1987): 30–34.

[31]For more, see Wolfram Eberhard, "Chinese Regional Stereotypes," *Asian Survey* 5 (December 1965): 596–608.

[32]Wang Dahua in *GZYJ* 8 (1988): 9; Li Jiangtao in ibid., pp. 4–8.

National policies to spur the commodity economy after 1977 affected Guangdong far more than most places. During the next ten years, for example, Shanghai's gross domestic product at nominal prices almost exactly doubled—but Guangzhou's rose four times.[33] From 1979 to 1986, the number of Guangzhou private firms soared by nearly 150 times.[34] Such changes outside the largest city of Guangdong were even faster, but regional capitals like Guangzhou receive emphasis in intellectuals' writings about cultural identity. Wang Bin, a teacher at the city's Zhongshan University, wrote of a "cultural break" (*wenhua duanlie*) that China suffered during the nineteenth and twentieth centuries. He was unsure where the nation's new cultural identity would come from (perhaps from tradition or the West, he speculated); but the place *to* which it would come was likely to be a coastal capital.[35]

Guangzhou was glorified by historian Ye Chunsheng because for many centuries it had been far from China's northern centers of "feudal influence."[36] Cultural change in the north was described by some Guangdong authors as too effete, too controlled by intellectuals. According to one Cantonese author, although his province lacked as much "culture fad" (*wenhua re*) as Beijing or Shanghai, it nonetheless enjoyed more progress in really basic values during the reform era. Just as the movement to write colloquial Chinese since 1919 had affected China's identity as a whole, he expected a new wave of "mass culture" (*dazhong wenhua*) to liberate the country further. He criticized northern intellectuals for fostering a "crisis culture" (*weiji wenhua*), which could certainly be symbolized by the Beijing television documentary *River Elegy*. What China needed, he thought, was more material change for ordinary people.[37]

The new regional culture of Guangdong was thus frankly praised as lowbrow. It was plebeian, less than fully cultivated, less aristocratic and

[33]Calculated from figures in Guangzhou Municipal Statistics Bureau, ed., *Guangzhou tongji nianjian, 1988* (Guangzhou statistical yearbook, 1988) (Beijing: Zhongguo tongji chuban she, 1988), p. 1; and Shanghai Municipal Statistics Bureau, ed., *Shanghai tongji nianjian, 1988* (Shanghai statistical yearbook, 1988) (Beijing: Zhongguo tongji chuban she, 1988), figs. 1–4.

[34]Efforts to calculate a comparable figure for Guangdong as a whole have thus far not borne fruit. These firms are called "*geti hu*." The "150 times" refers to a calculation that yielded 14,100 percent, albeit from a small base (and with no certainty that all firms at the beginning of the period were registered). Still, this increase was clearly greater than in the largest cities of north or east China. Yo Youjun and Li Yuanjiang in *GZYJ* 10 (1986): 13.

[35]In *GZYJ* 6 (1988): 34.

[36]Ye Chunsheng in *Kaifang shidai* (Open times) (hereafter *KFSD*) 5 (1989): 61–62.

[37]This southerner's hope for mass culture was an implicit critique of northern intellectuals' less democratic elite culture (*jingying wenhua*). See Huang Jianbin in *KFSD* 4 (1989): 49–51.

literary than either the dissident or official cultures of the north—and perhaps more democratic, pushing in directions like those of a different culture that Alexis de Tocqueville once praised for its justice (and condemned for its lack of excellence).[38] By the same token, the reforms weakened Guangdong's traditional emphasis on educational work. Many young people there avoided careers in teaching so that they might take up more lucrative jobs. A 1986 report said Guangzhou needed six thousand more teachers to staff its nine years of compulsory education.[39] The new era in the south was not mainly for intellectuals.

A 1986 survey of graduating high school students revealed that only 34 percent in Guangzhou vowed to retake university exams if they failed the first time, but the portion was 73 percent in Xi'an. Fully 26 percent of Guangzhou graduates were willing to seek their own jobs on a free market, but the portion in Xi'an was only 8 percent. In Guangzhou, 40 percent of the parents were content to let offspring decide their own careers; but in Xi'an, only 19 percent were. Similar Guangzhou polls, taken in 1981, showed only 1 percent of high school graduates wanted to become entrepreneurs; but by 1986, the figure had soared to 31 percent. When the same question was asked in 1986 Chengdu, only 10 percent replied they looked forward to being entrepreneurs.[40] This pattern was in stark contrast to Guangdong's historical record; a biographical dictionary of China's literary and political talents from 1840 to 1919 contained half again as many Cantonese entries as from the second-highest province.[41] During the five years from 1981 to 1986, the portion of Guangzhou people dissenting from the motto "Time is money, and efficiency is life" fell from 64 percent to 2 percent.[42]

[38]This comparison may discomfit scholars with investments in the continuity of cultures, but it would be a mistake to underestimate the ambition for systemic comparisons in Alexis de Tocqueville, *Democracy in America,* 2 vols., trans. Henry Reeve (New Rochelle, N.Y.: Arlington, 1966). Part of the problem is that many recent Americanists do not realize they must be implicit comparativists in order to communicate, even when they use only U.S. data. An exception, whose discussion of sideline audiences could be relevant to the China coast, is E. E. Schattschneider, *The Semisovereign People: A Realist's View of Democracy in America* (Hinsdale, Ill.: Dryden, 1975).

[39]Li Jiangtao in *GZYJ* 8 (1986): 4–8.

[40]Some shifts over time, shown in attitude surveys of this sort, may come not from basic changes of view but from changes in the freedom with which interviewees gave their own opinions rather than those they thought the interviewers wanted to hear—but shifts of either sort are evidence of cultural change in the same direction. See Yang Xianjun in *GZYJ* 9 (1986): 45–48.

[41]Dai Aisheng, Huang Hao, and Pan Zhijian in *Renmin ribao* (People's daily), overseas ed., May 28, 1986, p. 8, citing the *Zhongguo jindai shi cidian* (Dictionary of modern China), containing 185 Cantonese (15 percent of the whole sample) and 124 from the next then-province, Manzhou, out of twenty-one parts of the whole country.

[42]Yu Youjun and Li Yuanjiang in *GZYJ* 10 (1986): 13; see also n. 39.

In concrete terms, reforms brought problems, not just successes, to the south; but recent choices in the regional identity tolerated rather than solved them. Guangdong's grain deficit was huge by 1988, and its influx of mouths to feed was similar. Its environmental problems, according to one Zhongshan University professor, were the nation's worst. The average grades on the national university entrance exams were second from last among all provinces (only the Tibetans scored lower). In the five years after 1983, the numbers of Guangzhou graduates who passed national university exams steadily declined. On a list of China's ten largest cities by number of engineering technicians per capita, Guangzhou was at the very bottom.[43] Yet the south coast attracted talent from elsewhere. In the nineteenth century, at least fifty thousand Cantonese had immigrated to Shanghai;[44] but by the 1980s that tide had reversed. Almost sixteen thousand technical cadres then immigrated to Guangzhou alone. The influx to Shenzhen and Zhuhai was also great. Many ordinary workers also came (often without household registrations). This tide in Guangzhou meant that one of every thirty legal residents by 1989 (and a much greater portion of the illegal "black households") had arrived during the reforms.[45] By that year, this province of about sixty-five million provided work for more than five million non-Guangdong people.[46]

National identity.   Guangdong's patriotic identity has always retained a strong local flavor, perhaps because people near the edge of a nation have a relatively clear sense of other lands. Even after the mid-1989 political crackdown, PRC writers continued to describe a "Pearl River culture area."[47] Theorists from the north pointed out that Chinese culture is highly politicized, and politics there are often mooted in cultural terms. People's "state identities" (*guojia de rentong*), according to this northern line of thought, are more important in China than in other nations. Many millennia have seen official support for state identity there. Nationality, these writers say, is constructed by Chinese in three ways: blood kinship and assimilation, the spread of cultural norms of behavior, and especially the authority of the state. An emphasis on "blood identity" (*xueyuan rentong*) finds many expressions: "If a person isn't in my tribe, his heart must be different." A

43Jing Hong's interview with He Bochuan in *KFSD* 5 (1989): 29.

44Huang Chaomei in *KFSD* 2 (1989): 46.

45Ibid., p. 21.

46Feng Huajian and Mai Yechang in *Jiushi niandai* (The nineties) (Hong Kong) 7 (1989): 49.

47This area is the *zhujiang da wenhua quan*. Xiao Zhong in *Liaowang zhoukan* (Outlook weekly), November 27, 1989, p. 13.

stress on "cultural identity" (*wenhua rentong*) leads to the idea that China can be the "land of courtesy" (*liyi zhi bang*). Highlighting "identity through authority" (*quanwei rentong*), however, leads to a coercive, clientelist kind of solidarity.[48]

Yet state identity, defined this way, is the opposite of what most coastal people want. An anthropologist, reporting fieldwork in Guangdong, had to conclude: "A general impression one has is that there is a deep sense of distrust among the farmers towards the leaders and government. They feel that their lives have been manipulated in the name of socialism."[49] Rural industrialization alleviated these problems in the Pearl River Delta during the early 1980s. The relatively free, economics-oriented atmosphere of the south coast quickly became its most distinctive regional identity—or at least the part of that identity which received the most public emphasis at this time.

One analyst argued that China faces three great barriers in its political culture. The first is a "moralization of politics" (*zhengzhi de lunli hua*), caused by a strongly perceived need to have ethical leaders. The second is a "worship of the state" (*guojia chongbai*), which encourages the total submission of citizens; morals rather than institutions thus have the job of keeping both leaders and people good. The third barrier is a weakness of personal self-consciousness, developed under an "excessively stable structure" (*chao wending jiegou*) of rule over many centuries. Ideas and cultures do not, in this Guangdong writer's view, hold China back by themselves, but they are part of a syndrome that does so.[50]

This regional critique of a reportedly national construction of the state had concrete, nonideal aspects too. Like other provincial capitals, Guangzhou paid heavier taxes and other official extractions than did peripheral places in the province.[51] Ezra Vogel found that by 1985, for example, Guangzhou had less than double the industrial production of Foshan; but the capital was paying more than three times as much in taxes.[52] There were

---

[48]The striking saying reads "Fei wo zu lei, qi xin bi yi." See Liu Zehua, Ge Chuan, and Liu Gang in *Tianjin shehui kexue* (Tianjin social science) 2 (1988): 12–15.

[49]Helen F. Siu, "The Dilemma of Political Middlemen: Leadership in a Rural Commune during Socialist Transformations," in Göran Aijmer, ed., *Leadership on the China Coast* (Copenhagen: Scandanavian Institute of Asian Studies, 1984), p. 157, reporting on Huancheng, Guangdong. Similar notions are documented for a coastal city in White, *Policies of Chaos*.

[50]Rong Jian in *GZYJ* 9 (1987): 3–7.

[51]Lynn White, *Shanghai Shanghaied? Uneven Taxes in Reform China* (Hong Kong: University of Hong Kong, Centre of Asian Studies, 1989).

[52]Foshan, far from being atypically unlike the capital, was treated in fiscal matters relatively like it. The 1986 ratio of official budget revenues over expenditures was 2.0 for Guangzhou and

far more state enterprises in Guangzhou than in Foshan. Remittances from state firms were much greater than from collectives or private businesses, and the prices of such firms' products were officially set high. Heavily taxed administrative centers, on either the national or provincial levels, have not shown dynamic growth.

Differences between areas that interact more or less heavily with the state have long been common in China. On a small scale in every jurisdiction, the distinction between state-owned and collective or private firms reflects a parallel difference. Towns that are otherwise comparable can vary in this respect. For example in Guangdong, the urban districts in Jiangmen have far more state-affiliated institutions than in nearby Xinhui, which is mostly composed of independent agencies.[53] On a larger scale, cities such as Tianjin and Shanghai (and all provincial capitals as a group) are more tightly connected with the central bureaucracy and tax collectors than are other places.[54] The flexible "one country, two systems" notion developed for Hong Kong, Macau, and putatively Taiwan is an extension of this pattern of irregular state centralization.[55] Guangdong fits it, too.

Another example of the official tendency to use frontier buffers on the south China coast is the creation of Hainan Province from Guangdong's largest island, in April 1988. This was a project of northern reformers, and the island's administration had tensions with cadres in Guangzhou.[56] Despite such conflicts, Hainan's practical links with Guangdong became stronger during the reforms. Hong Kong and Macau will similarly become parts of the People's Republic administrative structure in 1997 and 1999, respectively; and media and trade from these Cantonese places deeply affect the ways Guangdong writers describe their province.

1.8 for Foshan; but for other cities, it was Jiangmen, 1.3; Shenzhen and Zhanjiang, 1.1; Maoming, 1.0; Zhuhai and Shaoguan, 0.9; and Shantou, 0.7. The rates for the prefectures were Huiyang and Zhaoqing, 0.7 and Meixian, 0.5; and for Hainan Administrative Region, only 0.4. Calculated from Guangdong Province Statistics Bureau, ed., *Guangdong sheng tongji nianjian, 1987* (Guangdong Province statistical yearbook, 1987) (Beijing: Zhongguo tongji chubanshe, 1987), p. 168. There is far less published information on the local identities of rural areas than of provinces as wholes, but available data suggest big subregional differences, especially in links with the state. See Ezra Vogel, *One Step Ahead in China: Guangdong under Reform* (Cambridge: Harvard University Press, 1989), chap. 6.

[53]Interview with an urban specialist in Hong Kong.

[54]These cities and Beijing are called "directly ruled" (*zhixia*) and have provincial status. Other whole provinces, such as Heilongjiang, have particularly close links to specific bureaucracies (in that case, the defense and oil ministries).

[55]See White, *Shanghai Shanghaied?*

[56]See Vogel's works, *One Step Ahead in China,* chap. 6, and *Canton under Communism* (Cambridge: Harvard University Press, 1969), e.g., p. 118.

Their national argument is that ethics in such places can legitimately, officially, usefully be different from morals inland or further north. A 1985 survey in Guangzhou showed that 85 percent of the city's radios, when turned on, were listening to Hong Kong stations.[57] Guangzhou's *Yangcheng Evening News,* at its height early in the decade, published 1.7 million issues per day and was the most widely circulated newspaper in all China.[58] By the late 1980s, this province published more journals than any other except Beijing. The variety of Guangdong publications doubled from 1980 to 1988. Only one-fifth of the printing houses there were owned by the state, and four-fifths were cooperative or private (a far larger percentage than in most provinces).[59]

Politics generally became less important in Guangzhou during the 1980s, and some reformers wrote with approval that individuals' pursuit of material wealth had displaced more social, communitarian interests there.[60] Journalists explicitly urged Guangzhou people to "minimize government and maximize society" (*xiao zhengfu, da shehui*).[61] A local author claimed that the diversification of Guangdong media gave people a tendency to think independently. Although local interests in national politics may have declined, Cantonese were willing by the mid-1980s to speculate about policy. They reportedly had a new tendency to speak as if they were more powerful: "If I were the mayor of Guangzhou . . ." or "If I were the factory director. . . ."[62] There is evidence that a "sense of civic competence" was rising on the PRC coast at this time,[63] although political participation still brought fewer rewards to independent people than did economic work.

Global identity. Partly because of its proximity to Hong Kong, which encouraged overseas Chinese and foreign visits to the province, world identity came naturally in Guangdong.[64] But none of this was new. Can-

[57]A slightly earlier survey averred that 40 percent of Guangzhou people regularly listened to such broadcasts, whereas in Chengdu the percentage was reportedly just 10. Yu Youjun in *GZYJ* 4 (1984): 18; Zhong Yuming in *Liaowang zhoukan,* November 27, 1989, p. 10.

[58]Xiao Zhong in *Liaowang zhoukan,* November 27, 1989, p. 13. Liu Binyan, China's most respected journalist despite his political dissent from the government, reported that for many years Guangzhou's *Yangcheng wanbao* has enjoyed an avid readership as far afield as Heilongjiang.

[59]Hua Xin in ibid., p. 11.

[60]See Huang Chaomei in *KFSD* 2 (1989): 22.

[61]Ibid., 3 (1989): 15–17.

[62]Li Xiaolu in *GZYJ* 8 (1987): 29.

[63]The phrase is from Gabriel A. Almond and Sidney Verba, *The Civic Culture* (Boston: Little, Brown, 1963), chap. 6.

[64]Yu Youjun in *GZYJ* 4 (1984): 18.

tonese traders long enjoyed far-flung cosmopolitan connections—including noble ranks in southeast Asian courts—and for centuries they ran shipping empires throughout East Asia. Before much Western contact, for example, they carried cargoes from Thailand to Japan, whose people did not attempt such trade because south Chinese lineages monopolized it (with no support from the Chinese government).[65] By the mid-1980s, Guangzhou was still receiving four times as many overseas visitors as Beijing, and it received five times as many as Shanghai.[66]

Economic opening to the world created an inherently unorthodox Chinese culture in Guangzhou. One recent writer claims that "commercialism" (*zhongshang zhuyi*) sums up the city's identity. More than 40 percent of Guangzhou's income comes from commerce, but less than 25 percent of all China's income is commercial.[67] Merchants classically have a lower social status in China than scholars; so intellectuals have chastized the city for its infatuation with trade. But a Zhongshan University instructor tried to rebut criticisms that Guangzhou had become a "cultural desert" (*wenhua shamo*), pointing out that the city has nightclubs, entertainment parks, and "merry places everywhere." This hedonist was unapologetic. He claimed that happiness is the city's "core value" and that Guangzhou not only has a culture; it has its own special kind. He openly praised cultures of "feeling" and "consumption" (*ganjue wenhua* and *xiaofei wenhua*), because such new superstructures create markets, helping the economy. These are mass rather than elite cultures. But, he said, much of American culture (more than the cultures of Europe) is also mass culture. When he claimed that Beijing and Shanghai have more developed elite cultures than Guangzhou, he intended a criticism of these more northerly cities.[68]

By 1989, a journal boasted that "Guangdong culture" provided the reform era's first truly modern teahouse with music, the first privately run ballroom, and the first large-scale, Disneyland-like amusement park.[69] Freedom and gaiety received cosmopolitan reputations in China by the 1980s. Opinion surveys showed Guangzhou to be far more worldly than

[65]Prof. Ishii Yoneo, a historian of Thailand at Kyoto University, reports that Southeast Asian cargoes arriving at Nagasaki during the Tokugawa period were ferried on "*Tōsen*" (*Tangchuan,* or "Tang" [Cantonese] ships).

[66]Many were from Hong Kong, and their role in cultural diffusion may have been as important as that of foreign visitors. Zhou Zangting in *GZYJ* 5 (1987): 36.

[67]Liu Meixiu in *KFSD* 3 (1989): 23–24.

[68]Qing Zhou in ibid., 58–60.

[69]Tian Feng and Xie Mingjia in *Guangdong shehui kexue* (Guangdong social science) 2 (1989): 135–40.

other places. When residents were asked whether they should mostly depend on themselves or on their collectives, the more individualist responses garnered a much stronger majority in Guangzhou than Chengdu.[70] This kind of identity can be deemed either progressive or libertine, and many Chinese think of all coastal cities in both these terms.

Cosmopolitanism became correct, in the 1980s essays of many China coast authors. The writer Wei Chengsi, for example, typified Shanghai culture (ambiguously called "*haipai wenhua*") as modern, urban, peripheral, complex, even pluralistic. This distinguished it from Beijing culture, which (as Lu Xun, modern China's greatest writer, had said in the 1930s) serves bureaucrats rather than businesses.[71] But the Shanghai-Guangdong difference by the 1980s was at least as great—and some Shanghai authors did not hide their regret at having lost much of their cosmopolitan tradition (and talented people) to the far south. They reported, for example, that the Cantonese area receives more time on central news broadcasts than East China, because Guangdong is now at all kinds of frontiers.[72] Although Shanghai writers look forward to the establishment of a "new Shanghai [or coastal] culture" (*xin haipai wenhua*), a southern author claims this has already been established—in Guangdong.[73]

Cosmopolitan and nativist identities are by no means exclusive. Often a single person can hold one or the other at different times. Among Guangzhou's masses, as among elite intellectuals, this fact has been evident for a century and a half.[74] Wang Bin in 1988 noticed that many previous coastal thinkers such as Yan Fu and Liang Qichao, who began by favoring the incorporation of modern foreign elements into Chinese culture, ended by advocating "restoration of the old" (*fu gu*). Recent philosopher Li Zehou advocates a reversal of the old modernizers' phrase "Chinese essence and Western use," saying the nation should work toward "Western essence and Chinese use." He could publish this only because he equates the "essence" of the West with Marxist modernization. But Wang Bin had doubts about this facile phrase; Marxism and modernization, he suggested, may not be equivalent. More important, Wang claimed that cultural change remains a big problem; the "transitional person" (*guodu ren*) tends to be in trauma.[75]

[70]Yo Youjun in *GZYJ* 4 (1984): 21.
[71]Wei Chengsi in *Shehui kexue* 1 (1986): 24–25.
[72]Li Tiangang in *Fudan xuebao: Shehui kexue ban* 3 (1988): 90–96.
[73]Zheng Fan in *Sixiang zhanxian* (Thought front) 3 (1988): 62.
[74]See Frederic Wakeman, Jr., *Strangers at the Gate: Social Disorder in South China, 1839–1861* (Berkeley and Los Angeles: University of California Press, 1966).
[75]*GZYJ* 6 (1988): 36. Wang quotes Le Zehou—and also Daniel Lerner—that a society with many "transitional people" would modernize; see p. 39.

Cosmopolitan identities are inherently multiple, but they are usual in the modern world. According to Lucian Pye, "Because identity involves the search for a sense of uniqueness, it is peculiarly difficult to arrive at any generalizations about the essential character of a resolved identity crisis"[76] Some reports speak approvingly of "Guangzhou culture" as an "alloy culture" (*hejin wenhua*) combining East and West, or a "window culture" (*chuangkou wenhua*).[77] Sheng Feng says change in China diffuses from the coast inland; so "peripheral culture" (*bianyuan wenhua*) has a transformative function for the whole country. Some writings adopt views of cultural diffusion, from A. L. Kroeber and others, to talk about the spread of ideas in China.[78] Guangdong is sometimes called the "test tube of a new culture" (*xin wenhua de shiguan*).[79] For Cantonese writer Huang Jianbin, its "melding of cultures" (*wenhua ronghe*) should not be rued—even if there were any practical way to avoid it—because it means progress.[80]

Taiwan and the Derecognition of 1979

Regional identity. On an island, as an ideal local identity is easy to define. Memories of the Hokkien and Dutch explorer-pioneers who came by water, the pirate-loyalist Zheng Chenggong (Koxinga), and the Japanese rule have all helped Taiwanese identify themselves historically. The 1945 liberation, the 1947 Guomindang (GMD) killing of islanders protesting corrupt governors, followed by the GMD's efforts of the 1950s to rebuild support through land reform and liberal economic laws—all these, plus decades of military threat from the mainland, have given Taiwanese families various senses of who they are.[81]

Diplomatic derecognition by the island's main protector, the United States, was just another shock in this series. Although the local air force has thus far been adequate for defense, 98 percent of China's people live across the water. The long-term prospects for maintaining Taiwan's system

[76]Lucien W. Pye, "Identity and the Political Culture," in Leonard Binder et al., eds., *Crises and Sequences in Political Development* (Princeton: Princeton University Press, 1971), p. 124.

[77]Wen Yanzi in *GZYJ* 5 (1986): 6.

[78]Sheng Feng in *Shehui kexue* 1 (1986): 20–23; Lu Yun in *Fudan xuebao: Shehui kexue ban* 3 (1986): 11–18.

[79]Zhou Zangting in *GZYJ* 5 (1987): 36.

[80]Huang Jianbin in *KFSD* 4 (1989): 51.

[81]For an overview of the period before the coverage in this chapter, see Lynn White, "The Political Effects of Resource Allocations in Taiwan and Mainland China," *Journal of the Developing Areas* 15 (October 1980): 43–66. A more general theory, suggesting how incursions shape identity, is in Lewis Coser, *The Functions of Social Conflict* (Glencoe, N.Y.: Free Press, 1956).

seemed, by 1980, very moot. A survey of attitudes on the island after derecognition, based on a carefully stratified sample, asked respondents to rank fifty public needs. "Unity on the island" against "threats from the mainland" dominated all four of the most frequent responses. The two needs awarded lowest priority on the long list both concerned repression of internal dissent.[82] Taiwan's people trusted each other, by this time, much better than they trusted outsiders.

Hu Fo, former chair of the Political Science Department at Taiwan National University, analyzed the 1980 Taiwan elections in relation to the loss of U.S. recognition. He concluded that the diplomatic break and the anti-GMD Kaohsiung incident together made voters concerned to elect candidates who could raise the international status of their system as a whole.[83]

The American shock at first provoked more discussions of policy than of identity. Although the decline of Taiwan's diplomatic recognition had come in many stages, not until 1983 did a major public debate about the island's identity begin. At that time, there was much in the press about "Chinese consciousness" and "Taiwan consciousness." The latter was said to rise as a response to greater international isolation. But this local awareness among islanders—post-1945 immigrants from the mainland, no less than pre-1945 Taiwanese families—was a result of the common external threat they all perceived. A Taiwan magazine called *Shenggen* (Roots) in 1983 published an issue with the title "Taiwanese Should Not Want Chinese Consciousness."[84] After that, the GMD government unsurprisingly closed the journal.

When elites joined this debate effectively, they did not deny the island's distinctiveness. A professor at the National Cheng-chi University admitted he had two "levels" of identity, Taiwanese and Chinese (and he said his aim was to move from the former to the latter).[85] State attempts to repress Taiwanese consciousness had for many decades been common. The Japanese had sponsored an "imperial subject consciousness" (*huangmin yishi*).

[82]Concerns about official corruption were expressed in the fifth-most-frequent response— a fairly high rating, suggesting some independence of these Taiwan respondents from fears of answering in a manner the government would not like. Yang Xiaorong in *Dongwu zhengzhi shehui xuebao* (Suzhou journal of social and political sciences) (Taipei) 3 (December 1979): 52–73.

[83]Hu Fo in *Shehui kexue lunzong* (Journal of social sciences) (Taiwan) 34 (June 1986): esp. 126.

[84]"Taiwan ren buyao Zhongguo yishi." Yin, "Taiwan de rentong weiji" (see n. 5), p. 264.

[85]Zhu Xinmin in Yang Qingsong, ed., *Taiwan mingyun Zhongguo ji* (Taiwanese fate and Chinese consciousness) (Taipei: Dunli, 1987), p. 69.

The GMD since 1945 had accented propaganda about mainland symbols, such as the Yellow and Yangzi rivers, urging the islanders to value their Chineseness.[86] This pattern bred dilemmas about identity. A mainlander living on Taiwan accused his fellow mainlanders of having "cultural schizophrenia" (*wenhua de jingshen fenlie zheng*) because they could not decide whether they wanted to be Taiwanese or Chinese.[87] The editor of the *Progressive News* (affiliated with the opposition Democratic Progressive party, or DPP) by 1987 called on *all* his fellow islanders to "make Taiwan home."[88]

Argument about identity was in the air. But not quite everyone on the island is simply mainlander or Taiwanese. President Le Teng-hui is a Hakka (from a pre-1945 immigrant family, but not from the long-dominant Hokkien Taiwanese group). Some post-1945 immigrants came from southern Fujian; so they are "mainlanders" but also native speakers of Hokkien/Taiwanese. Increased attention in the mid-1980s to the Malay-Austronesian "aborigines" suggests less about them than about Han islanders, who at this time published much about all problems of identity. The aborigines' "stigmatized identity" became subject to critical study, as did discrimination against low-income Hakkas. Anthropologist Xie Shizhong uses the ideas of Charles F. Keyes to describe emulation, by aborigines and Hakkas, of the island's dominant culture. Once social characterization becomes a topic, it applies to all groups. The culture with which many on Taiwan identified was still Chinese, but now also more local, in the words of sociologist Li Wenlang: "What they want to eat is no longer Sichuan *mapu doufu*, but now is Tainan *dandan mian*."[89]

National identity.   Because of the need to have a proficient government in a place undergoing quick economic change, because most of China is under a different regime, and because of Taiwan's security problem, national identity has been an issue on the island. But for many, nationality is an issue to defer. When a large number of Taiwan college teachers were asked in 1986 what problems they expected their island to face in the next five years, they overwhelmingly pointed to social concerns: pollution, crime, and unemployment. These items appeared on more than twice as

[86]Long Yingtai in ibid., p. 105.
[87]Long in ibid., p. 101.
[88]Lin Zuoshui in ibid., p. 98.
[89]Xie Shizhong, *Rentong de wuming: Taiwan yuanzhu min de zuchun de bianqian* (Stigmatized identity: The ethnic change of Taiwan aborigines) (Taipei: Zili Evening News, 1987), p. 5; Li Wenlang in Yang, *Taiwan mingyun Zhongguo ji*, p. 17.

many of the responses as did anxieties about the Taiwan independence question, which the respondents ranked least worrisome among a list of thirteen big issues. The interviewees also showed a lack of fear about direct military threats from the mainland during the next few years. This absence of concern did not come from any notion that their government had an effective policy toward the PRC—nearly half the respondents said they thought their government's stance was ineffective[90]—but apparently from a general sense they were well off and possibly from a desire not to think about the island's security problem.

Despite the signal success of government by mainlanders within Taiwan from 1950 to 1980, the large Hokkien- and Hakka-speaking communities still knew who they were. Taiwanese had long been skeptical of the GMD's "orphan ministers" (*gu chen*), who came to the island at midcentury and used to speak as if their hearts were set on returning to power in their mainland places of birth. Some of these officials reportedly considered the island dispensable, like a used toothbrush. So "toothbrushism" (*yashua zhuyi*) became a popular Taiwanese phrase with which to criticize mainlanders who did not commit themselves to the island.[91] But by the late 1980s, nearly three-quarters of the population had been born after 1950. As Li Wenlang shows, consciousness of "Taiwanization" (*Taiwan bentu hua*) correlated with local economic growth to make native Taiwanese realize they were first-class citizens on their island. They were no longer willing to "accept the insulting status of second-class citizen."[92]

Just as majority Taiwanese challenged minority mainlanders to become like themselves, many also saw a security value in avoiding hasty rhetoric that would deny their ancestral roots as Chinese. Even some artdent proindependence Taiwan writers did not challenge that the majority on the land is anthropologically Chinese. What they denied is the leap to political implications. As Lin Yuchun put it, "Having the same language and ethnicity does not require having the same state."[93] He pointed out that the GMD not only used to discourage Taiwanese from identifying themselves as such but also discouraged mainlanders from identifying with the island.

Many Overseas Chinese scholars have distinguished "levels" of Chinese identity based on categories such as citizenship, place of residence, ancestry,

[90]*Minyi yuekan* (Public opinion monthly) 5 (1986): 3–10.

[91]Li Wenlang in Yang, *Taiwan mingyun Zhongguo ji,* p. 17.

[92]Ibid., p. 18.

[93]"Tongwen tongzhong bubi tongguo." *Taidu jikan* (Independent Taiwan quarterly) (New York) 1 (1982): 113–14.

and strength of cultural identification.[94] Taiwan independence publications (embarrassed by the obviously Chinese language, religion, kin structure, and other standard anthropological traits of the majority on that island) have constructed taxonomies designed to show that no such trait can "prove" the need for a Chinese government on the island.[95] By the mid-1980s, one writer claimed that "Taiwan consciousness" (*Taiwan yishi*) had superseded Chinese identity among the island's youths.[96] At the same time, a Taipei magazine could publish a fairly objective, only somewhat negative history of the Taiwan Independence movement.[97] Overseas publications in Chinese dealt squarely with identity issues that threatened the state, for instance, with memories of the 1947 GMD shootings of Taiwanese. So much water had passed under so many bridges since that time, the authors of such histories were not all ostracized by the government.[98]

Chiang Kai-shek's son, Chiang Ching-kuo, speaking as president on Constitution Day in 1985, said he would be succeeded neither by a member of his own family nor by a military junta. Martial law ended in July 1987. The Taiwanese Hakka Lee Teng-hui became president constitutionally by January 1988. In his 1989 New Year's Day message, President Lee said the "Taiwan experience" should affect not just China, but developing countries around the world.[99] The obvious, much-envied economic success of Taiwan tended to fuse the local and cosmopolitan identities. The national level, in the middle, could be nearly finessed.

The opposition Democratic Progressive party looks inward, however. Its green-and-white party flag shows, at the center, an outline map of Taiwan. A party spokesman was asked whether this meant the DPP was uninterested in China. He coyly replied that when the government recovered the mainland, his party would put an outline map of China on its flag instead.[100] In the December 1989 elections, the DPP won six of the twenty-

[94]See, e.g., Singapore scholar Mai Liufang, writing in *Shehui kexue lunzong* 32 (September 1984): 63.

[95]A matrix of nationality types by such traits (and very like a homologous table from the Singapore writer cited in n. 94, but made for a different political purpose) is in Hong Zhesheng, Lin Zhetai, and Li Yongguang, *Taidu jikan* 4 (1982): 15.

[96]Shi Minhui, ed., *Taiwan yishi lunzhan xuanji* (Selections on the Taiwan identity debate), (Monterey Park, Calif.: Taiwan chubanshe, 1985), p. 1.

[97]Zeng Dexin in *Ren yu shehui* (Man and society) 2 (October 1984): 91–96.

[98]A prominent example is by Zhang Xucheng [Parris Chang] in *Taiwan wenhua* (Taiwan culture) (New York) 13 (September 1987): 13–20.

[99]Byron S. J. Weng in *China Update* (Fall 1989): 1, 10.

[100]An oral source, heard on Taiwan.

one county and city mayoralties (and an additional "nonparty" candidate received another). This meant a doubling of non-GMD representation in top local posts, which carry much patronage. In the Legislative Assembly, the GMD won 72 of the 101 seats; but 21 went to the DPP, and 8 more to unaffiliated candidates (fewer for the GMD than in any previous election). The opposition was exuberant. Lee Teng-hui's spokesman, while noting the GMD had not lost, described the opposition's advances as a "major attack."[101] Localism increasingly affects national identities on Taiwan, just as cosmopolitan views do.

Global identity. On Taiwan, world identity is now commercial and democratic. Free elections affect the views of foreign trading and military powers. Elections offer some external legitimacy, despite the chaos accompanying them and despite doubts about their cultural appropriateness. A democratic Taiwan is stronger, because its government can more credibly claim to represent the people. So long as the world saw Taiwan as controlled by a small group of GMD pensioners, then the Communist gerontocrats' rights to the island seemed altogether comparable. But as the island's government now must stand in contested elections, it can speak for the island more clearly. It is widely seen as more legitimate. Even leaders in Beijing may find it harder to claim (or believe) that the Chinese impulses of Taiwan's people for reunification with the People's Republic are repressed by the island's regime.

According to dissident Zhang Junhong (a sometime editor of opposition journals and a longtime resident of GMD jails), assessments of Taiwan's democracy depend on the extent to which elections are compatible with the form of Chinese culture that has emerged on the island. Zhang makes a humorous analogy to two sales reports about the prospects of exporting Taiwan shoes to Africa. One market researcher, after a trip, reported no chance at all of selling shoes there, because the Africans mostly go barefoot. But another, who also made the trip, came back ebullient about a huge market for shoes: the Africans clearly needed millions of pairs. According to Zhang, one could say Taiwan stands no realistic chance of developing democracy, because Chinese culture prevents that. Or alternatively, one could say Taiwan absolutely needs a democratic identification, no matter

[101]The DPP in Chinese is the Min Jin Dang. These elections covered the whole island except for the province-level cities of Taipei and Kaohsiung. See *Shijie ribao* (World journal) (New York), December 3, 1989, p. 1.

what its culture, because its fast-growing economy has pluralized the society and requires links with rich democracies abroad. Zhang's position is the latter. He says Taiwan has become a "world island" (*shijie dao*). Trade ties it to the United States and Japan, even if language also ties it to China.[102]

By the 1980s, Taiwanese were well aware of their island's prowess. Their place was prospering as the eleventh-largest trading country in the world, and by 1991 it apparently had the globe's largest currency reserves. The emergence of a two-party system made Taiwan resemble other nations that were deemed successful.[103] But local people's pride in cosmopolitan accomplishment was tempered by a sense they had for too long been manipulated by external powers. In 1983, public resentment of foreign politicians who were perceived as bullies, especially those in the United States, was still high. A Taipei survey asked, "Which world figure do you dislike most?" Jimmy Carter (who recognized the PRC) won by a landslide, with a disapproval rating almost twice that of runner-up Mao Zedong—followed, in order, by a most distinguished and catholic list: Richard Nixon, Henry Kissinger, and Joseph Stalin.[104]

Some foreign things were less bad, however. A Taiwan journal published, because its readers were clearly interested, detailed surveys on how French and Japanese identified themselves.[105] An analyst of cosmopolitan influences on Taiwan surveyed the effects of news reports, foreign movies, returned teachers and professionals, travel, and trade; and he found them all to be powerful, especially those coming through electronic media.[106] The islanders were so internationally minded, their leaders sought a plan to find a symbol for their uniqueness. Concerned about the island's identity, officials noticed that the United States had its Uncle Sam; Japan, its Tairô; France, its Marianne; the United Kingdom, its John Bull; and Russia, a polar bear. They decided Taiwan needed a similar emblem. A designer icon was required; so high bureaucrats, central and local together, sought an international artist with name recognition. They commissioned an American cartoonist, Ranan Lurie, to create a mascot. He drew and named "Cousin Lee" (Li biaoge), a jaunty figure clad in a martial arts suit, with a

[102]See Yang, *Taiwan mingyun Zhongguo ji*, p. 246.

[103]Li Wenlang in ibid., p. 16.

[104]We have a higher opinion of Carter; but for the delicious list, see *Minyi yuekan* 2 (1983): 4.

[105]Ibid., 8 (1986): 31–32.

[106]Lin Jiacheng in *Donewu zhengzhi shehui xuebao* 12 (1987): 262–63.

black belt, a pugnacious jutting chin, and haircut style that looks distinctively Taiwanese (not generally Chinese).[107] "Cousin Lee," the picture, was unveiled at a gala in 1985, attended by the mayor of Taipei and the presidential chief-of-staff. Within sixty days, a survey showed that four-fifths of urban Taiwanese had heard of Cousin Lee.[108] This cartoon, with fists flying, can well represent the dilemma in which Taiwan's people find themselves.

A Taiwan National University sociologist expressed resentment that foreigners and PRC spokespeople often refer to Taiwan as an "issue" or "problem." Instead, he pointed out, it is a place where people live. This island's inhabitants may develop an increasingly single identity because of external dangers.[109] Their situation, which has its perils, understandably affects their consciousness.

Hong Kong and Tiananmen, 1989

The sharpest recent change in a China coast identity is almost surely the 1989 Hong Kong case. Like any such event, this adjustment was partial, not wholly overturning the previous habits of China's third-largest city. It was spurred by a startling carnage in Beijing, twelve hundred miles to the north. But identity changes just partly, even when it changes most quickly. It is best seen when subject to historical shocks, but perhaps it can never be fully seen. In the 1989 case, Hong Kong reacted to Beijing's democracy movement and killings with a succession of the largest protest rallies ever held in the colony. Television in that city carried the same images of Tiananmen shown throughout the world (except in China)—but the other places were not scheduled to fall under the PRC government within eight years. The strain caused many in Hong Kong consciously to reevaluate their identities and their options for the future.

[107]A mascot with much cosmopolitan identity in the PRC after 1978 has been Monkey, from the classic film on a trip to India in search of sutras, the *Xi you ji* (Journey to the western lands). The Monkey meant modernization; and he has been pictured on billboards riding rockets, winning international sports matches, and generally aiding the emergence of a stronger China. He goes west—but not from the coast. Interestingly, the post-1978 fad for Monkey was somewhat displaced by a stress on figures like Ming seafarer Zheng He, e.g., in the TV documentary *He shang*. On Cousin Lee (spelled that way in English explicitly because the surname is also possible in that language), see *Taipei huakan* (Taipei pictorial), January 1986, pp. 32–33, which pictures Ranan Lurie along with notables such as Mayor Xu Shuide and Chief-of-Staff Shen Changhuan. For more of the public discussion about Cousin Lee, see *Guanghua* (Light of China) 11 (1986): 5–21.

[108]*Minyi yuekan* 2 (1986): 23.

[109]Shao Xinhuang in Yang, *Taiwan mingyun Zhongguo ji*, p. 161.

Regional identity. In Hong Kong local identity is very strong. The mountains and water, the wealth and opportunity, and the relative compactness of the city's elite make this place hard to leave, even for many who can easily do so. A 1985 survey shows that when a well-constructed sample of people in the colony had to choose between identifying as "Chinese" or "Hongkongese" (*Xianggang ren*), three-fifths chose to name themselves by their city.[110] Most interviewees disagreed with the statement "I am proud of the achievements of the PRC in the past several decades." Barely half agreed with the statement "I feel close to Chinese on the mainland."[111]

Some of this localism apparently comes from what the surveyors call "a fear of politics."[112] Hong Kong's Chinese elite was created by property-owning lineages that fled rebellions. Inland political upheavals from 1850 shaped local family traditions of deep conservatism. Fearsome campaigns during the first two decades of the People's Republic only strengthened this pattern in Hong Kong. Net immigration to the colony was highest at times of inland chaos, and the people who came were largely interested in protecting wealth and kin. Cultural symbols of this conservatism can be found in many aspects of Hong Kong and other prosperous China coast cities (for example, even in their architecture).[113] At the same time, Hong Kong people were aware that the Chinese government itself by the 1980s was becoming more conservative.

Guangdong was making quick economic progress. Toward the end of the decade, Hong Kong firms employed two million workers in that province (more than they hired in Hong Kong).[114] Some in the city could share the pride of a Guangzhou journal that said, "Hainan is Taiwanized, Shen-

---

[110]This was "an astonishingly large proportion of respondents," according to Lau Siu-kai and Kuan Hsin-chi, *The Ethos of the Hong Kong Chinese* (Hong Kong: Chinese University Press, 1988), p. 2. This book provides a wealth of statistical information on pre-1989 Hong Kong identity, and a repeat use of its questionnaires might provide some measure, useful for comparative studies, of how fast regional, state, and world identities can change in response to big shocks.

[111]This last proposition, innocuous and in that light garnering a weak 53 percent, did not require interviewees to specify the reasons for any closeness they might feel. Ibid., p. 180.

[112]Ibid., p. 76.

[113]Protection against robbers has been an enduring Hong Kong interest, even for relatively poor households. Few other parts of the world have such elaborate burglar alarms and universal window bars. This was not fertile ground for an extension of public trust in a civic culture. Architecture has been used as a symbol of colonial cultures in recent research on India, Shanghai, and other places. The method suggests some debt to Geertz, *Interpretation of Cultures* (see n. 18); see, e.g., Thomas R. Metcalf, *An Imperial Vision: Indian Architecture and Britain's Raj* (Berkeley and Los Angeles: University of California Press, 1988).

[114]Feng Huajian and Mai Yechang in *Jiushi niandai* 7 (1989): 49.

zhen is Hongkongized, Guangdong is Shenzhenized, and the whole country is Guangdongized."[115] Analysts saw a particular convergence between Guangzhou and Hong Kong.[116] This was localism, but with the locality expanded.

National identity.   Before Tiananmen, patriotic identity in Hong Kong followed these trends, and the most obvious links with China remained economic. Sophisticated but inconclusive surveys suggested that opinions in the city about democracy had broadened somewhat by 1987.[117] The Tiananmen tragedy quickly accelerated this pattern, because many Hong Kong elites and people were repelled by the incompetence and brutality they saw in the PRC government then. This politicization drove many to think about leaving the colony. It drew others to a more local politics. As legislator and Teachers' Union president Szeto Wah promised, "I swear to you all that I will stay in Hong Kong after 1997 even if [PRC premier] Li Peng remains in power then."[118] State and local identities became closer because of 1989, even as thousands of local leaders considered emigrating.

The two most senior Hong Kong Chinese legislators expressed this odd concurrent strengthening of regional, state, and world identities. They pleaded in Britain for "a home of last resort." In a formal message to a committee of Parliament, they proclaimed, "We are Chinese, we are proud to be Chinese. . . . We feel a deep sense of solidarity with the students in China, their bravery and their cause. We owe it to them, more than ever before, to demonstrate to Chinese leaders how democracy can work without becoming a threat to China and its sovereignty." They continued with the valid but complex claim that a right of exit would "encourage Hong Kong people and their children to commit themselves to a future in Hong Kong."[119]

Political identity after 1989 became more democratic because elections might strengthen local rule. In the mid-1980s, some local political scientists

[115]"Hainan Taiwanhua, Shenzhen Xiangganghua, Guangdong Shenzhenhua, quanguo Guangdonghua." Wu Ying in *KFSD* 2 (1989): 36–37. The shift in title, from *Guangzhou Research* to *Open Times,* suggests some of the change this journal documents.

[116]Li Changhong's interview with Feng Dawen in ibid., pp. 13–14.

[117]Charles F. Emmons, *Hong Kong Prepares for 1997: Politics and Emigration in 1987* (Hong Kong: Hong Kong University, Centre of Asian Studies, 1988), uses superb multivariate tests on attitude survey data in an attempt to relate confidence in Hong Kong to emigration and politics. In some cases, his hypotheses were not confirmed (or disconfirmed) in ways that Hirschman's theory, which we discuss in the next section, might have predicted.

[118]*South China Morning Post* (hereafter *Post*) (Hong Kong), June 5, 1989, p. 7, in *Foreign Broadcast Information Service* (hereafter *FBIS*), same day, p. 127.

[119]*Hongkong Standard,* June 20, 1989, p. 4, in *FBIS,* June 21, p. 83.

had argued that no major actor (not the People's Republic, not the Hong Kong people, not the British) could alter the city's type of regime significantly; so change would be limited. But the same analysts, writing before Tiananmen on the basis of surveys, had specified their "most significant finding" as follows:

> Many traditional [Chinese] political values have been retained. . . . However, the less-than-given authority of the colonial regime, its limited functions, and the changing political experience of Hong Kong Chinese have jointly worked to produce changes in these traditional political values. . . . Hong Kong Chinese are now less fearful of government and even expect fair treatment from it. . . . Accordingly, a constellation of proto-democratic values can be found in the ethos of the Hong Kong Chinese.[120]

During the heady spring of 1989, Hong Kong activists began to circulate petitions about PRC internal politics. One with thirteen thousand signatures demanded that the PRC institute a multiparty system throughout China, that freedoms of expression and assembly be guaranteed, and that prominent political prisoners be released. The petition's title was "Only When China Has Democracy Will Hong Kong Have a Democratic Future."[121]

The June 4 violence alienated many Hong Kong people, just as it also intensified their Chinese patriotism. One commentator described the dilemma of this schizophrenic political identity: "We abjure, we abjure, but still we must swear allegiance."[122] Such loyalty meant open involvement in PRC politics, with the aim of changing China's government (later to become Hong Kong's). Local legislator Martin Lee Chu-ming speculated that Hong Kong and parts of south China could ally against the north after 1997: "We speak the same dialect. . . . It's the sort of thing that can happen because Hong Kong's prosperity has rubbed off on Guangdong and Shenzhen."[123]

Other local leaders advised against interfering in PRC politics. Stephen Cheong, a member of Hong Kong's Legislative Council and a conservative, said in July 1989 that Hong Kong people should avoid expressing opinions

[120]See Lau Siu-kai and Kuan Hsin-chi, "Hong Kong after the Sino-British Agreement: The Limits to Change," *Pacific Affairs* 59 (Summer 1986): 214–36, and *Ethos of the Hong Kong Chinese*, pp. 190–91.

[121]*Shiyue pinglun* (October review) (Hong Kong), March 4, 1989, p. 17.

[122]"Buren, buren, hai xiu ren." *Mingbao yuekan* (Mingbao monthly) (Hong Kong) 8 (1989): 4.

[123]*Post,* August 3, 1989, pp. 1–2, in *FBIS,* same day, p. 58.

about politics inside China. He hoped Beijing authorities would repay this compliment by staying out of Hong Kong affairs.[124] But in late 1989 the *People's Daily* was openly asking whether Martin Lee and Szeto Wah had a "role conflict" (the colorful phrase was *jiaose chongtu*) between their political activities in Hong Kong and their duties on the Basic Law Drafting Committee, drawing the city's future constitution.[125] Many doubted PRC politicians could restrain themselves from expressing views on Hong Kong, even if the diverse local leaders all remained silent about China.

Political structure had been a major topic of public debate in Hong Kong long before 1989 (although in Beijing, scant discussion of constitutional proposals could be heard, even during the spring high tide of liberal expression). Institutional ideas abounded in the colony, as soon as the Sino-British Joint Agreement was signed. They were soon backed by exhaustive studies of the legal, social, economic, and other aspects of the coming structure.[126] Well before the mid-1989 violence in Beijing, a pessimistic and cautionary literature on Hong Kong's future, arguing that legal devices would likely prove inadequate to preserve a liberal regime, had also flourished.[127] The colonial government, aware that the PRC constitution contains ill-enforced provisions that resemble a bill of rights, decided in July 1989 to legislate a proper bill of rights on its own.[128] The main issue was how to write the local provisions so they might actually hold for the future.[129]

A professional poll in August 1989 showed that a strong majority of Hong Kong people favored the creation of political parties and that the degree of commitment to this idea correlated directly with household incomes. Two conservative legislative councillors had founded the Hong Kong Alliance in March. Another registered a think tank that resembled a party. During the Beijing demonstrations in May, two hundred Hong Kong liberal and labor groups formed the Alliance in Support of the Patriotic and Democratic Movement.[130] In September, two liberal legislators formed the Hong Kong Democratic Association, which became a

[124]*Post,* July 28, 1989, p. 7, in *FBIS,* same day, p. 60.

[125]*Renmin ribao,* overseas ed., November 8, 1989, p. 5.

[126]E.g., Peter Wesley-Smith and Albert Chen, eds., *The Basic Law and Hong Kong's Future* (Hong Kong: Butterworth, 1988).

[127]See the highly critical work of scholar-businessman George L. Hicks, *Hong Kong Countdown* (Hong Kong: Writer's and Publisher's Cooperative, 1989); also Raymonde Sacklyn, *The Dangers of the Basic Law (Draft)* (Hong Kong: Target, 1989).

[128]*Hongkong Standard,* July 7, 1989, p. 1, in *FBIS,* July 2, p. 67.

[129]See Wesley-Smith and Chen, *Basic Law and Hong Kong's Future.*

[130]*Post,* August 20, 1989, p. 1, in *FBIS,* August 2, pp. 70–71.

party for contesting elections. Martin Lee was the crucial member of this group, although his initial role was to recruit other liberals and prevent the democratic movement from splintering into factions.[131]

Hong Kong was becoming more liberal in politics, and 1989 obviously speeded the process. By August of that year, the Office of Members of the Executive and Legislative Councils (OMELCO) proposed that the number of directly elected seats in the legislature for 1991 be doubled from that proposed by a 1988 white paper. OMELCO, which includes strongly conservative business interests, also advocated that at least half the legislators be directly elected by 1995. A poll showed that 67 percent of Hong Kong residents thought the OMELCO pace of democratization for 1991 was about right; only 11 percent said it was too fast. The Group of 89, made up of conservative organizations, expressed disagreement, as did Beijing representatives. But most of the people polled said political development should occur despite opposition from Beijing.[132]

A prominent Hong Kong academic, Byron Weng, distinguished the city's major elites in categories both by their leftist, centrist, or rightist social policies and, more important, by their propensity to resist or accommodate Beijing. The most defiant group is openly pro-Taiwan (the Chinese Nationalist flag flew over sections of the post–June 4 protest parades in Hong Kong, although demonstrations on Taiwan were more muted, presumably because of the island's security interests). A second set of Hong Kong elites, only slightly more inclined to accommodate Beijing, are the "democratic" factions, led largely by lawyers and clerics. Third is the international community of business people, who try to steer clear of politics. The British colonial government and its associated banks must take a more openly accommodationist line. The fifth and sixth groups are easier to distinguish by their local policies than by their eagerness to cooperate with Beijing (which is high): the elite tycoons who deprecate democracy and need stability with the People's Republic for their profits, and the diplomatic and commercial representatives of Beijing in Hong Kong.[133] The most important swing elite among these is the conservative businessmen,

---

[131]*Post,* September 3, 1989, p. 1, in *FBIS,* September 6, p. 59.

[132]College-educated and high-income respondents were especially keen on political change, and the replies (collated by professional pollsters) were otherwise fairly invariant with respect to sectors, ages, and sexes. See *Post,* August 3, 1989, pp. 1–2, in *FBIS,* same day, p. 58.

[133]Weng Songran [Byron Weng] in *Jiushi niandai* 9 (1989): 46–49. An earlier, more complex but overly confident predictive attempt that uses similar categories is Bruce Bueno de Mesquita, David Newman, and Alvin Rabushka, *Forecasting Political Events: The Future of Hong Kong* (New Haven: Yale University Press, 1985), e.g., p. 114.

whose opposition to more democratic elections apparently comes from a fear of the instability such contests might cause and the constraints on local autonomy that might result. Their main disagreement with democrats is apparently about tactics, not about the goal of keeping control mostly local after 1997.

Democracy thus became a major focus of debate about identity in Hong Kong, as in Taiwan. Many residents (some businessmen, some intellectuals, some leftists) had long doubted its viability or aptness there, because this crown colony had scarcely more tradition of participatory politics than did China as a whole. Conservatives in Hong Kong also feared that competitive politicians might enlarge the government's social concerns and cause higher taxes, hurting the incentives to capital that let the city boom. This traditionalist view, dominant before mid-1989 and still enjoying much PRC and business support, had undergirded a quasi-class identity for Hong Kong, which is the richest Chinese city anywhere. Antipolitical logics seemed only sensible, for such an economic place.

After mid-1989, however, Hong Kong liberals could argue that more democratic participation could increase autonomy in the eventual SAR. The old, fully colonial structure, under which the governor had appointed his very "loyal opposition" in the legislature, had already become mixed by a diversification of councils and by the choosing of some legislators in occupational constituencies (lawyers, medics, accountants, and the like). This appointive structure could easily fail, however, to achieve the one goal for which a contested election is almost always good: to legitimate the autonomy of the winner. Vis-à-vis Beijing in future years, an independent voice for Hong Kong was seen by many as crucial. Elections might be subverted; but the system of appointments and constituency selections could be manipulated even more easily. To make the "two systems" part of the "one country, two systems" formula effective, some residents thought cordial links between Hong Kong and PRC elites would be enough. Others thought more democratic structures would become an unavoidable part of Hong Kong's identity, whether or not Chinese culture was favorable to it.

The September 1991 direct elections for the Legislative Council gave the democratic alliance led by Martin Lee a clear mandate from voters (sixteen of the eighteen elected seats), although the council has sixty members in all.[134] Public discussions of the structures through which the political

---

[134]Aside from the elected 18, functional constituencies chose 21, and the governor chose another 21 including himself as council president. Under the current unfinalized plans, the

identities of Hong Kong people might be expressed in the future are unusually sophisticated, and in this sense they are well in advance of parallel discussions in other parts of China's periphery, even though realization of serious plans for local power in a Chinese national framework is still very uncertain. Hong Kong has retained a very distinctive identity in past years such as 1949 and 1967, however; and in the future it might continue to do so.

Global identity. In Hong Kong, world identity has been partly expressed by the emigration of skilled residents. This phenomenon has the odd effect of strengthening local political participation there, for reasons explained below. After Tiananmen, doomsday humor tempered the towering anger that many kinds of Hong Kong leaders felt toward the PRC government (even though some business people could not show such sentiments in public). Some local writers claimed that both the British and Chinese governments cared little about Hong Kong. Deng Xiaoping had opined that it was good that the violence in Beijing had come to a head earlier rather than later; so Hong Kong wits joked that it would be better to leave the colony earlier rather than later.[135]

These threats were not idle. A mid-1989 poll in Hong Kong found that 12 percent of the six million people there already had residency rights overseas. Another 16 percent "definitely intended" to emigrate. A further 7 percent hoped at least to send some of their family out of the territory.[136] The emigrants were disproportionately well-educated, high-income professionals, so external governments understandably fostered their exit options. Canada refined its point system to monitor the queue for migration. Singapore announced a campaign to attract artisans; its consulate was so

---

council size will remain constant at 60 not including its president, and the elected/functional/appointed portions will be as follows: by about 1995, 20/30/10; and by about 1999, 30/30/0—except that appointed members will be selected in an electoral college nominated by an election committee that is apparently in turn to be generated by the executive. Credit is due to Professor Ian Scott of the Hong Kong University Department of Political Science for summarizing this situation, which might conceivably change if a later, more liberal Beijing government allows an acceleration of increase in the elected portion. The underrepresentation in government of Hong Kong's socially dominant middle class is explored in Ian Scott, *Political Change and the Crisis of Legitimacy in Hong Kong* (Hong Kong: Oxford University Press, 1988).

[135]*Nanbei ji yuekan* (South and North Pole monthly) (Hong Kong) 10 (1989): 19–21.

[136]The fact that this survey was by telephone makes it less random, although a strong majority of households in Hong Kong do have phones; see *Post,* July 28, 1989, p. 7, in *FBIS,* same day, p. 59.

beseiged that a temporary booth was built on the sidewalk outside, to hand out preliminary forms returnable by post. "Visa queues at the U.S. Consulate have more than doubled in recent weeks [after June 4], the *Post* reported.[137] Australia unveiled a "business migration plan" with a "rejection rate of less than five percent," under which applicants received Australian residence visas—after they invested half a million in Australian dollars.[138] Belize was less attractive, thus cheaper: only twenty-three thousand Hong Kong dollars for a passport and citizenship, with no residency requirement.[139] From the Hong Kong people's viewpoint, the problem with most of these plans was that a right to foreign abode was finalized only after the migrants stayed abroad for a long period. They could get no assurances about future residence overseas without actually leaving the colony, even if they did not yet, or surely, want to leave. But most, once away, did not come back.

The desperation, with some humor, in this exit was often obvious. In London, the British government (over objections from the colony's British governor) delayed promises of an automatic U.K. right of adobe for United Kingdom and colonies passport holders; so quaint plans proliferated. One group hoped to rent space for a new Hong Kong in the Western Isles of Scotland.[140] Horatio Cheung, of a consortium called Freedom of Movement, planned to set up a trust fund, to which families could give a thousand Hong Kong dollars yearly: "If three million people contributed to the fund, it would accumulate about three billion dollars a year." The group could then negotiate with Britain, Australia, Canada, New Zealand, or any other nation to accept residents in exchange for the money. The Right of Abode Delegation (or ROAD, a dedicated acronym) became fond of a site near Darwin, Australia, to be leased as a new British dependent territory.[141]

Departures from management jobs in the colony apparently strengthened PRC resolve to discourage the manpower drain (and the incentive to politics), even though Chinese officials did not publicly admit this. Many vocal Hong Kong people now seriously consider exit; and this option might at first be expected to reduce their interest in local politics. But the contrary occurs, for reasons parsed in a theory of Albert Hirschman. As exit

[137]*Post*, June 16, 1989, p. 5, in *FBIS*, June 29, p. 73.

[138]*Hongkong Standard*, October 5, 1989, p. 1, in *FBIS*, October 17, p. 58.

[139]*Asiaweek*, July 28, 1989, p. 28.

[140]A 1989 cartoon in the *Post* commented on this Scottish New Hong Kong by running a cartoon depicting a yuppie Hong Kong Chinese family, wearing their glasses but dressed in kilts beside their mandatory Mercedes, next to a rural Scottish road with a sign to "Loch Ma Chau" (after Hong Kong's Lok Ma Chau).

[141]*Post*, July 17, 1998, p. 1, in *FBIS*, same day, p. 74.

possibilities become more credible among valuable people who are increasingly dissatisfied, their local complaints become more frank and cogent, for two causes: First, people who can leave become braver in speaking their minds; if PRC reaction becomes too negative, they feel they can move safely away. Second, the complaints of potential defectors are especially telling, because PRC officials know that a major hemorrhaging of needed people from the city would ultimately reduce their own resources. The function relating dissatisfaction to the effectiveness of political "voice" is a discontinuous curve: It rises sharply just at the point where the discontented first know they must have a serious option to leave (which is however not yet finally taken). They speak louder then, and they are heard better then. In Hong Kong, the movement to guarantee local rights thus became stronger, very quickly, when "exit" became a more credible option to many local people, especially those with skills.[142]

The colony's top officials (Britons who sometimes wear ostrich feathers but may be closet democrats) pressed London to guarantee U.K. residency for top Hong Kong Chinese managers. In December 1989, some received this assurance, without any need to leave the colony even temporarily to assume such rights. Fully 225,000 promises of free entry to Britain were announced (including 50,000 future U.K. residency permits for "those who take prominent positions in Hong Kong between now and 1997"). These went to educated professionals' families, which many countries might be happy to dub citizens.

Beijing's economic interests were no doubt served by this British act, whose ostensible purpose was to encourage these productive people to remain in Hong Kong. But politics were more important than economics; so the PRC Foreign Ministry protested that London was in "gross violation" of the Sino-British accord: "Anyone caring for the future of Hong Kong cannot view this development with indifference."[143] These crucial local leaders, remaining at home in Hong Kong but free to leave, were now in a strong position to complain more effectively against any PRC policy they disliked. It should be no surprise that Beijing opposed the right of abode Britain offered to a relatively small part of the colony's people, because professionals who can leave can also speak effectively against any PRC faults.

The cosmopolitan identity of Hong Kong is evident because thousands

---

[142]See Albert O. Hirschman, *Exit, Voice, and Loyalty: Responses to Decline in Firms, Organizations, and States* (Cambridge: Harvard University Press, 1970), pp. 83 and passim. The same discontinuity was evident for East Germany, and astonished observers who were unaware of it, when the end of the Berlin Wall made exit a live option for many there.

[143]*New York Times,* December 31, 1989, p. 16.

of the most productive families there have strong links abroad. These global identities do not displace their political interests of either the local or Chinese kinds; on the contrary, they make for concurrent strengthened expression of them all. Identity is not zero-sum among sizes of collectivity. The Hong Kong government had for many years run advertising campaigns, communitarian and reminiscent of Victorian philanthropy, in an effort to persuade the family-centered, materialistic Hong Kong people to think of others outside their immediate families. But 1989 did far more to challenge and nurture Hong Kong people's interests in larger communities. Hong Kong people became more fully Chinese in that year, even while their disaffection with the Chinese government soared and while they looked internationally for safe havens they might later need.

The Role of Interface Identities

Not only do multiple identities coexist; in peripheral situations, they are mutually reinforcing. Identity on a coast may be inherently different from that in a more central place, because members can more seriously consider abandoning cultural or administrative aspects of the larger sphere. Perhaps they individually can leave (as some elites in Hong Kong do), or their military and economic position still keeps alternatives open (as in Taiwan), or their noncentral location allows a community to legitimate a special role for the larger country (as in these places and in Guangdong). Loyalty to any organized community depends partly on the degree to which a member sees it solving problems. If a peripheral member becomes progressively dissatisfied, the efficacy of complaint from there can rise in a discontinuous way: most quickly when political or physical defection becomes a live option.

Guangdong and Hong Kong are not about to leave China; and the chance of Taiwan doing so is low. But the ways in which these communities participate in the Chinese system are not entirely up to Beijing. Each of the peripheries is locally proud, and they are aware of each other. Chen Qiwei, a young Shanghai thinker, calls for regionalization of the Chinese economy.[144] He says the main problem in China's reform program is a lack of strategies for regional economic development, differentiated for each part of the country. There is no conflict between this program and affective

[144]Chen Qiwei, of East China Normal University, in *Xinhua wenzhai* 5 (1989): 30–32. By the winter of 1989, he was being criticized for his actions in the more liberal spring.

nationalism, if the special customs or products of different areas prove complementary.

Events such as those described here add layers of identity and allow identity to be studied. If coastal people become more disaffected, costs to the central government may exceed the benefits more quickly than elsewhere. Especially in running their own affairs, parts of the peripheral band can have their say—and what they say locally affects the rest of China by example. But circumference communities are not less loyal, as partial defection becomes a more realistic option for them and they become somewhat independent. These conditions make them participate in politics all the more, because such action becomes safer locally and more effective nationally.

The material and ideal sides of this participation are inextricable from each other. Concrete trade interests that allow profits and trust among Chinese in Guangdong, Hong Kong, Taiwan, and overseas also strengthen interregional and nationalist identities there. Distinguished spokesmen and academics from Hong Kong, Guangdong, Shanghai, and Taiwan have called for a "community of Chinese" (*Zhongguo ren gongtong ti*), which could cooperate especially in economic matters. A writer from a Hong Kong leftist think tank speculated that the future of the western Pacific Rim would be either "Japanese style" or "Chinese style" peace (*Rishi heping* or *Zhongshi heping*), and he frankly described the latter as "a system that would restore something like the offering of imperial tribute, so that China maintains the regional order of the Asian-Pacific area."[145] Some writers explicitly urge more liaisons between the three largest coastal ports (Hong Kong, Shanghai, and Dalian) because these are the harbors that can trade most easily with other places on the Pacific Rim. Hong Kong is said to be the natural "capital" of this Chinese international economic community—and these opinions were published on the mainland, though Hong Kong is not yet in the People's Republic.[146] Recipes for identities require concrete as well as normative ingredients.

The challenge of the coast threatens to modernize the old ideal claims to legitimacy which Chinese rulers and intellectuals have long held to be the moral basis of their polity. The periphery is in fact more democratic than the center, because a greater variety of people—not just officials, technocrats, and intellectuals—have more wealth, prestige, and power there. Harvard professor Tu Wei-ming has recently suggested how this process makes the periphery a new center: "The idea of the modern state involving

---

[145]Lin Jiang in *Weilai yu fazhan* (Future and development) 3 (1989): 10–11.
[146]Huang Zhilian in ibid., 2 (1989): 21–23.

power relationships based on competing economic and social interests is anathema to the Chinese cultural elite as well as the Chinese ruling minority. To them, the state—intent on realizing the historical mission to liberate China from threats of imperialist encroachment and the lethargy and stagnation of the feudal past—symbolizes the guardian of a moral order rather than the outcome of a political process."[147]

The peripheries may now be less afraid of the feudal past and the foreigners than of the national government. But at the same time, they do not exist without a center. Despite obvious and operational doubts about Beijing, the coastal communities look north as well as to each other. Ideas or benefits that encourage interactions between these regions come from outside China, from its widening buffer band, and from its center. Actual influences for change in mid-1980s China were of all these kinds. One PRC analysis cited a list of four such leverages, as various as the popular singer Deng Lijun, Jean-Paul Sartre, Alvin Toffler, and the special economic zones.[148] Some influences, especially in culture and affecting intellectuals, were not specific to coastal or southern regions; the others were mostly there.

Groups as various as northern reformers in Beijing and new rural industrialists in suburbs around northern and eastern PRC cities are peripheral politically, but they can now do more because of national examples from the south coast. They contribute to China's development along with Guangdong, Hong Kong, and Taiwan. The identities of nonintellectual workers, bureaucrats, and peasants are less easy to study. Intellectuals as a group may be more peripheral to modern Chinese society than they usually admit. Their self-consciousness *as* intellectuals often tends to overwhelm any other kind of self-awareness they have. Discourses on identity are often instrumentalist, but the old roles of Chinese intellectuals make this a particular problem for them.

River Elegy, the six-part television documentary produced in Beijing in 1988, spurred intense discussions of national identity among educated Chinese. This film had a conclusion that was cosmopolitan. The last episode, entitled "Azure Blue" (Weilan se), vividly depicted the Yellow River (a symbol for China throughout the series) moving into the world's billowing oceans, across which explorers such as Ming admiral Zheng He and Western explorers had sought their fortunes. The evocative presentation, allud-

---

[147]Tu Wei-ming, "Cultural China: The Periphery as the Center," *Daedalus* 120 (Spring 1991): 15–16.

[148]Pan Jianxiong et al. in *Shehui kexue yanjiu* (Social science research) 2 (1986): 61–65.

ing strongly to blue frontiers off the coast and the common redness of all people's blood, went beyond social analysis into a very broad cultural statement. But it affirmed China's need for democracy and science, and images of the coast and the ocean were explicitly mixed with these calls. As Pye has written of all modernizing societies, "Political systems cannot seek to advance by merely denying their past. Somehow or other, they must seek to come to terms with what they once represented even as they take on new forms and new content. . . . The identity crisis is thus a phase of growth that the political system must inevitably experience whenever its basic forms are substantially changed. It is a sign of growth and change, not of weakness or abnormality." Li Yongtai asserts that China's values do not necessarily converge with those of the West, but Chinese people nonetheless retain many options of identity, and they will choose among them.[149]

The multiple-level, mutually reinforcing, intense identities of south coast people have for centuries contributed crucially to the larger nation of which they now form the most dynamic part. These communities are at once regional, national, and cosmopolitan. They have helped to protect China's pride and strength, while absorbing new notions and resources from elsewhere. As the world's most populous country moves into the next century, all evidence suggests that boundary functions will remain lively on the China coast.

[149]Videotapes and published Chinese transcripts of *River Elegy* are now widely available, e.g., in Su Xiaokang and Wang Luxiang, eds., *He shang* (Hong Kong: Sanlian shudian, 1988); a précis in English is *China News Analysis* 1376, January 1, 1989, pp. 1–9. See Pye, "Identity and the Political Culture" (see n. 76), pp. 108, 111; and Li Yongtai in *Sichuan daxue xuebao: Zhe she ban* (Sichuan University journal: Philosophy and social science ed.) 2 (1989): 6. This choosing, existential role, personified in a Eurasian heroine, is aptly used as a metaphor for life itself in at least one novel on a distinctive part of Guangdong: Austin Coates, *City of Broken Promises* (Hong Kong: Oxford University Press, 1988).

中
國 8

China as a Third World State:
Foreign Policy and
Official National Identity

Peter Van Ness

One of the most consistent themes in Beijing's foreign policy statements over four decades of the People's Republic is the identification of China with the Third World. As Samuel Kim has put it, "If China's policy pronouncements are taken at face value, the centrality of the Third World is assured by three recurring themes: that China is a socialist country *belonging* to the Third World; that support for and solidarity with the Third World is indeed a basic principle in Chinese foreign policy; and that such identification will continue undiminished even if China becomes a rich and powerful state. . . . And yet," Kim continues, "China has emerged as perhaps the most independent actor in global group politics, a veritable Group of 1 (G-1)," and has maintained that independence, despite important changes in its foreign policy position, since the People's Republic of China's entry into the United Nations in 1971.[1] Moreover, as Michael Ng-Quinn has warned, China often puts on different faces to manipulate the world.

How can we resolve this contradiction? Do China's leaders truly identify the People's Republic as a Third World state? Or is the Chinese rhetoric about the Third World merely propaganda intended to create a Third World image of China in which the Chinese Communist party (CCP)

[1]Samuel S. Kim, "China and the Third World: In Search of a Peace and Development Line," in Kim, ed., *China and the World: New Directions in Chinese Foreign Relations,* 2d ed. (Boulder, Colo.: Westview, 1989), p. 148.

leaders do not themselves believe? We know from experience in analyzing the foreign policy of any modern state that official statements by policy makers do not necessarily reflect their perception or basic understanding of events. Official statements are often purposefully made to mislead or to create a certain image or impression. Official positions can mislead by what they include as well as by what they omit.[2]

Because the Chinese leadership invokes the history of Chinese humiliation at the hands of the Western powers, and *talks about* a common bond between China and all other nations similarly victimized does not necessarily mean that those same leaders, or the Chinese public for that matter, truly behave according to a shared identity with the Third World. Clearly, Chinese, especially older people, feel strongly about China's own century of humiliation; but it does not necessarily follow from that fact that they feel a common bond with the other, non-Chinese victims.

Kim and Lowell Dittmer, in their conceptualization of national identity, have emphasized its importance for establishing and maintaining domestic legitimacy, for specifying a country's global role, and for bolstering claims to international leadership. To this list of key concerns, I would add that we should investigate the relationship between a proclaimed national identity and the success or failure of a particular foreign policy line undertaken under its auspices. Most especially, what happens to national identity when the foreign policy line fails? Also, it is only realistic to assume, I think, that within any national leadership there are likely to be competing images of national identity which may become involved in struggles for power among political factions. Finally, we must, I would urge, continually exercise the foreign policy analyst's rule of thumb: always compare what foreign policy makers say with what they actually do. Do statesmen practice what they preach, or not? A more formal way of making the same point is to say that we should consistently compare "declaratory policy" with "operational policy."

When Sam Kim and Lowell Dittmer began this project, they proposed

[2]For example, during the period of the socialist camp line, virtually no claim was made in PRC official statements that Maoist theory had made a significant contribution to Marxist-Leninist ideology—to the point that Franz Schurmann in his research on China in the 1950s mistakenly inferred that the CCP leaders had accepted the notion that Mao's intellectual contribution was only to what he called "practical ideology," not to the more important and fundamental "pure ideology." Only after the Sino-Soviet dispute became an open conflict did it become apparent that the CCP had withheld such theoretical claims for Maoist ideology in deference to Moscow's leading role in the socialist camp. For Schurmann's definitions of pure and practical ideology, see his *Ideology and Organization in Communist China* (Berkeley and Los Angeles: University of California Press, 1966), p. 22.

that we conceive of China's national identity as a pyramid of four levels of variables "(beginning from the top): policies, principles, 'basic line' (*jiben luxian*), and world view (*shijie guan*)." To my mind, these variables constituted something closer to official ideology or what might be called "official national identity," namely, a sense of China articulated by government and party leaders as a part of their official responsibilities, a collectively determined official position regarding China's role in the world. This is not necessarily the same thing as national identity in the sense of what individual Chinese think about the global role of China, be they officials or everyday citizens. The debate prompted in 1988 by the television documentary *River Elegy* is a good example of the range of the more basic notions of Chinese identity.[3]

I therefore choose to begin my chapter with foreign policy and work back toward the more fundamental dimensions of official national identity—the deeper layers of the Kim-Dittmer pyramid—so as to illuminate how China's official national identity as a Third World state was employed by the leadership to enhance the legitimacy of the regime and to stake a claim for world leadership. In turn, I examine how the failure of a particular PRC foreign policy line seemed to reshape China's official national identity. My argument has three parts. First, I put the analysis into the perspective of a particular interpretation of forty years of PRC foreign policy. In that interpretation, I distinguish three "lines," one of which is the "Third World line" (1960–70). Second, I compare that line with the reform period, 1978–88, discussing what the implications of the market-reform strategy adopted during that decade were for the PRC's Third World identity. Third, I analyze the reemergence of an emphasis on China's Third World identity in the post–June 4 reaction to Western sanctions.

I must from the start be clear about what I mean by the term *Third World*. Usage of the term is usually ambiguous, and the ambiguities often disguise issues of substantial importance. There are at least five separate criteria generally used by analysts to identify countries of the so-called Third World: economic (poor and/or underdeveloped), cultural (non-Western), racial (nonwhite), political (nonaligned), and geographic (situated in Asia, Africa, or Latin America). Historically, the idea of a Third World emerged out of the independence struggles of societies dominated by Western impe-

---

[3]For one thoughtful commentary on the six-part television series and the debate it provoked, see Frederic Wakeman, Jr., "All the Rage in China," *New York Review of Books*, March 2, 1989, pp. 19–21.

rialism. The French apparently coined the term *tiers monde* in the mid-1950s after the first conference of Afro-Asian states at Bandung, Indonesia, in 1955.[4] The French term originally emphasized the idea of a third force or a group of states between, and distinctively apart from, the two major alliances of that time, the West and the socialist camp. The Chinese concept of a third world similarly envisages a grouping of states opposed to the two major world power centers—the alliances led, respectively, by the United States and the Soviet Union.

The intellectual roots of CCP ideology regarding the Third World are to be found principally in Mao Zedong's concept of "new democratic revolution," and the Maoist idea of China's relationship to the Third World is probably most fully stated in Lin Biao's 1965 essay on "people's war." The most famous formulation is in Mao's three-worlds theory, first publicly put forward by Deng Xiaoping in a speech to the Sixth Special Session of the United Nations General Assembly in 1974.[5] During the 1960s, the Maoist leadership put forward China as a model of Third World revolution that other countries in Asia, Africa, and Latin America might emulate.[6] To be "third world" meant to share a common sense of deprivation and exploitation at the hands of the rich and powerful. The Third World line in PRC foreign policy sought to shape the "have nots" of Asia, Africa, and Latin America into a revolutionary motive force to overturn the global status quo.

But is China in the eyes of its leadership essentially a Third World country as CCP propaganda has continually stated? No question points

[4]Paul Robert, *Dictionnaire alphabétique et analogique de la langue française* (Paris, 1969), s.v. "tiers monde."

[5]Mao Zedong, *Xin minzhu zhuyi lun* (On new democracy) (Yenan: Liberation Association, 1940); Lin Biao, "Long Live the Victory of People's War!" *Peking Review,* September 3, 1965, pp. 9–30; the official English translation of the Deng speech was published as a supplement to *Peking Review,* April 19, 1974, pp. 6–11. Also of theoretical importance for understanding the Maoist notion of the Third World is the concept of "intermediate zones"; see John Gittings, *The World and China, 1922–1972* (New York: Harper and Row, 1974) chaps. 11, 12, and Conclusion, and for an example of the concept applied, see *Renmin ribao* (People's daily), January 21, 1964, p. 1.

[6]The earliest statement of a Chinese revolutionary model to be published after the establishment of the People's Republic was in an address by Liu Shaoqi to the Asian and Australian Trade Union Conference convened in Beijing in November 1949; see *Xinhua yuebao* (New China Monthly), December 15, 1949, pp. 440–41. After the early 1950s, and until the 1960s, however, any claim to a uniquely Chinese revolutionary model was dropped from Chinese policy statements, apparently in deference to Soviet insistence on their particular notion of ideological orthodoxy; see n. 2.

more directly to the basic contradiction in China's global status. The two sides of the debate take familiar lines: Yes, China is non-Western culturally, nonwhite racially, has been the victim of Western imperialism, and is poor in per capita gross national product. But, no, China has the longest continuous political tradition in recorded history and an unsurpassed record of cultural achievement up through the eighteenth century; has since 1964 been a member of the exclusive club of nuclear weapons powers; is a permanent member of the U.N. Security Council; and is the world's most populous country, third largest in land area, and resource rich.

In this chapter I undertake to examine these issues and assess this debate in terms of a concept of official national identity, that is, the CCP leadership's image of China and its specification of the People's Republic role in the world. This is the party leadership's official answer to the questions: Who are we, and what should we collectively aspire to be? What is especially important about being Chinese, and what is it that most significantly distinguishes us Chinese from the rest of the world? For the PRC leadership, their answers to these questions must be tenable both domestically and internationally, in two very different political realms. As Kim and Dittmer have pointed out, a viable sense of national identity is vital domestically to securing the political legitimacy of a regime, and equally vital internationally as the political rationale supporting claims to international leadership.

Both Michael Hunt, when assessing Chinese national identity problems from the end of the Qing dynasty to 1949, and Merle Goldman, Perry Link, and Su Wei, when analyzing the late 1980s, focus on periods in Chinese history when the basic national identity was in dispute—times of crisis when the official definition of national identity and the leadership's answers to the key questions regarding China's collective identity were found to be politically untenable. As Arthur Waldron has commented, the significance of national identity involves a leadership successfully linking symbols to power, to performance.[7] In effect, from the founding of the CCP in 1921 until the Communist victory in 1949, the Guomindang and the CCP competed with each other to provide a new national identity for China, a convincing vision of a rich and powerful modern China—and a viable alternative to the Confucian sense of identity that had served Chinese so well for two thousand years. Now, in the 1990s, one reason that politics in China is so volatile and potentially explosive is that, once again, China's national identity is in dispute.

[7]Comment by Arthur Waldron at the Center for International Studies conference, Princeton, January 1990.

Forty Years of PRC Foreign Policy

Tables 1 and 2 summarize my interpretation of the history of PRC foreign policy, which I would like to propose as a basis for examining China's Third World identity. This interpretation focuses on analyzing China's foreign policy "lines" (*luxian*), with a foreign policy line understood as comprised of four parts: the CCP leadership's world view; the political-strategic component; the economic component; and a sense of China's global role (see Table 1). In the essay from which this interpretation is drawn, I have

Table 1. The three lines in Chinese foreign relations: Components

	Socialist-camp line (1950–57)	Third World line (1960–70)	Modernization/ opening to the West line (1978–88)
CCP leadership perception of the global system or world view	A world divided between capitalist and socialist camps	A world dominated by two imperialistic superpowers	A world shaped by superpower rivalry for hegemony
Political-strategic component of PRC foreign policy			
Basis of China's national security	Socialist-camp alliance	Third World coalition	Playing USA against USSR
Concept of world politics	Alliance confrontation (socialism vs. imperialism)	Structural transformation through class and national struggles	Balance of power/politics
Economic component of PRC foreign policy			
Strategy for domestic development	Command-economy model	Social-mobilization model	Market-socialism model
Source of technology and capital for development	Soviet Union and Eastern Europe	Self-reliance	USA, Japan, Western Europe, and U.N. agencies
China's global role	Junior member of the weaker coalition in an ideologically divided bipolar global system	Challenger of the superpower-dominated global system	Supporter of global status quo while focused on building domestic capabilities

Table 2. The relationship between international economic policy and political-military policy since 1950

Decade	International economic policy	Political-strategic policy	PRC foreign relations line
1950	Integration into the socialist-camp world economy (1950–59)	Strategic alliance with the USSR (1950–57)	Socialist-camp line (1950–57)
			Transition: Maoist concepts of "East wind over West wind" and Chinese road to socialism beginning in 1957–58
1960	Self-reliance (1960–77)	Third World anti-imperialist coalition (1958–70)	Third World line (1960–70)
1970			
		Détente with the USA (begun 1971)	*Transition:* PRC turns to USA to deter Soviet threat to China's national security, beginning in 1971
1980	Integration into the capitalist world market (1978–present)		Modernization/opening to the West line (1978–88)

presented data on the direction of PRC foreign trade, support for revolution, and Chinese economic aid to the Third World to demonstrate empirically the changes in Chinese foreign policy behavior.[8]

One way of analyzing a particular foreign policy line is to conceive of it as a form of national identity implementation, that is, a specification of roles for the People's Republic based on a given Chinese self-image. It is important, however, to distinguish between national-identity implementation and national-identity formation. For example, during Mao Zedong's rule in the People's Republic, he took upon himself almost exclusively the prerogative of defining China's official national identity. Implementation inevitably involved the entire official PRC apparatus as they attempted to

[8]Peter Van Ness, "Three Lines in Chinese Foreign Relations, 1950–1983: The Developmental Imperative," in Dorothy J. Solinger, ed., *Three Visions of Chinese Socialism* (Boulder, Colo.: Westview, 1984), pp. 113–42.

turn the collective image of China into viable political action, both domestically and internationally.

For the Chinese leadership, a foreign policy line is a unified, theoretically articulated, comprehensive design for dealing with the global system. Such a line begins with an analysis of the international situation. Then, on the basis of that analysis, the line prescribes a strategy for dealing with the principal problems that the analysis has identified. It is a paradigm or logically integrated model of foreign relations containing prescriptions for both political-strategic policies and international economic relations. There have been only three periods in the forty years of PRC history during which the party leadership implemented a comprehensive and consistent line in foreign relations. Each of the three lines was based on a different perception of the global system and China's role in it; and as can be seen from Table 1, each line constituted a different approach to dealing with the global environment. In terms of this particular interpretation, a foreign policy line requires that the components of political-strategic policy and international economic policy be compatible and synchronized.

Most analyses of Chinese foreign policy focus on the political-strategic component. There is good reason for this because defending the security of the state and society from unwanted foreign penetration is almost always the principal concern of the foreign policy makers of any country, and national defense has primarily to do with political-strategic considerations. It is also obvious, however, that the foreign policy of every modern state includes an economic component. Each state seeks to maximize the benefits it can derive from the global system for its economic development. Different development strategies call for different kinds of economic foreign policies. International economic policy for underdeveloped countries differs substantially from that for industrialized countries, because of the formers' relative poverty and limited opportunities for domestic capital accumulation and their technological backwardness.

Typically, Third World countries are preoccupied with maximizing access to foreign capital and technology for development and with expanding foreign markets for their exports in order to pay for the imported capital and technology. In addition to worrying about the terms of trade for their exports and imports, they are also especially concerned to avoid, to the greatest extent possible, vulnerability to outside influence (either world market influences or deliberate efforts by foreign states to affect their domestic situation) resulting from the conditions obtaining in their trade, foreign aid, and foreign investment relationships. In these respects, China is objectively a Third World country. There is no question that China is comparatively poor (twenty-first poorest at $330 of gross national product per capita among 121 reporting countries, according to the World Bank),[9] and despite its ranking as the world's third-most-important nuclear weapons power, the People's Republic is still in many respects underdeveloped. Yet to what extent does China identify as a Third World country? What is the substance behind the often repeated official statements that China is a developing country that belongs to the Third World—a "developing socialist country"?

During the forty years of the People's Republic, China's international economic policy and its political-strategic policy have followed different paths, responding to different circumstances and changing at different times. Inevitably there arise contradictions between these two foreign policy components, since the political-strategic component is shaped largely by what happens outside China in the global system, while the economic component is principally determined by the party leadership's assessment of domestic needs and choice of domestic development strategy. The leadership's attempts to give the impression in its public statements that at all times the Chinese state is implementing a consistent and comprehensive policy line, even though this is far from the case, especially in periods of transition from one line to another. PRC policy, like the policy of any state, must change in response to changing conditions.

Inferring more from PRC actions, then, than from CCP leadership statements, I argue that there have been only three periods since 1950 when China has implemented a comprehensive and consistent foreign policy line: 1950–57, the socialist-camp line; 1960–70, the Third World line; and 1978–88, the modernization/opening to the West line. In between have been periods of transition, during which PRC economic policy and its political-strategic policy were in contradiction with each other (see Table 2). Since the Beijing massacre of prodemocracy demonstrators in June 1989, party policy appears once again to have entered a period of transition.

Each of the three lines incorporated an analysis of the global system, integrated both economic and political-strategic components into a consistent world view and theoretical framework, and prescribed a particular role for China in global politics. The socialist-camp line conceived of China as a junior member of the Moscow-led alliance of communist party states in a bipolar (East versus West) world. The Third World line, alternatively,

[9]World Bank, *World Development Report, 1990* (New York: Oxford University Press, 1990), p. 178.

adopted a "have nots" against "haves" (South versus North) world view, according to which, China attempted to lead, in part by the example of its own experience, a Third World challenge to superpower control of the global system. Finally, the modernization/opening to the West line constituted a design that entailed joining the North while still talking about South versus North. This line aimed both to rely on the United States to deter possible Soviet threats to China's national security and to integrate the Chinese economy into the capitalist world market system. Each line was an effort to deal successfully at the same time with the competing demands of: (1) designing a viable global role for the People's Republic and (2) implementing an effective domestic strategy of socialist construction in a country that is both poor and the most populous in the world. When China's international economic policy and its political-strategic policy meshed, its foreign policy was stable: strategies to maintain national security and to serve the domestic development imperative were built into a common foreign policy line. When they diverged, the process of transition to something new began once again.

The Role of the Third World in Chinese Foreign Policy

During the socialist-camp line of the 1950s, China temporarily accepted the role of a dependent to the Soviet Union, showing deference to Moscow's ideological and foreign policy leadership. But as the differences between China and the Soviet Union grew in the late 1950s and finally lead to a break in relations in 1960, when Moscow withdrew its aid program from China.[10] Beijing shifted its strategic base of support away from the socialist camp in an attempt to build a broad coalition of radical forces in the Third World against the global status quo. At first, the main target was "U.S. imperialism." Later, especially after the outbreak of the Cultural

[10]Stress in the Sino-Soviet alliance reached the breaking point in 1960, when Moscow unilaterally withdrew its aid program and all its aid technicians from China in a matter of weeks, apparently in an effort to force the CCP back into the ideological fold. Compounded by problems resulting from the failure of Mao's Great Leap Forward, the Soviet aid withdrawal led to an estimated 47.5 percent drop in China's industrial output in one year, from 1960 to 1961, and a determination by the Maoist leadership to reject dependency on the Soviet Union and to undertake a new economic strategy of self-reliance. See Robert F. Dernberger, "Economic Policy and Performance," in Joint Economic Committee, U.S. Congress, *China's Economy Looks toward the Year 2000* (Washington, D.C.: U.S. Government Printing Office, 1986), 1:46.

Revolution in 1966, "Soviet revisionism" and ultimately "Soviet social imperialism" were also singled out for attack. A question that must be asked in hindsight is why China took such risks in confronting both of the world's two most powerful states at the same time. How did China's leaders think they might ever succeed? What was at stake from their point of view, and what does this tell us about China's Third World identity?

During the 1960s, Mao Zedong saw the Third World as presenting an opportunity to assert Chinese leadership and achieve a substantial measure of global power. As the Sino-Soviet dispute deepened, Beijing made a carefully conceived effort to create a new force in world politics to be comprised primarily of the colonial or newly independent countries of Asia, Africa, and Latin America. The Chinese saw the Third World as the area of greatest political opportunity on the contemporary world scene. It was a world in flux, one in which old political orders and alliances were crumbling and new ones being formed—where new friends could be won, old balances of power upset, and powerful new alliances established.

Capitalizing on the various appeals of the Chinese revolutionary experience before and after 1949, the Beijing government saw in the volatile conditions of Asia, Africa, and Latin America its best chance to influence world politics and to apply China's limited resources most fruitfully toward the attainment of foreign policy objectives. A measure of Chinese confidence in the political potential of Asia, Africa, and Latin America was the vision of the world put forward by Lin Biao in September 1965, which viewed North America and Western Europe as "the cities of the world" and Asia, Africa, and Latin America as "the rural areas of the world" which would ultimately encircle "the cities" with world revolution.[11]

The Chinese strategy may have been profoundly radical, but their tactics (except for the peak Cultural Revolution years of 1966–69) remained astutely pragmatic. By seeking to undermine the power and influence of the superpowers in the developing world, the Chinese hoped to alter the entire global power structure. Beijing sought to build broad alliances on several levels. Government-to-government relations, the granting of economic and technical assistance, the forming of new trade relations, the use of "people's diplomacy," as well as the support for revolutionary wars of national liberation—all played a part in Beijing's vigorous foreign policy offensive.[12]

Beijing had apparently come to believe that, compared with the relative

[11]Lin, "Long Live the Victory," p. 24.

[12]Peter Van Ness, *Revolution and Chinese Foreign Policy* (Berkeley and Los Angeles: University of California Press, 1970).

political stability of the industrialized countries of the West at that time, the conflicting political economic forces so evident in the new nations of Asia, Africa, and Latin America provided a vastly greater potential for radical change. Propelled into modernity by the trauma of World War II and the subsequent struggle for independence from Western colonialism, the Third World had become the scene of the most profound postwar political changes. As Lin Biao put it, "In the final analysis, the whole cause of world revolution hinges on the revolutionary struggles of the Asian, African and Latin American peoples who make up the overwhelming majority of the world's population."[13]

In appealing to the Third World, the Chinese focused essentially on local nationalistic aspirations and fears of renewed foreign domination. The basic cement of Beijing's desired alliance with the underdeveloped world was a common colonial experience and a continuing opposition to any form of foreign intervention or interference. Beijing stressed a common poverty and backwardness compared with the prosperous capitalist countries of the West and pointed to the danger of new colonial control by "economic imperialism."[14] The Chinese argued that each country of Asia, Africa, and Latin America should develop its own unique way of maintaining its national heritage and identity, free from the stifling influence of American "cultural aggression."[15] They said, in effect, borrow from the West if you will, but beware of becoming Westernized or coming under Western control. And, finally, Mao demonstrated that he was not above at least indirectly suggesting race as an issue if it might be useful. In a statement on American racial discrimination made before a large group of visiting Africans, he linked slavery and racial discrimination to U.S. imperialism, arguing that racial discrimination was a class phenomenon; and he called on people "of all colors in the world, white, black, yellow, brown, etc., to unite to oppose the racial discrimination practiced by U.S. imperialism."[16] China's appeal to the countries of the Third World during the 1960s amounted to an attempt to pit colonials against colonialists, "have nots" against "haves," colored against white, and East against West to unify the Third World into a new global political force.

[13]Lin, "Long Live the Victory," p. 24.

[14]See, e.g., Guo Wen, "Imperialist Plunder: Biggest Obstacle to the Economic Growth of the 'Underdeveloped' Countries," *Peking Review,* June 18, 1965, pp. 19–22, and June 25, 1965, pp. 19–22; and Nan Hanzhen's speech before the Afro-Asian Economic Seminar, published in ibid., March 5, 1965, pp. 16–26.

[15]*Shijie zhishi* (World culture) 20 (1965): 11–14.

[16]*Peking Review,* August 16, 1963, pp. 6–7.

Mao was prepared to incur the risk of opposing both superpowers at the same time because, in his view, the opportunity to take a leadership role in global politics and to enhance China's power was so great. As it turned out, he was wrong. The Third World line failed. Despite their admiration for China's audacity, few Third World countries were willing to follow China's lead and risk simultaneously opposing both the United States and the USSR, the world's two most powerful countries and the most important sources of much-needed economic and technical assistance for their development.

Moreover, by the mid-1960s, the escalation of the U.S. intervention in Vietnam threatened to lead to an American war with China, and Sino-Soviet differences had become so sharp during the Cultural Revolution that by 1969 it seemed clear that the Soviet Union was considering the option of a military strike against China's small nuclear weapons and missile-delivery system. Thus the PRC's Third World line had not only failed to unify the countries of the Third World into an antisuperpower global coalition but had put China's own national security at risk.

In an effort to deter the Soviets, the CCP under Mao in the late 1960s began to consider the possibility of an accommodation with the United States. For Mao, despite the strategic concessions the People's Republic was forced to make to consolidate the American deterrent to a possible Soviet attack on China during 1971 and 1972, the world role of an autonomous, self-reliant China was still central to his concept of Chinese national identity. It was only after Mao's death that the Deng Xiaoping leadership would implement an international economic policy that profoundly compromised that image.

During the modernization/opening to the West line of the reform decade 1978–88, China in fact turned its back on the Third World. The new post-Mao leadership still repeated many of the old 1960s slogans in Chinese propaganda (such as "self-reliance" and Third World solidarity against foreign threats to state sovereignty), but the entire thrust of PRC foreign policy had changed. International economic policies anathema under Mao Zedong's rule were vigorously pursued by the Deng Xiaoping reform leadership: establishing joint ventures in China with multinational corporations; joining the International Monetary Fund and the World Bank, the two key multilateral institutions linking the capitalist industrialized countries with the Third World; accepting long-term foreign loans; building a foreign tourist industry; importing foreign consumer goods for sale to Chinese citizens; and sending thousands of Chinese students and scholars abroad for academic training in capitalist countries.

China in the 1980s became a supporter of the global status quo as the party sought to ameliorate international conflict in its effort to use its foreign relations to achieve the greatest possible material benefit for its domestic economic and technology development. No longer the radical champion of the "have nots," the PRC was attempting as quickly as possible to join the "haves." The countries that became most important to China were those that had the capital and technology vital to PRC development. China had, in effect, adopted a "first world" policy.

The CCP's Response to Western Sanctions after June 1989

As Goldman, Link, and Su have argued, the prodemocracy protests of 1989 emerged as part of a quest for a new, post–Cultural Revolution national identity for China. The Beijing massacre and the suppression of the democracy movement have produced the most serious legitimacy crisis—and in that sense, national identity crisis—in the history of CCP rule. International events, especially the liberation of Eastern Europe, the collapse of the Soviet Union, and the international sanctions imposed on the People's Republic since the massacre, have deepened the internal crisis and raised serious doubts about the future of socialism in China.

In the competition within the top party leadership in the post-Mao period, different images of China's national identity have been put forward in the contest for power. Usually the issues in dispute involve both foreign policy and domestic concerns. In the final years of the 1978–88 reform decade in China one could identify within the party leadership three distinct positions on the controversial issues of market reform and the future of socialism: conservative, reform, and radical.[17] The conservative position was the orthodox view. Conservatives, often older party leaders who were veterans of the struggle for power before 1949 and who typically might have responsibilities in the military or public security organs, defended the party's monopoly of political power and the economic control maintained by the planning bureaucracy as hallmarks of what it means to be a socialist society. They cited ideological chapter and verse from Lenin (and sometimes even from Stalin and Mao) to defend their position and pointed to the party's achievements since winning power in 1949. Although they

[17]This typology is drawn from the more general analysis of leadership debates in socialist societies undergoing market reforms in Peter Van Ness, "Introduction," in Van Ness, ed., *Market Reforms in Socialist Societies: Comparing China and Hungary* (Boulder, Colo.: Rienner, 1989).

might have agreed to a minor role for the market in a socialist society, the conservatives generally saw systematic market reforms as a "capitalist" heresy, one that contained the danger of undermining party control and reversing progress already achieved on the road to communism.

Reformers, by contrast, pointed to the inefficiencies that had become apparent in the command economy and argued that the best way to restore vitality and initiative to China's socialist society in an increasingly competitive global environment was to introduce systemic market reforms. Moreover, they postulated that the prerequisite to socialist construction was a more substantial economic foundation (a more developed "forces of production") and argued that unless sustained and substantial economic growth was achieved, communism would continue to be postponed.[18] The reformers attempted to justify their initiatives in terms of Marxist ideology, even when their reform policies were designed to operate in terms of a logic borrowed from Western neoclassical economics.

Finally, many (but not all) of the radicals rejected Marxism as a philosophic orthodoxy for determining the future of socialist societies. The most prominent radicals were former or even current party members. Most would probably have agreed with radical Fang Lizhi, when he said in an interview, "Marxism is a thing of the past. It . . . belongs to a precise epoch of civilization which is over. It is like a worn dress that must be put aside."[19] The radical critique focused on political change: the democratization of what Marxists called "dictatorship of the proletariat" and what critics understood as totalitarianism. Radicals argued that the market reforms could never be successful without a basic political transformation. Their principal target was the party's monopoly of political power.

To summarize the basic differences among the three positions, the conservatives wanted to keep the Soviet-type system fundamentally intact (a

[18]For example, then–general secretary Zhao Ziyang in his report to the Thirteenth Congress of the CCP argued that "Marxist historical materialists have held all along that the productive forces are ultimately the decisive factor in socialist development. . . . Unless the productive forces are developed, there can be no socialist society, and socialism cannot advance from one stage to another until the realization of communism." He subsequently added: "Whatever is conducive to this growth [of the productive forces] is in keeping with the fundamental interests of the people and is therefore needed by socialism and allowed to exist. Conversely, whatever is detrimental to this growth goes against scientific socialism and is therefore not allowed to exist. *In these historical circumstances, the growth of the productive forces is the immediate and decisive criterion.*" Zhao, "Advance Along the Road of Socialism with Chinese Characteristics: Report Delivered at the 13th National Congress of the Community Party of China," *Beijing Review,* November 9, 1987, pp. i–xxvii; emphasis added.

[19]Tiziano Terzani interview with Fang Lizhi in *Far Eastern Economic Review,* October 22, 1987, p. 53.

little market reform perhaps, but nothing that would change the fundamentals of the system); the reformers wanted to change the operation of the economy to make it more efficient, while preserving the party's monopoly of political power and continuing to proclaim loyalty to Marxism; and the radicals wanted to throw out the entire Soviet-type social system, politics as well as economics, and begin with a democratization of the dictatorship of the proletariat.

To cite examples of those holding the three positions in China in 1987 just before the Thirteenth Party Congress: the then-veteran Politburo Standing Committee member Chen Yun and the National People's Congress Standing Committee chairman Peng Zhen were representatives of the conservative position; both Deng Xiaoping and his then–protégé, Zhao Ziyang, were prototypical reformers; and the jailed dissident Wei Jingsheng and the astrophysicist Fang Lizhi were two of the most prominent Chinese radicals. The Thirteenth Party Congress appeared to be a resounding victory for the reform position, especially when four key conservatives (Chen Yun, Peng Zhen, and ideologues Hu Qiaomu and Deng Liqun) were retired from their top party jobs. But in May 1989, in order to put together a party leadership coalition sufficient to oust Zhao Ziyang and willing to use force to suppress the democracy movement, Deng brought the conservatives back in.

The conservatives, the reformers, and the radicals each addressed questions of national identity differently, and only for the conservatives did a Third World identity for China seem positive or constructive. By contrast, the reformers identified with the east Asian newly industrialized countries (which are the exceptions rather than the norm of Third World development) as their implicit model; and many of the radicals aspired to China's full participation in global civilization, partaking of the best of culture wherever it was to be found rather than identifying with a more parochial and limited notion of national identity.

Over the decade of reform, the debate about China's future became increasingly heated as the problems of reform became more grave. The crunch came in 1988—in just the same way it had for Yugoslavia and Hungary, the two other communist states that had pioneered in implementing systematic market reforms.[20] Inflation, corruption, unemployment, budget and trade deficits, and increasing income inequalities had all become serious problems—but without enough of a market in place to

[20]See Van Ness, *Market Reforms*, especially Janos Kornai, "Some Lessons from the Hungarian Experience for Chinese Reformers," pp. 75–106.

truly force competition and increase economic efficiency. The party leadership had either to bite the bullet and push forward with the political reforms needed to make the transition across the structural threshold from what was still basically a command economy to what would be basically a market system, or the Chinese economy would teeter on that threshold, as Yugoslavia had for several years, suffering in many respects the worst of both economic worlds.[21]

Deng backed off. In September 1988, the party decided not to push forward with price reform, a key feature of the market strategy, and backed away from fundamental political change. And then the pressure began to build: from everyday citizens whose salary increases were lost to inflation and who were disgusted by official corruption, from innovative entrepreneurs strangled by party interventions, and from idealistic students eager to lead China into a better future.[22]

Since the massacre in June 1989, the new Jiang Zemin government has closed the door to dissent as a part of a countrywide repression, reversed the earlier political reforms, and attempted to reshape the objectives of economic reform. In trying to deny responsibility for the atrocities of June 1989, the regime has found itself confounded in contradictions of its own making.[23] In response to foreign condemnation of the official terror, and

[21]The Hungarian economist Janos Kornai, probably the most accomplished analyst of market reforms in socialist command economies, concludes in his most recent book that market socialism everywhere it has been attempted (including China) has failed. Contrary to his earlier advocacy of such reforms, Kornai is now convinced that, "the time has come to look this fact in the face and abandon the principle of market socialism." For Kornai, market reforms cannot successfully transform a command economy into an efficient and competitive economic system, and the only answer is full-scale privatization, "a free economy," which in turn, he argues, requires political democratization. His book is a prescription for achieving these fundamental changes: Kornai, *The Road to a Free Economy-Shifting from a Socialist System: The Example of Hungary* (New York: Norton, 1990), pp. 57–58.

[22]See Anita Chan, "The Challenge to the Social Fabric," *Pacific Review* (1989): pp. 121–31; Brian G. Martin, *China in Crisis: The Events of April–June 1989,* Current Issues Paper No. 1 (Canberra: Parliament of the Commonwealth of Australia, Legislative Research Service, 1989); John Fincher, "Zhao's Fall, China's Loss," *Foreign Policy* 76 (Fall 1989): 3–25; and Lowell Dittmer, "The Tiananmen Massacre," *Problems of Communism* 38 (September–October 1989): 2–15.

[23]The official CCP theoretical position supporting the policy changes appears in Jiang Zemin, "Speech at the Meeting in Celebration of the 40th Anniversary of the Founding of the People's Republic of China," *Beijing Review,* October 9, 1989, pp. 11–24. For analysis of the human rights situation, see Ann Kent, *Human Rights in the People's Republic of China: National and International Dimensions* (Canberra: Australian National University, Peace Research Centre, 1990); and for a commentary on the legal situation, see Jerome Alan Cohen, "Law and Leadership in China," *Far Eastern Economic Review,* July 13, 1989, pp. 23–24. See also "Beijing Reinforces Central Planners' Role and Extends Austerity," *International Herald Tribune,*

domestic passive resistance to the widening repression, a siege mentality has set in among the conservative party leaders in Beijing.

Mikhail Gorbachev's official visit to China in May 1989, intended by Deng Xiaoping as a celebration of a normalization of Sino-Soviet relations on Chinese terms (meaning the People's Republic had won Soviet concessions on all of the so-called three obstacles) and to form the basis for launching a truly "independent foreign policy," came in the middle of the embarrassing prodemocracy demonstrations. Humiliated by their inability to maintain order in the capital city, the leadership's subsequent use of force against what they called a "counter-revolutionary rebellion"[24] not only outraged the West but launched China on a repressive, antireform path directly counter to the direction of events in Eastern Europe. The conservatives seemed to want to shut the PRC off from both East and West.

Emerging in official PRC replies to the international sanctions imposed by the West on China since June 1989 are themes reminiscent of the 1960s. Once again we hear the protests about a Third World China under assault by Western imperialism. Charging the United States with interference in China's internal affairs and seeking to refute the Western concept of universal human rights, Yi Ding, for example, wrote that "third world countries, given their national conditions, stress collective rights. They regard collective human rights as the foundation of individual rights and the precondition for individuals to enjoy all rights and freedoms." Repeatedly, he invoked the Five Principles of Peaceful Coexistence, including the principle of noninterference in the internal affairs of other countries,[25] principles that originated in the early years of Afro-Asian solidarity.

China's democracy movement is described by the CCP as a premeditated

---

December 2–3, 1989, p. 19; and "China Harbors Last 'True Marxists,' Beijing's Economic Planner Says," *International Herald Tribune*, December 6, 1989, p. 2. For the CCP's official view of the atrocities, see Chen Xitong, "Report on Checking the Turmoil and Quelling the Counter-Revolutionary Rebellion," *Beijing Review*, July 17, 1989, pp. i–xx.

[24]For the best estimates of loss of life and the extent of the repression, see Amnesty International, *People's Republic of China: Preliminary Findings on Killings of Unarmed Civilians, Arbitrary Arrests and Summary Executions since 3 June 1989* (London: Amnesty International, August 1989); and Asia Watch, *Punishment Season: Human Rights in China after Martial Law* (New York: Human Rights Watch, February 1990). For the best analysis of where and when the killing took place in Beijing, see Robin Munro, "The Real Story of the Slaughter in Beijing," *Nation*, June 11, 1990, pp. 811–22.

[25]Yi Ding, "Opposing Interference in Other Countries' Internal Affairs through Human Rights," *Beijing Review*, November 6, 1989, pp. 10–12. Paradoxically, these are the same principles the CCP proclaimed so ostentatiously during the 1960s when meanwhile providing active support to revolutionary movements seeking to overthrow other Third World governments; see Van Ness, *Revolution and Chinese Foreign Policy*, esp. pt. II.

conspiracy that "colluded with foreign forces" to overthrow the Communist party and subvert Chinese socialism.[26] Once again, the image of a beleaguered Third World China defending itself valiantly against the sinister designs of Western imperialism is invoked.

The Future Viability of a Third World Identity

In the 1990s we may come to witness the complete collapse of any viable concept of Third World, not only as a result of the growing economic, political, and ideological differences among Third World countries themselves (already apparent for many years) but also because of the end of the Cold War competition between the United States and the Soviet Union. If indeed communism is dead as a viable alternative road to modernization, the idea of a *third* way loses all political meaning. Already several Marxist states in Africa have begun to reorient toward a market economy because of the Soviet collapse.[27] Most noticeable so far is the disappearance of the so-called strategic triangle. Robert Delfs observes: "The strategic triangle is gone, and with it China's influence on events outside the region. Western leaders no longer see any compelling logic to compromise or cooperate with China—hence the alacrity with which many agreed to economic sanctions over Tiananmen."[28]

To my mind, the central questions of Chinese national identity (as opposed to the official national identity put forward by the CCP leadership for policy purposes) focus on two issues: (1) how to relate to China's cultural tradition (illustrated by the debate prompted by *River Elegy*) and (2) the best strategies for achieving wealth and power (which virtually all Chinese seem to think are China's due). A Third World identity for China helps resolve neither issue. During the 1960s, China's attempt to lead the Third World and to shape the "have nots" into a third force in global politics failed. Moreover, during the reform decade Beijing gave up almost entirely on collective action and sought instead to join the "haves" by making a separate peace with the global status quo. If anything, China has shown that it wants desperately to escape from being Third World!

But how are we to interpret and understand official PRC claims to a Third World identity? Since in many respects China is still objectively Third

[26]Chen Xitong, "Report on Checking the Turmoil," pp. i–iv.
[27]Raymond Bonner, "African Democracy," *New Yorker,* September 3, 1990, pp. 93–105.
[28]Robert Delfs, "China 1990: Foreign Policy—Exit (World Stage Left)," *Far Eastern Economic Review,* August 23, 1990, p. 32.

World, is it not likely that party leaders truly identify China in those terms? Probably not.

Obviously we do not know what goes on in the minds of China's leaders, but let me suggest three reasons to be skeptical. First, virtually all Chinese leaders manifest in one way or another a national pride in being Chinese, an identification with the glories of China's past, and, one might say, a typical Chinese cultural arrogance. All of these traits point to a sense of China's uniqueness rather than of shared Third World characteristics. Thus when PRC leaders invoke a Third World official national identity, which domestically evokes memories of national humiliation, the result in terms of international relations is not necessarily a basic Chinese sense of common bond with the Third World.

Second, the Chinese have had great difficulties on a person-to-person basis translating their official policy of Third World solidarity into interpersonal cooperation and harmony. Chinese racist attitudes toward African blacks studying in China are a notorious example. Too often, when attempting to implement a PRC official identity as Third World, the Chinese sense of superiority and the expectation that others will defer to PRC leadership emerges through the rhetorical smoke screen. It is not surprising that Kim has found, in his empirical research on China's role at the United Nations, that when one presses beyond the rhetoric to investigate the People's Republic actions, China behaves not as a typical Third World country but, as Kim aptly puts it, as a Group of One (G-1).

Third, it is remarkable how completely the Third World line of the 1960s was replaced during the reform decade with policies that rejected de facto all the principles that earlier had been proclaimed as fundamental to Third World solidarity (common opposition to imperialism, self-reliant development, South-South cooperation, and so on). After Mao's death, when the opportunity became available for China to take the fast track to wealth and power by cooperating with the capitalist West instead of opposing it, China's Third World identity rapidly slipped away except for propaganda purposes.

Meanwhile, however, the propaganda statements repeatedly claiming for the People's Republic a Third World national identity are intended to tap basic feelings of Chinese nationalist sentiment and keep alive the option of a renewed effort to build coalitions among the countries of the Third World if necessary. In 1989, when relations with the superpowers rapidly deteriorated because of Western condemnation of the Beijing massacre and the beginning of the transformation of the Soviet Union and Eastern Europe, official CCP statements invoking a Chinese Third World identity once again emerged. But the reason for their reappearance, to my mind, is not because the Third World constitutes a fundamental dimension of Chinese identity but rather because, in a time of need, a conservative party leadership has fallen back on old symbols in the vain hope that they will still have some political usefulness.

Confounded by a national identity crisis of the most fundamental proportions, the CCP in 1990 is no more likely to be able to regain either domestic or international support by invoking the tattered slogans from the 1960s, urging Third World solidarity, than it is by rehabilitating the discredited Cultural Revolution role model Lei Feng, who has also been returned to the ideological fray. The Chinese people seem simply to be waiting—waiting for the ideologically bankrupt Long March generation of leaders to die, so that they can once again resume their search for a viable, modern national identity for China.

中
國 9

China's Multiple Identities
in East Asia: China
as a Regional Force

Robert A. Scalapino

"National identity," as I use the term, relates to the way in which a people, and especially a policy-making elite, perceive the essence of their nation in relation to others. It thus influences attitudes and policies alike, being the psychological foundation for the roles and behavior patterns of a country in the international arena. The concept must be used with caution. However vigilant, one is tempted to attach to the phrase an overweighting of that which is cohesive, hence collective, and uniform as well as permanent. Moreover, any attempt to transfer a concept of personal identity—itself replete with contradictions and change—to "national identity" is more likely to be misleading than helpful.

To use the phrase "national identity" is to speak in political terms, and in modern political terms, in the age when a greater number of citizens could be caused to grant the nation-state in which they lived legitimacy and allegiance (identifying with it) than in earlier times. The instrumentalities whereby such identification was achieved—some combination of coercion and persuasion—have been greatly abetted by advances in mass education and communication. Even here, however, a contradiction has developed. The contemporary information-communication revolution breaks down the exclusiveness and isolation that once afforded rulers the opportunity to mold their people with a minimum of external interference. Together with the degree to which economic intercourse is leaping over ideological-political boundaries virtually at will, the authority and, in legal terms, the sovereignty of the nation-state face parallel threats.

Current trends also cast a deep shadow of doubt over any "stage theory," whether applied to the development of identity or of political system. Decades ago, political events in both China and India (and before them, Russia) vitiated Marxist theory of the correlation between stages of economic development and political system. Moreover, a consciousness of national identity comes when a crisis is posed, internal or external. In essence, it is a response to a real or perceived challenge. Such a response occurs neither in stages nor in some preordained progression.

It is vital to understand that an elite—in this case, a political elite—must articulate a state's national identity. To be sure, to have validity, that identity must rest on certain predispositions rooted in race, culture (including religion or deeply implanted values), and broadly accepted goals. Each of these components, however, except race or ethnicity, is susceptable to change in varying degree. The latter is thus the one permanent factor in politics—and as contemporary events illustrate, frequently the most potent.

In this connection, it is important to distinguish between those subconscious or "natural" proclivities at the mass level that derive from a sense of commonality, whether of race, culture, class, or organizational unit (identifications that may lend themselves to national unity or division) and elite-promoted images that are projected to justify policies or to manipulate others. As noted, the latter succeed only if they have certain roots in the former; but the two are by no means identical, and not infrequently, a strong element of tension exists between them. The nation-state is only one competitive element in the quest for an individual's identification and loyalty, and in much of the world even today it is not the most powerful element in so far as the bulk of the people nominally under it are concerned—ethnic majorities as well as minorities.

Perhaps the most successful, if short-lived, effort to forge a concept of national identity was that of Adolf Hitler and his Nazi movement. With the ringing cry "One nation, one people, one leader" (Ein Reich, ein Volk, ein Führer) the Nazis succeeded in mobilizing a very large majority of German citizens (to be sure, only after outlawing all competing parties) by utilizing images of past injustices, racial superiority and, hence, the right to extirpate hostile forces and creeds, at home and beyond current boundaries. Yet this success lasted little more than a decade and, like a similar effort in Japan, ended in disaster. Nor can one be certain what twists and turns such a movement would have taken over a longer time had the Axis powers won the war, especially after Hitler had passed from the scene. Leadership in our times continues to vie with institutions in importance, and not only in societies where political institutions are weak.

In the final analysis, the concept of national identity must be used with the understanding that as a concept, it varies in political significance (priority and intensity) with the challenges immediately confronting the nation; that it is constantly in flux, being altered by a host of internal and external factors; that even in its most fundamental expression it is not without contradictions, some of them basic; and that the latter fact enables a political elite to play on its multiple and varied potentialities in fashioning images that will facilitate the exercise of power and the effectuation of policy.

Turning to the specific case of China, several themes have combined to provide the foundations of national identity throughout the twentieth century, with the political shifts from monarchy to Nationalist rule and thence to Communist dominance marked by both continuities and change. Two overriding concepts advanced by the political elites have been those of one nation composed of five primary races and of China as the Central Kingdom, the hub around which others revolve. The essence of modern Chinese nationalism has lain in these doctrines, garnished by the strong belief that a China destined by its superior culture to tutor (and in some degree, to control) others was being ravished by Western barbarians whose technological superiority gave them a power that neither their culture nor their methods of governance warranted. These themes represented a blend of China's traditional beliefs and its modern nationalism. Moreover, they meshed reasonably well with the xenophobic proclivities of the peasant masses. The Chinese peasant is suspicious of all that is "foreign," including those elements who came from beyond the immediate vicinity. For the peasant, moreover, governance has always been epitomized by personalities, not abstract institutions or law. Thus, for the elite, the concept of tutelage—raising the masses to political enlightenment—came naturally and was deeply implanted in the domestic policies of both Nationalists and Communists. Moreover, this concept could have a certain applicability to those "unenlightened peoples" on the peripheries of empire. Yet in the modern era, increased contact with the advanced industrial world, including growing portions of Asia itself, heightened the paradox between the tenacious belief in the innate superiority of China (its size, its civilization, its race) and the inescapable fact of its backwardness. Therefore, it is not surprising to find China's leaders playing on both of these themes in contrapuntal fashion or, more important, acting on them.

Against this background, let me turn to China's varied roles in the region of which it is a part and to the equally varied perceptions of those roles by China's neighbors. First, the importance of China to the rest of Asia is almost universally accepted—even a China uncertain of its course and lacking in the ability to project its authority far beyond its boundaries. Its physical scale, its aggregate statistics—economic and military as well as demographic—and the cultural legacy it has bequeathed to many of the other Asian societies guarantee that China will be accorded the status of a regional power.

The extent to which it is prepared to play that role can be debated.[1] If we explore the military dimensions of China's power, a mixed picture emerges. The Chinese People's Liberation Army bloodied Indian forces in the Himalayan border clashes of 1962 but fared poorly in 1979 against seasoned Vietnamese forces. Yet when Chinese naval forces seized several atolls in the South China Sea, Hanoi found it prudent to rest with protests, and the formidable forces that China kept on the Sino-Vietnamese border required a sizable Vietnamese border guard until rapprochement between the two governments. Despite its limited military reach, moreover, the People's Republic continues to expand its nuclear weaponry, albeit at a level far below that of either the United States or Russia. If it can be argued that nuclear weapons have declined in credibility except as a deterrent, the fact that China is East Asia's only nuclear state confers a "big power" status on it as a member of the still relatively exclusive nuclear club.[2] Moreover, recent moves to develop a blue-water navy suggest that the People's Republic intends to back up its interests with military power.

There are countervailing factors. As is well known, even the small states surrounding China have formidable military forces, generally more modern than those of China. The two Koreas, for example, have military forces out of all proportion to their populations, as does Taiwan. Japan, moreover, has a small military force almost wholly defensive in structure but with the most modern equipment. These circumstances, together with the prevailing alliance structure in the region, limit China's potential mlitary reach. Yet as we have seen, when China has been prepared to take risks or accept considerable losses, it has committed its military forces outside its borders.

---

[1] For diverse positions, see Commission on Integrated Long-Term Strategy, *Discriminate Deterrence* (Washington, D.C.: Pentagon, January 1988); Donald S. Zagoria, "China and the Superpowers: Recent Trends in the Strategic Triangle," in Robert A. Scalapino et al., *Asian Security Issues: Regional and Global* (Berkeley: University of California, Institute of East Asian Studies, 1988); Samuel S. Kim, ed., *China and the World: Chinese Foreign Policy in the Post-Mao Era* (Boulder, Colo.: Westview, 1989); and Harry Harding, ed., *China's Foreign Relations in the 1980s* (New Haven: Yale University Press, 1984).

[2] See John Lewis and Xue Litai, *China Builds the Bomb* (Stanford: Stanford University Press, 1988).

Currently, tension is lower with potential adversaries including Vietnam and Taiwan. The premium is on handling the People's Republic's domestic problems, with the military's domestic role uncertain. Thus the image projected is that of a benign China, prepared to abide by the Five Principles of Coexistence. Yet no small neighbor can be certain of the future.

In the economic realm also, China's status as a regional power is subject to varying interpretations. The quantitative gains in gross national product during the reform era after 1979 are well known, as is the onset of a plethora of problems by 1987, necessitating economic retrenchment. The People's Republic's economic progression has been spasmodic, well characterized by the phrase "two steps forward, one step backward," with "planning" subject to some of the same vagaries that apply to "law" in China. Nevertheless, in this land of 1.1 billion people, the aggregate statistics are impressive and the growth spurts suggestive of a strong potential, given proper policies. If the pledge of Deng Xiaoping and his associates is achieved, China's gross national product in the year 2000 will reach U.S. $1,100 billion, placing China in fifth position in the world in aggregate gross national product. But even in that event, the Chinese themselves will still be poor, with per capita income about U.S. $900 annually. It is this situation that enables Chinese leaders to identify their nation simultaneously as great, entitled to respect—and a part of the backward world. There can be no doubt, however, that some Asian states court the giant even when it is sick, with visions of a better future periodically dashed and then resuscitated.

In the political sphere, any portrayal of China's regional power status must also take full account of its complexities. The early years witnessed a simultaneous espousal of cosmopolitanism via Marxism-Leninism led by the "Great Soviet Union" and the creation of a sphere of influence within east Asian communism. Weak in virtually every sense, the young People's Republic used radical rhetoric to establish its revolutionary credentials abroad and backed that rhetoric by providing diverse forms of assistance to communist movements throughout East Asia.[3] Subsequent events provided eloquent evidence of the results. As Beijing's quarrel with Nikita Khrushchev unfolded, the People's Republic was able to carry most Asian Communist parties with it, including those of Indonesia, Vietnam, and North Korea.

---

[3] A detailed examination of this period is given by Jay Taylor, *China and Southeast Asia: Peking's Relations with Revolutionary Movements,* expanded ed. (New York: Praeger, 1976).

See also Melvin Gurtov, *China and Southeast Asia: The Politics of Survival* (Baltimore: Johns Hopkins University Press, 1962).

Naturally, China's policies during these years created enemies in at least equal numbers to friends. While the People's Republic called for a sweeping global revolution, most leaders of the new Asian nations believed that they had had their revolution, and they did not wish to be toppled by communists, indigenous or otherwise. Moreover, the historic concern with Chinese expansion, fed by the resentment of the overseas Chinese economic dominance, further clouded the picture in Southeast Asia.

The PRC leaders, however, had more than one string to their bow. As a prelude to the 1955 Bandung conference, Zhou Enlai—together with Jawaharlal Nehru and U Nu—fashioned the Five Principles of Peaceful Coexistence. Here was a formula, reemphasized in recent years, for harmony among nations operating under separate systems. In its origins, moreover, it had strong regional connotations despite the universal applicability proclaimed. Through Zhou, the People's Republic was asserting that it was prepared to live at peace with its neighbors, notwithstanding basic ideological and institutional differences. If Bandung and the Five Principles subsequently had limited influence, it was because most Asian leaders were never certain as to whether China was placing its priorities on comrade-to-comrade, people-to-people, or state-to-state relations. In reality, of course, it varied its priorities depending on the situation, keeping all its options open in a period when its economic and strategic strength was limited.

China's influence—or at least a convergence of views—with the two other prominent Leninist states of East Asia has risen since the advent of Mikhail Gorbachev, at least temporarily. On the one hand, the People's Republic under Deng pioneered in economic reform before the recent East European-Soviet efforts and, accompanying this, allowed some political opening. These moves, at least the former, had an impact on North Korea and Vietnam. On the other hand, a majority of Beijing's leaders, along with those in Pyongyang and Hanoi, were appalled by political developments in the Western Leninist states after 1985.

A growing ideological gap thus developed, with the east Asian Leninist leaders proclaiming that the dictatorship of the Communist Party would be rigorously upheld and "bourgeois liberalism," a form of "extreme Westernization," would be combated. An appeal to xenophobia emerged, with the assertion that the choice was between independence and a return to China's state of subordination to the imperialists who were now seeking to subvert socialism by "peaceful evolution." Only the Mongolian People's Republic (MPR)—long intimately connected with the USSR—started down a separate path, followed later by the Kampuchean People's party of the Phnom Penh government.

At the same time, the PRC sought to maintain an earlier stance of shifting from comrade-to-comrade to state-to-state relations everywhere and, in this manner, behaved like a "bourgeois" state. Thus Beijing currently proclaims that revolution cannot be exported and, as far as can be determined, has recently confined revolutionary assistance in the region to the Khmer Rouge (as well as Norodom Sihanouk) under special circumstances. Even an end to that aid was pledged at the end of 1991. Diplomatic relations have been established with all the east and south Asian states except South Korea (out of deference to the North) and a few South Pacific states. In sum, China has increasingly established itself as a part of the prevailing regional order rather than as a revolutionary agent. Relations with certain states, to be sure, remain less than satisfactory because of past issues, but normalized relations with Vietnam have been reestablished and overtures to India are periodically made. Meanwhile, relations have been stabilized with Russia and the Mongolian People's Republic, and despite the ideological cleavage, Beijing's leaders have signaled that they do not want to engage in polemical battles.

Predictions regarding China have always been hazardous and never more so than today. Some observers have forecast a unified, powerful China by the early decades of the twenty-first century—a China that would have the capability of deeply influencing every aspect of other Asian states.[4] Other observers have raised doubts about the ability of this massive society to coordinate and sustain policies, or to maintain unity. They foresee a protracted period of instability and forced concentration on domestic problems. Some even predict disintegration and a period akin to the "warlordism" of the 1920s. It is possible, of course, that elements of the less extreme forecasts can be melded: a China with continuing serious internal problems but a nation that still manages to gain in overall power and the capacity to project that power. An analogy might be India—its domestic problems persist but it has demonstrated a capacity to play a role of rising importance in the Asian subcontinent and the Indian Ocean.

Whatever the future holds, two facts important to China's regional influence today must be reiterated. First, the Chinese—or more accurately, those who directly or indirectly shape attitudes and policies—perceive their nation as influential or at least as worthy of being influential, and they behave accordingly. Second, virtually all China's neighbors accord the People's Republic a healthy respect, using that phrase in a nonnormative sense. No Asian leader dismisses the People's Republic of China as unimportant to the future of its neighbors. Moreover, both the United States

---

[4]See, e.g., Commission on Long-Term Integrated Strategy, *Discriminate Deterrence*.

and Russia treat the People's Republic as a major nation having global as well as regional consequence.

With these generalizations providing the setting, let me examine the current policies and perceptions of the People's Republic as they pertain to individual Pacific-Asian states and the key determinants that shape them. Unlike India in its region, China is not in a position to play a hegemonic role in either northeast or Southeast Asia because of the immediate presence of Japan and Russia, with the United States a third Pacific-Asian power having vital interests in the region.

Toward the three latter nations, China's policies have gravitated in the direction of a nonhostile, nonaligned, yet nonequidistant position containing as low risks as possible. Earlier policies served PRC interests less well. The initial alliance with the USSR, grounded in a combination of ideological, security, and developmental considerations, temporarily served certain purposes, but after only a decade, it collapsed because of the tensions derived from the increasingly different priorities of the two states and the strains of PRC dependence on Soviet domestic as well as foreign policies in a tempestuous era.[5] Khrushchev, the Soviet Union's first reformer, wanting to revitalize an economy in significant trouble, preferred détente with the United States over the risk of war on behalf of China. Nor was he prepared to accord the People's Republic that degree of equality and consultation in the course of his break from Stalinism that the strongly nationalist Mao required. Thus a combination of differently perceived national interests and idiosyncratic behavior patterns produced the cleavage. In retrospect, however, the separation was inevitable at some point. Two major states living cheek by jowl with each other, striving to build a national identity and possessing very different cultures, stages of development, and degrees of military power can only be allied when they possess a common enemy. The United States played that role initially but later gravitated toward a more complex policy.

In the decade of the 1960s, PRC foreign relations were dominated by strong elements of romanticism and xenophobia, garbed in ideological raiment. Identifying itself with the newly discovered Third World, the People's Republic took a "plague on both your houses" approach to the USSR and the United States. The satisfaction of such a policy in terms of "self-reliance" and independence was offset by the fact that the Third World

---

[5]The classic account is Donald S. Zagoria, *The Sino-Soviet Conflict, 1956–1961* (Princeton: Princeton University Press, 1962); for a Soviet version, see O. B. Borisov and B. T. Koloskov, *Soviet-Chinese Relations, 1945–1980* (Moscow: Mysl, 1971).

could serve neither the developmental nor the security interests of the People's Republic, and most efforts to move closer to the "Second World," namely, capitalist Western Europe and Japan, were hampered by the deep hostility characterizing Sino-American relations.

When Mao and his associates were finally confronted with the possibility of a conflict with the USSR in 1969, ideology and xenophobic Sinocentrism had to give way to pragmatic, interest-oriented policies, revealing once again that adaptive quality that recurrently saves the Chinese from prolonged extremism. Thus the pendulum swung. Improving relations with the United States enabled China to enter the wider world, with ties reestablished or strengthened with Western Europe and Japan. And by the end of the 1970s, Deng Xiaoping and some others were calling for a global alliance, led by the United States, against Soviet hegemonism.

Yet this position was unlikely to survive beyond the immediate threat because it entailed a high-risk, high-cost PRC foreign policy at the very time China's leaders perceived a critical need to place top priority on domestic reforms. By the early 1980s, international conditions were favorable for making a shift. The United States had reestablished clear military primacy in the Pacific-Asian theater; Leonid Brezhnev had held out a small olive branch to China; and dramatic advances were being made by the market economies in Asia as well as in the West.

China proceeded to define its position as that of nonalignment, announcing that it was prepared to open relations with any nation on the basis of the Five Principles of Peaceful Coexistence. Subsequently, PRC leaders outlined the three conditions that the Soviet Union had to meet if Sino-Soviet normalization were to be achieved: reducing border forces, withdrawing from Afghanistan, and inducing the Vietnamese to end their Cambodian involvement. As progress was made on these conditions, normalization ensued, climaxed by Gorbachev's mid-1989 visit to Beijing.

Meanwhile, China combined "nonalignment" with a decided tilt to the United States and Japan. PRC policies toward the major states had evolved in relatively sophisticated fashion. Economic and strategic needs were reflected in the relations cultivated with the two major market economies.[6] Whether measured in trade figures, technology transfer, the training of scientists and technicians, or military purchases and contacts, PRC relations with these two nations dwarfed other foreign ties. And through these

---

[6]On policy toward the United States, see various articles in *Asian Survey, Beijing Review,* and *International Studies* (Beijing); on Japan, see Allen S. Whiting, *China Eyes Japan* (Berkeley and Los Angeles: University of California Press, 1989).

growing connections and those with other market economies, China was gradually drawn into the institutions of economic significance at the regional and global levels, thereby becoming at least a peripheral part of the market-dominated international order. Meanwhile, as relations with the USSR improved, marginal but useful economic benefits accrued, together with a release from some of the previous military pressures and the achievement of a new flexibility in choosing positions on international issues.

Suddenly, in the spring of 1989, a combination of external and domestic developments threatened these policies. The global crisis in Leninism combined with the political relaxation and economic malaise characterizing China to induce divisions among Chinese leaders and rising public unrest. When to this volatile scene were added errors of judgment and policy, the result was the June 4 repression. For the PRC leaders in power, the crisis had become an issue of survival. For much of the world, and especially the West, it became an issue of human rights. Bitterness and mutual recrimination followed.

PRC leaders—weak, uncertain, and feeling beleaguered—responded in predictable fashion. They demanded that "interference in China's internal affairs" cease, displaying some of the old rhetoric, replete with xenophobic overtones. Face was involved. Thus, the insistence was that the United States take the first steps to make amends. Major nations led by the United States, it was proclaimed, had shifted from "military hegemonism" to "peaceful evolution," but the intent was the same: to overthrow socialism.[7]

Through such rhetoric, Chinese leaders—in concert with their North Korea and Vietnamese counterparts—voiced their alarm at what was happening in the Western Leninist societies including the old USSR and their fear that in the process of an economic turning out, "subversive" political themes would contaminate the citizenry and especially the younger educated generations. An effort was made to partially exempt the Japanese, with the implication that they had been dragged more or less unwillingly into concurrence with the human rights protests.

Yet at the same time, PRC officials were repeatedly proclaiming that the government intended to continue to promote an economic turning out, focusing on a growing interaction with the market economies at all levels. It heralded any evidence of new U.S. or Japanese investment. Moreover, in a variety of concrete steps, certain agencies promoted continuing PRC-U.S.

[7]One example among many is contained in Jiang Zemin's speech of September 29, 1989, reprinted in *Beijing Review,* October 9, 1989, pp. 11–24. See also Winston Lord, "China's Big Chill," *Foreign Affairs* 68 (Fall 1989): 1–26; and my "Asia and the United States: The Challenges Ahead," ibid., 69 (Spring 1990): 89–115.

cultural relations, albeit with new restrictions and clearances relating to students and visiting scholars, some of which predated the June events.

In truth, there now appeared to be not one but many Chinas: the center versus the provinces and municipalities; official versus unofficial linkages; and even within the official community, a diversity of views and policies. Since this is clearly a transitional period with future leaders and policies in doubt, one cannot predict China's relationships with the other major Pacific-Asian societies in the period ahead. China's national interests would, however, dictate a broad continuance of the foreign policies established in the early 1980s with such modifications as changing conditions demand but no fundamental shifts. This assumes, of course, the continuance of leaders who are private pragmatists and a China that continues to be more or less whole.

To buttress its position with the major states and as evidence that economics challenges politics for priority in Chinese foreign policy despite the resurgence of ideology for domestic consumption, PRC leaders in recent years have undertaken a radical shift in policies toward the so-called newly industrial economies (NIEs). Setting aside ideological and strategic barriers, Beijing has dramatically expanded economic and cultural relations with South Korea, Taiwan, and Singapore, as well as with Hong Kong. It should be quickly noted that such developments have been enthusiastically supported, often initiated, by the private sector of these societies, with either limited interference or support from the governments concerned.

China's practical policies are underwritten by the theme that economics can be separated from politics. Thus the political positions of North Korea are regularly espoused and South Korean leaders or policies periodically criticized, even as trade with the South hovers around three billion dollars (1989) and cultural contacts expand. To be sure, since the June 4 massacre, China has exhibited some caution in its policies toward the Republic of Korea (ROK) and has drawn closer to the Democratic People's Republic of Korea (DPRK) politically, but diverse contacts with the South continue, including trade and visitations. Some ten thousand Koreans went back and forth between China and South Korea throughout 1989. In sum, China continues to follow a de facto two-Koreas policy. Anxious to keep the North by its side in this period of global Leninist crisis, Beijing may not grant official recognition to the Republic of Korea quickly, but its desire for peace on the Korean peninsula and its willingness to interact with South Korea on many levels have been repeatedly demonstrated.[8]

[8]The background is sketched in Young Whan Kihl, *Politics and Policies in Divided Korea* (Boulder, Colo.: Westview Press 1984), as well as in Steven I. Levine, "China in Asia: The PRC

Even more dramatic developments have taken place in recent years in relations between the People's Republic and Taiwan.[9] Here, trade has also approached five billion dollars per annum, with investment from Taiwan going into Fujian and Guangdong in ever-increasing amounts. More than one million people from Taiwan have visited the People's Republic in the past few years, with a handful of PRC citizens allowed to come to Taiwan. Both sides continue to criticize each other in political matters, often with strong ideological overtones. Taiwan, moreover, has recently twisted the dragon's tail by getting five small states to grant it official recognition in exchange for economic assistance. The People's Republic has promptly broken relations with these countries, reiterating its opposition to a "two-Chinas" policy. Its formula for reunification remains "one country, two systems."

More worrisome for the People's Republic, several important European and Asian nations have been upgrading their relations with Taiwan, responding to its economic dynamism. Moreover, Taiwan's leaders, emulating South Korea, have embarked on their own *Nordpolitik,* directing attention to Eastern Europe, Russia, and even Vietnam. In sum, Taiwan's economic strength is breaking down political barriers while the People's Republic is lacking the capacity to employ retaliatory measures; indeed, through its own economic relations with Taipei, Beijing is a part of the broader pattern.

Cross-contacts, moreover, are leading away from, rather than toward, reunification, at least in the near term. In contrast to developments relating to the two Germanies which led to institutional fusion, the situation between the divided states of Asia, the PRC-Taiwan included, is one of increasing institutional-systemic separation, thereby making difficult any advance beyond the highly questionable "one nation, two systems" formula. Beijing authorities insist that negotiations take place between parties, whereas President Lee Teng-hui, while significantly modifying the "three nos" policy toward the People's Republic (no official contact, no negotiations, no compromises), has proposed a dialogue between the two *govern-*

---

as a Regional Power," in Harding, *China's Foreign Relations.* On the negative side, see Yu Shaohua, "Political Crisis in South Korea," *Beijing Review,* October 30, 1989, pp. 14–16.

[9]For the Taiwan perspective on relations with the People's Republic, see President Lee Teng-hui's inaugural speech of May 20, 1990, published in full in *Newsletter* (Taipei), May 31, 1990, pp. 1–5, and in the same issue, a summary of Lee's press conference on May 22, pp. 5–9. The PRC perspective can be found in a report by Jiang Zemin, "Party Chief Stands for One China and Two Party Negotiation," *Beijing Review,* June 18, 1990, p. 7; and Guo Xiangzhi, "Prospects for Relations between the Two Sides of the Strait in the 1990s," *Liaowang* (Outlook), May 14, 1990, pp. 21–22.

ments providing the Beijing government renounces the use of force against Taiwan, ends its policy of seeking to isolate Taiwan internationally, implements political democracy, and adopts an open economic system. Naturally, PRC authorities have rejected the conditions as well as the concept of governmental negotiations, which, they point out, constitutes advocacy of two Chinas. In practical terms, however, an unofficial dialogue is underway, buttressed by a rapidly growing network of economic and cultural ties. Yet polls in Taiwan show that to know the People's Republic better is not to love it more. Those who have visited the mainland from Taiwan are even more opposed to reunification than those who have not made the trip.

Increasingly worrisome to Beijing, moreover, is the Taiwan independence movement, spurred forward both by international developments—especially the dismemberment of the old Russian empire—and by the demise of first-generation mainland refugees on Taiwan. This movement is still supported by only a small minority of the Taiwanese, but under certain circumstances it could grow.

Toward a third NIE, Hong Kong, the reunification issue has been settled in formal terms, with reversion scheduled for 1997. Yet with political issues added to economic ones, especially since the events of 1989, the People's Republic faces the task of rebuilding its credibility in order to contain an accelerating brain that seems likely to reduce Hong Kong's educated professional and managerial classes to a dangerously low level. Beijing's pledge of extensive autonomy and support for Hong Kong's capitalism "for fifty years" must be evaluated alongside its insistence that PRC troops will be stationed in the territory and that Hong Kong cannot serve as a source of interference in PRC politics. Thus the question remains, What will China inherit when this territory reverts to the People's Republic in a very few years?

Yet another Chinese enclave exists in the form of Singapore, a city-state surrounded by a Malay sea. More successfully than most other Asian states, Singapore has practiced a de facto "one China, one Taiwan" policy. Anxious to create a Singaporean identity and avoid internal factionalism, Lee Kuan Yew long restricted cultural relations with other Chinese societies, especially the People's Republic. Yet trade grew, and Lee himself interacted personally with both Taipei and Beijing while proclaiming that Singapore would be last among the five Association of Southeast Asian Nations (ASEAN) (Brunei excluded) to recognize the People's Republic. Recognition finally took place. Meanwhile PRC leaders displayed remarkable public tolerance for Singapore's domestic and foreign policies, allowing not a word of public criticism to be uttered.

Thus, among the multiple Chinas of Asia, a modus vivendi between rising economic and cultural interaction and continuing political separatism is maintained, with systemic developments—economic as well as political—not conducive to a closer identity, at least for the present, despite the expanding network of ties. As in the case of the Korean people and those of Vietnam (even after reunification) as well as the Germans, the sense of belonging to a single race and cultural tradition has been made much more complex for the Chinese by the political divisions and the radically different stages of economic development that have accompanied those divisions. Yet for Beijing, a certain cultural identity with the other Chinas supports the pragmatic policies currently being pursued.

Ironically, in contrast to relations with the NIEs, PRC relations with the other Leninist states of Asia have been periodically cool-to-hostile at various points in the past. Ideological commonality was earlier overridden by considerations born out of practical economic and strategic concerns. The concept of a unified socialist world has now vanished, although the remaining Leninist states of Asia—together with Cuba—are making an effort to revitalize their mutual relations in response to the adverse international currents. Thus improvements have taken place, although none of these states have genuinely close ties. Soviet domestic policies and the increasingly bold overtures of Russia to the Republic of Korea together with the upheaval in Eastern Europe have caused Kim Il Sung to seek closer relations with the People's Republic once again. Yet in dealing with the North Koreans, China's leaders reveal their mastery of separating words from actions. Verbal criticism of the ROK government is stepped up, and fealty is sworn to central DPRK positions on American troop withdrawal and reunification. But while there is some reduction in the more forward evidences of PRC-ROK intercourse, the basic economic and cultural ties are maintained, as we have seen—and they dwarf those with North Korea. Pyongyang, it might be noted, is not fooled by China's sweet talk. It deeply resents the growing PRC relations with the South. Not merely in quantity but also in quality of relationships, the difference is pronounced. For example, apart from official visits—which are regular—contacts between PRC and DPRK scholars, technicians, and commercial representatives are minimal in comparison with similar Chinese–South Korean categories.[10]

Meanwhile, PRC relations with the Mongolian People's Republic have warmed from the deep freeze that prevailed at the height of the Sino-Soviet hostilities. The first cultural troupes from Outer Mongolia have visited

[10]See Robert A. Scalapino and Hongkoo Lee, eds., *North Korea in a Regional and Global Context* (Berkeley: University of California, Institute of East Asian Studies, 1986).

China, and diplomatic relations have been restored to normalcy, with the new Mongolian chairman of the Presidium of the Great Hural, Ochirbat, having visited Beijing in the spring of 1990, and other official visits following. The Soviet pledge that eventually all USSR troops would be withdrawn from the MPR by the end of 1991 makes it incumbent on the Mongolians to improve relations with Beijing. Yet the deep suspicion of Chinese irredentism lives on in Ulaanbaatar, and Russia remains the only credible protector of the Mongol nation. Hence, no intimacy can be expected in the Chinese-Mongolian relationship despite—or perhaps because of—the fact that there are more Mongols within the People's Republic of China than in the MPR. Historical racial-cultural rivalry and the fear of the reassertion of Chinese imperialism have rendered past systemic similarities meaningless. Now, moreover, the MPR is pursuing political patterns influenced by *glasnost,* including a multiparty system, thereby separating itself from other Asian Leninist states (except the Phnom Penh government), at least for the present. Nevertheless, by pursuing better relations with the Mongols while remaining alert to a greater Mongol nationalism, Beijing can possibly hasten the advent of the Mongolian People's Republic as a true buffer state rather than a Russian ally, and that would suit the new Mongolian government as well. At present, Ulaanbaatar, well aware of the turmoil inside the old Soviet Union, is seeking safety not merely in creating friendly relations with China but in cultivating both Koreas, Japan, and the United States.

China's relations with Vietnam—and by extension, with Cambodia—reinforce the central point advanced earlier.[11] Hanoi's historical museum is replete with a detailed visual account of heroic Vietnamese warding off Chinese invasions. Chinese leaders until recently denounced Hanoi's leaders, both privately and publicly, as ungrateful for the major assistance given them in their conflict with the French, the South Vietnamese, and the Americans. They were defined as "tricky," not to be trusted, and above all harboring hegemonic ambitions with respect to Cambodia and Laos. Bilateral PRC-Vietnam talks have however resulted in a restitution of normal relations, as noted earlier. Yet mutual trust and warmth will not come quickly, even if the Cambodian settlement holds. The dilemma for Vietnam has been acute. To live in a state of high hostility with the neighboring

---

[11]An illustration of the continuing Chinese hostility to Vietnam can be seen in Chen Jiabao, "Vietnam's 'Final Withdrawal' a Hoax," *Beijing Review,* October 16, 1989, pp. 16–17. See also William J. Duiker, "Looking Beyond Cambodia: China and Vietnam," *Indochina Issues* 88 (June 1989).

People's Republic was to condemn itself to militarism, poverty, and insecurity. Yet to abandon its historical ambitions for priority in Cambodia and Laos—positions held by the Vietnamese for both economic and security reasons—has been anathema. For the present, the dilemma appears to have been resolved in favor of accommodation with the northern giant. The rapidly declining Russian interest in encircling China via a ring of alliances and Hanoi's urgent need to repair its disastrous economic situation by turning outward to the market economies induced a Vietnamese compromise on Cambodia minimally satisfactory to Beijing. This relation, however, is likely to be a delicate one for the long term.

Further to the west, PRC relations with the Kabul government in the Najibullah era were marked by minimalism and hostility. While Beijing has very limited common political interests with the various mujahideen factions, its perceived strategic interests lie in seeing an Afghanistan that is not closely aligned with Russia or India. Such an Afghanistan would create additional pressure on Pakistan, a nation most useful to China in geopolitical, strategic terms—both as counterweight to India and as an Islamic friend visible to China's own Islamic population directly to the north.

In sum, one can look in vain for signs of the genuine comradeship or international socialist solidarity once promised by Marxist-Leninist doctrines. If community is being built, it is through the Asian regional organizations and their global counterparts with a strong market orientation. Indeed, Asia's Leninist societies, having achieved only thin relations with each other, resting primarily on common efforts to shore up battered ideological defenses, look at such organizations with increasing longing.

It remains to examine China's policies toward the nonsocialist developing states of Asia, those societies labeled Third World, a term more misleading in its gross simplification than helpful. It is here that the People's Republic has displayed the greatest policy shifts in the decades from the 1950s to the 1990s. As noted earlier, ideological garments have been largely cast aside, except for verbal adherence to the side of the South in North-South matters. In Southeast Asia, China combines many of the behavioral patterns characteristic of a government that views itself as entitled to major power status with the policies of a state pursuing perceived national interests irrespective of the ideological or political inconsistencies. Thus, Indonesia, like Singapore, is cultivated despite obstacles, and alignment with a somewhat uneasy Thailand is heralded. Even Malaysia with its smouldering Malay-Chinese ethnic tensions and wariness toward Beijing is treated with consideration. In sum, China works assiduously to establish its credentials as a peaceful, constructive nation, prepared to coexist harmoniously with its ASEAN neighbors.[12] In the aftermath of June 4, ties with Myanmar (Burma), another state threatened with pariah status because of its repressive, xenophobic policies, were renewed. Through official visits, military sales, and border trade agreements, relations have been advanced.

At the same time, China demonstrates on occasion that it is not a nation with which one should trifle. Ground is not given with respect to territorial issues, the South China Sea atolls being a case in point. While China has agreed to set aside the sovereignty issue for the present while joint development gets underway, Chinese spokesmen make it clear that title to these atolls belongs to China and will not be relinquished. States that violate China's perceived interests are treated to Beijing's wrath—not merely Vietnam but also the Philippines, which was publicly scolded after its foreign minister visited Taiwan unofficially.

The states of this region can thus never forget that a massive state exists nearby, and despite all the rhetoric about peaceful coexistence and historic friendships, that state intends to preserve (and expand?) its perceived interests. Thus, the ASEAN community, in one form or another, advances balance-of-power doctrines, whether through efforts to retain an American presence; the desire to keep Vietnam a viable, independent entity; or the commitment to the strengthening of ASEAN itself. Whatever it may say and whatever the restrictions on its reach, the PRC is destined to be regarded by most of the southeast Asian states, irrespective of their political system, as a major power potentially or actually intrusive and, hence, in some degree, a threat. The PRC presence in the South Pacific is as yet modest and contested by Taiwan. With the larger states of this vast region, however, China has established useful ties.

South Asia represents a more complex picture. There, the central factor is the existence of a single dominant state, India, and its determination to play a hegemonic role largely to the exclusion of other major states. In effect, India has enunciated a Monroe Doctrine for the region. Its intervention—albeit initially requested—in Sri Lanka and the Maldives, its punishment of Nepal, the periodic tension and persistent uneasiness in its relations with Pakistan all testify to India's insistence that New Delhi be acknowledged as the principal authority in the subcontinent, the existence of the South Asian Association of Regional Cooperation notwithstanding.[13] The expansion of

---

[12]See, e.g., Lin Xiaocheng, "A Brief Analysis of the Progress and Experience of the ASEAN Countries in the Industrialization Process," *International Studies* 4 (1989): 22–41.

[13]See Zheng Ruixiang and Dong Manyuan, "Developing Friendly Sino-Indian Relations on the Five Principles of Peaceful Coexistence," *Foreign Affairs Journal* 12 (June 1989): 64–70.

the Indian navy, moreover, signals the commitment to extend that authority to the Indian Ocean and possibly beyond.

The PRC is not in a position to challenge India in these respects, nor is there any desire to concentrate on such a goal. Yet Chinese interests in its own Himalayan borders have been accentuated because of the Tibetan problem. The great majority of Tibetans resent Chinese rule now as in the past. The basic incompatibility between Tibetan and Han cultures cannot be bridged, at least for the foreseeable future, and to Tibetans, the exiled Dalai Lama is a sacred symbol. The fact that he—and a significant number of Tibetan refugees—are resident in India and that contacts between them and their homeland serve to keep the political pot simmering rankles Beijing. Long ago, in the days of loudly heralded Indian-Chinese friendship, Nehru acknowledged that Tibet was a part of China. Yet India has had a deep suspicion of Chinese activities in the Himalayan region, especially Nepal, and the memory of the bitter defeat in the military conflict over the border in 1962—a controversy still unresolved—has contributed greatly to the coolness in Sino-Indian relations, as have Beijing's close ties with Pakistan.

Indeed, the People's Republic of China more than any other outside nation, even the United States, has sought "friendly relations" with almost all of the south Asian states that New Delhi considers in its orbit. Premier Li Peng's visit to Bangladesh, Nepal, and Pakistan in November 1989 was but one example of China's cultivation of key nations in the region. Meanwhile, although Rajiv Gandhi's earlier visit to Beijing produced many effusive statements about relations based on peaceful coexistence, concrete results were minimal.

The improvement in Sino-Soviet relations has also worried India's leaders. When in India in 1988, Gorbachev refrained from pledging full support to New Delhi in its controversy with Beijing. Moreover, the dismemberment of the Soviet Union renders the past alignment of India with Moscow increasingly meaningless. In addition, India's recent shift from Laskian socialist ideals to a more open market economy—if it lasts—will cause India to relate more closely to the advanced states, possibly vying with China for investment and technology.

Historically, China and India met at two intersections. Across lofty mountains and the vast arid plains beyond, Indian Buddhism made its way into the Celestial Kingdom several thousand years ago, with Buddhist monasteries gradually dotting the Tibetan and west China landscapes. Meanwhile, in Southeast Asia, a cultural faultline was established, with Chinese influence predominant in North Vietnam and certain other enclaves, and with Indian influence strong from Burma to Cambodia and, in certain periods, Indonesia.

In modern times, India has played an exceedingly limited role in Southeast Asia, concentrating on the south Asian subcontinent. But whenever China appears to be more actively involved with Burma (Myanmar), Indian antennae go up. It has not been forgotten that Chinese assistance was earlier given to tribal groups such as the Naga to soften India's Assam border. Moreover, past assistance to the Burmese Communists, encamped near the China border and with strong minority components, represented another threat in New Delhi's eyes. Warmer relations between the Rangoon government and Beijing worry New Delhi. New Delhi's close relations with Vietnam and its early recognition of the Heng Samrin government in Phnom Penh are additional evidences of its earlier alignments. Geopolitics has thus melded with cultural and ideological penetrations to shape Sino-Indian relations for millenia, down to the present.

In summarizing China's role as a regional force, one is required to acknowledge that the People's Republic plays upon a variety of images, whether sincerely perceived or cultivated to influence others. One identity is that of China, the great power—seat of culture and transmitter of values, once Confucian, later Marxist-Leninist. Since this perception cannot be completely abandoned, the humiliations of the twentieth century have produced deep and lasting scars. Yet when its national interests—as its leaders define these—are at stake, or when a severe loss of face is threatened, Beijing is sometimes prepared to act in imperious fashion even now, whatever the costs. It is this perception of grandeur and a self-confidence that defies all obstacles which concerns China's neighbors most as they contemplate the possible scenarios of the twenty-first century.

The identity that generally dominates the Communist elite, however, is that of a nation—and a people—whose very survival is threatened by the inroads, militant or peaceful, of "Westernism," that set of beliefs and institutions proclaimed incompatible with Chinese needs and values. When the national identity is encapsulated in the phrase "beleagured nation," a defensive, xenophobic response is natural, yet one that encourages the effort to achieve identity with other "oppressed nations." The tension within China in regard to this identity has, however, increased mightily in recent years, as a growing portion of the educated elite openly challenge the image of a "progressive China" threatened by "reactionary" ideas. On the contrary, they see themselves as a part of backward nation at a dead end, therefore desperately in need of a massive transfusion of new ideas, policies, and institutions.

In truth, such a countervailing view has been present in Chinese elite circles for more than one hundred years. Hence the successive influence of Western liberalism, Russian-modified Marxism, and more recently, either parliamentarism or the authoritarian pluralism characteristic of the most rapidly developing societies of Asia. And from this latter perception China can learn not merely from the advanced West and Japan but also from South Korea and Taiwan.

To the extent that China's current sense of identity is strongly imbued with modern nationalism, to the degree that Chinese leaders and citizens place primary emphasis on China, the new nation-state, attitudes and policies are marked by a shift from the belief in a rightful suzerainty over lesser cultures to an emphasis on such international norms as sovereignty and the equality of all nation-states. Rather than emphasize China's legitimate prerogatives as leader of the region, Chinese spokesmen place stress on China's right to conduct its internal affairs without external interference and on the other assertions contained in the Five Principles of Peaceful Coexistence. One can debate the degree to which this new identity, late in coming, is being undermined by the forces of economic interdependence and the global stream of information that has come to bombard virtually everyone. New institutions that will modify or limit national sovereignty are developing, some official, some unofficial. Major portions of China are being incorporated into the natural economic territories (NETs) that are emerging. Guangdong–Hong Kong–Taiwan is one example; Liaoning–South Korea will be another, along with Fujian-Taiwan. How will these economic entities interrelate with the political entities we call nation-states? Political issues are also increasingly becoming internationalized, as the Helsinki Agreement and the Strategic Impediments Initiative dialogue between the United States and Japan illustrate. Thus the tension between nationalism and internationalism will impinge full force on the national identity crisis.

As already indicated, it is not necessary to argue that the diverse identities harbored in the collective Chinese psyche constitute a unique condition. On the contrary, in one degree or another, this condition is characteristic of all nations today, and especially large, important ones. Moreover, like other states, China pursues two primary goals in its domestic policies: development and security. These goals have played a critical role in shaping PRC foreign policies at all times, with the relative emphasis given each varying with changes in the domestic and international environment. With security threats, at least external ones, diminished, the focus has been increasingly on development, with foreign policies caused to serve as handmaiden to this priority. It is this fact that accounts for the strenuous effort by Beijing leaders to insist that China can turn outward economically—even to such nations as the United States and Japan—without being corrupted by their political ideas, provided the citizenry, and especially the intellectuals, are properly educated. Economic relations with the NIEs, too, proceed in near-complete disregard of ideological or political considerations, while relations with neighboring Leninist states, even Russia, have been constrained by the limited economic opportunities offered.

Security, however, has not disappeared from PRC leaders' consciousness. Indeed, it is woven into the fabric of economic and political policies. To obtain technology from advanced Pacific-Asian states, to develop economic links with Taiwan, to draw overseas Chinese into special economic zones are security-related actions. Beyond this, China, like other major states, evidences continuous concern about its borders. Most border disputes have been resolved, but there remain areas of contention, not only with India and, on a minor scale, with Russia and the Central Asian Republics, but also with Japan, Vietnam, Malaysia, and the Philippines. Beyond this, questions arise, especially in Russian, Mongolian, Korean, and Vietnamese minds, as to whether at some future time, the Chinese will assert claims to portions of areas to the north and south once considered part of the Chinese empire or under Chinese suzerainty. Some Russians remember Mao's reported assertion in darker days, "We have not yet presented them (the Russians) with our full bill."

Border issues are thus inextricably connected with those broader considerations commonly labeled "buffer state" desires. The People's Republic of China has been confronted in the past with a 4,500-mile border to its north and west with a single empire, the Soviet Union. Along its border, only a limited buffer state structure was possible. This is now changing with the establishment of independent central Asian republics along with the changed status of the Mongolian People's Republic. The likely instability of central Asia, however, may not be conducive to tranquility, especially if the Islamic peoples of this region seek to advance their separate identity. The difficulties in creating a security structure to the south beyond Tibet (itself a buffer in earlier times) are also transparent, given India's position. In the past, the Korean peninsula and Southeast Asia—historic spheres of influence for China—have represented extensions of power when China was strong. The periodic wooing of North Korea and the determination to prevent Vietnam's dominance over Indochina, since shifted to an interest in improving relations with Hanoi in exchange for Cambodian "neutralization," are testimony to China's continuous interest in these areas. They are also the reasons for the anxieties of the small states, especially those in Southeast Asia. But the apprehensions extend to Moscow as well. PRC leaders insist that they will *never* be hegemonists. Some neighbors remain skeptical.

In certain respects, China's policies toward the region of which it is a part have undergone remarkable changes in the four decades since the People's Republic was established. The shifts have been from aligned revolutionary to nonaligned pariah, to outward bound and available, to nonaligned but tilted toward dynamic economies. Each phase has been shaped by a combination of domestic and external stimuli and accompanied by appropriate ideological supports. To be sure, irrationality born from the weaknesses and errors of leadership has played a significant role on occasion. But throughout these decades, the combined goals of development and security, fluctuating in the priorities assigned, have persisted and generally been the principal factors shaping both the foreign and domestic policies of this massive society.

In effectuating these goals, China's diverse images of itself and the world are transmitted through behavior patterns still strongly linked to an ancient political culture. Hence the essence of PRC foreign policy can only be understood by interrelating those persistent goals that China shares with many other states, the patterns of behavior drawn from its slowly changing culture, its sense of the attributes of the Chinese race, its scale and geopolitical position, and the varied influences of a revolutionary international environment.

It is also from these factors that China's varying national identities manifest themselves, given voice by successive elites and sustained in varying degrees by the citizenry at large. China, the superior; China, the backward; China, the proud; China, the despairing; China, the uncertain; China, the principled; China, the pragmatic—all are aspects of China's identity as perceived within and observed without, depending on diverse times and circumstances. And each has played its part in this nation's unfolding foreign policies.

中
國 10

Whither China's Quest
for National Identity?

Samuel S. Kim and Lowell Dittmer

Historically, war has performed a critical role in the shaping of national identity. In the nineteenth century, when the nationalization of the state was in full swing in the West, practically all the new nations had wrenching problems with national identity. Finding an ideal into which they could transform themselves was difficult enough. Creating a national self-consciousness, a sense of identity, required differentiation from other communities, which is more easily accomplished in the face of internal or external threats. Resort to collective violence can sharpen an us/them dualism in its most absolutist form. As the historian Michael Howard has observed, "No Nation, in the true sense of the word, could be born *without* war," and "no self-conscious community could establish itself as a new and independent actor on the world scene without an armed conflict or the threat of one."[1] World War II became a benchmark in the reconstruction of national identity. The remaking of physical and political boundaries of empires, states, and nations inevitably posed crises of national self-inclusion and self-definition for all the participants. Both winners and losers had to reaffirm or revise their national role conceptions in the postwar world order.

Samuel S. Kim acknowledges the support of the Peter B. Lewis Fund of the Center of International Studies, Princeton University; Lowell Dittmer acknowledges the research support of the MacArthur Group for International Security Studies at the University of California at Berkeley.

[1]Michael Howard, "War and the Nation-State," *Daedalus* 108 (Fall 1979): 102.

The study of identity, too, owes its initial impetus to individual and collective identity crises set in motion by this nationalistic global war. Although Emile Durkheim, Sigmund Freud, and George Mead provided important conceptual antecedents,[2] the study of identity as a serious social science enterprise is largely a post–World War II development. Since its initial formulation in the writings of Erik Erikson in the mid-1940s, the concept of identity has come into use by many scholars from various disciplines, methodological orientations, and even political leanings. Andrew Weigert and his colleagues treat the concept as a bridge that links the psychological study of the individual and the sociological study of symbolic interaction. At the micro level, identity is the enduring source of human motivation and behavior, confirming what human beings imagine to be true about themselves, in their own eyes and in those of their significant others. The meaning of life is thus derived from individuals' interaction with significant others. At the macro level, identity is "a deeper cultural code of personal meanings that relate the individual to the most general level of societal meanings."[3]

Following Freud, psychologists have generally tended to study identity in terms of inner processes. The dynamic source of identity is attributed to a biopsychological drive in the individual self, not to a social system's need for stability and predictability, even if its enactment often meets societal needs for solidarity and collective action. Sociologists often conceptualize identity as shared beliefs and sentiments and also as enacted social roles and statuses that maintain the social order. It is what Durkheim called "collective conscience"—the glue, or organic solidarity, of dissimilar individuals of the same community which "connects successive generations with one another"—that sociological theorists are most concerned with. Political scientists have generally studied identity as a political resource in state forming, nation building and modernizing, and democratic political processes. Some of them have applied role theory, a variant and corollary of identity theory, in the study of comparative foreign policy. Most recently, identity theory has found its way into international relations theory. In a pioneering work, William Bloom addresses the long-standing theoretical problem of aggregating from individual attitudes to mass behavior by

[2] See Emile Durkheim, *The Division of Labor in Society,* trans. George Simpson (New York: Free Press, 1964); Uri Bronfenbrenner, "Freudian Theories of Identification and Derivatives," *Child Development* 31 (1960): 15–40; and George H. Mead, *Mind, Self, and Society* (Chicago: University of Chicago Press, 1934).

[3] Andrew Weigert, J. Smith Teitge, and Dennis W. Teitge, *Society and Identity: Toward a Sociological Psychology* (Cambridge: Cambridge University Press, 1986), pp. 27–28.

applying identity theory both to nation building and to international relations.[4]

Identity theory postulates that:

1. There is a universal human biopsychological need for a sense of identity/difference so that ambiguities and uncertainties can be minimized and human life rendered more meaningful and manageable.
2. The construction of identity to realize this sense of identity/belonging begins with the establishment of the categories of self and other as mutually conflictive yet interdependent, each depending on and partaking of the other (for although identity begins in differentiation, it cannot be confirmed and legitimized without internalizing the mores, symbols, and behavioral patterns of significant others).
3. An identity is an ongoing negotiating process through the cycles of human life to enhance physical and psychological survival, security, and well-being, in the course of which the self attempts, especially in those problematic moments of ambiguity, to secure an identity that others do not bestow while others attempt to bestow an identity that the self does not appropriate.
4. Identity enactment is situation-specific; that is, threats to, and opportunities for the enhancement of, security function as catalysts for identity mobilization.
5. All identifications, from an individual nuclear family to the global system, are a series of relationships with positive or negative reference groups.
6. People with the same or shared identification generally tend to pool their resources to act in concert for the enhancement of their common identity.[5]

[4]Durkheim, *Division of Labor in Society*, pp. 79–80. For the political scientists, see, e.g., Karl W. Deutsch, *Nationalism and Social Communication* (Cambridge: MIT Press, 1953); Dankwart A. Rustow, *A World of Nations: Problems of Political Modernization* (Washington, D.C.: Brookings Institution, 1967); Lucian W. Pye, "Identity and the Political Culture," in Leonard Binder et al., eds., *Crises and Sequences in Political Development* (Princeton: Princeton University Press, 1971), pp. 101–34; Sidney Verba, "Sequences and Development," in ibid., pp. 283–316; Anne Norton, *Reflections on Political Identity* (Baltimore: Johns Hopkins University Press, 1988); Walker Connor, *The National Question in Marxist-Leninist Theory and Strategy* (Princeton: Princeton University Press, 1984), and "Ethnonationalism," in Myron Weiner and Samuel Huntington, eds., *Understanding Political Development* (Boston: Little, Brown, 1987), pp. 196–220; William E. Connolly, *Identity\Difference: Democratic Negotiations of Political Paradox* (Ithaca: Cornell University Press, 1991); Carl Backman, "Role Theory and International Relations," *International Studies Quarterly* 14 (September 1970): 310–19; Kal J. Holsti, "National Role Conceptions in the Study of Foreign Policy," ibid., 233–309; and Stephen G. Walker, ed., *Role Theory and Foreign Policy Analysis* (Durham, N.C.: Duke University Press, 1987). See William Bloom, *Personal Identity, National Identity and International Relations* (Cambridge: Cambridge University Press, 1990).

[5]This formulation of identity theory draws on, but alters, the expositions of Bloom, Connolly, Erikson, Hoover, Norton, and Weigert et al. See nn. 3 and 4; Erik H. Erikson, *Childhood and Society*, 2d ed. (New York: Norton, 1963); and Kenneth R. Hoover, *A Politics of Identity: Liberation and the Natural Community* (Urbana: University of Illinois Press, 1975).

Drawing on the Durkheimian notion that a social entity has its own life and organizational needs distinguishable from the sum of its constituent parts, national identity is the characteristic collective behavior of the national system as a whole, in interaction with other subnational, national, and international systems, flowing from the totality of shared attributes and symbols of a solidarity political group known as a "nation-state." Focused on systemic behavior, then, national identity, in our conceptualization, encompasses more than Sidney Verba's analytic definition of it as a "set of individuals who fall within the decision-making scope of the state."[6] More important, it involves national essence—the core sentiments and symbols of the state—with which a mass of people most commonly identify and on the basis of which they have contracted to live together and to act in concert to defend and protect their common identity. National identity theory seeks to define the necessary and sufficient conditions for establishing such a relationship between a citizenry and its state, not only in terms of what the state *is* (as represented by the myths, rituals, flag, constitution, and anthem that relate how the nation-state came to be and what it stands for) but also in terms of what the state *does* (via its role performance in domestic and foreign policy).

Embedded in a fully formed national identity is a sense of a distinctive international mission. For its members, national identity is not an end in itself but a means of participating in that transcendental mission which is generally thought to be essential to fulfillment of the universal human need for collective security. Like personal identity, national identity cannot be constructed, let alone enacted, in isolation. In isolation there is only anomie, not identity. Like personal identity, national identity too becomes fully activated when faced with a threat or an opportunity in its environment. Identity mobilization presupposes that members of the society have already made a preliminary identification with the solidarity group through political socialization, internalizing the core beliefs, sentiments, and symbols of the nation-state.

This refinement of the concept suggests again the insufficiency of the Pye-Verba analytic concept of national identity: to wit, that no single set of attributes (a common language, a common religion, a common territory, and the like) is sufficient to the creation and maintenance of a viable national identity. To their concept we have added the synthetic requirement that there be a substantive core with which the nation can identify in its most abiding and inclusive sense. A national identity, once congealed, may

[6]Verba, "Sequences and Development."

be expected to provide a basis for reasonable expectations concerning state behavior under various contingencies, or at least to set the outer limits for such behavior; that is, a state as the agent of national identity is expected by its citizens to act at home and abroad to safeguard the integrity of the national essence. But the theory does not presuppose the modalities or the outcomes of the nation-state identity dynamic; for identity mobilization is situation specific (Frank Borman, looking at the planet Earth from 240,000 miles away, could grasp a global human identity). National identity mobilization is also subject to leadership styles, particularly of "founding fathers," as a crucial intervening variable. Given such variables, responses to an identity threat may be expected to vary from one extreme, of inertial absorption, to the other extreme, of a fundamental transformation of national identity, with a marginal shift of policy options and strategies being the most likely response.

National identity theory postulates, however, that domestic societal factors are generally more important than external systemic ones in the formation of national identity, whereas external systemic factors generally take precedence in determining the outcomes of national identity role enactments. Just as the domestic culture defines the identity options open to an individual at a given time, the international system too can condition, if not completely dictate, what viable national identity role options are open to a nation-state at any point in that state's international life. As a result—most dramatically illustrated by the sudden shift of Soviet national identity from a superpower donor to a Third World supplicant—national identity may vary over time as a nation's capabilities shift and its status changes.

The construct of national identity is still beset with certain conceptual and definitional difficulties. The main problem is the indiscriminate interuse of the terms *nation* and *state*. It is difficult to escape from the terminological confusion that arises when "nation" is used to mean "state," as in "subnational," "national," "international," and "transnational" actors and systems.[7] "Nation" is a sociopsychological concept referring to a self-conscious and self-differentiating community of people bound together by common history and solidarity. The original meaning of the English word *nation*—from the Latin verb *nasci* (to be born)—was simply a "group of people born in the same place." With the universalization of the national ideal and the nationalization of the state in the nineteenth century, cata-

[7]See Hugh Seton-Watson, *Nations and States: An Enquiry into the Origins of Nations and the Politics of Nationalism* (Boulder, Colo.: Westview, 1977); and F. H. Hinsley, *Sovereignty,* 2d ed. (Cambridge: Cambridge University Press, 1986).

lyzed by the French Revolution and the Napoleonic Wars, this original meaning became progressively blurred and saturated by competing notions of what the ideal nation ought to be. This development has led David Kertzer to argue that "the nation itself has no palpable existence outside the symbolism through which it is envisioned . . . symbolism is the stuff of which nations are made." The construction of nation-states in Europe was a hazardous—and often "nation-destroying"—process, as Walter Connor demonstrates.[8] Of some five hundred or so political units in Europe in 1500, for instance, only about twenty-five survived this process to exist as nation-states in 1900.[9]

"State" is a legal concept referring to an internationally recognized political entity possessing tangible territorial, demographic, and governmental attributes. To muddy the waters, the relationship between nation and state seems both ambiguous and interdependent, as the state has indeed become the sovereign center of self-conscious collective action in the formation and presentation of national identity. Of course national identity can be talked and debated about by any solidarity group, but it cannot easily rise in politics without state sponsorship.

It is generally accepted that the Peace of Westphalia (1648) marked the point of transition from the unipolar, papal hierarchical world order of the medieval West dominated by the image of a Eurocentric Christian commonwealth, to the modern state system. Hence the Westphalian system and the state system have become synonymous.[10] Yet the nation-state (or the state-nation, to be chronologically more accurate), in any version recognizable to us today, is hardly older than the American Constitution and the French Revolution, both born in 1789 and both setting in motion the long and still-incomplete process of nationalizing the state system.[11]

[8]David I. Kertzer, *Ritual, Politics, and Power* (New Haven: Yale University Press, 1988), p. 6; Walker Connor, "Nation Building or Destroying?" *World Politics* 24 (April 1972): 336: "Since most of the less developed states contain a number of nations, and since the transfer of primary allegiance from these nations to the state is generally considered the *sine qua non* of successful integration, the true goal is not 'nation-building' but 'nation-destroying.'"

[9]See Charles Tilly, ed., *The Formation of National States in Western Europe* (Princeton: Princeton University Press, 1975), pp. 15, 38–39.

[10]Richard A. Falk, "The Interplay of Westphalia and Charter Conceptions of International Legal Order," in Richard A. Falk and Cyrus E. Black, eds., *The Future of the International Legal Order*, vol. 1, *Trends and Patterns* (Princeton: Princeton University Press, 1969), pp. 32–70. Martin Wight rejects this generally accepted view, arguing instead that the French-Spanish struggle over Italy in 1494 marked the beginning of the modern state system and that "at Westphalia the state system does not come into existence; it comes of age." Wight, *Systems of States* (Leicester: Leicester University Press, 1977), p. 152.

[11]E. J. Hobsbawm, *Nations and Nationalism since 1780: Programme, Myth, Reality* (Cambridge: Cambridge University Press, 1990).

Moreover, the concept of nation has permitted more than one definition because there are all sorts of nations. A nation is not a plant that grows "naturally" into any preprogrammed form or shape. Nation building is a highly indeterminate process intermeshing changing patterns of internal and external structural dynamics. Connor, a leading authority on the concepts of "nation" and "ethnonationalism," comes to three conclusions: (1) The simplest and ultimate statement about a nation is that "it is a body of people who feel that they are a nation" and are "characterized by a myth of common descent." (2) There are at least five kinds of "peoples" making up five kinds of nations: "prenations/potential nations; nations; offshoot nations; diasporas; and members of immigrant societies." (3) More than anything else, it is the myth of common ancestry as the defining characteristic of the nation which provides a master key to the study of the global upsurge in ethnonational movements and identities.[12]

The concept of the state is no less ambiguous and problematic. The multiple meanings accorded to a "true" state are legion and thus pose a major obstacle to formulating international relations theory.[13] World War II set off a global tidal wave of decolonization and a subsequent explosion of membership in the family of "nations" in the postwar era. The number of U.N. member states had more than tripled, from the original 51 to 179 in mid-1992. Only a tiny fraction of the member states can be said to embody the totality of the "nation" they pretend to represent in the world organization. Third World states lack, in many cases, some of the classical statehood attributes that characterized the "sovereign" European states that emerged in the seventeenth and eighteenth centuries. States may be formed either through the creation of a new one or the federation or division of existing ones. As a primary juridical person and subject in international law, a state, by evincing several characteristics it shares in common with other states, such as territory, population, government, and sovereignty (as stipulated in Article 1 of the 1933 Montevideo Convention on the Rights and Duties of States), fulfills the basic requirements for entrance into the international community. Yet the general picture of contemporary states, judged in terms of the classical statehood attributes, is very confusing. If the quintessence of

---

[12]Connor, "Ethnonationalism," pp. 203, 206, 208.

[13]Yale Ferguson and Richard Mansbach cite at least ten competing notions of the state, all of which are being inescapably shaped by "the norms, ideologies, and political aspirations that animate the practitioners and scholars in our field." Given this conceptual chaos, the best we can do, they argue, is to treat the state not as an independent variable but merely as a concept describing a situation of "*relative* political institutionalization, power, and vulnerability across the millennia." See Ferguson and Mansbach, *The Elusive Quest: Theory and International Politics* (Columbia: University of South Carolina Press, 1988), chap. 5, pp. 111–42; quotation at p. 125.

a true statehood is "sovereignty"—independence of action from external control and yet distinct from its domestic society—how many contemporary states can be said to fulfill this inordinate requirement in an interdependent world? Nearly two dozen of the U.N. member states have a population of only about 250,000. Focusing on state sovereignty merely begs the question of whether a state possesses "paper sovereignty" or real sovereignty. Despite such ambiguities, one central government as the authoritative agent of allocating values in domestic society and conducting foreign relations in the international (interstate) system is the core requirement of contemporary statehood.[14]

The fact that only a small fraction of potential nations have made a successful transition to nation-states by becoming member *states* of the United Nations suggests a critical role of the state in the construction and enactment of a national identity. Nation building without state sponsorship is a nonstarter. Indeed, one of the major functions of the state has been to express a sense of political and social identity of its citizens. At the same time, most nation-states today include within their jurisdiction more than one nation, or potential nations. A multinational state is the norm, and a true nation-state, where a state's jurisdiction coincides perfectly with its own nation and homogeneous people (like Iceland, Japan, Norway), is an exception. As the internationally recognized center of collective action and as the generally recognized locus of the most fundamental us/them divide in our times, the state constantly manipulates, and is also increasingly being manipulated by, a national identity dynamic in both domestic and international politics. As we suggested in the introductory chapter, national identity is and becomes, ultimately, the concordant relationship between nation and state that obtains when a mass of people identify with what the state is and does.

In a statecentric world, the state, with its legitimate monopoly on violence and its controlling interest (ranging from strong influence to monopoly, depending on the type of regime) in "normative power" in terms of manipulating the national symbol system, plays a determining role in the construction and management of a national identity dynamic. A national identity without state power or sponsorship faces a Sisyphean struggle to emerge in politics. As E. J. Hobsbawm sharply argues, "Nations do not make states and nationalisms but the other way round."[15] Likewise, a

[14]Eric A. Nordlinger notes, "Quite simply, the state is made up of and limited to those individuals who are endowed with society-wide decisionmaking authority." Nordlinger, *On the Autonomy of the Democratic State* (Cambridge: Harvard University Press, 1981), p. 11.

[15]Hobsbawm, *Nations and Nationalism,* p. 10.

transnational or supranational identity encounters even more daunting difficulties because of the absence of a world government and shared transnational sentiments, symbols, and rituals in world politics. A stateless person in the statecentric world is a nonperson. In a multicentric "postinternational" world where what James Rosenau calls "sovereignty-bound" (state) actors compete with "sovereignty-free" (nonstate) actors, however, the centrality of the state is more problematic and multiple identities are feasible.[16] In an age of global communication producing a transparency revolution, the politics of national identity encounters the growing disjunction between "global time and political place," as William Connolly puts it, in a world "in which state power is simultaneously magnified and increasingly disconnected from the ends that justify its magnification."[17]

National identity theory merely posits that the more closely the inclusion/exclusion criteria of national self-identity (however the state chooses to draw them) comport with the constituent emotional and symbolic elements of national self-definition, the firmer the national identity; the more secure the national identity, the more predictable the state's behavior.

Despite its terminological ambiguity, the concept of identity presents both the challenge and the chance to construct general propositions about the changes and continuities in China's enactment of its national essence. As a bridging concept, identity provides a cross-cultural comparative framework through which Sinology can be squared with the circle of Western social and behavioral sciences. Identity can link the symbolic and behavioral dynamics of a people, their nation-state, and the world at large. In short, identity theory is a missing link for integrating the study of relevant aspects of political culture, role theory, realpolitik and idealpolitik perspectives on national interest and purpose, and long-term continuities amid historical flux, as the essays in this book have amply demonstrated.

China's Identity in Historical Perspective

Does China have an identity crisis? The answer depends on which aspect or aspects of the question one wishes to address. The question is elusive partly because identity is a relative, not an absolute, concept and partly because national identity enactment is changing and situation specific. Whereas China scholars have not been oblivious to the subject's impor-

[16]For his drastic reconceptualization, see James Rosenau, *Turbulence in World Politics: A Theory of Change and Continuity* (Princeton: Princeton University Press, 1990).

[17]Connolly, *Identity/Difference*, pp. 206, 216.

tance, they have rarely addressed it explicitly. As Wang Gungwu reminds us, for the Chinese themselves the concept of identity was too abstract; thus the term (*rentong*) did not even exist before the 1980s. As a technical term, *rentong,* meaning "to identify that which is the same," "is yet to be used in ordinary speech."[18] White and Li (Chapter 7) illustrate the extent to which the concept has wormed its way into the thinking of some Chinese writers. Is this not a sign that China—at the very least, the southern peripheries of China—is finally coming to grips with its national identity problematic?

Writing in 1968, Lucian Pye argued that modernization has created an acute authority crisis, not an identity crisis, for the Chinese. For Pye, "the critical difference between the Chinese and most of the other developing countries begins with the fact that the Chinese have been generally spared the crises of identity common to most other transitional systems." He also (more controversially) advances a theory of ethnocentric determinism: the Chinese national identity is "derived less from the content of culture, which is always somewhat vague and ambiguous, and more from the fact of race, which is biologically unambiguous."[19] Twenty-years later, Pye softened and shifted his view, linking identity with legitimacy: "China's identity problem, which is at the core of its legitimacy difficulties, is manifestly obvious, but few in China dare give voice to it."[20]

To advance beyond this still-sketchy commentary, it is necessary to begin from a diachronic perspective. Without some historical perspective on change and continuity, it is far too easy to exaggerate either the possibilities for or the constraints against the creation of a new Chinese national identity. What Karl Marx once said about human history-making power may well be applied to the study of Chinese national identity: "Men make their own history, but they do not make it just as they please; they do not make it under circumstances chosen by themselves, but under circumstances directly encountered, given, and transmitted from the past."[21] In short, we need to be sensitive to those forces and elements that appear to have been most influential in the shaping of Chinese national identity, the enduring sense of Chinese essence (*guocui*) as a singularly important "we" (the Chinese world) against "them" (the barbarian world).

[18]Wang Gungwu, "The Study of Chinese Identities in Southeast Asia," in Jennifer W. Cushman and Wang Gungwu, eds., *Changing Identities of the Southeast Asian Chinese since World War II* (Hong Kong: Hong Kong University Press, 1988), pp. 16–17.

[19]Lucian W. Pye, *The Spirit of Chinese Politics: A Psychocultural Study of the Authority Crisis in Political Development* (Cambridge: MIT Press, 1968), pp. 5, 55.

[20]Lucian W. Pye, *The Mandarin and the Cadre: China's Political Cultures* (Ann Arbor: University of Michigan, Center for Chinese Studies, 1988), p. 167.

[21]Karl Marx, *The Eighteenth Brumaire of Louis Napoleon,* in Lewis Feuer, ed., *Basic Writings on Politics and Philosophy: Karl Marx and Friedrich Engels* (New York: Doubleday, 1959), p. 320.

With admirable clarity, Ng-Quinn (Chapter 2) has delineated the base-line for the diachronic analysis of Chinese national/state identity, drawing behavioral referents from premodern Chinese history until the Ming dynasty. The formation of the Chinese state as well as the crystallization of the Chinese *guocui* occurred more or less synchronously during the period of the Three Dynasties of Xia, Shang, and Zhou. Middle Kingdom (Zhong-guo), still the Chinese term for "China" today, first appeared during the Spring and Autumn and Warring States period and referred to the core cultural area in the middle of a greater "all-under-heaven" (*tianxia*). Refuting Pye, Ng-Quinn demonstrates that it is not "race" (since most of China's fifty-six component ethnic groups are Mongoloid in race) but acceptance of the state as an embodiment of the combination of many common elements of the population that constitutes the Chinese identity. From the beginning, the Chinese state was pivotal to defending and protecting the integrity of Chinese identity, for at least three reasons of state: physical survival, national distinctiveness, and primacy (the supremacy of the national interest). It was just such a synthetic sense of state unity irrespective of internal differences and an abiding sense of preference for differential interaction with other states on the basis of cultural compatibility—and not any ethnocentric identity—which made premodern China invulnerable to an identity crisis. Cognitively, "state," "world," and "culture" were enmeshed, even if empirically the Chinese state had to interact with other states in the real world.

In fact, both internal and external factors have reflected and effected the formation of the Chinese state and the construction of the Chinese identity. If the formation of the Chinese state was facilitated by a competitive external environment, the construction of the Chinese *guocui* grew out of language, customs, values, religion, history, and the drive for biologic and social perpetuation. Once congealed, however, the self-identity of premodern China, remained firm and stable, at least in its core. Of course the changing external environment, Ng-Quinn argues, caused the same Chinese identity/difference to adopt various national role conceptions—expansive, complacent, or regulatory—to meet situational contingencies. In short, premodern China was firm in its self-identity but flexible in its mobilization of self-identity, and herein lies the main explanation for the perpetuation of the Chinese state.

Ng-Quinn's is a largely primordialist interpretation: that the core determinants of Chinese identity is essentially *affective,* based on unity and culture in existence since the period of Xia, Shang, and Zhou. This "national" identity served as Durkheim's "collective conscience," bonding the Chinese population, at least psychologically and hence immutably, while roles as manifest behavior mobilizing state identity can and do change. Like an individual, a state can enact various roles without modifying its identity. This anchored identity provides stability and predictability, helping to perpetuate the state as circumstances change.

The historian Ping-ti Ho suggests an alternative explanation for the longevity of Chinese identity. Its roots are to be found in the dynamic interplay of three factors: (1) one of the most successful agricultural systems in the world; (2) a primordial religious belief in the necessity of continuing patrilineal descent lines which generated powerful social and biologic pressures to perpetuate the collective social body as a civilizational state; and (3) a language system so unique in concept and form that it promoted and preserved the distinctive identity of Chinese civilization. Owing to the synergy of "these factors involving the biologically necessary, the socially essential, and the culturally basic, the Chinese civilization has been able periodically to revitalize itself and to retain its discernible identity even today."[22]

Of course premodern China had relatively easy trials and tribulations. A real test for Chinese national identity did not come until the Opium War (1839–42), which marked for China's anti-imperialist revolutionaries the epochal transition from the premodern to the modern eras in Chinese history. The strength and persistence of the traditional Chinese civilizational identity were most dramatically revealed during the first half of the nineteenth century, when China was faced with a continuing threat from the dynamic and expansionist West. The stage was set for confrontation as more and more Westerners began to arrive in China in the wake of the McCartney mission in 1793, which had sought to open China to diplomacy and free trade. Inevitably, the Chinese world and the Western world, with their distinct claims of superiority based on different world views and identities, collided head on. A letter from a British Christian missionary to the home office in London (ca. 1869) speaks directly and powerfully to the two irreconcilable identifications: "Are we not much superior to them [the Chinese]? Are we not more manly, more intelligent, more skillful, more human, more civilized, nay, are we not more estimable in every way? Yes, according to our way of thinking. No, *emphatically* no, according to theirs. And it would be nearly as difficult for us to alter our opinion on the subject as it is for them to alter theirs."[23]

[22]Ping-ti Ho, "The Chinese Civilization: A Search for the Roots of Longevity," *Journal of Asian Studies* 35 (August 1976): 547–54; quotation at p. 554.

[23]Griffith John to the London Missionary Society, in R. Wardlaw Thompson, ed., *Griffith John: The Story of Fifty Years in China* (New York: A. C. Armstrong, 1906), p. 254.

What is so striking about the traditional Chinese image of world order—at least the high Qing scholar-gentry enactment of Chinese identity which became predominant in the nineteenth century and seemed designed to support Manchu rulers as the legitimate heirs and defenders of the great Chinese tradition—is the extent to which it was colored by the assumptions, beliefs, sentiments, and symbols of the Confucian self-image.[24] Indeed, this nineteenth-century Chinese image of world order was no more than a corollary of the Chinese internal order and thus an extended projection of the Chinese civilizational identity. What is even more striking is the absence of a nationalistic dynamic in the enactment of the nineteenth-century Chinese identity; for judging by the contemporary usage, the Chinese identity as mobilized in specific response to the Western threat was more civilizational than national. As in days of yore, that civilizational identity was presumed to reproduce itself in a concentrically larger expandable circle as the correct cosmic order. There was no awareness of a need for a foreign ministry in the universal Chinese state. When in 1839 the British superintendent of trade in China, Charles Elliot, urged the viceroy of Canton, Deng Tingzeng, to settle the differences between the "two nations" by peaceful means, the latter is reported to have been greatly confused by the term *two nations,* which he mistook for England and the United States. Relying on this incident and other documentary and behavioral referents of Qing diplomacy in the nineteenth century, Immanuel C. Y. Hsü flatly declares, "Doubtless, Imperial China was not a nation-state."[25]

Of course, imperial China in the nineteenth century was as much a nation-state as any European one, perhaps more so in terms state and nation concordance. The Sino-Western conflict in the nineteenth century was not so much an international conflict as it was a system-to-system conflict, a mismatch between Western nationalism and Chinese culturalism. The so-called tribute system (a term coined by Western Sinologists for complex, practical, and institutional expressions that constituted the method of managing external, that is, barbarian, affairs) made no "realist" sense. But it served a vital symbolic function by exemplifying and legitimizing the myth

[24]On the traditional Chinese world order, see John K. Fairbank, ed., *The Chinese World Order: Traditional China's Foreign Relations* (Cambridge: Harvard University Press, 1968); and Samuel S. Kim, *China, the United Nations, and World Order* (Princeton: Princeton University Press, 1979), chap. 1, pp. 19–48. For an alternative interpretation based on more recent historiography, see Michael Hunt, "Chinese Foreign Relations in Historical Perspective," in Harry Harding, ed., *China's Foreign Relations in the 1980s* (New Haven: Yale University Press, 1984), pp. 1–42.

[25]Immanuel C. Y. Hsü, *China's Entrance into the Family of Nations: The Diplomatic Phase, 1858–1880* (Cambridge: Harvard University Press, 1960), p. 13.

of Qing China as the universal state governed by the Son of Heaven. As John Fairbank reminds us, even during the golden era of the Sinocentric world order, however, "China's external order was so closely related to her internal order that one could not long survive without the other."[26] In other words, even imperial China with all its pretensions of normative self-sufficiency could not really live in isolation; it needed outside barbarians in order to enact and validate the integrity of its identity/difference.

The crushing defeats China suffered in a series of military confrontations with the West in the 1840s and 1850s failed to modify the Sinocentric image of outlandish barbarians. The psychological security of Chinese identity anchored in the center of a universal state ruled by the Son of Heaven resisted any attempt to construct a new Chinese national identity. At the heart of the repeated failures of Chinese reformers' responses to the Western challenge and the collapse of the traditional Chinese world order lies the failure to establish synergism between Western ideas and Chinese values and to reconstruct the national identity to be responsive to a clear and continuing threat to the integrity of the Chinese state. The so-called *tiyong* dilemma—Chinese learning for cultural identity and Western learning for its practical utility—could not be resolved. Indeed, to advocate departing from the ideological continuity of tradition and reconstructing the national identity was viewed not as expressing a necessity for survival but as an ultimate betrayal of raison d'état. The alien Qing (Manchu) dynasty (1644–1911) cannot be singled out as the only culprit in the national disaster. The Manchus as alien conquerors were ever-mindful of the fate of Mongol rule (1279–1367) and determined to rule China by Chinese virtues (and vices). By the midnineteenth century, the triumph of Chinese civilization over the Manchu was nearly complete, with the abolition of Manchu even as a secondary official language. "If the government of the Ch'ing had faults," confessed the reformer Kang Youwei, "they were the ancient faults of the Han, T'ang, Sung, and Ming—'It was not a special Manchu system.'"[27]

In terms of national identity theory, however, the lesson of China's failure to respond to the Western challenge in the nineteenth century seems somewhat complicated by the manifest inability and unwillingness of the alien dynasty to mobilize Chinese identity in nationalistic terms. If the stability of national identity is critically dependent on the state-nation concordance, its effective mobilization in world politics is critically depen-

[26]John K. Fairbank, "A Preliminary Framework," in Fairbank, *Chinese World Order* (see n. 24), p. 3.
[27]Quoted in Mary C. Wright, *The Last Stand of Chinese Conservatism: The T'ung-Chih Restoration, 1862–1872* (Stanford: Stanford University Press, 1962), p. 53.

dent on its role commitments suiting its role capabilities. It has been suggested that a change in foreign policy behavior is a reflection of the incongruence between self and role which results from overcommitment to a particular set of national role obligations.[28] In other words, late Qing China was faced not so much with crises of self-inclusion as with crises of national purpose and state survival. The gap between its identity commitments and identity capabilities widened to the point where the Chinese state could no longer defend the integrity of its self-identity against the Western onslaught aimed at remaking China. Thus, contrary to the Pye thesis, Qing China's identity crisis came late in its life cycle and emanated from the progressive widening of the discrepancy between promise and performance until it was unbridgeable. As a case in point confirming the Habermasian nexus of identity and legitimation crises, the Chinese system in the twilight phase of Qing rule could no longer cope with *neiluan* (internal disorder) and *waihuan* (external calamity) without relinquishing its identity.[29] The need for adaptive behavior forced a deviation from valued norms that Qing China could no longer afford.

At long last, modern Chinese ethnonationalism was born in the wreckage of the traditional Chinese world order. Ironically, it was Japanese, not Western, imperialism that delivered another blow through its decisive victory in the Sino-Japanese War of 1894–95. By the turn of the century the cumulative impact of the unequal treaty system, coupled with the rise of expansionist Japan, had irreparably undermined the Sinocentric world order and Qing China. A new generation of young ethnonationalists came along, searching for a new strategy for making China strong and powerful again and achieving national respect, freedom, and equality in the international community.[30] Paradoxical as it may seem, in order to cope with wrenching ambiguities and uncertainties created by China's encounter with the other (Western) world, to fight fire with fire as it were, the Chinese were forced to accept such Western concepts as nation, sovereignty, race, citizenship, and identity. The quest for Chinese *national* identity in a modern sense finally began at the turn of the century with the popularization among Chinese intellectuals of such modern terms as *minzu* (literally, "clan people" by connoting the notion of "nation") imported from the writings of the

[28]Backman, "Role Theory and International Relations," p. 316.

[29]See Jürgen Habermas, *Legitimation Crisis,* trans. Thomas McCarthy (Boston: Beacon, 1973).

[30]This is one of the major themes in Sun Yat-sen's *San min zhuyi* (The three principles of the people); see Sun Yat-sen, *San Min Chu I: The Three Principles of the People,* trans. Frank W. Price (Shanghai: Commercial Press, 1932).

Japanese Meiji period. The term *Zhonghua minzu* (Chinese people or nation) was closely associated with nationalistic writings warning of the clear and present danger of national annihilation under external invasion. Zhang Taiyan, one of the leading intellectuals of the time, introduced the concept of *Zhongguoren* (people of the Middle Kingdom, or Chinese people). Zhang's vague but inclusive definition, according to David Wu, "marks the beginning of a modern concept of Chinese national identity. Later efforts were made both in and out of China, through intellectual discourses and government promotions, to construct a Chinese identity based on his nationalistic view."[31]

The crisis of a weak state becomes a focal point of angst over Chinese national identity in the turbulent transitional period from late Qing China to the founding of the People's Republic in 1949. As Hunt shows (in Chapter 3), a dominant feature of the Chinese quest for national identity during this period was a preoccupation with creating and maintaining a strong and unified state. *Aiguo zhuyi* (patriotism, or literally the "ideology of loving the country") rather than "nationalism" became the more acceptable and unifying term to express loyalty to China and a desire to serve it. At any rate, Hunt argues, patriotism is a better term for describing and explaining the particular characteristics of the Chinese search for national identity. Given the state's pivotal role in both historical fact and historical myth, in its civilizational greatness and territorial conquests, the quest for a national identity that is state centered and state strengthening is hardly surprising.

For the first time in Chinese history, there also emerged in the writings of the politically engaged intellectuals and policy influentials a general agreement on the importance of "the people," perhaps a popular sovereignty with Chinese characteristics. A strong state required not only institutional reform but also a popular base of state sovereignty, as echoed in Kang Youwei's memorial asserting "that all the countries in the world today which have held to old ways have without exception been partitioned or put in great danger." As Wilson suggests (in Chapter 5), however, if the substance of Kang's memorial is revolutionary, moving well beyond the more modest changes advocated by the earlier self-strengthening reformers, the style and form of his remonstrating is still old-fashioned.

According to Hunt, a strong state imperative raised several unavoidable but elusive and paradoxical challenges: Can (old) China be saved without

[31]David Yen-ho Wu, "The Construction of Chinese and Non-Chinese Identities," *Daedalus* 120 (Spring 1991): 161.

destroying important parts of it? Is state transformation possible without either societal transformation at home or allies abroad? To save China and defend and protect the integrity of the Chinese national identity, Hunt says, left patriots no choice but to put their faith in Russia, one of China's most dangerous neighbors. The successful Bolshevik revolution and the humiliating Versailles settlement led many patriots to a drastic redefinition of the world situation. Li Dazhao, most notably, found it necessary to subordinate popular and regional unity to social revolution and internationalism. For China to survive in a "robbers' world" required nothing less than the synergy of radical popular resistance at home and revolutionary allies abroad.[32] Li's revolutionary vision and strategy of making China strong and powerful resonate in the ideological transformations of Li's disciple, Zhang Guotao, and Mao Zedong. Indeed, in Hunt's essay we see the beginning of China's proletariat internationalism and the construction of a new national identity as a socialist state.

Hunt presents a fascinating account of the process of conceptual transformation through which Mao in the 1910s arrived at his thesis that a strong state was the key to the livelihood of the people and China's survival. As early as 1914, Mao was convinced that the destruction of China could be averted, even if he was not yet sure how such a national salvation could be achieved. Two years later, Mao was completely converted to the statist imperative. By 1920, Marxism was wedded to Mao's strong-state patriotism, or as Hunt puts it, Mao's patriotism led to revolution and internationalism.

In perhaps his most illuminating essay on the subject of Chinese national identity (written in October 1938, while China was at war with Japan), Mao comes to terms with the problem of the compatibility of patriotism and Marxist Internationalism by asking, "Can a Communist, who is an internationalist, at the same time be a patriot?" Mao first responds with the theoretical clarification (the beginning of the Sinicization—qua Maofication—of Marxism) that "the theory of Marx, Engels, Lenin and Stalin is universally applicable," to be sure, but to be regarded "not as a dogma, but as a guide to action." (Parenthetically, the Maoist notion that Marxism is not a dogma but a guide to action has resonated so often in Deng's comments and speeches in the post-Mao era that the uninitiated can easily take it as the essence of post-Mao Dengism.) Mao then argues:

---

[32]For another analysis of contemporary Chinese foreign policy in terms of the dangers and opportunities presented by a "robbers' world," see Edward Friedman, "Maoist and Post-Mao Conceptualizations of World Capitalism: Dangers and/or Opportunities," in Samuel S. Kim, ed., *China and the World: New Directions in Chinese Foreign Relations,* 2d ed. (Boulder, Colo.: Westview, 1989), pp. 55–85.

Being Marxists, Communists are internationalists, but we can put Marxism into practice only when it is integrated with the specific characteristics of our country and acquires *a definite national form. . . . For the Chinese Communists who are part of the great Chinese nation, flesh of its flesh and blood of its blood,* any talk about Marxism in isolation from China's characteristics is merely Marxism in the abstract, Marxism in a vacuum. Here to apply Marxism concretely in China so that its every manifestation has *an indubitably Chinese character,* i.e., to apply Marxism in the light of China's specific characteristics, becomes a problem which it is urgent for the whole Party to understand and solve. Foreign stereotypes must be abolished, there must be less singing of empty, abstract tunes, and dogmatism must be laid to rest; they must be replaced by *the fresh, lively Chinese style and spirit which the common people of China love.* To separate international content from national form is the practice of those who do not understand the first thing about internationalism.[33]

The demise of the traditional Chinese world order and the collapse of the Qing dynasty in its wake made it relatively easy for Chinese patriots of all ideological persuasions to agree on the strong-state thesis as a fundamental point of departure. But constructing a new Chinese national identity based on a new national symbol system proved much more difficult. As Hunt reminds us, the disagreement among Chinese patriots centered on three questions vital to making China strong and powerful again: What ideology would prop up the state and give its rejuvenating process legitimacy and direction? Where would the new leadership positions come from and by what rules of entry and play in the governmental institutions? and Who were the "people," and what would be the proper basis for their relationship to the state? The disagreements these questions engendered can be reduced to system-reforming as against system-transforming approaches. Ultimately, the CCP's system transformers prevailed over the Guomindang (GMD)'s system reformers. The founding of the People's Republic of China signaled to the world a new Chinese state based on a new national identity. China finally emerged from a century of national humiliation proclaiming its new national identity.

Although writing of different periods of Chinese history, both Ng-Quinn and Hunt approach the subject of national identity from an essentially realist, state-centered perspective but arrive at somewhat different conclusions. Despite the many variations on the realist paradigm in international relations, its core assumptions stress the centrality of the state as a unitary, rational actor, the supremacy of national interests, and the primacy

[33]"The Role of the Chinese Communist Party in the National War, October 1938," in *Selected Works of Mao Tse-Tung,* vol. 2 (Beijing: Foreign Languages Press, 1965), pp. 196, 208, 209–10, emphasis added.

of realpolitik over idealpolitik. For Ng-Quinn, the Chinese state played a central role in the creation and perpetuation of Chinese identity during much of the premodern period. In the Qing-Republican transitional period, as Hunt shows, Chinese national identity was less self-evidently primordial and more subject to reconstruction in the course of political and intellectual struggle over the competing notions of how to make the Chinese state strong and prosperous.

Watson, a cultural anthropologist, presents a powerful reminder that there is another story to tell, or at least another way of telling the same story (Chapter 4). A genuine puzzle for him is the same enduring China puzzle that has fascinated and frustrated Western Sinologists since the early Jesuits began to write about the Middle Kingdom. What was the glue (Durkheim's collective conscience) that held Chinese society together for so many centuries? The durability of Chinese society and culture, and the continuity of Chinese cultural identity, are all the more remarkable, as Watson puts it, for existing in a country of continental dimensions, mutually unintelligible languages, and an amazing array of ethnic differences.

For Watson, national identity is a modern concept; for it presupposes the existence of a modern, media-conscious state actively involved in nation-building and modernization processes. A shared sense of cultural identity predated the construction of a national identity in China and thus conditioned it. Yet the processes of constructing a unified culture (a cultural identity) and a nation-state concordance (a national identity) are similar except in one important respect. Like national identity, cultural identity too does not grow "naturally" in any society; it has to be negotiated, transacted, and achieved. The critical difference lies in the actors involved in the two different but overlapping processes. While the state played a dominant role in creating, nurturing, and promoting a national identity, ordinary people of every description (farmers, artisans, shopkeepers, midwives, silk reelers, laborers, and the like, both male and female) played an equally central role in the promotion and perpetuation of cultural identity. In short, Watson's is a different level of analysis, proceeding as it does from the bottom-up populist or anthropological perspective instead of the more common top-down state-centered, realist perspective.

What is Chinese culture or Chinese cultural identity? Watson shies away from earlier Tylorian primordialist notions that culture is something preordained or immutable or a set of traits that people inherit passively from ancestors.[34] Rather, he conceptualizes culture as an ongoing, collective

[34]See A. L. Kroeber and Clyde Kluckholm, *Culture: A Critical Review of Concepts and Definitions* (New York: Random House, 1952), pp. 81–88.

enterprise that must be renegotiated by each new generation. Nor is culture exclusively a product of elite endeavors. Ordinary people actively participate in the construction of a unified culture by following a system of shared practices or rites. Orthopraxy (correct practice) rather than orthodoxy (correct belief) was the principal means of constructing and maintaining cultural unity and cultural identity in the late imperial China. And this sense of Chinese cultural identity is still very much alive in Taiwan, Hong Kong, Singapore, and rural areas of the People's Republic of China. The seemingly unchanging Chinese culture is a renewable resource giving new meanings about being and becoming Chinese in a changing world.

One is and becomes Chinese and achieves Chinese cultural identity (*wen*) by understanding and performing key rituals associated with the life cycle—the rites of birth, marriage, death, and ancestor—in the proper and accepted manner. In essence, one becomes Chinese by *acting* Chinese. Rites rather than beliefs—participatory practice rather than adherence to values—is really what make one Chinese. It is also the performance of rites rather than the conversion to a received dogma that works as the glue that holds Chinese society together. In conducting funeral rites, for example, it is the primacy of ritual practice, rather than the preoccupation with beliefs, that has made it possible for imperial authorities, local elites, and ordinary people to agree and unite.

Yet Chinese orthopraxy as the principal means of cultural integration allows for great variation within an overarching structure of unity, leaving considerable scope for the expression of what outsiders might see as chaotic regional and ethnonational cultural diversity. Watson finds the genius of the Chinese approach to the perpetuation of cultural identity in this variation within unity: a unified Chinese cultural system so flexible that those calling themselves Chinese can participate in a unified, centrally organized culture while they simultaneously celebrate their local or regional distinctiveness. Interestingly enough, one also finds variation within unity resurrected in contemporary Chinese foreign policy in the form of the firmness/flexibility dialectical code of conduct: that China is always firm on matters of principles but most flexible in their application in specific situations—a code resonating with the Maoist notion of Marxism as a guide to action.

The important point here is that the imperial state was always concerned with proper ritual form (*li*) rather than substantive content (inner belief) in maintaining the social order. In practice, however, the distinction between form and content is difficult to draw when the value of "harmony" (*he*) is constantly promoted by the state as the proper form of all human relations. Indeed, harmony in a great variety of manifest symbolic forms has been all pervasive, Arthur Wright claims, "in innumerable era names, place names, personal names, street, palace, temple, and studio names throughout Chinese history."[35] Tellingly enough, the Board of Rites (Libu) was in charge of handling external affairs by enforcing the proper performance of rites and rituals in the acceptable Chinese way (for example, the performance of the kowtow: three kneelings and nine prostrations). According to Watson, the decline of state power during the nineteenth century, although a major preoccupation for historians of Qing China, had little effect on the stability and integrity of Chinese cultural and civilizational identity because the Chinese people continued to identify themselves as representatives and transmitters of a grand civilization, irrespective of political developments. Even at the level of ordinary rural Cantonese, Watson argues, society without *li* invites *luan* (chaos), and *luan* conjures up fears of banditry, famine, and cannibalism (the ultimate symbol of social breakdown). Although Watson deals largely with the construction of a unified culture in late imperial China, he draws a very important conclusion for the People's Republic. The Maoist preoccupation with orthodoxy (and we might add post-Tiananmen China's return to it) is a clear deviation from the very practical and participatory principles that held Chinese society and culture together for so many centuries.

A New National Identity or the Old Imperial One?

Looking at four decades of the PRC as a whole, it is striking to observe how Pye's notion of a national identity crisis as typically arising early in nation-state development has been reversed in the PRC case. As with Qing China, a national identity crisis was virtually absent in the early days of the People's Republic. More than any event, the 1989 Tiananmen massacre reflected and affected a profound crisis of national self-definition. To be sure, there was an earlier national identity crisis in 1957, when China began to experiment with several competing notions of state comportment. Then the Cultural Revolution set in motion what Goldman, Link, and Su (Chapter 6) call an identity crisis of great depth and scope. A series of three belief crises (*sanxin weiji*)—the crisis of belief (*xinyang*) in Marxism, the crisis in faith (*xinxin*) in socialism, and the crisis in trust (*xinren*)—began slowly chipping away at the acceptance of the People's Republic as an authentic

---

[35] Arthur F. Wright, "Struggle v. Harmony: Symbols of Competing Values in Modern China," *World Politics* 6 (October 1953): 34.

socialist state. But Tiananmen may be said to have dramatized the China's *neiluan* (internal disorder) for both domestic and global audiences. In the process, the Chinese communist state, in order to legitimate itself, was forced to act out its national identity on the losing side of an emerging post–Cold War world order.

Faced with the dual crises of legitimation and identity, the government has revived fundamentalism in the form of assaults on the so-called peaceful evolution (*heping yanbian*) strategy of the capitalist West in general and capitalist America in particular. The pre-Tiananmen notion that there is neither an international enemy nor foreign aggression standing in the way of China's modernization drive is being criticized as one of the major causes of the present predicament.[36] The revised definition of the world situation, according to a classified Communist party document, rejects the core assumptions of the world peace/development line (mid-1984 to mid-1989), warning instead that world politics has entered a new phase of "the struggle between the two systems." Although varying "in its form, intensity and the tactics employed," we are told, the two-system struggle "will be sharper, more complex and more intense than before."[37] In terms of the synthetic definition set forth in Chapter 1, then, the People's Republic has recently entered the most problematic phase to date in its developmental trajectory. The sound and fury of official response to the challenge of national purpose and direction only underlines the depth and scope of this unprecedented identity crisis. Yet so far this reorientation seems to be for domestic consumption only, giving rise to a curious phenomenon: a new weltanschauung (or rather, a reincarnation of an old one) without operational foreign policy consequences—pure domestic symbolism.

To appreciate this identity crisis fully, one must return to the beginnings of the Chinese communist state. The national identity of the People's Republic was based on the complete repudiation of the identity of the previous GMD government and its international comportment. The clarity of national purpose, a charismatic leader at the helm, and the identification of the international positive and negative reference groups all led to confident public pronouncement on what the new Chinese state was all about and intended to do. Already, months before formal establishment of the People's Republic on October 1, 1949, Mao had declared that all Chinese

[36]For an exploration of the extent to which the post-Tiananmen Chinese leadership is mired in a legitimation-cum-identity crisis, see Samuel S. Kim, "Peking's Foreign Policy in the Shadows of Tiananmen: The Challenge of Legitimation," *Issues & Studies* 27 (January 1991): 39–69.

[37]Quoted in *New York Times,* November 11, 1990, pp. 1, 11.

"must lean either to the side of imperialism or to the side of socialism. Sitting on the fence will not do, *nor is there a third road.*"[38] Such a two-world theory was congenial to the redefinition of the national self in terms of the "principal contradiction" in the world. Mao's defining role in the formulation and presentation of a new national identity was made clear in his "standing up" proclamation of the founding of the People's Republic: "Our nation will no longer be an insulted nation; we have stood up." Mao's authority, as Frederick Teiwes suggests, was forever legitimized by the magnitude of the 1949 revolutionary victory and was "so great as to sustain the leader's charisma even in the face of major subsequent failures during the socialist era."[39]

In some respects, the Korean War came as a blessing in disguise, providing, as it did, both testing and validating of the adopted PRC national identity. As Mao later recalled, it was only by intervening in the Korean War that Beijing was able to demonstrate, to Stalin's satisfaction, that Mao was not another Tito—and China not another Yugoslavia. The Korean War thus consolidated the Moscow-Beijing axis on a foundation of shared values and shared fears. At the same time, the Korean question, as Zhou Enlai put it, "is not simply a question concerning Korea, it is related to the Taiwan issue."[40] The entry of the United States into the Korean War also helped Mao to answer with ease and clarity his perennial question for the Chinese revolution and thus "to unite with real friends in order to attack real enemies."[41] The Korean War provided the exogenous trigger for national identity mobilization, and it confirmed for the national self and "significant others" that China could indeed stand up for the integrity of its new national identity as a revolutionary socialist state against the world's most powerful antisocialist superpower.

[38]*Selected Works of Mao Tse-Tung,* vol. 4 (Beijing: Foreign Languages Press, 1961), p. 415, emphasis added.

[39]Mao Zedong, quoted in John Bryan Starr, *Continuing the Revolution: The Political Thought of Mao* (Princeton: Princeton University Press, 1979), p. 276; Frederick C. Teiwes, *Leadership, Legitimacy and Conflict in China: From a Charismatic Mao to the Politics of Succession* (Armonk, N.Y.: M. E. Sharpe, 1984), p. 49.

[40]Zhou Enlai, quoted in Hao Yufan and Zhai Zhihai, "China's Decision to Enter the Korean War: History Revisited," *China Quarterly* 121 (March 1990), p. 103. This study, based on recently released PRC documents and memoirs, comes to the conclusion that "the reasons why China entered the Korean War were primarily security" (p. 115).

[41]In the opening line of Volume 1 of *Selected Works,* Mao writes, "Who are our enemies? Who are our friends? This is a question of the first importance for the revolution. The basic reason why all previous revolutionary struggles in China achieved so little was their failure to unite with real friends in order to attack real enemies" (Beijing: Foreign Languages Press, 1965), p. 13.

Identity Changes and Continuities

Proceeding from the premise that national identity is in large part cultural identity typed in "significant cultural meanings," Wilson (Chapter 5), unlike Watson, probes core Chinese values and beliefs that guide role relationships as his way of empirically testing and validating change in Chinese national identity. Significant cultural meanings constitute the operational core of national identity, the basis for distinctive patterns of behavior both individual and societal. For empirical validation of changing cultural meanings and role relationships, however, Wilson turns to China's legal development, as the law in any society reflects and effects structural and content changes in the cultural meanings of rights and duties. The traditional Chinese legal conception depended on clear definition and firm enforcement of social status and hierarchy, with absolute obedience as the supreme virtue. In the traditional Chinese normative order, Wilson explains, the determination of right and wrong stressed derelictions of obligations as required by *li* (proper form) above the actual nature of a transgression, wrongdoing was determined not by the commission of certain acts but by the violation of the obligations associated with filial piety.

Starting from this traditional legal baseline, Wilson argues, a transformation in the cultural meanings of rights and obligations has clearly taken place during the post-Mao era. In the first thirty years of communist rule, especially during the period from 1958 to 1978, the emphasis in relations between the government and people—and between state and nation—continued to stress class status and citizen obligations, while "rights," especially "negative rights," were generally disregarded.[42] And the concept of equality before the law was nowhere to be found, in theory or practice. As late 1979, as shown by Wilson's essay and also by the PRC refusal to sign any of the U.N.-sponsored multilateral human rights conventions, human rights were still defined as given and regulated by the state, not "heaven-given." Consistent with both the dominant tradition of Confucian humanism and Marxist proletarian egalitarianism, "human rights" were still conceptualized as more collective than individual, more social and economic than civil and political, more needs-based than rights-entitled, and more duties-oriented than rights-centered.

Nonetheless, against this obligation-centered tradition, China has taken

---

[42]On "positive rights" and "negative rights" in Chinese human rights thinking and practice, see Richard W. Wilson, "Rights in the People's Republic of China," in James C. Hsiung, ed., *Human Rights in East Asia: A Cultural Perspective* (New York: Paragon House, 1985), pp. 109–28.

a legal leap at home and abroad in the 1980s. However frail this rule of law is in China, the restoration and rejuvenation of law have produced important and far-reaching ripple effects, the Tiananmen bloodletting notwithstanding. Nowhere is a new conception of rights and duties more apparent, according to Wilson, than in family relations, where traditional biases based on age and gender are being increasingly replaced by equality as a new basis for solidarity. The Chinese people still identify with the civilizational greatness of China's legacy, but they do so with a new world view. The world, according to the Chinese people, no longer pivots around the Middle Kingdom nor their own cultural meanings around the Chinese state (the point also stressed by Goldman, Link, and Su). With obligation no longer serving as the main operational code of conduct came a profound change in the way Chinese see themselves and their place in a changing world. They are evolving a new sense of national identity based on equality of persons combined with communitarian ideals. In short, Wilson seems to confirm the proposition that national identity enactment is situation specific.

This unfolding drama of normative transformation is nowhere clearer than in a comparison of the way people framed their dissent in the late nineteenth century and today. In striking contrast to the reformer Kang Youwei's 1897 memorial with its traditional obsequious tone, the demands of the students in the spring of 1989 asserted the constitutional rights of citizens and requested dialogue on the basis of full equality. The student-led democracy movement of 1989 was also notably devoid of xenophobic or self-assertive nationalism. In a country with no strong pacifist tradition to speak of, the Chinese students seem to have learned from the post-Vietnam, post-Afghanistan international climate a remarkable lesson: how to conduct one of the most disciplined and nonviolent democratic movements to appear anywhere in modern history. They resorted to the hunger strike as a new form of peaceful remonstration and empowerment. Even after the bloody suppression, Yan Jiaqi and Wuer Kaixi reaffirmed in a joint declaration "rational, peaceful and non-violent methods. China's contemporary history has taught us that the use of violence against violence and the theory that 'power grows out of the gun barrel' will not lead China to true freedom and democracy. This is also the firm belief of the martyrs of June 4."[43] Wilson reminds us that, paradoxical as it may seem, the government also appealed for support in the name of the law, justifying its bloody military suppression as necessary for maintaining law and order, and that

[43]The text of "Joint Declaration" is published in *Hongkong Standard,* July 5, 1989, p. 8.

for the party-state-government to have done so is to reveal a profound shift in cultural meanings.

Although Wilson's essay is largely limited to changing cultural meanings of rights and duties, the 1980s, especially from mid-1986 to mid-1989, has also witnessed some incremental shifts and modifications in Chinese thinking on human rights.[44] Thanks to expanding global-local linkages, the Chinese government has been forced to shift its approach from outright denial and repression to a more diversified and opportunistic one. Apparently sensing that human rights can be made an important resource in the positive presentation of Chinese national identity, the Chinese government has undertaken a slow, reluctant, and almost forced expansion of the concept of human rights, reflected in its greater participation in the activities of U.N. human rights organs; its increasing acceptance of certain select global human rights principles and norms; and its softer, albeit increasingly less effective, response to the ever-growing human rights demands at home.

As late as 1979, the PRC government dismissed the Universal Declaration of Human Rights as a means of safeguarding the bourgeois dictatorship of capitalist states and as a cover to legitimize ideological infiltration of socialist countries.[45] By 1982, China seems to have realized that human rights have become an integral part of world politics—that what a state is and does with respect to human rights affects not only the condition and fate of its people but also its international image and reputation.[46] China's human rights promises and performance became an integral part of the presentation of its national identity in world politics. Hoping to enhance China's international reputation, the Chinese government in the 1980–88 period ratified or acceded to seven multilateral human rights conventions on women, racial discrimination, refugees, apartheid, genocide, and torture.

Conceptually and legally, China crossed the Rubicon in the protection of *individual* human rights when it signed in 1986 (and ratified in 1988) the Convention against Torture and Other Cruel, Inhuman or Degrading Treatment or Punishment. By dint of its ratification of the antitorture

[44]See Samuel S. Kim, "Thinking Globally in Post-Mao China," *Journal of Peace Research* 27 (May 1990): 191–209.

[45]See Xiao Weiyun, Luo Haocai, and Wu Jieying, "How Does Marxism Look at the 'Human Rights' Question?" (in Chinese), *Hongqi* (Red flag), May 1979, pp. 43–48.

[46]See, e.g., Wei Min, "Tantao youguan renquan de jige wenti: Jinian 'shijie renquan xuanyan' tongguo sishi zhounian" (An inquiry into some problems on human rights: In commemoration of the 40th anniversary of the adoption of the 'Universal Declaration of Human Rights'") *Renmin ribao* (p daily), 1988, p. 4.

convention, China could no longer seek, as a matter of legal principle, the sanctuary of domestic jurisdiction nor excuse itself by citing the structural violence of colonialism and imperialism or its own cultural and social constraints. With the Tiananmen massacre, China's official thinking on human rights simply backslid to the 1979 position,[47] while many prominent students and intellectuals were making a great leap forward and outward, thinking globally and acting globally in the elusive quest for a more democratic national identity.

Goldman, Link, and Su (Chapter 6) discuss this major transformation in the Chinese intellectuals' quest for national identity. For the majority of the politically engaged intellectuals, it is the "country" (the Han Chinese nation), not the PRC party-state, that has become the most significant reference group for their individual and collective loyalty and identification. As the slogan goes, "We love our country, but we hate our government." Patriotism as the rallying force behind Chinese national identity mobilization has come to be equated with loyalty to society and country as distinguished from party, government, and state. Viewed against the longstanding state-society and state-nation concordance and the Chinese intellectual tradition of dedication to serving the state, this is indeed a radical change in the conceptual evolution of China's intellectual community. The proposition that the contest between ethnocentric loyalty and statecentric loyalty is a mismatch because the latter almost invariably loses out finds support in the post-Mao Chinese case.[48] What is most revealing about this post-Mao disjuncture between nation and state is that the Han Chinese have been so dominant within their own nation-state that the two kinds of loyalties have long remained largely overlapping, leaving only discontented minority nationalities, most notably the Tibetans, to vie in such a contest.

Yet the process of the intellectuals' normative transformation was very gradual, evolving from the Democracy Wall and scar literature in the late 1970s to the growing alienation of the mid-1980s and finally the massive protests of 1989. Goldman, Link, and Su view Chinese intellectuals' efforts to forge a new post–Cultural Revolution identity for themselves as a protracted and agonizing process. In the first stage, intellectuals of all generations tended toward a kind of socialist restorationism, a return to the golden age of the early 1950s, when socialism in its original "pure"

[47]See Jiang Bin, "'What are Socialist Human Rights?'" (in Chinese) *Jiefangjun bao* (Liberation Army daily), August 11, 1989, pp. 1–2; and Yi Ding, "Guoji guanxi zhang de bu yanshe neizheng yuanze" (The principle of noninterference in international relations), *Renmin ribao*, August 25, 1989, p. 7.

[48]For ample testimony for this proposition, see Connor, "Ethnonationalism."

form was believed to have served as the symbolic anchor and ark of the PRC's national identity. *Butian* ("repair heaven") and *chaitian* ("dismantle heaven") vied as system-repairing (and system-saving) as against system-dismantling (and system-transforming) options, although most intellectuals still favored the system-reforming restorationist approach. The upsurge of post-Mao scar literature, based on the twin themes of the horrors of the Cultural Revolution and idealized memories of early socialism, showed a general orientation toward socialist restorationism.

The second stage (1982–88) witnessed a series of debates on socialist alienation, different kinds of loyalty and identity, and traditional culture and national character, and a bewildering array of Western ideas and theories including convergence theory. Between 1979 and 1983, some six hundred articles on the phenomenon of socialist alienation were published.[49] Although Wang Ruoshui and Zhou Yang still believed that humanism embedded in Marxism could be revived as the way of relegitimating Chinese socialism, the hardline ideologues put an end to the alienation debate by launching the campaign against spiritual pollution. Bai Hua's "Unrequited Love" and Liu Binyan's "The Second Kind of Loyalty" got caught up in the vortex of national identity politics, revealing and intensifying the growing nation-state cleavage.

One troublesome irony emerges from the Goldman/Link/Su essay: the more the hardliners insisted on the inalienability and unity of patriotism, party, nation, and state, the more they succeeded in achieving exactly the opposite. While still united on the desirability and irreversibility of post-Mao reforms and the opening to the outside world, Chinese intellectuals began slowly to doubt the basic assumptions of the *butian* approach. As late as the mid-1980s, as Goldman, Link, and Su suggest, there still existed a substantial continuity in the intellectuals' identification with the state. Intellectuals maintained this identification because of their belief that they had a vital state-serving and state-saving role to play and because they knew that the state itself was largely supporting reform, notwithstanding the cruel treatment it had repeatedly inflicted on them over the years. After January 1987, when Hu Yaobang, Liu Binyan, Fang Lizhi, and Wang Ruowang were made the scapegoats for the student demonstrations in December, troubling doubts about the intellectuals' identity as system-saving restorationists began to surface. By the summer of 1988, according to

[49]Center of Philosophical Studies, the Shanghai Academy of Social Sciences, *Rendaozhuyi he yihua sanshi ti* (Thirty topics on humanitarianism and alienation) (Shanghai: Shanghai renmin chubanshe, 1984).

Goldman, Link, and Su, the working compromise based on the triangular structure of party-country-intellectual began to crumble.

The suppression of the alienation debate was not the end of all debate. The party's lurching alternation between repression and relaxation gave rise to another and deeper debate, under the rubric of "culture fever" (*wenhua re*) (or "searching-for-roots fever"). Once again Chinese intellectuals began to ask the century-old cultural and historical questions about the root causes of their national identity predicament. This round of agonizing focused on the proper cultural foundation for processes of nation building and modernization reform, and it culminated in the television documentary *He shang* (River elegy, or The river dies young) in June 1988. The series generated a great stir of both horror and applause among Chinese at every level of society and everywhere—mainland, Taiwan, Hong Kong, and overseas. For at least several months in the second half of 1988, *River Elegy* brought the whole Chinese-speaking world into the game.

Judging on the medium used, the message conveyed, and the reaction evoked, *River Elegy* certainly played a trailblazing role in the politics of Chinese national identity exploration. It is a vivid testimony to the coming of the modern media/transparency revolution to post-Mao China. Television documentary programs can bridge the great chasm between elite and mass culture. Arguably, *River Elegy* comes close, faute de mieux, to being the functional equivalent of a national referendum on the symbol system of Chinese identity. The Yellow River, the Great Wall, and the Chinese dragon were depicted as emblematic of a self-enclosed peasant culture under the oppressive yoke of authoritarian rule. Far from showing national prowess, these omnipresent symbols, so beloved by Western tourists, were dramatized as symbolizing China's conservatism, backwardness, tyrannical rule, and impotent national defense as well as smothering the gentler, kinder, and more humane aspects of the national spirit.

In one of the most telling passages, from Part 1, "Xun meng" (In search of a dream), Su Xiaokang, the principal writer of the script, quoting Toynbee (but also drawing from Shakespeare's *Julius Caesar*), observes that "the most useful function of an external enemy is to merely deliver the final blow to a society that has already committed suicide but still has not drawn its last breath." In Part 6, "Weilanse" (Azure blue), the Yellow River flows into the open Pacific Ocean, symbolizing the "azure" global civilization of the twenty-first century. Then comes the clarion call for a new identity, for the Chinese to move from here to there—from the Yellow River culture to the blue sea under the azure sky. It is a call for a major transformation of the civilizational identity. Standing at the crossroads between civilizational decay and collapse and cultural renaissance, China needs another May Fourth movement to create a new culture on the foundation of science and democracy.[50] Of course this message, echoing Lu Xun's "Ah-Qism," is hardly new, but "what is unprecedented," as a commentator observed in *China Daily,* "is the fact that millions of ordinary people have been led to think about such crucial issues by a most effective modern instrument of mass communication."[51]

Apparently *River Elegy* has powerfully fascinated national imagination, becoming an immediate success. Local television stations in Shanghai and Shenzhen repeated the series in July, and videotapes and the book edition of the script together with commentaries went on sale in Beijing. The China Central Television Station in Beijing, the original sponsor and producer of the program, decided in response to hundreds of letters from viewers to have a second run in August. Within a few months, reprints of the original script and pirated copies of the videotape also became widely available in street-corner shops in Taipei.[52] After a brief period of initial hesitation, an unprecedented wave of interest and publicity unfolded in the Chinese press, with the grand national debate lasting for several months.[53]

In the end, *River Elegy* seems to have underlined the absence of national consensus on the core symbols of Chinese national identity. Like truth, its message lies in the eyes of the beholder. Supporters and detractors can at least agree that television has become an important mass communication medium through which the traditional cultural gulf between the masses and the elite can be bridged and, by implication, Chinese national identity can be reassessed, reappropriated, and reconstructed. Two PRC publicists, writing in the same issue of *Qiushi* (Seeking truth) in October 1988, present sharply contrasting views. For Tian Benxiang of the China Arts Research Institute, the series powerfully projected the spirit of critical rationality, a will to national self-strengthening through the vigorous implementation of reforms and opening to the world so as to empower China to rise up again in the family of nations. A great national self-criticism such as this reflects

[50]Su Xiaokang and Wang Luxiang, eds., *He shang* (River elegy) (1988; reprint, Taipei: Jinfeng chuban youxian gongsi, 1990), pp. 20–21, 96.

[51]Commentator, "Yellow River Complex," *China Daily* (Beijing), August 12, 1988, p. 4.

[52]Kim bought with ease a Taiwan reprint (102d printing!) of the book (see n. 50) and two video cassette tapes (all six parts in two tapes) in Taipei in June 1990. Judging by the bibliographic information in this copy, the 102 reprintings occurred between October 1988 and April 1990.

[53]See Alice De Jong, "The Demise of the Dragon: Backgrounds to the Chinese Film, 'River Elegy,'" *China Information* 4 (Winter 1989–90): 28–43.

and affects a great national self-confidence, he asserts. As in the Chinese word for "crisis," *weiji,* which embodies the duality of danger and opportunity, behind the critical rationality of *River Elegy,* according to Tian, there is a great sense both of national mission and of national crisis in respect to the fate of both the nation and the prospects for reform. Stripped to its core, then, *River Elegy,* for Tian, is essentially self-strengthening, not self-subverting. For Qi Fang of the CCP's Propaganda Department, however, the series is nothing less than a self-negating nihilist exercise. The strength for national revival can come only from Chinese culture; no nation has ever relied on self-negation to achieve national development. By describing Chinese culture as "yellow" (and thus fully negating it) and by Western culture as "azure" (and thus fully endorsing it), Qi argues, the authors of *River Elegy* show the poverty of a Sinocentric world view.[54]

The treatment of *River Elegy* inevitably changed with the political shifts in turbulent Chinese domestic politics. The series' strongly proreform orientation and a dozen or so favorable references to such reformers as Deng Xiaoping and Zhao Ziyang at first provided a measure of official protection. Besides, as Harry Harding shows, Deng has repeatedly warned against a closed-door mentality, attributing "the slow pace of China's modernization to its international isolation from the middle of the Ming dynasty through [the] Opium War, and from the Sino-Soviet split of the late 1950s through the Cultural Revolution."[55] During the second half of 1988, PRC vice-president Wang Zhen was the only self-styled cultural point man fulminating on the antitraditional and antichauvinist tone of *River Elegy,* while *China Daily* and politburo member Hu Qili defended the series as a health exercise in free debate and speech.

As Goldman, Link, and Su suggest, *River Elegy* was at one and the same time the culmination and termination of several years of "culture fever." The three petitions of early 1989 calling for amnesty and release of political prisoners are a benchmark in the intellectuals' quest for a distinct, separate, and autonomous identity for themselves. That they took up the case of Wei Jingsheng, the archetypal system dismantler, is another indication of radical normative change. For the first time, as Goldman, Link, and Su put it, Chinese intellectuals began in large numbers to confront the issue of the "original face" of China's Marxist system. For the first time, Chinese intel-

---

[54]Tian Benxiang, "On 'River Elegy'" (in Chinese), *Qiushi* (Seeking truth), October 1988, pp. 28–33; Qi Fang, "My Views on 'River Elegy' and the Discussion It Has Evoked" (in Chinese), ibid., pp. 34–39.

[55]Harry Harding, *China's Second Revolution: Reform after Mao* (Washington, D.C.: Brookings Institution, 1987), p. 133.

lectuals began to transcend the dialectic of *butian* versus *chaitian,* since both terms pertain to identification with the state. Conceptually at least, Chinese intellectuals could no longer regard party, state, and nation as one, and for the first time in the history of the People's Republic, some elite intellectuals had joined prodemocracy demonstrations. Goldman, Link, and Su argue that this radical transformation, though informed by Western ideas and the developments in Eastern Europe and the Soviet Union, was largely shaped and determined by the intellectuals' own experience and suffering.

And yet in the wake of the Tiananmen massacre, the hard-line government launched major assaults on *River Elegy* as integral part of its anti–Zhao Ziyang campaign. "If Zhao Ziyang had laid a theoretical foundation for the transformation of China's ideological and political work," the Chinese people were now told, "Su Xiaokang and other River Elegy writers had just put this transformation into practice to cater to Zhao Ziyang's needs in transforming ideological and political work."[56] The new party line on *River Elegy,* reflecting the new party line in intra-elite conflict and cleavage, characterized the program as a big propaganda coup for bourgeois liberalism which had provided theoretical and emotional preparation for the June 4 turmoil. A multitude of calls have been issued for the study of China's cultural heritage. Starting on August 9, the *Beijing wanbao* (Beijing evening post) alone is reported to have carried an article a day, for 101 days, pointing out the scholastic and historical fallacies and ideological distortions of the television series.[57] As a product of bourgeois liberalism, *River Elegy* was also linked to the strategy of co-optation through peaceful evolution peddled by international reactionary forces. Paradoxically, the "new" communist state, in a desperate and promiscuous search for relegitimation, has changed its tune and become the self-styled defender of the national identity and symbol system of the old China.

China's Identity as a Socialist State

Even before the demise of the Second (Socialist) World in 1989 and 1990 and the collapse of Soviet communism in 1991, post-Mao China was already in an ideological bind, and the contradictions in China's self-proclaimed identity as a socialist and proletarian state were everywhere for everyone to see. Although the dictatorship of the proletariat has always been a myth in

[56]*Beijing Domestic Service in Mandarin,* October 20, 1989, in *Foreign Broadcast Information Service* (hereafter *FBIS*), October 31, 1989, p. 64.

[57]See *Renmin ribao,* December 19, 1989, p. 6.

China, albeit a necessary and legitimizing one, there was at least some normative and symbolic basis for the proletarian identity in the Maoist period. During much of the 1950s, China's proletarian identity was mobilized in domestic and foreign policy to symbolize its solidarity with the Soviet Union. Then the searing Sino-Soviet conflict required that China's international socialist identity progressively nationalized. In the 1980s, China's socialist identity suffered steady burnout just when China's working class itself was rapidly expanding owing to the post-Mao reforms and growing involvement with the global political economy. This evolution of socialist identity can be seen in both symbolic and policy domains.

In symbolism, rituals, and language, Beijing fostered the creation of an international socialist identity. As Steven Levine suggests, red, the color of revolution, became the symbolic core of Chinese socialism: "The red flag of the People's Republic of China, the red neckerchiefs of the young Pioneers, the little red book of quotations from Chairman Mao, and the countless red banners that floated above every demonstration are just a few examples among many showing how the Chinese Communists identified themselves and their cause through the use of the color red."[58] During the heyday of the Cultural Revolution, the slogan "Chairman Mao is the reddest sun of the East" circulated throughout China. After the Sino-Soviet conflict, however, the international socialist symbols underwent a process of "nationalization or indigenization" with "the subordination of the international socialist symbols of the first decade of the PRC to nationalist symbols celebrating China's own past, including the history of the CCP, its leaders and its martyrs."[59] In the post-Mao era, Beijing launched yet another round of symbolic deconstruction and reconstruction, devaluing socialist symbols, rituals, and language and identifying the party-state as the sovereign agent making China a powerful and prosperous country. After Tiananmen, the leadership retreated to the old Stalinist slogan that "only socialism can save China." Thus has China's socialist identity shifted from the first phase of full acceptance in the 1950s; to the second phase of toleration in the 1960s and 1970s; to the third, and presumably final, phase of rejection, or acceptance only under duress, in the 1980s and early 1990s.[60]

The images and symbols of heroic workers as vanguards of world socialist revolution have virtually vanished from the actual policy, if not com-

---

[58]Steven I. Levine, "China and the Socialist Community: Symbolic Unity" (Paper presented at the Conference on China's Quest for National Identity, January 25–27, 1990, Princeton University), p. 2.

[59]Ibid., pp. 28–29.

[60]Ibid., p. 43.

pletely from the official self-definition, of post-Mao China. Article 1 of the constitution still proclaims, "The People's Republic of China is a socialist state of the people's democratic dictatorship led by the working class and based on the alliance of workers and peasants." And yet there is today only one kind of proletarian China, the one that is becoming a proletarian state in a new way by vigorously peddling its cheap labor as a comparative advantage in international markets. Thanks to post-Mao China's U-turn away from paternalism or patrimonialism—and this is what Chinese workers understand by "socialism"—to the commodification of labor, a large section of the Chinese working class remains alienated from the reform program.[61]

The phenomenon of deepening socialist alienation in the post-Mao era is not confined to the politically engaged intellectuals. In a curious mixture of market and paternalism, the "socialist" state "has literally sold off its patrimonial rights to transfer *hukou* [residential or household registration] to capitalist investors," says Richard Kraus. The emergence of such a freewheeling capitalist labor market produced the new phenomenon of a floating migrant population (estimated at 50 million) of peasants searching for higher wages in urban areas. Some 2.5 million people moved illegally to Guangdong in the last three weeks of February 1989, after Chinese New Year. The problem of a floating migrant population is but one symptom of the deepening and widening social malaise; others are massive illiteracy (which has increased 10 percent during the Deng decade), demographic explosion, environmental degradation, rising surplus labor, and unemployment. The extent to which China's identity as a proletarian state has faded is also suggested, Kraus points out, by the unprecedented antisocialist personnel policy on the shop floor: "Hire the children, but fire their mothers."[62]

Internationally, too, post-Mao China in 1978–79 made a sudden and dramatic change from aid giving to aid seeking. Since 1979, China has joined the Third World competition to export coolie labor, under the guise of promoting "international labor cooperation" (*guoji laowu hezuo*). The total number of Chinese experts and workers abroad under such contracts increased from about eighteen thousand between 1979 and 1981, to thirty-one thousand in 1983 and fifty-nine thousand by the end of 1985. From 1979 to 1985, the total value of labor service contracts was $5.1 billion. Early in 1988, China had over seventy "international economic cooperation corpora-

[61]Richard C. Kraus, "China's Identity as a Proletarian State" (Paper presented at the Conference on China's Quest for National Identity).
[62]Ibid.

tions," which had signed more than four thousand labor contracts with over one hundred countries. The Soviet Union became a market for the exportation of cheap Chinese labor in late 1988, when China signed an agreement to send ten thousand workers to Siberian timber projects. In the five years from 1982 to 1987, the total value of labor contracts reached $7.03 billion (at an annual average of $1.4 billion).[63]

"Sell the Mercedes-Benzes to pay the national debt!" shouted several thousand Beijing citizens as they marched into Tiananmen Squre in May 1989. A more desperate and sinister effort to sell its coolie labor—and to cope with its external debt crisis—followed the June 4 massacre. In August 1989, the Chinese government through Chinter, a Chinese-owned company in Brussels, made an offer of cheap convict labor from Chinese prisons (at about one-fifth of the going rate in Europe) to Swedish auto giant Volvo in return for building a factory in China. Capitalist Volvo rejected the offer as smacking of "[socialist?] slave labor." In July 1989 the presence of mainland Chinese prostitutes in Taiwan became public, and some of them sued for return to Fujian and compensation.

"The system of exploitation of man by man has been eliminated," states the preamble to the PRC constitution, "and the socialist system securely established." And yet by shifting from paternalism to the market, the central government has effectively deprived workers of welfare state protection against abuses by their employers. What happens to China's identity as a proletarian state when the only executions made public in the post-Tiananmen reign of terror were of working-class youth, not of students? Tellingly, such a differentiation between workers and intellectuals serves the interests of both the political elite and the intellectual elite. Vigorous claims of greater status and power by China's intellectuals and merchants have largely been made at the expense of the working class. Here we begin to see the problematic meaning of the "science and democracy" movement led by China's politically engaged intellectuals since the May Fourth movement in 1919.

Multiple Chinas?

White and Li (Chapter 7) address both theoretical and empirical issues in the study of Chinese identity by applying various identity concepts and propositions to China's peripheral regions in the south: Guangdong, Hong

---

[63]Samuel S. Kim, *The Third World in Chinese World Policy* (Princeton: Princeton University, Center of International Studies, 1989), pp. 38–39.

Kong, and Taiwan. China's "national" or "core" identity can be more sharply focused when it is juxtaposed and contrasted with alternative peripheral identities. By delineating the boundary role of "interface identities" through the concept of periphery, White and Li go some distance in addressing the level-of-analysis problems in the study of national identity. These outlying coastal areas, constituting the windows of opportunity to or the pathways of penetration from the outside world, embody both primordial and situational dimensions of Chinese identity. The situation of coastal Chinese on the southern periphery makes them particularly important as zones of interface defining the Chinese state's relationship with the outside world, as sources of social experiments, and as sources of ideological contamination. (The original four special economic zones were established "safely" near Hong Kong and away from the political center.) White and Li take up the proposition that a new threat or danger can trigger identity enactment or reconstruction, as they focus on three key events that generated questions about identity: the rise of extensive commodity markets in 1978, which provided an opportunity in Guangdong; the U.S. derecognition in 1979–80, which amounted to a threat in Taiwan; and the Beijing spring and summer of 1989, which appeared as both a threat and an opportunity in Hong Kong.

Without entirely rejecting the primordialist claim, because identity cannot be changed completely, easily, or frequently, White and Li nonetheless proceed from a more flexible, dynamic, and contextual premise. Their central argument is that national identity is not the only identity option open to coastal Chinese because the Chinese nation-state is not the only, or even the most important, *experienced* reality in their psychocultural consciousness and historical time. According to White and Li, then, identity, or at least the enactment of identity, is largely situational. The analyst can not observe and describe particular identities, either personal or collective, apart from the experiences that shape them and the situations that evoke them. An enacted identity thus has to be situation specific. Whereas from the perspective of Chinese national identity per se, these three regions on the periphery constitute a permeable membrane through which innovation may penetrate to stimulate or challenge the center, from a regional perspective there are multiple claims to identity. Coastal people and groups can choose or alter their identity options to meet or redefine their current needs. Like their compatriots in Southeast Asia, coastal Chinese in the three outlying areas experience the simultaneous coexistence of regional, national, and world identities, and these multiple identities are mutually reinforcing.

Although all three regions seem to have embraced regional, national, and world identities in a mutually reinforcing way, their enactment is situation specific. State-centered political identity is less salient in Guangdong with the rise of a more assertive commercial civil society. An interface identity, or a "window culture" combining East and West, is thriving. When China's national identity dynamic and its perennial reunification drive is seen from a coastal perspective, the concept of one China seems like a myth that papers over economic, political, and identity disparities and tensions between coastal and inland China. The center's reunification drive resembles a Daoist paradox: doing less and less is really achieving more and more. To hold together different parts of a whole, one must let them go (or the Sinatra doctrine of laissez-faire applied to multiple Chinas).[64]

In the Taiwan case, according to White and Li, the much-envied economic success (Taiwan's average per capita income is about $10,000, when the black economy is factored in, compared with China's $350) made possible a fusion of local and cosmopolitan identities while finessing the central issue of national identity. Moreover, the challenge of defining and enacting an authentic national identity seems perennially elusive. The shock of American derecognition first provoked more discussions of policy than of identity. By 1983, however, a major debate on identity began to unfold with no resolution in sight. Taiwan's search for its own authentic identity even led to the adoption of the distinctively Taiwanese Cousin Lee as a national icon.

At the official government level, the attempt of the People's Republic to impose its conception of national identity through the "one country, two systems" formula served as the catalyst for Taiwan's own search for reunification formulas. President Lee suggested a "one country, two governments" formula (in effect, "one nation, two states"), and Premier Hau Po-tsun has since proposed a "one country, two regions" formula, a more practical formula for a bicoastal relationship between island China and coastal China that is however still totally unacceptable to Beijing.[65] In search of a more visible and dignified international role, Taiwan even presented a new identity as "Customs Territory of Taiwan, Penghu, Kinmen and Matsu" in applying for membership in the 108-member General Agreement on Tariffs and Trade—only to provoke Beijing's fury about the

---

[64]See Manuel Maisog, "The Reunification of China: A Historical Perspective" (Senior thesis, Woodrow Wilson School of Public and International Affairs, Princeton University, 1989).

[65]For Beijing's total rejection see *Renmin ribao,* overseas ed., May 3, 1990, p. 5.

"creeping officiality" of Taipei's flexible diplomacy. Even since the Beijing carnage, Taiwan finds itself unable to gain much in diplomatic recognition or enhanced and national identity from the self-inflicted international isolation of its old communist foe, partly because of its own anachronistic pretensions—its claim, for instance, to rule both Mongolia and Tibet. By its own reckoning, the Republic of China is the second-largest country in the world, with Tibet and the Mongolian People's Republic constituting nearly 42 percent of its more than 11.4 million square kilometers.[66] Taiwan's national identity crisis is essentially one of inclusion.

For the people of Hong Kong, the Beijing spring and summer of 1989 was indeed a crisis in the Chinese sense of the term *weixian* (danger), but it presented not only danger but also opportunity, for their own national identity mobilization. The result, White and Li suggest, is an odd concurrent strengthening of regional, state, and world identities, but in a way that leads to competition among them rather reinforcing of one another. The 1989 Beijing crisis actually became the catalyst for the rediscovery in Hong Kong of a national identity that had seemed to be fading away. In a 1985 survey, for example, three-fifths of a well-constructed sample of people in the colony identified only with Hong Kong, and most interviewees disagreed with the statement "I am proud of the achievements of the PRC in the past several decades." The June 4 carnage, while it alienated many Hong Kong people severely, also intensified their Chinese patriotism. Like mainland intellectuals, people in Hong Kong began to differentiate between their love of country (their ethnocentric Han identity) and their hatred of the Beijing government (a state-centered identity). Tellingly, the Hong Kong people's "voice" gained credibility as exit options became more available. Still, the chance of any of the three coastal regions leaving China is slight. One thing remains fairly certain, White and Li conclude: coastal China's interface function remains crucial to the politics of Chinese national identity mobilization.

If multiple identities can coexist and even complement each other to some extent among coastal Chinese, the same cannot be said of China's non-Han minority peoples in the strategic borderlands of Tibet, Xinjiang, and Mongolia. The official identification of China, canonized in the constitution, is that "the People's Republic of China is a unitary multinational state [*tongyi de duo minzhu guojia*], created in common by its various nationalities." This self-identity too is a legitimating myth, not an experienced reality. In the south, as Watson suggests in his essay, non-Han

[66]According to Wu Hau-peng, chairman of the Taiwan's Mongolian and Tibetan Affairs Commission; see Lincoln Kaye, "China's Minorities Problems Are No Help to the KMP," *Far Eastern Economic Review,* May 17, 1990, p. 22.

peoples offered little resistance, and over a thousand-year period, the vast majority have forfeited their ethnic and cultural identities through intermarriage, enforced Sinicization, or political domination. In the steppes and the highlands of the north and west, however, Chinese culture did not prevail, and the non-Han border peoples still fiercely resist assimilation into Han society.

The basic dilemma lies in the fact that China's minorities, more than eighty million people (or about 8 percent of the total population), reside in the "autonomous" regions that account for roughly 64 percent of its area.[67] In the 1930s and 1940s the CCP, for both ideological and strategic reasons, recognized the importance of an active synergy between people's wars of liberation and ethnocentric nationalism and promised the right of self-determination. Immediately after assuming power in 1949, as Walker Connor argues, the CCP changed its party line from advocating the right of self-determination to promoting the notion of a single, indivisible China.[68] This dramatic turnabout is revealed in a cable from the central party propaganda office of the New China News Agency to the Northwestern branch office:

> Today [October 1949] the question of each minority's "self-determination" should not be stressed any further. In the past, during the period of civil war, for the sake of strengthening the minorities opposition to the Guomindang's reactionary rule, we emphasized this slogan. This was correct at the time. But today the situation has fundamentally changed. . . . For the sake of completing our state's great purpose of unification, for the sake of opposing the conspiracy of imperialists and other running dogs to divide China's nationality unity, we should not stress this slogan in the domestic nationality question and should not allow its usage by imperialists and reactionary elements among various domestic nationalities. . . . The Han occupy the majority population of the country, moreover, the Han today are the major force in China's revolution. Under the leadership of the Chinese Communist Party, the victory of China's peoples democratic revolution mainly relied on the industry of the Han people.[69]

---

[67]See *Xinjiang ribao* (Xinjiang daily), May 4, 1990, p. 4, in *FBIS,* June 25, 1990, pp. 55–56. As recently as 1985, the minority population was only 67 million people, or 6.7 percent of the total. *Questions and Answers about China's National Minorities* (Beijing: New World, 1985), p. 1.

[68]Connor, *National Question,* pp. 67–100.

[69]Quoted in Dru C. Gladney, "The Peoples of the People's Republic: Finally in the Vanguard?" *Fletcher Forum of World Affairs* 12 (Winter 1990): 70. See also June Teufel Dreyer, *China's Forty Million: Minority Nationalities and National Integration in the People's Republic of China* (Cambridge: Harvard University Press, 1976); Fei Xiaotong, *Toward a People's Anthropology* (Beijing: New World, 1981); Thomas Heberer, *China and Its National Minorities: Autonomy or Assimilation?* (Armonk, N.Y.: M. E. Sharpe, 1989); and Ma Yin, ed., *China's Minority Nationalities* (Beijing: Foreign Languages Press, 1989).

Upon the founding of the People's Republic of China, more than four hundred self-styled non-Han ethnic groups applied to the new Chinese state for official recognition as minority nationalities, and only fifty-four of them received official state approval. Over the next forty years, only one other group managed to obtain state recognition, even though fifteen groups are still on an official application list and over 799,705 people were listed as "unidentified" in the 1982 census.[70] From the very beginning, the state has taken on itself the hegemonic task of legislating claimants' minority nationality status as an integral part of its nationalistic drive toward a single, unified, multinational Chinese state. It is only within this overarching framework that people have been permitted to seek state recognition of their self-defined identity. In an obvious attempt to emphasize China's policy of special benefits to minorities, *China Daily* (Beijing) reported on July 27, 1990, that some five million "Chinese people" had already asked to have their "nationality identity" changed, without saying how many actually succeeded in obtaining such state recognition.

The implication is that some Han Chinese simply wanted to take advantage of special benefits in such areas as education and birth control but that "a large-scale change-over" can result in a chain of problems. With regard to birth control, the article points out that China's ethnic minority population now accounts for "about nine per cent of China's 1.1 billion people," a 2.3 percent increase over the 1985 estimate.[71] What this article fails to say (and what the state's nationality policy refuses to recognize) is the well-established fact that ethnic minorities in any state show substantially less loyalty toward the state than do the dominant majority group and that their ethnonational demands are more political than economic.[72] If the Western co-optation strategy can never work in changing China's self-defined national identity as a socialist state, there is no reason to believe that China's coercive assimilation strategy for handling its minority nationalities can work any better.

The upsurge of ethnonational demonstrations and movements in Tibet in March 1989 and in Xinjiang in April 1990, both quickly and mercilessly suppressed by Chinese authorities, serve as a reminder that communist China is no more successful than its Soviet and East European counterparts in squaring deviant nationality practice with the idealized theory of proletarian globalism. For better or for worse, ethnocentric identity is a per-

[70]Dru C. Gladney, "Dialogic Ethnicity: The State and National Identity in China" (Paper presented at the Conference on China's Quest for National Identity) (see n. 58).

[71]*China Daily* (Beijing), July 27, 1990, p. 3.

[72]See Connor, "Ethnonationalism."

ceived reality that cannot be easily remolded or erased by even so powerful a global ideology as Marxism. In the Tibet case, the spark that alarmed China and triggered the violent reaction was the hoisting of a Tibetan flag above the Jokhang Temple in Lhasa on February 7, 1989.[73] The violence in Xinjiang is reported to have erupted when ethnic Kirgiz Muslims, asserting their non-Chinese identity, balked at being given new "Chinese identity cards."[74] For the first time, some Chinese leaders, especially those in Xinjiang, are waking up to the fact that political and ethnonational upheavals in the Soviet Union and Eastern Europe are having a destabilizing impact on China's minority nationalities. In the face of such an identity challenge, the state response has always been, and continues to be, refractory. Given the demonstrated inability of any communist state to wipe out ethnonational consciousness, doing more and more may result in achieving less and less.

Embodied in the notion of multiple Chinas is the idea of diaspora China, made up of an estimated thirty-six million people of Chinese ancestry—often referred to as *huaqiao* (overseas Chinese or sojourners only temporarily away from the homeland)—scattered throughout the world. How they maintain or lose their identities is another dimension of China's quest for national identity. Although the identity dynamics of overseas Chinese vary greatly between and within regions and over time, the available evidence suggests that there are seveal identity principles at work. First, *huaqiao*'s individual and collective identities are consciously espoused at those moments of close encounter with the enigma of otherness—"in those moments of ambiguity where one is other to oneself, and in the recognition of the other as like," as Anne Norton puts it.[75] The rise of modern nationalism and the threat of external invasion endangering the Chinese state combined with so much cultural and racial discrimination in host countries during the late Qing and early Republican period catalyzed the *huaqiao*'s serach for their *gen* (roots). Seeking and asserting Chinese national identity through rediscovery of *gen* became a survival strategy for *huaqiao* working classes abroad. It is through this synergistic interplay between primordial ancestral ties and specific situations that so many *huaqiao* became aware of their Chineseness and came to assert their Chinese identity more vigorously than Chinese within China. That made them, as Wang Gungwu says, "backbone of Chinese nationalism and of the anti-Manchu and, later, the anti-imperialist movements."[76]

[73]*New York Times,* August 14, 1990, p. A3.
[74]Ibid., April 23, 1990, p. A3; *South China Morning Post* (Hong Kong), April 13, 1990, p. 10.
[75]Norton, *Reflections on Political Identity,* p. 7.
[76]Wang Gungwu, "Among Non-Chinese," *Daedalus* 120 (Spring 1991): 142.

Second, the Chinese in the diaspora have demonstrated their adaptability to the changing situations in both the Chinese state and their host countries by experimenting and embracing various identities for various purposes. Like their compatriots in coastal China, the overseas Chinese in Southeast Asia have adopted multiple identities based on experience in order to cope with ambiguities and uncertainties as situations changed. They seem to thrive by adopting coexisting ethnic, national, local, cultural, and class identities.[77] Paradoxically, some overseas Chinese in Southeast Asia have chosen to leave China altogether and emigrate again, to freer Western democracies, especially those in North America, in the hope of preserving a measure of Chinese identity for their posterity.

The quest for Chinese identity among Chinese-Americans, too, takes the form of an adaptive interplay between the primordial pull of the homeland (the ancestral village, the Chinese race, China as a nation, the Chinese government, and Chinese culture) and the situational push of local conditions, including changes in Sino-American relations. Ling-chi Wang has suggested that at least five different identities have appeared among Chinese-Americans—"the sojourner mentality; assimilator; accommodator; ethicly proud; and uprooted"—each being defined by its relation to Chinese *gen*. Although each identity is a product of a specific historical situation, all five "are found among the Chinese in the United States today and all are still changing and interacting with each other, sometimes in peaceful coexistence and at other times in conflict."[78]

Third, the Chinese state, by virtue of its physical and demographic size, long history, and civilizational greatness, has had an invisible hand in the formation and restructuring of the *huaqiao*'s national identity in the diaspora during much of the twentieth century. But thanks to the ideological misappropriation of the national identity dynamic over the years, especially during the Cultural Revolution and post-Tiananmen periods, it is now the Han Chinese nation and cultural identity, not the PRC state or state/nation identity, that is the primary locus of overseas Chinese sentiments and loyalty. Indeed, credibility in the quest for Chinese identity may have already shifted from the center to the periphery, as the center has forfeited its ability, wisdom, and legitimate authority. Tu Wei-ming explains that it is by rediscovering and renewing cultural, not national, identity that Chinese intellectuals outside mainland China are seeking "to build a transnational

---

[77]Wang, "Study of Chinese Identities in Southeast Asia" (see n. 18), pp. 1–21.

[78]L. Ling-chi Wang, "Roots and Changing Identity of the Chinese in the United States," *Daedalus* 120 (Spring 1991): 184, 192.

network for understanding the meaning of being Chinese within a global context."[79]

The Presentations of National Identity in Foreign Relations

China's quest for national identity is no longer, if it ever was, a purely domestic problem.[80] All national identities are contested in a distinct but changing international environment. In the Chinese case, the enactment of national identity is complicated by Beijing's enduring reunification dilemma. Identification as a unitary, multinational state remains essential but elusive. Transforming the divided polity of multiple Chinas and multiple systems into the united polity of one China with two systems—peacefully if possible and with force if necessary—has become one of the three pronounced objectives of post-Mao Chinese foreign policy.

China's twin identifications with the Third World and as a socialist country together constitute one of the most enduring themes in Chinese foreign policy pronouncements. Van Ness (Chapter 8) examines the relationship between this proclaimed national identity and the success or failure of a particular foreign policy line following from that assertion of identity. In doing so, he presents a diachronic interpretation of the forty years of PRC foreign policy. For the Chinese leadership, he explains, a foreign policy line represents a unified, theoretically articulated, comprehensive design for dealing with the global system, and it has four parts: the CCP leadership's world view; the political-strategic component; the economic component; and a sense of China's global role. In short, a foreign policy line reflects the official national identity that the Chinese leadership would like to enact in the international arena—the image it wants to project on the world stage. It is the official CCP answer to the questions Who are we, what do we collectively aspire to, what is special about being Chinese, and what most distinguishes us from the rest of the world? Van Ness warns us that this official national identity does not necessarily coincide with what *individual* Chinese, officials or citizens, think about China's global role.

Van Ness makes a useful distinction, however, between national identity formation and national identity implementation. A particular foreign policy line is better conceived of as a form of implementation, specifying and

[79]Tu Wei-ming, "Cultural China: The Periphery as the Center," ibid., p. 22.
[80]See Chih-yu Shih, *The Spirit of Chinese Foreign Policy: A Psychocultural View* (London: Macmillan, 1990).

ordering national roles emanating from a given Chinese national identity. Whereas Mao as paramount leader could play an exclusive, defining role in Chinese national identity formation, implementation necessitated the involvement of the entire diplomatic establishment, domestically and internationally.

There have been only three basic foreign policy lines, according to Van Ness, corresponding to three periods of PRC foreign policy: the socialist-camp line (1950–57), the Third World line (1960–70), and the modernization/opening to the West line (1978–88). The intervening years were periods of transition, with various dimensions of Chinese foreign policy in contradiction with each other. Van Ness sees the 1960s as the golden age of the Third World line, with Mao following a daring dual-adversary stategy vis-à-vis the superpowers because the opportunity to lead in Third World politics and thus to enhance China's power and identity seemed to him so great. For Mao, the Third World, like the Chinese peasantry, was a blank plate inviting a great leader to etch upon it the blueprint for the most promising world system. There is a sense in which Mao can be said to have succeeded in his antihegemonic strategy in that his Third World line seems to have impressed both superpowers, leading the United States to overestimate the Chinese threat while at the same time causing the Soviet Union to start its military build-up along the Sino-Soviet borders. In the end, however, as Van Ness argues, Mao miscalculated. The Third World line not only failed to create a credible antisuperpower coalition, but more seriously it put China's national security at risk.

Mao had to make strategic concessions to the United States in order to deter a possible Soviet attack. And yet a transition to the modernization/opening to the West line was not yet possible, Van Ness argues, because the global role of an autonomous, self-reliant China was still central to Mao's concept of Chinese national identity. Paradoxically, it was during this "transition" in the Van Ness periodization that the Third World was for the first time recognized for its distinct, independent, and positive identity, rather than as an intermediate zone or hotbed of socialism. According to Mao's three-worlds theory, the Third World was the prime motive force for transformation. It was only after the ascendancy of Deng as the new paramount leader in 1978 that transition to the new lines would become possible.

Despite lip service to the old 1960s slogans, the entire thrust of PRC foreign policy changed during the Deng decade. China, according to Van Ness, turned its back on the Third World and supported the global status quo. Yet Beijing maintained, all the same, an abiding identification with the

Third World, which reflected the emotional/moral dimension of China's national identity, stunted but not erased by the post-Mao modernization line. This sense of being unjustly oppressed and exploited by the imperialist predators, bespeaking a deep underlying sense of vulnerability and grievance, is so deeply encoded in Chinese historical consciousness that it can wane or wax in response to changing circumstances but never completely disappear as a determinant of Chinese national identity.

In the final years of the Deng reform decade, Van Ness sees three contending elites—the conservatives (Chen Yun, Peng Zhen, Deng Liqun), the reformers (Deng Xiaoping, Zhao Ziyang, and Hu Yaobang), and the radicals (Wei Jingsheng, Fang Lizhi)—each addressing the challenge of Chinese from its own perspective. China's Third World identity had positive connotations only for the conservatives. Reformers could identify only with the East Asian newly industrialized economies untypical of the Third World. Many of the radicals looked toward full participation in global civilization, eschewing any merely parochial notion of national identity.

Although China's Third World identity made a comeback of sorts in post-Tiananmen China, Van Ness is skeptical about its viability. Without the bipolarized "Yalta system" between the two superpowers, the idea of a third global force loses much of its normative and geopolitical meaning. A Third World identity hardly seems relevant for reconciling tradition and modernity or for formulating the best strategies for achieving the wealth and power the Chinese consider China's due. In concept and behavior, as Van Ness reminds us, the Chinese, with their cultural arrogance and racist attitudes toward African blacks, have not found it easy to carry out official policy on Third World solidarity. During the Deng reform decade, Beijing in effect embraced a "first world" policy while its Third World identity withered away. Meanwhile, the Chinese people, concludes Van Ness, must wait for the ideologically bankrupt Long March generation of leaders to die before they begin again to search for a modern national identity.

Even more revealing and ironic in post-Tiananmen Chinese foreign policy is the monumental contradiction between combating the Western "peaceful evolution" strategy and espousing "peaceful coexistence" as the only way to a new international order. All the self-confident certainties and moralism so characteristic of much of Chinese foreign policy over the years have vanished. Perhaps the deepest cause of angst over Chinese national identity is as an awareness that China has been inferior to the Western powers in the very domain of normative politics and the very principles of proper behavior which Confucianism has held to be the hallmark of China's civilizational greatness. Even in the normative domain of global politics—

and this is the locus of China's Third World policy—China's power and influence is negligible.[81] As Tu reminds us, it is this "asymmetry between the centrality of its [China's] magnetic pull in cultural China and the marginality of its significance to the 'global village' as a whole" that demands analysis and contemplation both from the "second symbolic universe" (overseas Chinese) and "third symbolic universe" (non-Chinese China hands in the non-Chinese world engaged in China scholarship, trade, and diplomacy).[82]

As if to add insult to injury, the traditional Chinese concept of *lai hua*—the smug assumption that the outside barbarians could not help but be transformed by the awe-inspiring virtue of Chinese culture—and the Sun Zi strategy of winning war without firing a single shot would seem to have worked all too well in peacefully melting socialism in Eastern Europe and in its very epicenter, the Soviet Union. The demise of the Second (socialist) World clouds the concept of a *third* world, which only adds to the ambiguity of China's own identity and role in world politics. The withering of both socialism and the socialist world has forced China's Third World policy into a double bind.

Scalapino (Chapter 9) begins with some useful caveats about national identity and its application to Chinese foreign relations. First, he cautions against a free-wheeling use of the concept, especially leaping from "personal identity" to "national identity." Second, he warns against an overly state-centered notion of national identity. Thanks to the contemporary information and communication revolution, political rulers no longer enjoy the hegemonic power to remold national identity with a minimum of external interference. Put differently, the Maoist opinion of the Chinese people as "poor and blank," perfect candidates for ideological and identity transformation and mobilization is no longer valid in post-Mao China. Third, Scalapino, like Van Ness, White, and Li, makes a distinction between two levels of national identity, between mass identifications that derive from a sense of commonality (and may lend themselves to either national unity or division) and those identifications promoted by the elite to justify policies or to manipulate the populace. The two levels can be mutually complementary but are by no means identical. Fourth, like White and Li, he argues that the nation-state is not the only available "significant other" on which people can bestow loyalty and with which they can

---

[81] See Samuel S. Kim, *China In and Out of the Changing World Order* (Princeton: Princeton University, Center of International Studies, 1991).

[82] Tu, "Cultural China," p. 16.

identify. In many parts of the world and for many ethnic majorities as well as minorities, the nation-state is not necessarily the most powerful reference group. And finally, Scalapino, like several contributors to the volume, takes an essentially contextual as against primordialist approach. For him, national identity formation and enactment are constantly in flux because subject to a host of internal and external factors. Even in its most fundamentalist form, national identity is not without contradictions.

Still, he proceeds from the premise that the concept of national identity can help illuminate how people see and define their nation-state in relation to others; for he believes that national identity influences attitudes and policies alike because it is the psychological foundation for a country's roles and behaviors in the world. In the specific case of China, Scalapino argues that political elites have advanced two overriding concepts: one nation composed of five primary races, and China as the Central Kingdom around which others revolve. Against this historical conceptual background, he examines how China's national identity is enacted through various national roles in East Asia and how those roles are perceived by China's Asian neighbors. Because of its sheer physical size the importance of China to the rest of Asia is almost universally accepted. The total power in demographic, geopolitical, military, and economic terms coupled with the cultural legacy it has bequeathed to many Asian societies guarantee that China will be accorded the status of a regional power, even if the extent to which it is prepared to play such a role is debatable. At the same time, China's dual status in the international pecking order—a poor developing country in per capita terms and a giant in aggregate terms—makes it possible for Chinese leaders simultaneously to claim respect as a great nation and membership in the backward world. Whatever the future holds and whatever the "reality" of actual power and influence, Beijing acts as if it has already become a great power and is indeed being treated as such by virtually all its Asian neighbors. More improtant, Scalapino argues, the United States and Russia treat China as a nation of both global and regional importance.

Since the Tiananmen hammer blow, the world at large has learned to be skeptical of the myth of one China. Beijing can be observed drawing on a variety of images and roles to influence its Asian neighbors. One China still supports Pyongyang's quest for absolute legitimation while another China follows a de facto two-Koreas policy. The same Janus-faced approach can be seen in Beijing's carrot and stick policy toward Taiwan. Even in official China there has arisen an uneasy merger of positive and negative images of Japan, greatly complicating any assessment of the future course of China's Japan policy or of the extent to which Japan has become a positive or negative reference group in the development of Chinese national identity.[83] In China's relations with other Asian communist regimes, one searches in vain for any signs of socialist solidarity or proletarian internationalism. In effect, "proletarian internationalism" has been redefined to encompass any forces that advocate national independence and progressive change on the basis of equal rights. China now judges the foreign policy of another state, Zhao Ziyang declared in his 1986 "Report on the Work of the Government," by the criterion of "whether it helps to maintain world peace, develops friendly cooperation among nations and promotes world economic prosperity."[84] Of China's multiple identities, concludes Scalapino, the dominant one in the eyes of the Chinese leadership is its ethnocentric Han identity, which is threatened by the inroads of Western beliefs and institutions incompatible with Chinese needs and values.

Scalapino sees the tension between nationalism and internationalism as entering full force into the national identity crisis, with serious implications for the peaceful resolution of many territorial disputes with and irredentist claims against Beijing's neighbors. Internal and external factors, functioning as both cause and effect, lead to constant reconstruction of the repertoire of China's national identities. Given China's multiple national identities and the demonstrated volatility and unpredictability of turns and twists in Chinese foreign policy (in Scalapino's words, "from aligned revolutionary to nonaligned pariah, to outward bound and available, to nonaligned but titled"), predicting the shape of things to come is like predicting the course of moving targets of undetermined trajectories. Scalapino concludes without venturing a prediction.

Though not specifically addressed in this volume, the theories of Marxism-Leninism have clearly had a major effect on the evolution of a contemporary Chinese political identity. China's young revolutionaries were impressed with Marxism-Leninism's claim to have scientifically analyzed the pattern of economic modernization and determined the historically "correct" way of achieving industrial prosperity amid justice for all, and they firmly rejected the "capitalist" road" at several critical junctures. Having blocked or at least impeded what might have otherwise been the most "natural," free-market path to economic development, Marxist doctrine offered few clues to the future; China's revolutionary leadership could only turn for guidance to the example of countries that had already embraced socialism.

[83]See Allen S. Whiting, *China Eyes Japan* (Berkeley and Los Angeles: University of California Press, 1989).

[84]Zhao Ziyang, "Report on the Work of the Government," *Beijing Review,* April 21, 1986, p. xvii.

The Soviet Union was thus revolutionary China's first model.[85] Soviet political institutions were superimposed on China in the process of "socialist construction" and have subsequently been altered only marginally. Indeed, in the Gorbachev years, the Soviet Union deviated further from the original Stalinist model that did China, at least politically speaking. The sudden collapse of Soviet communism left Beijing with no positive international reference group, forcing the government to retreat into the precarious Stalinist "socialism in one country" line of defense.

And yet it is well known that after the first few years of socialist fraternity, when the Soviet Union sent China hosts of advisors and launched a major effort to jump-start industrialization, relations between the two countries have been troubled, much as British-American relations in the century after independence were disturbed by a legacy of imperial nurturance on Britain's part which recognized no distinct U.S. national identity, making the United States extremely sensitive and resentful. As Levine observed, "The socialist identity that China assumed in the 1950s was an *apprentice* or *dependent* identity in which the PRC as a subordinate partner in the hierarchic international community system accepted tutelage from the Soviet Union in the guise of elder brother."[86] This sensitivity to junior partnership and the concomitant dependent identity was further complicated by the PRC's determination to adhere to Marxism-Leninism and indeed to persevere in the realization of socialism and communism essentially as Lenin and Stalin had envisaged it.

The conflicting requirements of ideological legitimacy and national identity have been reconciled in at least two ways.[87] In domestic policy the CCP regime made significant marginal adjustments to the Stalinist paradigm of command planning, while recoiling from any shift substantial enough to throw its socialist identity into question. During the Maoist period this shift was accomplished through the Great Leap Forward and the Cultural Revolution experiments and involved the devolution of many aspects of planning and administration to local levels and a much greater emphasis on equal distribution (of education and culture as well as consumer commodities) than has characterized Soviet socialism. During the post-Leap recovery and again in the post-Mao period the adjustments involved the

---

[85]In 1953, for instance, the CCP publicly pronounced that "the primary issue before us is to learn from the Soviet Union. . . . We must set going a tidal wave of learning from the Soviet Union on a nationwide scale, in order to build up our country . . . 'follow the path of the Russians,'" Editorial, *Renmin ribao,* February 14, 1953, p. 1.

[86]Levine, "China and the Socialist Community," p. 41.

[87]See Lowell Dittmer, *Sino-Soviet Normalization and Its International Implications, 1945–1990* (Seattle: University of Washington Press, 1992).

adoption of a rather substantial market and quasi-private sector, particularly in the agriculture, service, and small-scale manufacturing, in an ardent quest for a "social market" economy like that pioneered in Eastern Europe. These experiments permitted the People's Republic to assert its own national identity without abandoning socialism—by pursuing what was known as "socialism with Chinese characteristics." In foreign affairs the CCP leadership redefined China's stance toward two significant "reference groups": the socialist world and the Third World. In its relationship to the socialist world China drew a "principled" distinction between itself and the Soviet Union, condemning its former mentor for the ideological heresies of "revisionism" and "social hegemony" and proclaiming China's support for a truer and purer vision of socialism. China's position split the communist bloc after the early 1960s into an orthodox majority led by Moscow and a radical minority (including Albania and some Asian communist parties) led by Beijing. In its relationship to the Third World, China assumed the role of trailblazer of a new road to rapid transformation from underdevelopment to industrialized socialism via an initial violent breakthrough followed by permanent revolution. By popularizing the Chinese model in the Third World, the People's Republic was able to assume an international leadership role its limited strategic and economic resources would otherwise have scarcely permitted, thereby also usefully dramatizing its new national identity.

Thus the pretense of "normalizing" Sino-Soviet relations with the restoration of party-to-party relations in May 1989 is misleading because it suggests a return to a normal state that has never in fact existed. Both countries disavowed the norms of socialist internationalism they claimed to adhere to in the 1950s and agreed to the Five Principles of Peaceful Coexistence which China uses as the political equivalent of most-favored nation treatment, (meaning China promised to treat the USSR like any other country). Now that the revolt against orthodox Leninism has swept Eastern Europe and even many erstwhile adherents in the Third World (for example, Mozambique, Angola, and Nicaragua), China searches for a new socialist identity without an international reference group.

Future Prospects

What does the future hold for China's quest for national identity? The contributors to this volume are in general agreement that post-Tiananmen China is faced with an unprecedented national identity crisis, even though they may disagree about its main causes. It seems that at least one of the causes of this crisis is conceptual. Marxism is perhaps poorly suited to a state-centered quest for national identity; for its theory says the state, or the nation-state, is the instrument of exploitation of man by man and therefore is a transitory phenomenon with no positive functions and destined to wither away. Yet the common denominator of all the so-called Marxist states has until recently been a swollen state and a spent society, turning Marxist theory on its head. For Marx, the state was to be transcended by civil society. His Italian disciple Antonio Gramsci developed this theme in the twentieth century (and in a prison cell), stressing civil society's political and cultural supremacy over the state. Ironically and revealingly, as one writer commented with regard to recent events, "It was Gramsci's analysis that was adapted by East European intellectuals in formulating their strategy for challenging state power and legitimacy."[88]

The basic dilemma of post-Mao China is what to do about its apparent inability to completely embrace or reject socialism. For practical reasons post-Mao Chinese leaders could engage in endless doubletalk on socialism. A post-Tiananmen editorial in *Renmin ribao* (People's daily) charged that, at an internal party meeting in early 1987, even Zhao Ziyang had proposed abandoning the adherence to socialism on the grounds that nobody knew any more what socialism or the socialist road really meant.[89] And yet abandoning the legitimating prop of socialism in any direct manner would be an act of ideological and political suicide akin to that of the "self-strengthening" reformers of the nineteenth century. The post-Mao system can no longer cope with systemic problems without infringing on or giving up its identity as a socialist state.

Another indication of deepening anxiety about the possibility of national disintegration is the revival of interest, at least among some expatriated reformers, in a federalist approach, an idea that first came and went during the chaotic warlord decade of the 1920s. In a speech delivered at the First Congress of Chinese Students and Scholars in the United States, held in Chicago in July 1989, Yan Jiaqi proposed " 'federalism' (*lianbang guojia*) under a democratic system as the best hope both for reforming China's internal politics and ultimately for resolving the problems of Hong Kong, Taiwan and Tibet."[90] It should be noted that Yan is speaking directly to

[88]James M. Skelly, "From Rousseau to Gramsci," *Deadline,* November–December 1989, p. 11.

[89]"Zhiyou shehuizhuyi caineng fazhan Zhongguo" (Only socialism can develop China) (editorial), *Renmin ribao,* July 22, 1989, p. 1.

[90]Cited in Arthur N. Waldron, "Warlordism versus Federalism: The Revival of a Debate?" *China Quarterly* 121 (March 1990), p. 116. In the 1930s and 1940s, Mao Zedong himself entertained federalist ideas; see Stuart R. Schram, "Decentralization in a Unitary State:

post-Tiananmen China's crisis of national identity and unity in his capacity as an exiled democratic leader, not to any international or global federalism. Despite his disdain for traditional Chinese political culture, Yan's ideas on democracy and federalism seem still wedded to the long-standing Chinese preoccupation with the ways and means of establishing national unity and of making China once again a rich and powerful country.[91]

The lack of international enemies and reference groups seems to leave China no choice but to resort to tradition to ground its national identity, as evidenced in the assaults on *River Elegy*. The quest for national identity, blocked in one dimension, compensates in another.

Several aspects of national identity call for more. First, we need to know whether there is a predictable sequence or pattern of national identity development. The model of individual psychogenetic maturation presumes so, but phylogeny does not necessarily replicate ontogeny, and any extrapolation from the individual to the group can only be a basis for tentative hypotheses. The crises model pioneered by Pye, Verba, and their followers also assumes a predictable sequence of tasks and crises in political development, and this model is more empirically based. Yet its concept of national identity is somewhat different from the one we have found useful, and the evidence accumulated in this volume shows how difficult it is to reduce the identity problem to one of developmental sequence. Scalapino, for one, emphatically rejects the idea of a normal developmental sequence, asserting that, inasmuch as a concern with national identity arises only in the context of external threat, identity is a strictly contingent variable.

It is certainly true that outside threats tend to provoke a greater concern with identity; take, for example the intensified search for American identity since the rise of Japan and the Pacific Rim. But we need to investigate other possible outside stimuli. We have already suggested that international opportunity—the opening of the Western frontier to American "manifest destiny," for example, or the Soviet rise to international leadership in the wake of the destruction of the Axis powers—may have a major impact on national identity. Surely, too, it would be foolish to foreclose the possibility of identity-affecting crises from within as well as from without, economic depression, for example, resulted in significant regime changes to shore up

---

Theory and Practice, 1940–1984," in Schram, ed., *The Scope of State Power in China* (Hong Kong: Chinese University Press, 1985), pp. 81–83.

[91]See David Bachman and Dali Yang, trans. and eds., *Yan Jiaqi and China's Struggle for Democracy* (Armonk, N.Y.: M. E. Sharpe, 1991).

national identity in Italy, Germany, Japan, and the United States; differential economic prosperity and the fear of being left behind contributed to equally significant regime changes in the Soviet Union and Eastern Europe. In further work on this topic, it may be useful to differentiate between domestic threats or opportunities and international ones, or between what we have called crises of self-definition and crises of inclusion. There may well be some predictable sequence of domestic identity development, for example, and crises of inclusion may be more likely at some (early) stages than others, whereas crises of self-definition or international disturbances or opportunities may be more unpredictable. If there is a pattern to identity development, the next logical question would be what forms of identity pathology (including, of course, "crises") are liable to occur at each stage of development.

Another question to pursue is how national identity comes to be defined in any given political system. The foregoing chapters have touched on some of what we might call the sentimental attributes of national identity: strength, compassion, justice, and stability. These attributes are not displayed together, as a peacock displays his tail feathers, but selectively, as a key or tonal center emerges from a musical scale. How does a given nation-state arrive at its own repertoire of attributes? And what are the tactics and policy consequences of selecting a particular home key? If the elite picks the wrong key for a particular occasion—uncompromising sternness where compassion is called for, tears where a joke would work better—the resulting politics will be out of tune—which brings us to a related problem. Although we have characterized national identity as a willed synthesis between nation and state, its construction is pursued simultaneously by two architects: from the top down by the state, from the bottom up by the nation. How well the synthesis works can vary considerably. We have argued that linguistic and subcultural diversity is not the insuperable obstacle to national cohesion it is generally assumed to be, in view of the demonstrated capacity of a heterodox citizenry to override such differences and identify with common mythologized experiences, values, and collective interests. Yet at the very least we may hypothesize that the existence of such coherent national or ethnic subcultures establishes an alternative nexus for loyalty, which may on occasion outbid identification with the center. This is only one aspect of the juncture between state-centered and nation-based identity that requires fuller exploration; for even in countries characterized by relative national and ethnic homogeneity, such as South Korea, the state may become politically alienated from its citizenry, with a resulting deflation in sense of national identity.

Our purpose in this book is to raise new issues; it would certainly be premature to try to provide any definitive answers as yet. We believe we have taken a "great leap" forward (or at least a considerable one) in analyzing a hitherto neglected dimension of China's nation-building experience, but we can claim credit for "one small step" in the understanding of national identity.

Index

Abnormal psychology, 144
Afghanistan, 230
Africa, as part of Third World, 196–97, 204–5
African blacks (studying in China), 213
Afro-Asian conference (1955), 197
Ah Q, 131, 266
Aiguo zhuyi (patriotism), 63, 252
Albania, 286
Alienation, 128, 136, 138, 140, 141, 148, 150, 264; alienation debate, 264–65
Alliance in Support of the Patriotic and Democratic Movement, 184
Alloy culture, 173
American identity, 288
Analects, 99
Analytic philosophy, 144
Anti-Rightist Campaign (1957–59), 128
Asia, as part of Third World, 196–97, 204–5
Association of Southeast Asian Nations (ASEAN), 277; neighbors, 231
Authority, 153; *tianzi*, 129

Badao (way of hegemony), 52
Bai Hua, 132, 133–35, 140, 264
Bandung, Indonesia, 197; conference, 220
Bangladesh, 232
Bei Dao, 129, 148
Beijing massacre (1989), 202, 207, 209, 213
Belgium, 11
Bellah, Robert, 158
Benjamin, Walter, 144
Bing Xing, 148

Blood identity, 167
Bloom, William, 238
Board of Rites (Libu), 257
Bolshevik Salute, 131
Borman, Frank, 241
Bourgeois liberalization, 135, 140
Bourgeois liberation, 132
Brezhnev, Leonid, 223
Buddhism, 52
Burma, 233
Butian ("repair heaven"), 129, 137, 148, 149, 264, 268

Cambodia, 229–30
Canada, 11; francophone, 8
Cantonese identity and separatism, 164
Castro, Fidel, 17
CCP. *See* Chinese Communist Party
Central Asian Republics, 235
Chaitian ("dismantle heaven"), 129, 148, 149, 264, 268
Chang, K. C., 42
Chen Duxiu, 70–71
Chen Qiwei, 190
Chen Shizhong, 141, 143
Chen Xilian, 130
Chen Yun, 281, 209
Cheng Zhongying, 108, 113
Chengdu, 166
Cheong, Stephen, 183
Cheung, Horatio, 188
Chiang Ching-kuo, 177
Chiang Kai-shek, 68

Chinese Communist Party (CCP), 2, 20, 126, 194, 197–99, 202, 206, 212–14, 254; conservatives (in leadership), 207, 211; radicals, 208; reformers, 208; Thirteenth Party Congress, 209
Chinese essence. *See Guocui*
Chinese-Americans, 278
Chinter, 271
Chu, Godwin, 113, 117
Civil liberties, 148
Coastal Chinese, 155, 161, 163, 169, 172, 191–93, 272
Coexistence, 55
Cold War, 28, 212
Collective identity, 4
Comintern, 14
Communist Youth League, 5
Comrade-to-comrade relations, 220
Concept of a unified socialist world, now vanished, 228
Confucianism, 45–46, 52, 107, 110; Confucian sense of identity, 99, 198
Cong Weixi, 131
Congruence, Eckstein's theory of, 24
Connolly, William E., 245
Connor, Walter, 10, 242–43, 275
Constitution, of People's Republic of China, 271
Control theory, 144
Convict labor, 271
Cosmopolitan identity, 173, 177; of Hong Kong, 189
Cosmopolitanism, 160, 172
Counter-revolutionary rebellion, 211
Cousin Lee (Li Biaoge), 179, 180
Crisis in trust (*xinren*), 129
Crisis of belief (*xinyang*) in Marxism, 129
Cross-contacts, 226
Cult: of the individual, 142; of the personality, 138
Cults, 94
Cultural identity, 80, 168, 255–56
Cultural Revolution, 101–2, 122, 125, 127–30, 142, 195, 285
Cultural unification, 88
Culture, Chinese, 81, 85, 93, 160, 255
Culture fever, 143, 265, 267
Cyprus, 8
Czechoslovakia, 2

Da tong (great community), 60
Dalai Lama, 232
Dalian, 191
De facto two-Koreas policy, 225
de Gaulle, Charles, 17

Declaratory policy, 195
Democracy, 138, 144, 150, 161, 183, 186, 193
Democracy Wall, 128, 135; movement (1979), 128, 132
Democratic Progressive party (DPP), 175, 177, 178
Deng Liqun, 139, 192, 209, 281
Deng Tingzeng, 249
Deng Xiaoping, 21, 121–23, 131, 134–36, 139–40, 142, 145, 148, 150, 187, 197, 206, 209–11, 219, 223, 280, 281; regime of, 127, 128
Derrida, Jacques, 144
Detente, with United States, 200
Diaspora China, 277
Dictatorship of the proletariat, 208
Di'er zhong zhongcheng (second kind of loyalty), 141, 143, 152
Ding Ling, 140
Domino, George, 113
Dong Zhongshu, 41
Dragon, symbol of China, 265
Dumont, Louis, 97–98
Durkheim, Emile, 238, 247, 255; Durkheimian concept of social entities, 240

East Asian Co-Prosperity Sphere, 26
East Wind over West Wind, 200
Eastern Europe, 2, 199, 207, 211, 213, 286, 289
Eckstein, Harry, 24
Economic imperialism, 205
Edwards, John, 10
Elite cultures, 171
Elliot, Charles, 249
Engels, Friedrich, 253
Enloe, Cynthia, 159
Erikson, Erik, 3, 155–57, 238
Ethnonationalism, 35, 243
Existentialism, 140

Fairbank, John, 250
Fang Lizhi, 144, 145, 149, 151, 208–9, 264, 281; open letter of, 148
Federalism (*lianbang guojia*), 287
Feng Guifen, 64
Fifth modernization, 130
Filial piety, 19, 104, 107
Five Principles of Peaceful Coexistence, 211, 220, 234
Foreign policy line, Chinese, 195, 201
Four Cardinal Principles, 132, 136
Four "fundamental forms" of national identity crisis, 7
France, 179
Freud, Sigmund, 144, 238; Freudianism, 140
Funeral rites, 87

Futurism, 144

Gaenslen, Fritz, 113
Gandhi, Mohandas, 4
Gang of Four, 137, 142
García Márquez, Gabriel, 144
Geertz, Clifford, 159
Gellner, Ernest, 8–9
gen (roots), 277, 278
Germany, 26–28, 289; German nationalism, 15
Global identity, 178, 187
Global Leninist crisis, 225
GMD. *See* Guomindang
Goddess of Liberty statue, 122
Gorbachev, Mikhail, 136, 147, 220, 223, 211
Gramsci, Antonio, 287
Great Leap Forward, 101, 127, 138, 142, 285
Great power, China as, 283
Great Wall, 265
Group of 89, 185
Group of 1 (G-1), 194, 213
Guangdong, 90, 155, 161, 163, 191, 271–72
Guangzhou, 164–66, 170; culture, 173
Guocui, 18–20, 22, 246–47. *See also* National essence
Guojia (government or state), 134
Guomindang (GMD), 132, 134, 173–78, 198, 254, 258

Habermasian nexus of identity and legitimation crises, 251
Hainan Province, 169
Hakka, 175, 176
Hale, Edward Everett, 5
Han Chinese, 86, 94
Hau Po-tsun, 273
He shang. See River Elegy
Hegel, G. W. F., 3
Heidegger, Martin, 3
Heng Samrin, 233
Herbst, Jeffrey, 8
Herdsman's Story, The, 131
Hirschman, Albert, 188
Hitler, Adolf, 4, 161, 216
Ho, Ping-ti, 248
Hobsbawm, E. J., 244
Hokkien-speaking communities, 176
Hong Kong, 5, 23, 85, 155, 170, 180, 191, 225, 227, 256, 265, 271, 274, 287; Hong Kong Democratic Association, 184; Hongkongese, 181
Horowitz, Donald, 160, 161
Howard, Michael, 237

Hsu, Immanuel C. Y., 249
Hu Feng, 127
Hu Fo, 174
Hu Jiwei, 137, 140, 150
Hu Qiaomu, 139, 209
Hu Qili, 145, 267
Hu Yaobang, 120, 122, 128, 133, 135, 139, 140, 144, 147, 149, 264, 281
Hua Guofeng, 130
Huang Jianbin, 173
Huaqiao (overseas Chinese), 277
Human rights, 148, 211
Humanism, 138
Hundred Flowers movement, 127
Hundred-Day Reform, 118–19
Hungary, 209

Ideals of Confucianism, 126
Identification, 19, 30; as a process, 155
Identity, 154; choices offered by, 161; crisis, 4, 6, 7, 11, 24; defined, 155; theory, 238
Identity-altering events, 163
Inclusion: crises of, 27; critera for, 9, 10, 27
Independent integrity, 149
India, 11, 17, 43, 218, 221–22, 230–33, 235
Individualism, 140
Information theory, 144
Information-communication revolution, 215
Intellectual community, 125
Intellectuals, 20–21, 79, 125, 148, 192; identity of, 146, 264
Intelligentsia, 20
International reference group, 16
International relations, 238
International relations theory, 238, 243
International Monetary Fund, 206
Irredentism, Chinese, 229
Italy, 28, 289

James, Harold, 15, 160
Japan, 11, 26, 54, 65, 75, 179, 199, 216, 218, 222–23, 234–35, 288–89
Japanese investment, 224
Jiang Zemin, 149, 210
Jiben luxian (basic line), 196
Jin Yaoji, 159
Jokhang Temple, 277
Just and equal society, 126

Kafka, Franz, 144
Kang Youwei, 64, 74, 118–19, 250, 252, 261
Kertzer, David, 242
Keyes, Charles F., 175
Khrushchev, Nikita, 141, 219, 222

Kim Il Sung, 228
Korea. *See* North Korea; South Korea
Kroeber, A. L., 173

Lacan, Jacques, 144
Lao Mu, 148
Laos, 230
Lasswell, Harold, 25
Latin America, as part of Third World, 196–97, 204–5
Law, 152
Leadership, 216
Lee, Martin Chu-ming, 183–86
Lee Kuan Yew, 148, 227, 273
Lee Teng-hui, 175, 177, 226
Legitimacy, 191; crisis of, 9
Lei Feng, 21, 141, 143, 214
Lenin, V. I., 142, 207, 253; Leninism, 286
Lhasa, 119, 277
li, 99–100, 110, 107, 256, 260
Li Dazhao, 70–71, 253
Li Peng, 121–22, 149, 232
Li Shuxian, 149
Li Wenlang, 175, 176
Li Yongtai, 193
Li Zehou, 144–46, 148, 172
Liang Qichao, 69, 74, 172
Lin Biao, 197, 204, 205
Lin Yuchun, 176
Linguistic philosophy, 144
Liu Binyan, 131, 140–45, 147, 150, 152
Liu Xiaobo, 144, 151, 152
Liu Zaifu, 144
Local identity, 177
Localism, 178
Long March, 134; generation (of leaders), 214
Lu Xun, 131, 172, 266
Luther, Martin, 4
Luxian. *See* Foreign policy line

Macau, 169
McCartney mission (1793), 248
Madsen, Richard, 102
Malay-Austronesian "aborigines," 175
Malaysia, 230, 235
Maldives, 231
Mang Ke, 148
Mao Zedong (Mao), 73–74, 126–30, 138, 141–42, 197, 200, 213, 223, 252, 259, 280; regime of, 128
Maoism, 129, 130
Marcuse, Herbert, 144
Martial law, 122
Marx, Karl, 139, 246, 253

Marxism, 73, 138, 208–9, 234, 253, 287
Marxism system, 147, 267
Marxism-Leninism, 2, 128, 233, 284–85
May Fourth movement, 30, 68, 70, 73–75, 143, 149, 267, 271
Mead, George, 238
Meineke, Friedrich, 160
Mencius, 41, 154
Ming dynasty, 34, 46, 111, 148
Minorities, in China, 275
Modernism, 140, 144
Modernization, 160
Mongolia, 274; Mongolian People's Republic (MPR), 220–21, 228
Montevideo Convention on the Rights and Duties of States, 243
Mozi, 41
Myanmar (Burma), 231

Napoleon, 161
Nation, 158, 241, 243; differentiated from "state," 34
National boundaries, 6, 23
National character, 24
National distinctiveness, 37–38
National essence, 18, 22–23
National identity, 1–2, 5–7, 9–10, 13, 22, 24, 31–33, 44, 80, 104, 167, 182, 215, 217, 240; as behavior, 34; crisis of, 286; mobilization of, 241; theory of, 240–41, 245, 250
National People's Congress, 209
National role, 15, 33; conceptions of, 33, 247
Nationalism, 9, 35, 58, 160, 191, 217, 252, 261
Nationality, 167
Nation-state, 25, 29, 155, 159, 216
Nazi movement, 216
Nehru, Jawaharlal, 161, 232
Neoconfucianism, 41–42
Neodaoists, 41–42
Nepal, 232
New Authoritarianism, 148
New Criticism, 144
New Culture movement, 69
New democratic revolution, 197
Newly industrial economies (NIEs), 2, 16, 209, 225, 228, 235
Ni Yuxian, 141–43
Nietzsche, Friedrich, 25, 144
Nolan, Philip, 5
Non-Han ethnic groups, 276
North Korea, 220, 225, 228, 235
Northern Ireland, 8
Norton, Anne, 9, 277
Nu, U, 220
Nuclear weapons power, 202

Office of Members of Executive and Legislative Councils (OMELCO), 185
Official national identity, 196, 198, 212
One-ism, one party, one leader, 136
Operational policy, 195
Opium War, 248
Opposition, intellectuals as, 153
Orthodoxy (correct belief), 84, 99, 256
Orthopraxy (correct practice), 84, 96, 99, 256
Overseas Chinese, 277; in Southeast Asia, 278

Pakistan, 230–32
Parsons, Talcott, 157
Party-country-intellectuals, 147
Party-state, 25, 127
Patriotism, 127, 133; defined, 150
Peace of Westphalia (1648), 242
Peaceful evolution (*heping yanbian*), 258
Peng Zhen, 209, 281
People's diplomacy, 204
People's Liberation Army, 218
People's war, 197
People-to-people relations, 220
Petitions, 148, 151, 183
Philippines, 235
Pocock, David, 98
Political prisoners, 148
Political scientists, 238
Political socialization, 21, 26
Post–Cultural Revolution identity, 128
Postmodernism, 144
Poststructuralism, 144
Preez, Peter du, 33
Premodern Chinese national identity, 40
Primacy of maintaining the state, 39
Primordialist interpretation, 247
Prodemocracy protests (1989), 207
Psychologists, 238
Psychosocial identity, 3
Purge of Hu Yaobang, 145. *See also* Hu Yaobang
Pye, Lucian, 8, 173, 246, 247, 257, 288
Pye-Verba definition of national identity, 6–8, 11–13, 30, 240

Qi Fang, 267
Qing (Manchu) dynasty (1644–1911), 34, 62, 67, 76, 111, 148, 250
Qu Yuan, 21, 133
Quasi-class identity for Hong Kong, 186

Realist paradigm, 254
Reception theory, 144
Reference group, 15
Reflective literature (*fansi wenxue*), 130

Regional culture of Guangdong, 165
Regional identity, 163, 181
Regulatory national role of state, 53
Rentong, 246
Restorationism, 129, 130, 136
Reunification, 226
Rigby, T. H., 29
Right of Abode Delegation (ROAD), 188
Ritual, 81
River Elegy (*He shang*), 23, 145–46, 150, 165, 192, 196, 212, 265, 266, 288
Robbe-Grillet, Alain, 144
Role theory, 238, 245
Russia, 12, 67, 69, 179, 221–22, 235
Rustow, Dankwart, 11

Sanctions (after June 1989), 207, 211, 212
Sanxin weiji, 129, 157
Sartre, Jean-Paul, 144, 192
Scar literature, 128, 130
Schwartz, Benjamin, 40, 99
Science and democracy, 266
Searching-for-roots fever, 143
Second kind of loyalty. See *Di'er zhong zhongcheng*
Self-definition, crises of, 27
Self-reliance, 25, 206
Semiotics, 144
Shakespeare, *Julius Caesar*, 265
Shanghai, 164, 169, 191; culture, 172
Shao Yanxiang, 148
Sheng Feng, 173
Shenggen (Roots), 174
Shenzhen, 167
Shijie guan (world view), 196
Singapore, 148, 225, 227, 256
Sinocentric world view, 267
Sino-Indian relations, 232
Sino-Soviet dispute, 204
Sino-Soviet normalization, 223
Sino-Soviet relations, 232
Sino-Vietnamese, 218
Social Science Research Council (SSRC), 77–78
Socialism, 138, 147, 287
Society, 125, 126
South Africa, 6
South China Sea, 218
South Korea, 221, 225, 228, 234
Southeast Asia, 272; Chinese in, 161
Sovereignty, 34, 216, 234, 243, 244
Soviet Union, 2, 69, 73, 197, 199, 200, 203, 206–7, 211–13, 222, 285, 286, 289; as model, 126; revisionism in, 204; as social imperialism of, 204

Special economic zones, 272
Spengler, Oswald, 4
Spiritual Pollution Campaign (1983), 139, 145
Spratley Islands, 6
Sri Lanka, 28, 231
Stage theory, 216
Stalin, Josef, 161, 207, 253
Stalinist paradigm of command planning, 285
State, 32, 34, 35, 125, 126, 129, 241–42, 243, 286; Chinese, 148, 247, 278; expansion, 45; identity, 13, 168. *See also* National identity
Statecraft approach, 64
State-to-state relations, 220
Structuralism, 144
Student-led democracy movement of 1989, 261
Su Xiaokang, 23, 265, 268
Sun Yat-sen, 68, 73, 150, 161
Supranational or world identities, 160
Surrealism, 144
Switzerland, 11
Synthetic definition, 12, 14
Systems theory, 144
Szeto Wah, 182, 184

Taiwan, 23, 73, 155, 173, 191, 218, 225–26, 227, 234–35, 256, 265, 271–73, 283, 287; independence movement, 227
Taiwanization, 176
Tang Yijie, 148
Teiwes, Frederick, 259
Thailand, 230
Theory of ethnocentric determinism, 246
Third Reich, 6
Third World, 10, 194–214, 222, 230, 282, 286
Third World line (1960–70), 280
Three belief crises (*sanxin weiji*), 129, 257
Three-worlds theory, 197
Tian Benxiang, 266–67
Tiananmen (1989), 17, 180
Tianjin, 169
Tianxia ("all under heaven, the world"), 126, 129
Tibet, 54, 235, 274, 276, 287; Tibetans, 232, 277
Tito, 259
Tocqueville, Alexis de, 166
Toffler, Alvin, 192
Tongzi restoration (1860s), 64
Totalitarianism, 208
Toynbee, Arnold, 265
Tradition, Chinese, 145, 146, 288
Traditional Chinese views of identity, 154
Tu Wei-ming, 191

Tutelage, concept of, 217
Two Koreas, 218

United Kingdom, 179, 188; residency permits, 189
United Nations, 194, 197–99, 213
United States, 2, 11, 16, 21, 26–27, 173, 179, 197, 199, 200, 206, 211–12, 222–23, 235, 280, 289; imperialism of, 203, 205
Universalistic ethic, 18
Unrequited Love, 132

Verba, Sidney, 240, 288
Versailles settlement, 68
Vietnam, 25, 49, 93, 206, 220, 221, 229, 235
Vogel, Ezra, 168
Volvo, 271

Wan Li, 143
Wang, Ling-chi, 278
Wang Bin, 157, 158, 165, 172
Wang Dongxing, 130
Wang Gungwu, 161, 246, 277
Wang Meng, 130, 131, 140, 144
Wang Ruoshui, 136, 137, 140, 264
Wang Ruowang, 145, 264
Wang Zhen, 139, 146, 267
Wangdao (way of true or benevolent kingship), 52
War, 237–38
Weber, Max, 144
Wei Chengsi, 172
Wei Jingsheng, 128, 129, 132, 148, 209, 267, 281
Wei Yuan, 64
Weigert, Andrew, 157, 238
Weiji, 4, 267
Weng, Byron, 185
Western Europe, 199, 223
Westernization, 146
Westin, Charles, 156
Whyte, Martin, 101
World Bank, 202, 206
World identity, 178
Wright, Arthur, 257
Wu, David, 252
Wu De, 130
Wu Zuxiang, 148

Xi'an, 166
Xie Shizhong, 175
Xiliang, 67
Xingjiang, 276

Yan Fu, 172
Yan Jiaqi, 287

Yang, C. K., 94
Ye Chunsheng, 165
Ye Jianying, 142
Yellow River, 265
Yi Ding, 211
Young, Crawford, 159, 160
Yuan Mu, 122
Yugoslavia, 2, 17, 28, 209, 210, 259

Zhang Guotao, 72–73, 253
Zhang Jie, 148
Zhang Junhong, 178
Zhang Taiyan, 252

Zhang Xianliang, 131
Zhang Zhidong, 67
Zhao Ziyang, 122, 133, 140, 144–45, 149, 209,
    281, 284, 287
Zheng Chenggong, 173
Zheng He, 192
Zhongguoren (Chinese people), 252
Zhonghua minzu (Chinese nation), 252
Zhou Enlai, 75, 137, 220, 259
Zhou Gucheng, 160
Zhou Yang, 137, 139, 140, 264
Zhuhai, 167
Zuguo (motherland), 134

Books Written under the Auspices of the
Center of International Studies
Princeton University
1952–1991

Almond, Gabriel A. *The Appeals of Communism*. Princeton: Princeton University Press, 1954.

Kaufmann, William W., ed. *Military Policy and National Security*. Princeton: Princeton University Press, 1956.

Knorr, Klaus. *The War Potential of Nations*. Princeton: Princeton University Press, 1956.

Pye, Lucian W. *Guerrilla Communism in Malaya*. Princeton: Princeton University Press, 1956.

Cohen, Bernard C. *The Political Process and Foreign Policy: The Making of the Japanese Peace Settlement*. Princeton: Princeton University Press, 1957.

De Visscher, Charles. *Theory and Reality in Public International Law*. Translated by P. E. Corbett. Princeton: Princeton University Press, 1957; rev. ed. 1968.

Weiner, Myron. *Party Politics in India: The Development of a Multi-Party System*. Princeton: Princeton University Press, 1957.

Corbett, Percy E. *Law in Diplomacy*. Princeton: Princeton University Press, 1959.

Knorr, Klaus, ed. *NATO and American Security*. Princeton: Princeton University Press, 1959.

Sannwald, Rolf, and Jacques Stohler. *Economic Integration: Theoretical Assumptions and Consequences of European Unification*. Translated by Hermann Karreman. Princeton: Princeton University Press, 1959.

Almond, Gabriel A., and James S. Coleman, eds. *The Politics of the Developing Areas*. Princeton: Princeton University Press, 1960.

Kahn, Herman. *On Thermonuclear War*. Princeton: Princeton University Press, 1960.

Butow, Robert J. C. *Tojo and the Coming of War*. Princeton: Princeton University Press, 1961.

Knorr, Klaus, and Sidney Verba, eds. *The International System: Theoretical Essays*. Princeton: Princeton University Press, 1961.

Snyder, Glenn H. *Deterrence and Defense: Toward a Theory of National Security*. Princeton: Princeton University Press, 1961.

Verba, Sidney. *Small Groups and Political Behavior: A Study of Leadership*. Princeton: Princeton University Press, 1961.

Modelski, George. *A Theory of Foreign Policy*. New York: Praeger, 1962.

Paret, Peter, and John W. Shy. *Guerrillas in the 1960's*. New York: Praeger, 1962.

Almond, Gabriel A., and Sidney Verba. *The Civic Culture: Political Attitudes and Democracy in Five Nations*. Princeton: Princeton University Press, 1963.

Burns, Arthur L., and Nina Heathcote. *Peace-Keeping by United Nations Forces*. New York: Praeger, 1963.

Cohen, Bernard C. *The Press and Foreign Policy*. Princeton: Princeton University Press, 1963.

Dunn, Frederick S. *Peace-Making and the Settlement with Japan*. Princeton: Princeton University Press, 1963.

Falk, Richard A. *Law, Morality, and War in the Contemporary World*. New York: Praeger, 1963.

298

Knorr, Klaus, and Thornton Read, eds. *Limited Strategic War*. New York: Praeger, 1963.

Rosenau, James N. *National Leadership and Foreign Policy: A Case Study in the Mobilization of Public Support*. Princeton: Princeton University Press, 1963.

Sklar, Richard L. *Nigerian Political Parties: Power in an Emergent African Nation*. Princeton: Princeton University Press, 1963.

Black, Cyril E., and Thomas P. Thornton, eds. *Communism and Revolution: The Strategic Uses of Political Violence*. Princeton: Princeton University Press, 1964.

Camps, Miriam. *Britain and the European Community 1955–1963*. Princeton: Princeton University Press, 1964.

Eckstein, Harry, ed. *Internal War: Problems and Approaches*. New York: Free Press, 1964.

Paret, Peter. *French Revolutionary Warfare from Indochina to Algeria: The Analysis of a Political and Military Doctrine*. New York: Praeger, 1964.

Rosenau, James N., ed. *International Aspects of Civil Strife*. Princeton: Princeton University Press, 1964.

Thornton, Thomas P., ed. *The Third World in Soviet Perspective: Studies by Soviet Writers on the Developing Areas*. Princeton: Princeton University Press, 1964.

Falk, Richard A., and Richard J. Barnet, eds. *Security in Disarmament*. Princeton: Princeton University Press, 1965.

Ploss, Sidney I. *Conflict and Decision-Making in Soviet Russia: A Case Study of Agricultural Policy, 1953–1963*. Princeton: Princeton University Press, 1965.

Sprout, Harold, and Margaret Sprout. *The Ecological Perspective on Human Affairs, with Special Reference to International Politics*. Princeton: Princeton University Press, 1965.

von Vorys, Karl. *Political Development in Pakistan*. Princeton: Princeton University Press, 1965.

Black, Cyril E. *The Dynamics of Modernization: A Study in Comparative History*. New York: Harper and Row, 1966.

Eckstein, Harry. *Division and Cohesion in Democracy: A Study of Norway*. Princeton: Princeton University Press, 1966.

Knorr, Klaus. *On the Uses of Military Power in the Nuclear Age*. Princeton: Princeton University Press, 1966.

Bienen, Henry. *Tanzania: Party Transformation and Economic Development*. Princeton: Princeton University Press, 1967.

Gordenker, Leon. *The UN Secretary-General and the Maintenance of Peace*. New York: Columbia University Press, 1967.

Hamilton, Richard F. *Affluence and the French Worker in the Fourth Republic*. Princeton: Princeton University Press, 1967.

Hanrieder, Wolfram F. *West German Foreign Policy, 1949–1963: International Pressures and Domestic Response*. Stanford, Calif.: Stanford University Press, 1967.

Kunstadter, Peter, ed. *Southeast Asian Tribes, Minorities, and Nations*. Princeton: Princeton University Press, 1967.

Miller, Linda B. *World Order and Local Disorder: The United Nations and Internal Conflicts*. Princeton: Princeton University Press, 1967.

Rosenau, James N., ed. *Domestic Sources of Foreign Policy*. New York: Free Press, 1967.

Wolfenstein, E. Victor. *The Revolutionary Personality: Lenin, Trotsky, Gandhi*. Princeton: Princeton University Press, 1967.

Young, Oran R. *The Intermediaries: Third Parties in International Crises*. Princeton: Princeton University Press, 1967.

Bader, William B. *The United States and the Spread of Nuclear Weapons*. New York: Pegasus, 1968.

Black, Cyril E., Richard A. Falk, Klaus Knorr, and Oran R. Young. *Neutralization and World Politics*. Princeton: Princeton University Press, 1968.

300

Falk, Richard A. *Legal Order in a Violent World*. Princeton: Princeton University Press, 1968.

Gilpin, Robert G. *France in the Age of the Scientific State*. Princeton: Princeton University Press, 1968.

Ullman, Richard H. *Anglo-Soviet Relations, 1917–1921*. Vol. 2, *Britain and the Russian Civil War: November 1918–February 1920*. Princeton: Princeton University Press, 1968.

Barros, James. *Betrayal from Within: Joseph Avenol, Secretary-General of the League of Nations, 1933–1940*. New Haven: Yale University Press, 1969.

Black, Cyril E., and Richard A. Falk, eds. *The Future of the International Legal Order*. Vol. 1, *Trends and Patterns*. Princeton: Princeton University Press, 1969.

Hermann, Charles. *Crisis in Foreign Policy: A Simulation Analysis*. Indianapolis, Ind.: Bobbs-Merrill, 1969.

Knorr, Klaus, and James N. Rosenau, eds. *Contending Approaches to International Politics*. Princeton: Princeton University Press, 1969.

McAlister, John T., Jr. *Viet Nam: The Origins of Revolution*. New York: Knopf, 1969.

Rosenau, James N., ed. *Linkage Politics: Essays on the Convergence of National and International Systems*. New York: Free Press, 1969.

Smith, Jean Edward. *Germany beyond the Wall: People, Politics and Prosperity*. Boston: Little, Brown, 1969.

Tucker, Robert C. *The Marxian Revolutionary Idea: Essays on Marxist Thought and Its Impact on Radical Movements*. New York: W. W. Norton, 1969.

Waterman, Harvey. *Political Change in Contemporary France: The Politics of an Industrial Democracy*. Columbus, Ohio: Charles E. Merrill, 1969.

Young, Oran R. *The Politics of Force: Bargaining during International Crises*. Princeton: Princeton University Press, 1969.

Black, Cyril E., and Richard A. Falk, eds. *The Future of the International Legal Order*. Vol. 2, *Wealth and Resources*. Princeton: Princeton University Press, 1970.

Falk, Richard A. *The Status of Law in International Society*. Princeton: Princeton University Press, 1970.

Gurr, Ted Robert. *Why Men Rebel*. Princeton: Princeton University Press, 1970.

Knorr, Klaus. *Military Power and Potential*. Lexington, Mass.: D. C. Heath, 1970.

McAlister, John T., Jr., and Paul Mus. *The Vietnamese and Their Revolution*. New York: Harper and Row, 1970.

Whitaker, C. Sylvester. *The Politics of Tradition: Continuity and Change in Northern Nigeria, 1946–1966*. Princeton: Princeton University Press, 1970.

Black, Cyril E., and Richard A. Falk, eds. *The Future of the International Legal Order*. Vol. 3, *Conflict Management*. Princeton: Princeton University Press, 1971.

Frankel, Francine R. *India's Green Revolution: Political Costs of Economic Growth*. Princeton: Princeton University Press, 1971.

Gordenker, Leon, ed. *The United Nations in International Politics*. Princeton: Princeton University Press, 1971.

Sprout, Harold, and Margaret Sprout. *Toward a Politics of the Planet Earth*. New York: Van Nostrand Reinhold, 1971.

Black, Cyril E., and Richard A. Falk, eds. *The Future of the International Legal Order*. Vol. 4, *The Structure of the International Environment*. Princeton: Princeton University Press, 1972.

Garvey, Gerald. *Energy, Ecology, Economy*. New York: W. W. Norton, 1972.

Bebler, Anton. *Military Rule in Africa: Dahomey, Ghana, Sierra Leone, and Mali*. New York: Praeger, 1973.

Knorr, Klaus. *Power and Wealth: The Political Economy of International Power*. New York: Basic Books, 1973.

Morse, Edward L. *Foreign Policy and Interdependence in Gaullist France*. Princeton: Princeton University Press, 1973.

Tucker, Robert C. *Stalin as Revolutionary 1879–1929: A Study in History and Personality*. New York: W. W. Norton, 1973.

Ullman, Richard H. *Anglo-Soviet Relations, 1917–1921*. Vol. 3, *The Anglo-Soviet Accord*. Princeton: Princeton University Press, 1973.

Bienen, Henry S. *Kenya: The Politics of Participation and Control*. Princeton: Princeton University Press, 1974.

Laszlo, Ervin. *A Strategy for the Future: The Systems Approach to World Order*. New York: G. Braziller, 1974.

Massell, Gregory J. *The Surrogate Proletariat: Moslem Women and Revolutionary Strategies in Soviet Central Asia, 1919–1929*. Princeton: Princeton University Press, 1974.

Rosenau, James N. *Citizenship between Elections: An Inquiry into the Mobilizable American*. New York: Free Press, 1974.

Vincent, John R. *Nonintervention and International Order*. Princeton: Princeton University Press, 1974.

Black, Cyril E., Marius B. Jansen, Herbert S. Levine, Marion J. Levy, Jr., Henry Rosovsky, Gilbert Rozman, Henry D. Smith II, and S. Frederick Starr. *The Modernization of Japan and Russia*. New York: Free Press, 1975.

Eckstein, Harry, and Ted Robert Gurr. *Patterns of Authority: A Structural Basis for Political Inquiry*. New York: John Wiley and Sons, 1975.

Falk, Richard A. *A Global Approach to National Policy*. Cambridge: Harvard University Press, 1975.

Kalicki, Jan H. *The Pattern of Sino-American Crises: Political-Military Interactions in the 1950s*. New York: Cambridge University Press, 1975.

Knorr, Klaus. *The Power of Nations: The Political Economy of International Relations*. New York: Basic Books, 1975.

Sewell, James P. *UNESCO and World Politics: Engaging in International Relations*. Princeton: Princeton University Press, 1975.

von Clausewitz, Carl. *On War*. Edited and translated by Michael Howard and Peter Paret. Princeton: Princeton University Press, 1976.

Gordenker, Leon. *International Aid and National Decisions: Development Programs in Malawi, Tanzania, and Zambia*. Princeton: Princeton University Press, 1976.

Bissell, Richard E. *Apartheid and International Organizations*. Boulder, Colo.: Westview Press, 1977.

Garvey, Gerald. *Nuclear Power and Social Planning: The City of the Second Sun*. Lexington, Mass.: D. C. Heath, 1977.

Garvey, Gerald, and Lou Ann Garvey, eds. *International Resource Flows*. Lexington, Mass.: D. C. Heath, 1977.

Forsythe, David P. *Humanitarian Politics: The International Committee of the Red Cross*. Baltimore, Md.: Johns Hopkins University Press, 1977.

Murphy, Walter F., and Joseph Tanenhaus. *Comparative Constitutional Law Cases and Commentaries*. New York: St. Martin's Press, 1977.

Sigmund, Paul E. *The Overthrow of Allende and the Politics of Chile, 1964–1976*. Pittsburgh: University of Pittsburgh Press, 1977.

Bienen, Henry S. *Armies and Parties in Africa*. New York: Africana Publishing Co., Holmes and Meier, 1978.

Sprout, Harold, and Margaret Sprout. *The Context of Environmental Politics*. Lexington: University Press of Kentucky, 1978.

Ahmed, S. Basheer. *Nuclear Fuel and Energy Policy*. Lexington, Mass.: D. C. Heath, 1979.

302

Kim, Samuel S. *China, the United Nations, and World Order*. Princeton: Princeton University Press, 1979.
Billington, James H. *Fire in the Minds of Men: Origins of the Revolutionary Faith*. New York: Basic Books, 1980.
Davison, W. Phillips, and Leon Gordenker, eds. *Resolving Nationality Conflicts: The Role of Public Opinion Research*. New York: Praeger, 1980.
Falk, Richard A., and Samuel S. Kim, eds. *The War System: An Interdisciplinary Approach*. Boulder, Colo.: Westview Press, 1980.
Hsiung, James C., and Samuel S. Kim, eds. *China in the Global Community*. New York: Praeger, 1980.
Johansen, Robert C. *The National Interest and the Human Interest: An Analysis of U.S. Foreign Policy*. Princeton: Princeton University Press, 1980.
Kinnard, Douglas. *The Secretary of Defense*. Lexington: University Press of Kentucky, 1980.
Kruglak, Gregory T. *The Politics of United States Decision-Making in United Nations Specialized Agencies: The Case of the International Labor Organization*. Washington, D.C.: University Press of America, 1980.
Ozbudun, Ergun, and Aydin Ulusan, eds. *The Political Economy of Income Distribution in Turkey*. New York: Holmes and Meier, 1980.
Ramberg, Bennett. *Destruction of Nuclear Energy Facilities in War: The Problem and the Implications*. Lexington, Mass.: D. C. Heath, 1980.
Bienen, Henry S., and V. P. Diejomaoh, eds. *The Political Economy of Income Distribution in Nigeria*. New York: Holmes and Meier, 1981.
Falk, Richard A. *Human Rights and State Sovereignty*. New York: Holmes and Meier, 1981.
Gilpin, Robert G. *War and Change in World Politics*. Cambridge: Cambridge University Press, 1981.
Mittelman, James H. *Underdevelopment and the Transition to Socialism: Mozambique and Tanzania*. New York: Academic Press, 1981.
Rozman, Gilbert, ed. *The Modernization of China*. New York: Free Press, 1981.
Tucker, Robert C. *Politics as Leadership*. Columbia: University of Missouri Press, 1981.
Abdel-Khalek, Gouda, and Robert L. Tignor, eds. *The Political Economy of Income Distribution in Egypt*. New York: Holmes and Meier, 1982.
Hillal Dessouki, Ali E., ed. *Islamic Resurgence in the Arab World*. New York: Praeger, 1982.
Onuf, Nicholas G., ed. *Law-Making in the Global Community*. Durham, N.C.: Carolina Academic Press, 1982.
Falk, Richard A. *The End of World Order*. New York: Holmes and Meier, 1983.
Knorr, Klaus, ed. *Power, Strategy, and Security*. Princeton: Princeton University Press, 1983.
Laursen, Finn. *Superpower at Sea*. New York: Praeger, 1983.
Aspe, Pedro, and Paul E. Sigmund, eds. *The Political Economy of Income Distribution in Mexico*. New York and London: Holmes and Meier, 1984.
Baehr, Peter R., and Leon Gordenker. *The United Nations: Reality and Ideal*. New York: Praeger, 1984.
Garvey, Gerald. *Strategy and the Defense Dilemma*. Lexington, Mass.: D. C. Heath, 1984.
Grieco, Joseph M. *Between Dependency and Autonomy: India's Experience with the International Computer Industry*. Berkeley: University of California Press, 1984.
Hallenberg, Jan. *Foreign Policy Change: United States Foreign Policy toward the Soviet Union and the People's Republic of China, 1961–1980*. Stockholm: University of Stockholm, 1984.

Kim, Samuel S. *The Quest for a Just World Order*. Boulder, Colo.: Westview Press, 1984.

Krepon, Michael. *Strategic Stalemate: Nuclear Weapons and Arms Control in American Politics*. New York: St. Martin's Press, 1984.

Bienen, Henry S. *Political Conflict and Economic Change in Nigeria*. London: Frank Cass, 1985.

Rozman, Gilbert F. *A Mirror for Socialism: Soviet Criticisms of China*. Princeton: Princeton University Press, 1985.

Bermeo, Nancy G. *The Revolution within the Revolution: Worker's Control in Rural Portugal*. Princeton: Princeton University Press, 1986.

Black, Cyril E. *Understanding Soviet Politics: The Perspectives of Russian History*. Boulder, Colo.: Westview Press, 1986.

Cohen, Stephen F. *Sovieticus: American Perceptions and Soviet Realities*. New York: W. W. Norton, 1986.

Falk, Richard A. *Reviving the World Court*. Charlottesville: University Press of Virginia, 1986.

Fleming, James E.; William F. Harris, II; and Walter F. Murphy. *American Constitutional Interpretation*. Mineola, N.Y.: Foundation Press, 1986.

Kabashima, Ikuo, and Lynn T. White, III, eds. *Political System and Change*. Princeton: Princeton University Press, 1986.

Kohli, Atul, ed. *The State and Development in the Third World*. Princeton: Princeton University Press, 1986.

Oye, Kenneth A., ed. *Cooperation under Anarchy*. Princeton: Princeton University Press, 1986.

Falk, Richard A. *The Promise of World Order: Essays in Normative International Relations*. Philadelphia: Temple University Press, 1987.

Falk, Richard A., and Mary Kaldor, eds. *Dealignment: A New Foreign Policy Perspective*. Oxford: Basil Blackwell, 1987.

Fischer, Dietrich; Wilhelm Nolte; and Jan Øberg. *Frieden gewinnen: Mit autonomen Initiativen aus dem Teufelskreis ausbrechen*. Freiburg: Dreisam-Verlag, 1987.

Fischer, Dietrich, and Jan Tinbergen. *Warfare and Welfare: Integrating Security Policy into Socio-Economic Policy*. New York: St. Martin's Press, 1987.

Gersovitz, Mark, and John Waterbury, eds. *The Political Economy of Risk and Choice in Senegal*. London: Frank Cass, 1987.

Gilpin, Robert G. *The Political Economy of International Relations*. Princeton: Princeton University Press, 1987.

Gordenker, Leon. *Refugees in International Politics*. New York: Columbia University Press, 1987.

Issawi, Charles P. *An Arab Philosophy of History*, rev. ed. Princeton: Darwin Press, 1987.

Kohli, Atul. *The State and Poverty in India: The Politics of Reform*. New York: Cambridge University Press, 1987.

Nilsson, Ann-Sofie. *Political Uses of International Law*. Lund, Sweden: Dialogos, 1987.

Rozman, Gilbert F. *The Chinese Debate about Soviet Socialism, 1978–1985*. Princeton: Princeton University Press, 1987.

Suleiman, Ezra N. *Private Power and Centralization in France: The Notaires and the State*. Princeton: Princeton University Press, 1987.

Tucker, Robert C. *Political Culture and Leadership in Soviet Russia from Lenin to Gorbachev*. New York: W. W. Norton, 1987.

Ullman, Richard H., and Mario Zucconi, eds. *Western Europe and the Crisis in U.S.-Soviet Relations*. New York: Praeger, 1987.

Walt, Stephen M. *The Origins of Alliances*. Ithaca, N.Y.: Cornell University Press, 1987.

Calder, Kent E. *Crisis and Compensation: Public Policy and Political Stability in Japan, 1949–1986*. Princeton: Princeton University Press, 1988.

Falk, Richard A. *Revolutionaries and Functionaries: The Dual Face of Terrorism*. New York: E. P. Dutton, 1988.

Kohli, Atul, ed. *India's Democracy: An Analysis of Changing State-Society Relations*. Princeton: Princeton University Press, 1988.

Bienen, Henry S. *Armed Forces, Conflict, and Change in Africa*. Boulder, Colo.: Westview Press, 1989.

Burke, John P., and Fred I. Greenstein. *How Presidents Test Reality: Decisions on Vietnam, 1954 and 1965*. New York: Russell Sage Foundation, 1989.

Cohen, Mark R., and Abraham L. Udovitch, eds. *Jews among Arabs: Contacts and Boundaries*. Princeton: Darwin Press, 1989.

Colburn, Forrest, ed. *Everyday Forms of Peasant Resistance*. Armonk, N.Y.: M. E. Sharpe, 1989.

Falk, Richard A. *Revitalizing International Law*. Ames: Iowa State University Press, 1989.

Giorgis, Dawit Wolde. *Red Tears: War, Famine, and Revolution in Ethiopia*. Trenton, N.J.: Red Sea Press, 1989.

Hall, John A., and G. John Ikenberry. *The State*. Minneapolis: University of Minnesota Press, 1989.

Mujal-León, Eusebio, ed. *The USSR and Latin America: A Developing Relationship*. Boston: Unwin Hyman, 1989.

White, Lynn T., III. *Policies of Chaos: The Organizational Causes of Violence in China's Cultural Revolution*. Princeton: Princeton University Press, 1989.

Brown, L. Carl. *Centerstage: American Diplomacy since World War II*. New York: Holmes and Meier, 1990.

Colburn, Forrest D. *Managing the Commanding Heights: Nicaragua's State Enterprises*. Berkeley: University of California Press, 1990.

Downs, George W., and David M. Rocke. *Tacit Bargaining, Arms Races, and Arms Control*. Ann Arbor: University of Michigan Press, 1990.

Herbst, Jeffrey. *State Politics in Zimbabwe*. Berkeley: University of California Press, 1990.

Kohli, Atul. *Democracy and Discontent: India's Growing Crisis of Governability*. Cambridge: Cambridge University Press, 1990.

Lifton, Robert J., and Eric Markusen. *The Genocidal Mentality: Nazi Holocaust and Nuclear Threat*. New York: Basic Books, 1990.

Suleiman, Ezra N., and John Waterbury. *The Political Economy of Public Sector Reform and Privatization*. Boulder, Colo.: Westview Press, 1990.

Tucker, Robert C. *Stalin in Power: The Revolution from Above, 1928–1941*. New York: W. W. Norton, 1990.

Bachman, David, and Dali Yang, translators and eds. *Yan Jiaqi and China's Struggle for Democracy*. Armonk, N.Y.: M. E. Sharpe, 1991.

Bachman, David. *Bureaucracy, Economy, and Leadership in China: The Institutional Origins of the Great Leap Forward*. Cambridge: Cambridge University Press, 1991.

Bienen, Henry, and Nicholas van de Walle. *Of Time and Power*. Stanford: Stanford University Press, 1991.

Black, Cyril E., Louis Dupree, Elizabeth Endicott-West, Daniel C. Matuszewski, Eden Naby, and Arthur N. Waldron. *The Modernization of Inner Asia*. Armonk, N.Y.: M. E. Sharpe, 1991.

Tullis, LaMond. *Handbook of Research on the Illicit Drug Traffic: Socioeconomic and Political Consequences*. Westport, Conn.: Greenwood Press, 1991.

Danspeckgruber, Wolfgang, ed. *Emerging Dimensions of European Security Policy*. Boulder, Colo.: Westview Press, 1991.

Grossman, Gene M., and Elhanan Helpman. *Innovation and Growth in the Global Economy*. Cambridge: MIT Press, 1991.

Schneider, Ben Ross. *Politics within the State: Elite Bureaucrats and Industrial Policy in Authoritarian Brazil*. Pittsburgh: University of Pittsburgh Press, 1991.

Thelen, Kathleen A. *Union of Parts: Labor Politics in Postwar Germany*. Ithaca, N.Y.: Cornell University Press, 1991.

Bermeo, Nancy, ed. *Liberalization and Democratization: Change in the Soviet Union and Eastern Europe*. Baltimore: Johns Hopkins University Press, 1992.

Bienen, Henry, ed. *Power, Economics, and Security: The United States and Japan in Focus*. Boulder, Colo.: Westview Press, 1992.

Falk, Richard. *Explorations at the Edge of Time: The Prospects for World Order*. Philadelphia: Temple University Press, 1992.

Gordenker, Leon, and Peter R. Baehr. *The United Nations in the 1990s*. New York: St. Martin's Press, 1992.

Grossman, Gene M., ed. *Imperfect Competition and International Trade*. Cambridge: MIT Press, 1992.

Issawi, Charles; Cyril E. Black; Jonathan E. Helmreich; Paul C. Helmreich; and A. James McAdams. *Rebirth: A History of Europe since World War II*. Boulder, Colo.: Westview Press, 1992.

Marx, Anthony W. *Lessons of Struggle: South African Internal Opposition, 1960–1990*. New York: Oxford University Press, 1992.

Rozman, Gilbert. *Japan's Response to the Gorbachev Era, 1985–1991*. Princeton: Princeton University Press, 1992.

Volker, Paul, and Toyoo Gyohten. *Changing Fortunes: The World's Money and the Threat to American Leadership*. New York: Random House, 1992.

Library of Congress Cataloging-in-Publication Data

China's quest for national identity / edited by Lowell Dittmer and Samuel S. Kim.
  p. cm.
  Includes bibliographical references and index.
  ISBN 0-8014-2785-1. — ISBN 0-8014-8064-7 (pbk.)
  1. Nationalism—China. 2. National characteristics, Chinese. I. Dittmer,
Lowell. II. Kim, Samuel S., 1935– .
JC311.C45764 1993
320.5′4′0951—dc20   92-27284